The Sport Mega-Events of the 2020s

This book explores various social, cultural, political and economic issues through the lenses of various sport mega-events in the twenty-first century, including the Olympic Games, and the World Cup and European Championships in football. In a time where sport mega-events are closely followed by controversies, legacy discourses and questions of their governance, the chapters within this book showcase why sport mega-events continue to ignite important questions for scholars, commentators, fans and sport and political authorities.

By covering various topics emerging around sport mega-events such as physical activity, legacies, rhetoric, media coverage, environmental impacts, diplomacy and spectators' experiences, this book breaks new ground as it considers a range of longstanding and emerging socio-political issues relating broadly to the staging of spectacular sport mega-events in the present day.

This is a fascinating reading for students and researchers situated in sociology, sport management, event management, political science, sport studies, sport business, urban studies and leisure studies. The chapters in this book were originally published as a special issue of *Sport in Society*.

Jan Andre Lee Ludvigsen is Senior Lecturer in International Relations and Politics with Sociology at Liverpool John Moores University, UK. His research fields are within the sociology and politics of sport and he has authored four books in this area.

Joel Rookwood is Lecturer in Sport Management at University College Dublin in Ireland and a visiting fellow in Sport Management and Marketing at the University of Vic – Central Catalunya in Spain. Joel's research interests include sports mega-events, international development, the football industry and sports governance, areas in which he has published widely.

Daniel Parnell is Associate Professor in Sport Business at the University of Liverpool Management School, UK. Dan's research interests lie in business management, policy, and social and economic networks in sport.

Sport in the Global Society: Contemporary Perspectives

Series Editor: **Boria Majumdar**, *University of Central Lancashire, UK*

The social, cultural (including media) and political study of sport is an expanding area of scholarship and related research. While this area has been well served by the *Sport in the Global Society* series, the surge in quality scholarship over the last few years has necessitated the creation of *Sport in the Global Society: Contemporary Perspectives*. The series will publish the work of leading scholars in fields as diverse as sociology, cultural studies, media studies, gender studies, cultural geography and history, political science and political economy. If the social and cultural study of sport is to receive the scholarly attention and readership it warrants, a cross-disciplinary series dedicated to taking sport beyond the narrow confines of physical education and sport science academic domains is necessary. *Sport in the Global Society: Contemporary Perspectives* will answer this need.

The Potential of Community Sport for Social Inclusion
Exploring Cases Across the Globe
Edited by Hebe Schaillée, Reinhard Haudenhuyse and Lieve Bradt

The Professionalization of Action Sports
The Changing Roles of Athletes, Industry and Media
Edited by Guillaume Dumont and Holly Thorpe

Interrelationships Between Sport and the Arts
Edited by Jonathan Long and Doug Sandle

The League of Ireland
An Historical and Contemporary Assessment
Edited by Conor Curran

Forced Migration and Sport
Critical Dialogues across International Contexts and Disciplinary Boundaries
Edited by Ramón Spaaij, Carla Luguetti and Nicola De Martini Ugolotti

The Sport Mega-Events of the 2020s
Governance, Impacts and Controversies
Edited by Jan Andre Lee Ludvigsen, Joel Rookwood, Daniel Parnell

Methodological Advancements in Social Impacts of Tourism Research
Edited by Manuel Alector Ribeiro and Kyle Maurice Woosnam

For more information about this series, please visit:
www.routledge.com/Sport-in-the-Global-Society--Contemporary-Perspectives/book-series/SGSC

The Sport Mega-Events of the 2020s
Governance, Impacts and Controversies

Edited by
Jan Andre Lee Ludvigsen, Joel Rookwood
and Daniel Parnell

LONDON AND NEW YORK

First published 2024
by Routledge
4 Park Square, Milton Park, Abingdon, Oxon OX14 4RN

and by Routledge
605 Third Avenue, New York, NY 10158

Routledge is an imprint of the Taylor & Francis Group, an informa business

Introduction, Chapters 1, 3–5, 7 and 9 © 2024 Taylor & Francis
Chapter 2 © 2021 Themis Kokolakakis and Fernando Lera-López. Originally published as Open Access.
Chapter 6 © 2021 Christina Philippou. Originally published as Open Access.
Chapter 8 © 2021 Joel Rookwood. Originally published as Open Access.

With the exception of Chapters 2, 6 and 8, no part of this book may be reprinted or reproduced or utilised in any form or by any electronic, mechanical, or other means, now known or hereafter invented, including photocopying and recording, or in any information storage or retrieval system, without permission in writing from the publishers. For details on the rights for Chapters 2, 6 and 8, please see the chapters' Open Access footnotes.

Trademark notice: Product or corporate names may be trademarks or registered trademarks, and are used only for identification and explanation without intent to infringe.

British Library Cataloguing in Publication Data
A catalogue record for this book is available from the British Library

ISBN13: 978-1-032-59381-4 (hbk)
ISBN13: 978-1-032-59382-1 (pbk)
ISBN13: 978-1-003-45445-8 (ebk)

DOI: 10.4324/9781003454458

Typeset in Minion Pro
by Newgen Publishing UK

Publisher's Note
The publisher accepts responsibility for any inconsistencies that may have arisen during the conversion of this book from journal articles to book chapters, namely the inclusion of journal terminology.

Disclaimer
Every effort has been made to contact copyright holders for their permission to reprint material in this book. The publishers would be grateful to hear from any copyright holder who is not here acknowledged and will undertake to rectify any errors or omissions in future editions of this book.

Contents

Citation Information vii
Notes on Contributors ix

Introduction—The sport mega-events of the 2020s: governance, impacts and controversies 1
Jan Andre Lee Ludvigsen, Joel Rookwood and Daniel Parnell

1 Can international sports mega events be considered physical activity interventions? A systematic review and quality assessment of large-scale population studies 8
Michael Annear, Shintaro Sato, Tetsuhiro Kidokoro and Yasuo Shimizu

2 Sport legacy impact on ethnic minority groups: the case of London 2012 26
Themis Kokolakakis and Fernando Lera-López

3 Residents' perceptions of sporting events: a review of the literature 44
Balázs Polcsik and Szilvia Perényi

4 "Winning the women's world cup": gender, branding, and the Australia/New Zealand *As One 2023* social media strategy for the FIFA Women's World Cup 2023™ 64
Adam Beissel, Verity Postlethwaite and Andrew Grainger

5 Media coverage and public opinion of hosting a women's football mega-event: the English bid for *UEFA Women's Euro 2022* 95
Jonathan Rocha de Oliveira, Maria Thereza de Oliveira Souza and André Mendes Capraro

6 Anti-bribery and corruption in sport mega-events: stakeholder perspectives 115
Christina Philippou

7 Uniting, disuniting and reuniting: towards a 'United' 2026 133
Nicholas Wise and Jan Andre Lee Ludvigsen

8 From sport-for-development to sports mega-events: conflict, authoritarian modernisation and statecraft in Azerbaijan 143
Joel Rookwood

9 Predicting climate impacts to the Olympic Games and FIFA Men's World Cups from 2022 to 2032 163
Walker J. Ross and Madeleine Orr

Index 185

Citation Information

The chapters in this book were originally published in the journal *Sport in Society*, volume 25, issue 4 (2022). When citing this material, please use the original page numbering for each article, as follows:

Introduction
The sport mega-events of the 2020s: governance, impacts and controversies
Jan Andre Lee Ludvigsen, Joel Rookwood and Daniel Parnell
Sport in Society, volume 25, issue 4 (2022), pp. 705–711

Chapter 1
Can international sports mega events be considered physical activity interventions? A systematic review and quality assessment of large-scale population studies
Michael Annear, Shintaro Sato, Tetsuhiro Kidokoro and Yasuo Shimizu
Sport in Society, volume 25, issue 4 (2022), pp. 712–729

Chapter 2
Sport legacy impact on ethnic minority groups: the case of London 2012
Themis Kokolakakis and Fernando Lera-López
Sport in Society, volume 25, issue 4 (2022), pp. 730–747

Chapter 3
Residents' perceptions of sporting events: a review of the literature
Balázs Polcsik and Szilvia Perényi
Sport in Society, volume 25, issue 4 (2022), pp. 748–767

Chapter 4
"Winning the women's world cup": gender, branding, and the Australia/New Zealand As One 2023 social media strategy for the FIFA Women's World Cup 2023™
Adam Beissel, Verity Postlethwaite and Andrew Grainger
Sport in Society, volume 25, issue 4 (2022), pp. 768–798

Chapter 5
Media coverage and public opinion of hosting a women's football mega-event: the English bid for UEFA Women's Euro 2022
Jonathan Rocha de Oliveira, Maria Thereza de Oliveira Souza and André Mendes Capraro
Sport in Society, volume 25, issue 4 (2022), pp. 799–818

Chapter 6
Anti-bribery and corruption in sport mega-events: stakeholder perspectives
Christina Philippou
Sport in Society, volume 25, issue 4 (2022), pp. 819–836

Chapter 7
Uniting, disuniting and reuniting: towards a 'United' 2026
Nicholas Wise and Jan Andre Lee Ludvigsen
Sport in Society, volume 25, issue 4 (2022), pp. 837–846

Chapter 8
From sport-for-development to sports mega-events: conflict, authoritarian modernisation and statecraft in Azerbaijan
Joel Rookwood
Sport in Society, volume 25, issue 4 (2022), pp. 847–866

Chapter 9
Predicting climate impacts to the Olympic Games and FIFA Men's World Cups from 2022 to 2032
Walker J. Ross and Madeleine Orr
Sport in Society, volume 25, issue 4 (2022), pp. 867–888

For any permission-related enquiries please visit:
www.tandfonline.com/page/help/permissions

Notes on Contributors

Michael Annear, Faculty of Sport Sciences, Waseda University, Tokyo, Japan.

Adam Beissel, Department of Sport Leadership & Management, Miami University, Oxford, OH, USA.

André Mendes Capraro, Physical Education Department, Federal University of Paraná, Curitiba, Paraná, Brazil.

Jonathan Rocha de Oliveira, Physical Education Department, Federal University of Paraná, Curitiba, Paraná, Brazil.

Maria Thereza de Oliveira Souza, Physical Education Department, Federal University of Paraná, Curitiba, Paraná, Brazil.

Andrew Grainger, School of Sport, Exercise and Nutrition, Massey University, Palmerston North, New Zealand.

Tetsuhiro Kidokoro, Physical Fitness Research Institute, Meiji Yasuda Life Foundation of Health and Welfare, Tokyo, Japan.

Themis Kokolakakis, Sheffield Hallam University, Sheffield, UK.

Jan Andre Lee Ludvigsen, School of Humanities and Social Sciences, Liverpool John Moores University, UK.

Fernando Lera-López, Institute for Advanced Research in Business and Economics and Department of Economics, Public University of Navarra, Pamplona, Spain.

Madeleine Orr, Faculty of Management, University of British Columbia, Kelowna, BC, Canada.

Daniel Parnell, Centre for Sport Business, University of Liverpool Management School, University of Liverpool, UK.

Christina Philippou, Accounting and Financial Management, University of Portsmouth, Portsmouth, UK.

Szilvia Perényi, Department of Sports Management, University of Physical Education, Budapest, Hungary.

Balázs Polcsik, Doctoral School of Sport Sciences, University of Physical Education, Budapest, Hungary.

Verity Postlethwaite, Independent Scholar, Worcester, UK.

Joel Rookwood, School of Public Health, Physiotherapy and Sports Science, University College Dublin, Ireland.

Walker J. Ross, Florida Southern College, Barney Barnett School of Business and Free Enterprise, Lakeland, FL, USA.

Shintaro Sato, Physical Fitness Research Institute, Meiji Yasuda Life Foundation of Health and Welfare, Tokyo, Japan.

Yasuo Shimizu, Division of Arts and Sciences, International Christian University, Tokyo, Japan.

Nicholas Wise, School of Community Resources and Development, Arizona State University, Phoenix, AZ, USA.

Introduction—The sport mega-events of the 2020s: governance, impacts and controversies

Introduction

As the guest editors of this Special Issue in *Sport in Society*, we would like to begin this editorial by paraphrasing sociologist Maurice Roche, who must be considered a key scholar in the social and historical study of mega-events. For Roche (2000), who initially and predominantly focused on the Olympics and World Fairs, mega-events constitute some of the modern society's great *shows*. In his 2000 book, Roche further concluded *vis-à-vis* mega-events that '[w]e are likely to see much more of them, in both "official" and "alternative" forms, as "global society" and its culture begin to take on a more patterned and institutionalised character in the early generations of the twenty-first century' (p. 235).

Fast forward 20 years, and the social scientific study of sport mega-events has increasingly taken new turns and followed new avenues. As Roche (2017) argued more recently, mega-events always have the capacity to surprise us and provide us with a glimpse of broader processes and tendencies at play in the global life. Here, we concur with Roche and, in distinctive ways, this Special Issue is firmly rooted in such perspective. Sport mega-events, in our view, can help us better understand and make sense of the world that we live in. However, if we are to expand our knowledge on exactly *how* or *why* mega-events have the capacity to surprise us and tell us new things about societies, then we would argue that a continued and comparative study of mega-event is as necessary as it is scholarly important in the current world.

It is well-established that sport mega-events are socially, culturally, financially, politically and historically important and valuable. For example, in the modern world, sport mega-events are commonly utilized by states as tools for soft power, nation branding and public diplomacy (Rookwood and Adeosun 2021). Events are collectively memorized and work as reference points in communities' social calendars and in the broader public structuring of time (see Roche 2003). And, indeed, each sport mega-event is filled with anticipation of sporting success, Olympic records, defining moments and atmospheric expectations.

Though, sport mega-events must not be unequivocally glorified. They have also been subject to increased opposition, criticism and scrutiny. These typically relate to their astronomical economic costs, their physical, social and spatial impacts on public space and their failure to produce those 'legacies' that regularly are promised or exaggerated in the bidding stages (Boykoff 2020). All these social realities feed into the three subthemes of this Special Issue. These include *governance*, *impacts* and *controversies*. As we argue, these three themes will follow most – if not all – mega-events in the 2020s. Simultaneously, these subthemes often inter-link and may reinforce each other, as we will unpack further next.

Governance

All mega-events involve complicated and long-lasting bidding, planning and construction phases. Commonly, mega-events provide cities with an opportunity to revitalise urban spaces and increase tourism, and often involve some of the largest security operations in the world.

Further, mega-events are – as mentioned – increasingly used as political tools and for purposes of soft power on the international scene. The actors involved within a mega-event's planning are multiple and diverse. While mega-events are hosted by cities or countries, they are simultaneously administered by sport governing bodies and organised by local organising committees. Then, sport mega-events are typically sponsored by gigantic international corporations and broadcasted by powerful media giants. Moreover, throughout the Covid-19 pandemic, the staging of events was also largely guided by the World Health Organization's guidelines (Lee Ludvigsen 2021). One key question is thus how sport mega-events are *governed*. Especially when considering the multitude of public and private actors that are involved in the staging of events and their decision-making processes. Furthermore, questions may also be asked around the transparency and regulation of mega-events. As Horne and Manzenreiter (2006, 18) remind us:

> Sports mega-events have been largely developed by undemocratic organizations, often with anarchic decision-making and a lack of transparency, and more often in the interests of global flows rather than local communities

As Pierre Bourdieu (1998) alluded to in his piece on the 'Olympic spectacle', sport governing bodies, such as IOC have become commercial enterprises and, as Boykoff (2016, 136) writes, 'only about half of the IOC's revenue comes from granting television rights, while corporate sponsorship makes up 45 percent and ticket sales only 5 percent'. Indeed, the increased commercialism and lack of transparency have proved highly problematic. It has meant that mega-events like the football World Cup and the Olympic Games have been subject to much public criticism over the lack of transparency, allegations of bribery (Sugden and Tomlinson 2017; Boykoff 2020) and the strict conditions that event owners place upon their bidders and potential hosting countries (Włoch 2013). In that sense, it is completely prudent to ask: 'Given all the unpredictability and uncertainties surrounding major international sports mega-events, why do governments and cities compete for the right to host them?' (Horne 2007, 85). Indeed, as Paulsson and Alm (2020) recently observed, some countries have – in order to avoid political risk at national and local level – withdrawn their Olympic bid considerations or applications following the lack of public support.

It may be argued that sport mega-events can work as a microcosm for the wider power relations and governance structures that exist within the world (of sports). Critical voices including sport-related social movements (Norwegian Supporters Alliance 2021), athletes, journalists (Zirin 2016) and academics (Boykoff 2020; Sugden and Sugden 2020) have called for reforms in the current governance of neoliberal mega-events. Even still, a number of sport mega-events tend to leave behind 'white elephants' (Horne 2007) and are often associated with substantial cost overruns that, first and foremost, are felt by the local populations and communities.

Against this reality, Müller (2015, 15) concludes that: 'Radical changes to the rules of the games – in how mega-events are planned, awarded, and governed – are needed'. Further, Müller argues that, '[d]ebates and actions to counteract the mega-event syndrome must start now, early in the bid phase, when the basic parameters can still be changed' (ibid.). As such, it is hoped that the papers of this special issue can tie into and contribute to these *debates* and *actions* regarding mega-event governance and regulation, to facilitate a more transparent and sustainable future for sport mega-events. This naturally links up to our next subtheme, which is impacts.

Impacts

Sport mega-events are typically framed in terms of *impacts* and attempts to engender positive 'legacies'. In generic terms the notion of 'impact' is often applied in reference either to having a marked effect or influence, or to the action of entities coming forcibly into contact. This definitional variance may be helpful in the applied context of sport mega-events. The intended outcomes of mega-event hosting often include asserting influence, such as over national and international audiences. However, some of the unintended adverse consequences of such events can serve as by-products of collisions between different organisations, personnel, policies, and priorities. Rather than being manifest as rigidly polarised positions, a more nuanced interpretation might suggest that mega-event impacts can vary significantly. For instance, a sports facility constructed to stage a mega-event might incur considerable cost, in terms of financial outlay and the conditions for, treatment of and risks to the workforce involved in its construction. As what has become an archetypal example, Qatar's forthcoming 2022 FIFA Men's World Cup has been widely criticised in relation to related human rights abuses, in addition to allegations of bribery, corruption, and discrimination (Khalifa 2020).

In different circumstances the long-term usage and implications of such facilities can propel sports performers, organisations and investment. The City of Manchester Stadium (as it was known before naming rights changed due to Etihad's sponsorship agreement) was initially proposed as an athletics arena in Manchester's failed bid for the 2000 Summer Olympics, and was converted to a football ground after staging the 2002 Commonwealth Games. It subsequently became the home of Manchester City Football Club, helping attract investment which has propelled the club from the second tier of English football in 2002 (and indeed the third tier in 1998) to become five-time Premier League champions since. There are of course a litany of examples of stadia constructed for mega-events that have not been well utilised or served to promote sport participation and performance levels in the long term. As previously noted, sport mega-event literature details numerous cases of such 'white elephants', as Drummond and Cronje (2019) argue.

Legacy claims can include references to sustained usage of purpose-built facilities and other infrastructural investments, stressing quantitatively projected economic benefits, which can underestimate costs and overstate the potential advantages. In cases where there is a failure to yield positive legacies and impacts this can hinder development in sporting, economic and political contexts, amongst others. Prioritising the expenditure of public money to finance infrastructural construction can deplete resources elsewhere, restricting spending on healthcare, housing and education, for instance. Such decisions can adversely impact upon political leaders if the benefits of hosting an event that their administration has overseen are not widely perceived to outweigh the costs.

Realistically, sport mega-events should positively impact a broad range of communities. Long-term requirements should drive short-term investment and event organisers should prioritise the economic viability of events, working with key stakeholders such as sports federations, political organisations, broadcasting and media companies and commercial partners. For host nations, impacts should be informed by key objectives including the staging of safe, profitable, memorable and innovative events with sustainable outcomes and legacies which promote and increase opportunities to participate in sport and physical activity and improve national elite sport performance levels. It is also reasonable to expect successful mega-events to facilitate modernisation, trade, tourism and revenue growth within host nations and cities.

Controversies

In terms of controversies, sport mega-events have been the sites for a number of controversial moments through the history (see e.g., Boykoff 2016). Whilst an exhaustive list of 'controversies' related to sport mega-events is beyond of this paper's remit, controversies may be both sporting related and non-sporting related. In recent times, these include cases of doping, allegations of bribery or corruption (Philppou, this issue) and human rights breaches (Boykoff 2016).

Furthermore, some of the contentious consequences of mega-events may also be the displacement of social groups or communities in order to 'sanitize' or 'clean up' event cities and their spaces and places.

As Müller (2015) asserts, '[m]ega-events are exceptional happenings and so, too, is the time during which the hosts prepare for them [...] Many governments pass laws that introduce exceptions in areas such as taxation, immigration, property rights, urban planning, and freedom of speech'. For example, in a case study of London's 2012 Olympics, Watt (2013) explores the experiences of displacement of lower-income East Londoners against the backdrop of positive 'legacy' discourses. As such, Watt argues that wider neoliberal processes such as gentrification can be accelerated by events such as the Olympics. This again led to a local community disconnected and spatially excluded from the Olympic-related changes. Similarly, Zirin (2016) explore exceptional processes of militarization and gentrification in the cases of the 2014 World Cup and 2016 Olympics in Brazil, and he notes how many local residents felt excluded from the wider sporting spectacles, which were locally resisted. Thus, the contemporary controversies of mega-events are often tightly linked up to their governance and impacts and collectively underpin – as we previously contended – *why* a continued academic engagement with sport mega-events is imperative.

This special issue: an overview

In this special issue, titled *The Sport Mega-Events of the 2020s: Governance, Impacts and Controversies*, we have included a number of articles that capture forthcoming sports mega-events in the 2020s. Whilst some of the papers are case studies focusing specifically one mega-events, some of the papers will focus more specifically on issues or controversies that arise in line with contemporary sports mega-events and their housing. Furthermore, some of the papers also take a 'step back' and look at recently staged mega-events to see what these may tell us about the next decade.

As we discussed above, mega-events are usually hosted to have a short or long-term *impact*. 'Impacts', much like 'legacies', are contested and may however transcend diverse fields, including health, physical activity and education. So, Annear, Sato, Kidokoro and Shimizu tap into existing debates surrounding physical activity legacies that often are promoted in the housing of sports mega-events. Drawing from a systematic review, the authors question whether sports mega-events can be considered physical activity interventions. Naturally, the findings of Annear et al. will be of high relevance for scholars, but also for policy-makers, event planners and cities pursuing the prestigious hosting rights of future mega-events. Similarly, Kokolakakis and Lera Lopez also investigate sport mega-event 'legacies'. The authors remain mainly focused on London's 2012 Olympics and how the types of 'legacies' have impacted ethnic minority groups and sport participation.

Mega-events have long-lasting social impacts on their local communities and the host city residents. A central scholarly question that remains is thus what local residents feel about their cities staging sport mega-events. As such, the paper by Polcsik and Perenyi provides the first comprehensive literature review which systematically explores the published literature on residents' perceptions between 2000 and 2020. With their findings and conclusions, this paper may thus be integral to the development and definition of future research directions. Following this, Beissel, Postlethwaite and Grainger's article turn towards the FIFA 2023 Women's World Cup in football. This event's hosting rights were awarded to Australia and New Zealand, and by exploring bid books, relevant web sites and social media discourses surrounding this bid, the paper examines the communicated hosting visions of the event promoted as '*As One*'. This paper and its material give unique insight into the importance of social media in building popular narratives around 'legacies' and situates the event within the wider political and cultural frames of the Asia-Pacific. Meanwhile, Olveira, Souza and Capraro examine aspects of media coverage ahead of the 2022 women's Euros which England will be the host of.

Then, as we stated, mega-events are often surrounded by *controversies*. This includes allegations of bribery, corruption and abuse of power. Seeking to explore the darker side of sport mega-events, Philppou explores stakeholder perspectives of bribery. Drawing from interviews with anti-corruption specialists, sporting officials and other stakeholders, Philippou highlight some of the key issues related to corruption and bribery and proposes some potential solutions. Again, these practical solutions can have large-scale implications and could ensure increased transparency and oversight in the world of sports mega-events.

The final three papers are structured around sport mega-events' politics and *governance*. The paper by Wise and Ludvigsen examines the upcoming men's FIFA 2026 World Cup that will be co-hosted by Canada, Mexico and the US. This will be the first time a World Cup is co-hosted by three countries, and this particular mega-event has been surrounded by political rhetoric and possesses unique geographical features. For Wise and Ludvigsen, the political and cultural journey towards 'United 2026' – as the bid was promoted as – may be situated in a political and historical context, with the NAFTA agreement that initially was signed by Bill Clinton. Their paper traces this bid's political underpinnings and, as the event approaches in time, Wise and Ludvigsen also offer some tentative pathways for empirical research on this event, and the geopolitics of mega-events more widely. Rookwood's article is also concerned with some of the political impacts and motives of sport mega-events. Rookwood explores the roles of sport mega-events in Azerbaijan and how mega-events are deployed to leverage political influence within and beyond the country's region in the present-day. The recent years have seen sustainability and the environment feature regularly in the public rhetoric of international sporting organisations. In this context, Walker and Orr explore the environmental conditions that may be of relevance for policy makers and planners for their event contingency plans. The immediate issues which Walker and Orr touch upon include heat conditions and poor air quality in relation to event cities. Yet they also reflect on the long-term consequences of this and the importance of designing climate-resilient events in the 2020s and beyond. Consequently, this article marks the closure of this special issue.

Into the 2020s and beyond

As we are writing this editorial paper, the 2020 UEFA European Championships in men's football and the 2020 Olympics in Tokyo (both staged throughout June, July and August 2021) have just concluded amidst the Covid-19 pandemic. Whilst the respective events' closing ceremonies served as symbolic *ends* to the two events; closing ceremonies – for fans, commentators and athletes alike – concurrently symbolize a *start* of a new period, and generate levels of anticipation, hope and expectation for the *next* sports mega-event that is pinpointed in the sporting calendar. Whilst it must be recognized that the two mega-events mentioned above provided many athletes, coaches, spectators and TV viewers with memorable moments amidst a challenging pandemic period, these events were simultaneously controversial. In the UK, 9,000 Covid-19 cases were linked to the Euro 2020 fixtures post-event (The Guardian 2021), whilst the Tokyo Olympics were staged despite widespread public opposition to the event across the host country (Lee Ludvigsen and Parnell 2021). Upon reflection, it feels appropriate for us to conclude by reiterating that sport mega-events *matter*. They matter sociologically, politically, culturally and economically. As Horne and Manzenreiter (2006: 1) argue, 'sports "mega-events" are important elements in the orientation of nations to international or global society'. Sport mega-events also entertain us and enable defining moments and long-lasting memories (Giulianotti 2019). That is one reason why our social calendars – as mentioned – circulate around these gigantic and all-consuming occasions and projects (Roche 2003).

Whilst the academic lexicon of studies on sports mega-events may be considered to be well-established, has grown immensely throughout the 2000s and 2010s, and boasts a number of key publications (e.g., Roche 2000; Horne and Manzenreiter 2006; Boykoff 2020), it still remains imperative that this field continues to develop in line with external and internal trends and developments. This includes but is not limited to environmental changes (Ross and Orr, this issue), emerging technologies and digital media (Woods and Ludvigsen 2021), Covid-19 (Parnell et al. 2020) and athlete and civic activism that emerges in responses to neoliberal sport mega-events (Boykoff 2020). Throughout the 2020s and beyond, we remain certain that sport mega-events still will generate new and complex questions speaking to their governance structures, their emerging controversies, and their impacts.

Such perspective guides this Special Issue's key aims, which revolve around, firstly, to mark a new and significant path in the social study of sport mega-events. Secondly, the Special Issue seeks to illuminate some of the most pressing issues that emerge around contemporary mega-events and demonstrate how an analysis of these issues in sport, can facilitate an understanding of these issues more broadly, and how we see the modern world. Through a fascinating range of transnational, contemporary and inter-disciplinary contributions in this issue – that are both empirical, conceptual and theoretical in their nature and approaches – we remain optimistic that this Editorial and Special Issue as a whole and, *most importantly*, the separate articles featuring within it, can influence and shape the (ever-)evolving research agenda over the new decade. A decade that consists of exciting, revealing and defining sport mega-events that have taken place, or will take place across global cities like Tokyo, Beijing, Paris, Los Angeles and Milano, only to name a few.

Disclosure statement

No potential conflict of interest was reported by the author.

References

Bourdieu, P. 1998. *On Television*. Translated by P. Ferguson. New York: New York Press.
Boykoff, J. 2016. *Power Games: A Political History of the Games*. London: Verso.
Boykoff, J. 2020. *NOlympians: Inside the Fight against Capitalist Mega-Sports in Los Angeles, Tokyo and Beyond*. Nova Scotia: Fernwood.
Drummond, R., and J. Cronje. 2019. "Building a White Elephant? The Case of the Cape Town Stadium." *International Journal of Sport Policy and Politics* 11 (1): 57–78. doi:10.1080/19406940.2018.1508053.
Giulianotti, R. 2019. "Football Events, Memories and Globalization." *Soccer & Society* 20 (7–8): 903–911. doi:10.1080/14660970.2019.1680490.
Horne, J. 2007. "The Four 'Knowns' of Sports Mega-Events." *Leisure Studies* 26 (1): 81–96. doi:10.1080/02614360500504628.
Horne, J., and W. Manzenreiter. 2006. "An Introduction to the Sociology of Sports Mega-Events." *The Sociological Review* 54 (2_suppl): 1–24. doi:10.1111/j.1467-954X.2006.00650.x.
Khalifa, N. A. D. 2020. "Analysis of the Impediments to the Effective Management of Mega Sporting Events: A Case of the FIFA 2022 World Cup in Qatar." *European Journal of Business and Strategic Management* 5 (1): 70–95.
Lee Ludvigsen, J. A. 2021. "When 'the Show' Cannot Go on: An Investigation into Sports Mega-Events and Responses during the Pandemic Crisis." *International Review for the Sociology of Sport* 1–18.
Ludvigsen, J. A. L., and D. Parnell. 2021. "Redesigning the Games? The 2020 Olympic Games, Playbooks and New Sports Event Risk Management Tools." *Managing Sport and Leisure*: 1–13. doi:10.1080/23750472.2021.1928538.

Müller, M. 2015. "The Mega-Event Syndrome: Why So Much Goes Wrong in Mega-Event Planning and What to Do about It." *Journal of the American Planning Association* 81 (1): 6–17. doi:10.1080/01944363.2015.1038292.

Norwegian Supporters Alliance. 2021. "Statement from Norwegian Football Supporters." https://www.fotball-supporter.no/2021/05/26/statement-from-norwegian-football-supporters/

Parnell, D., P. Widdop, A. Bond, and R. Wilson. 2020. "COVID-19, Networks and Sport." *Managing Sport and Leisure*: 1–7. doi:10.1080/23750472.2020.1750100.

Paulsson, A., and J. Alm. 2020. "Passing on the Torch: Urban Governance, Mega-Event Politics and Failed Olympic Bids in Oslo and Stockholm." *City, Culture and Society* 20: 100325–100328. doi:10.1016/j.ccs.2019.100325.

Roche, M. 2000. *Mega-Events and Modernity: Olympics and Expos in the Growth of Global Culture*. London: Routledge.

Roche, M. 2003. "Mega-Events, Time and Modernity: On Time Structures in Global Society." *Time & Society* 12 (1): 99–126. doi:10.1177/0961463X03012001370.

Roche, M. 2017. *Mega-Events and Social Change: Spectacle, Legacy and Public Culture*. Manchester: Manchester University Press.

Rookwood, J., and K. Adeosun. 2021. "Nation Branding and Public Diplomacy: Examining Japan's 2019 Rugby World Cup and 2020 (21) Olympic Games in the Midst of a Global Economic Downturn and the COVID-19 Pandemic." *Journal of Global Sport Management*: 1–21. doi:10.1080/24704067.2021.1871860.

Sugden, J. P., and J. T. Sugden. 2020. "Critical Reflections on the Future of Global Sport Governance in a post-Covid-19 World: Levelling the Field." In *Sport and the Pandemic*, edited by P. M. Pedersen, B. J. Ruihley and B. Li, 157–164. London: Routledge.

Sugden, J., and A. Tomlinson. 2017. *Football, Corruption and Lies: Revisiting 'Badfellas', the Book FIFA Tried to Ban*. London: Routledge.

The Guardian. 2021. "9,000 Covid Cases Linked to Euro 2020 Games in Mass Events Scheme." https://www.theguardian.com/world/2021/aug/20/9000-covid-cases-linked-to-euro-2020-games-in-mass-events-scheme.

Watt, P. 2013. "It's Not for Us." *City* 17 (1): 99–118. doi:10.1080/13604813.2012.754190.

Włoch, R. 2013. "UEFA as a New Agent of Global Governance: A Case Study of Relations between UEFA and the Polish Government against the Background of the UEFA EURO 2012." *Journal of Sport and Social Issues* 37 (3): 297–311. doi:10.1177/0193723512467192.

Woods, J., and J. A. L. Ludvigsen. 2021. "The Changing Faces of Fandom? Exploring Emerging 'Online' and 'Offline' Fandom Spaces in the English Premier League." *Sport in Society*: 1–16. doi:10.1080/17430437.2021.1904902.

Zirin, D. 2016. *Brazil's Dance with the Devil: The World Cup, the Olympics and the Fight for Democracy*. Chicago, IL: Haymarket Books.

Jan Andre Lee Ludvigsen

https://orcid.org/0000-0002-0085-2321

Joel Rookwood

https://orcid.org/0000-0002-6510-4519

Daniel Parnell

https://orcid.org/0000-0001-5593-0633

Can international sports mega events be considered physical activity interventions? A systematic review and quality assessment of large-scale population studies

Michael Annear, Shintaro Sato, Tetsuhiro Kidokoro and Yasuo Shimizu

ABSTRACT
Amidst ongoing debate about the viability of physical activity (PA) legacies associated with hosting international sports mega events, this systematic review explores quantitative evidence from population studies that utilize repeated measures. This review is guided by the PRISMA protocol and includes article quality evaluation techniques from health intervention research. Structured Boolean searches were conducted across six databases and grey literature sources. In total, 12 studies were identified from the last two decades across four event typologies. Among these studies, 9 were evaluated as being of higher quality, but only 4 employed standard definitions or measures of PA. Among the higher quality studies, two-thirds found no evidence for statistically significantly PA legacies, although gaps and limitations precluded definitive assessment. Common concerns include limited evaluation of covariates, sweeping conclusions based on insufficient evidence, arbitrary conceptualization and operalization of PA, and lack of triangulation. Research recommendations for resolving the impasse are proposed.

Introduction

Contested physical activity legacies

There is ongoing debate in the event management, sport science and public health literature regarding the possibility of achieving population physical activity (PA) legacies as an outcome of sports mega evet hosting. Regular PA refers to habitual and sustained participation in sport, exercise, leisure time activities or active travel that increases breathing rate, heart rate and energy expenditure (World Health Organization 2019). Such activity is associated with confirmed physical and mental health benefits (Garber et al. 2011; Colberg et al. 2016; Rebar et al. 2015), opportunities for social networking and the development of significant life meaning (Beaton et al. 2011; Wong et al. 2018). If significant population-level increases in PA could be realized as a result of hosting large sporting events, meeting or exceeding international guidelines for volume and intensity, it would represent a tremendous return on community investment as well as a powerful public health legacy. For the purposes of the present review, sports mega events are defined as fixed-duration and costly international competitions that are organized by a special authority over defined development and promotion (pre-hosting) and post-hosting time periods, which yield the highest levels of media coverage and impacts for the host community (Byers, Slack & Parent, 2012; Muller, 2015; Rogerson, 2016). This definition is operationalized to include the 10 largest international sports competitions involving the highest levels of athlete and spectator attendance, greatest media coverage, and largest economic impacts. Based on global sports impact reports (Sports Marketing Intelligence 2017), such events include the Summer Olympic and Paralympic Games, Winter Olympic and Paralympic Games, FIFA Football World Cup, Rugby World Cup, Commonwealth Games, Student Games (Universiade), World Games, Pan-American Games, and Asian Games. Events considered for this review included multiple-sport or single-sport events with global participation or multiple-sport continental/regional events (Sports Marketing Intelligence 2017). Single-sport continental or regional events were not included in the review (e.g., European Football Championship, Ryder Cup of Golf or World Series of Baseball) as they typically involve a smaller number of participant and host countries.

Since the turn of the century, there has been a growing focus on legacy planning associated with mega event hosting. For example, since the Sydney 2000 Olympics, cities that bid for the rights to the Games are required to submit proposals outlining how they plan to leverage the event to achieve wider societal outcomes (International Olympic Committee 2017). Legacy plans for the forthcoming Tokyo Olympics (delayed to 2021 due the global COVID-19 pandemic) are no exception and include objectives relating to population health and sports participation as measures of hosting success as well as economic, educational and social development goals (Tokyo Organizing Committee of the Olympic and Paralympic Games 2016). Mega event legacy has been defined in several ways, although most definitions refer to tangible and intangible outcomes across a range of domains, including community sport participation, economic development, urban regeneration, education and others, that unfold in the months and years after hosting (International Olympic Committee 2017; Bason and Grix 2018). The achievement of population PA is a common legacy objective founded upon such theoretical perspectives as the demonstration (trickle-down) effect, the festival effect, and the social ecological model (Weed et al. 2015; Kurumi, Wu and Sato 2018; Hiller and Wanner 2015). These perspectives hypothesize that through athlete role modelling, the creation of an exciting or convivial atmosphere, or infrastructure changes and facility development, hosting a sports mega event creates the conditions to facilitate widespread changes in behaviour (Veal, Toohey, and Frawley 2019; Weed et al. 2015).

There are a growing number of studies and reviews that have been undertaken in the last two decades to explore the PA-related legacies of sports mega-events (Annear et al. 2019; Weed et al. 2015; Weed et al. 2012; Mahtani et al. 2013; McCartney et al. 2010). Based on emerging epidemiological data, public health researchers have surmised that current PA-related legacy effects appear to currently be '… more rhetoric than reality' (Bauman, Bellew, and Craig 2014, 243), while sport policy researchers have asserted that, if properly leveraged, mega events '…may be a justifiable investment in sport participation terms' (Weed et al. 2015, 195). Existing reviews and commentaries have been limited, however, by a consistent failure to distinguish between a diversity of research designs (e.g., cross-sectional vs longitudinal) and quality parameters (e.g., convenience sampling vs population sampling). Few reviews include article quality assessments, and none differentiate between designs that can, or cannot, determine objective legacy effects. This manuscript attempts to progress the current debate concerning the influence of mega-event hosting on population PA by focusing on large and methodologically rigorous studies (as determined by evaluation scores on an international measure of article quality) from the last two decades.

Review question, originality and rationale

The overarching question that guided this systematic review is as follows: what population-level, quantitative evidence exists to support or refute assertions that hosting the largest international sports events provide measurable and significant increases in community PA participation? Within this overarching question are several implicit secondary queries: 1) How has PA legacy been operationalized and measured in quantitative, population-level studies? 2) Can a statistically significant PA legacy effect be attributed to hosting the largest global sports events? 3) What are the gaps and limitations across study designs and outcome measures within the current literature? and 4) Where should researchers focus their efforts to definitively address the issue of PA legacy effects in the coming years.

A unique element of the present review is the focus on the evaluation of quantitative research studies that utilize representative national or subnational samples and which include a temporal component in their data collection (e.g., pre-post, longitudinal, experimental or cohort level data). Studies based on such designs provide the highest level of evidence for determining statistical significance, effect magnitude and potential causality, which allow researchers to make objective determinations concerning the potential impacts within particular legacy domains (Shintaro et al. 2020; Oshimi, Harada, and Fukuhara 2016). Another novel feature of this review is the inclusion of a robust health intervention assessment tool (the Downs and Black checklist) to identify studies of relatively higher and lower methodological rigor, which also requires assessment of studies that have comparable experimental or intervention-type designs (involving repeated measurement) that is typical of quantitative research (e.g., considering a mega-event as a time-bound intervention to promote health-related behaviours). While acknowledging the growing body of qualitative scholarship that examines mega-event legacies (Carter and Lorenc 2015), this study explicitly aims to evaluate and compare studies that report objectively measured and statistically significant effects at the population level. Beyond the focus on quantitative research, a final unique feature of the research was the inclusion of only the largest sports mega event types, including Olympic and Paralympic Games, Football and Rugby world cups and related competitions as defined in global sport impact assessments (Sports Marketing Intelligence 2017).

Methods

Review and assessment protocols

This study was informed by and structured using the PRISMA (Preferred Reporting Items for Systematic Reviews and Meta-Analyses) guidelines for the conduct of systematic reviews and meta analyses (Liberati et al. 2009) as well as the Downs and Black checklist for Quality

Assessment in intervention-type studies (Downs and Black 1998). The PRISMA guidelines are one of two best-practice checklists for systematic reviews that inform design, execution and reporting of systematic reviews and meta analyses (Liberati et al. 2009). In practice, the PRISMA guidelines set forth 27 reporting criteria (addressing rationale, methods, design, results, discussion, ethics and other matters) that review authors should report to ensure transparency and repeatability of research processes. The Downs and Black Checklist is a reliable and valid measure of research quality and risk of bias (methodological rigor) in health-related intervention studies that include both randomized and non-randomized designs (Downs and Black 1998). Because hosting a sports mega-event is often framed by researchers, either explicitly or implicitly, as a type of intervention to promote health-related behaviours, this is an appropriate tool to assess quality in quantitative research undertaken to examine so-called legacy effects.

Search strategy and data extraction

The systematic review procedures included structured searches of six databases that provided a balance between comprehensive and specialized information in relation to both sport and health-related research, including the Cochrane Database of systematic reviews, PubMed/Medline, Sport Discuss, Scopus, Google Scholar, and the Olympic World Library. Searches of the grey literature were also conducted by the authors to identify potentially relevant studies that were not readily accessible through database searches. In the context of the present study, grey literature searches included evaluation of reference lists of closely related research articles (Annear et al. 2019; McCartney et al. 2010; Veal, Toohey, and Frawley 2019; Weed et al. 2015) and consultations with academic experts.

A Boolean search string was developed that included combinations of relevant search terms, which were developed in consultation with members of the research team. The following search string and keywords were used: 'Mega event OR Olympic OR Football OR Rugby OR Games (inclusive of such terms as Commonwealth Games, Paralympic Games, Student Games, World Games, Asian Games or Pan-American Games)' AND 'Sport OR physical activity OR exercise' AND 'legacy OR outcome OR participation' AND 'population OR intervention OR experiment OR longitudinal OR survey'. Searches were conducted and completed in November and December 2020 to provide a complete 20-year search period (January 2000–December 2020). All data were extracted by the first author using pre-formatted excel data tables and confirmed by co-authors from full text versions of the included manuscripts.

Inclusion criteria (screening and eligibility assessment)

Six initial inclusion (screening) criteria were used to evaluate the relevance of studies identified via Boolean searches. These criteria included the following: studies published in peer-reviewed academic journals, studies published in English, studies published on or after the year 2000 (a 20-year range was selected as the year 2000 the first year that legacy plans became a requirement for cities bidding to host the Olympics), quantitative studies based on self-reports or direct measurement, studies that explore a common PA domain as an outcome variable or covariate (e.g. sport, exercise or active leisure participation), and studies related to hosting one of the largest global sporting events, including the Olympic Games, Commonwealth/Pan American/Asian/Student/World Games, Football World Cup and/or Rugby World Cup.

Following the stage one screening criteria, a further three eligibility criteria were then applied to identify studies that met the requisite criteria related to the level and mode of measurement. These criteria included the following: studies that involve large and representative populations/datasets (at a municipal, regional or national level), studies that include either experimental, longitudinal or cohort study designs related to mega-event hosting impact (with multiple data collection points), and studies that report summary statistics of PA or related concepts (either for a total population or sub-groups).

Manuscript quality assessment

Article quality was assessed using the Downs and Black quality index (Downs and Black 1998). This index scores manuscript quality based on the following criteria: reporting, external validity, internal validity, and power. As a relatively small number of studies met the initial inclusion criteria, the Downs and Black index was used primarily as a tool for assessing the relative merits and potential biases of included studies from the point of view of health intervention research. Cut points for article quality were based on those published elsewhere (Hooper et al. 2008). Downs and Black score ranges were given corresponding quality levels as previously reported: excellent (26–28), good (20–25), fair (15–19) and poor (≤14).

Data synthesis and evaluation

A narrative synthesis was used for data integration in this study, which is consistent with the analytic approach of other recent systematic reviews conducted in sport and health studies (Heneghan et al. 2020; Tassignon et al. 2019). Narrative synthesis refers to interpretive evaluation that consolidates results based on a diversity of methodological backgrounds or measurement typologies (Harden and Thomas 2005). This type of analytic strategy is used as a pragmatic alternative to statistical meta-analyses when there are limits or inconsistencies among the extracted data (Snilstveit, Oliver, and Vojtkova 2012). Narrative synthesis was necessary in the present review for several reasons, including a lack of consistent PA measures, variations in measurement mode (e.g., annual sport participation frequencies, daily step counts, weekly PA or energy expenditure estimates etc.), and wide diversity of summary statistics (e.g., percentages, odds ratios, correlation coefficients and effect sizes). Narrative synthesis was supported by evaluation of article quality with the Downs and Black checklist, which permitted reliable and comparative estimations of research rigor and limitations.

Results

Search and screening results

After structured database searches, examination of the grey literature and removal of duplicates, 33 articles were identified for potential inclusion in the review based on consideration of title, keyword, and abstract information (see Table 1). Following initial screening, each manuscript was reviewed in full. Among this set of manuscripts, 21 were excluded on one of the following grounds: only descriptive statistics were provided, studies reported perceptions or attitudes related to PA rather than behaviour change, or design elements biased the potential effect of mega-events (e.g., providing vouchers for participation in fitness classes during a mega-event). Following screening and eligibility assessment, 12 studies were included in the final analysis (see Figure 1 and Table 2).

Article quality assessment

The twelve included studies were subjected to quality assessment using the Downs and Black checklist for health-related intervention studies. Scores ranged from 13 (poor) to 21 (good). Nine studies were identified as being of fair or good methodological and reporting quality (Aizawa et al. 2018; Berger et al. 2019; Perks 2015; Sandercock, Beedie, and Mann 2016; Craig and Bauman 2014; Potwarka and Leatherdale 2016; Kokolakakis, Lera-López, and Ramchandani 2019; Kokolakakis and Lera-Lopez 2020; Bauman, Bellew, and Craig 2014). A further three studies were of comparatively poorer quality (Pappous and Hayday 2016; Veal, Toohey, and Frawley 2012; Frawley and Cush 2011). The nine higher quality studies represented largescale quantitative analyses of mega event impacts. In contrast, the three lower quality studies included mixed methods and case study data, which often only extended to descriptive evaluations of temporally comparative data (e.g., percentage change from pre- to post-event). It is important to emphasize that a rating of *poor* in the article quality assessment is not an indictment of research design. Rather, it is a measure of the extent to which the study design conforms to recommended best practice when conceptualized and assessed as intervention research.

Event type and location

Published studies that employed population-level and longitudinal/cohort designs most commonly addressed PA legacies associated with the Summer Olympic and Paralympic Games (see Table 3). Smaller numbers of studies were identified that addressed the Winter Olympic and Paralympic Games, Rugby World Cup and Commonwealth Games. Despite the prevalence of studies of the Olympic and Paralympic Games, no studies were identified from the Rio de Janeiro (2016), Beijing (2008), or Athens (2004) Summer Olympic and Paralympic Games. Nor were any studies located from the Salt Lake City (2002), Turin (2006), Sochi (2014) or Pyeongchang (2018) Winter Olympic and Paralympic Games.

Table 1. Databases searched and articles recovered during initial screening.

Database name	Articles identified	Initial inclusions
Cochrane database (systematic reviews)	0	0
Olympic World Library	18	4
Web of Science	258	10
PubMed (incl. MEDLINE)	19	3
SportDiscus	58	1
Google Scholar	100	8
Grey literature searches	11	11

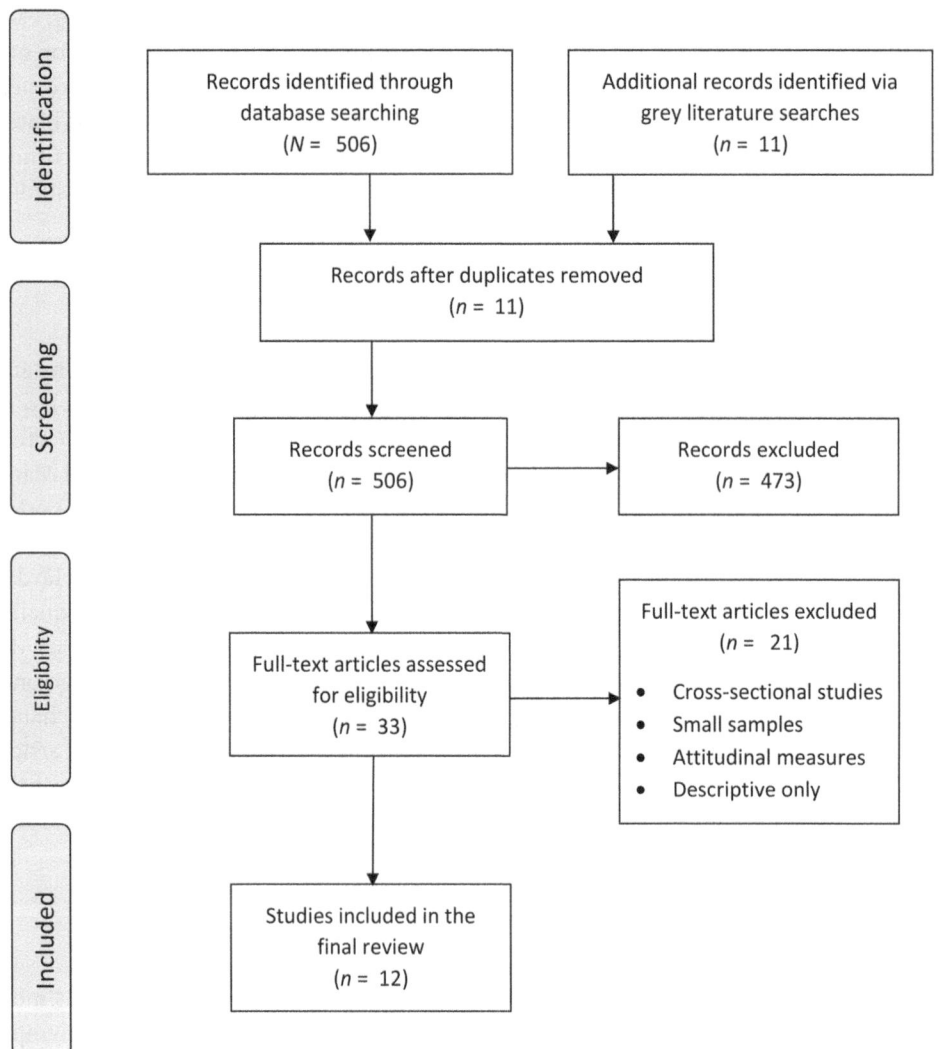

Figure 1. PRISMA data extraction and screening flow diagram.

Furthermore, no studies were identified that addressed other mega sports events, such as the Football World Cup, Asian Games, Pan-American Games, Student Games (Universiade) or World Games.

Discussion

Summary of evidence

Among the studies identified in the review process, nine (75%) were regarded as being of higher research quality (fair-good quality assessment), while three (25%) provided lower-quality evidence. Among the nine higher quality studies, six (67%) reported no association between event hosting and higher levels population PA in the months and years

Table 2. Summary of the characteristics and quality scores for studies included in the systematic review ($n = 12$).

Reference	Event / location	Participants	Design and follow-up period	PA outcome measure	Salient finding	PA legacy assessment	Quality score
1. Aizawa et al. (2018)	1964 Tokyo Olympics Japan	Adults, 40 years and older in wave 1 (1994) $N > 1500$	National sport survey Cohort study (multi-wave follow-up over a 50-year period) 1994 / 2004 / 2014	Self-reported annual sport participation frequency	After controlling for demographics and other determinants of sport participation, individuals who experienced the Tokyo 1964 Olympic Games participated in sport more frequently than other generations.	Positive	Good (20 / 28)
2. Bauman, Bellew, and Craig (2014)	2000 Sydney Olympics Australia	Adults, 18–75 years $N > 3500$	National survey – oversampling in NSW/ACT Longitudinal (pre-post event) 1999 / 2000 (within 12 months of hosting)	Self-reported weekly PA minutes	There were no significant effects of the Olympics on physical activity participation among adult Australians, measured 6 weeks after the end of the Games.	Nil	Fair (17 / 28)
3. Berger et al. (2019)	2012 London Olympics United Kingdom	Children, 11–14 years $N > 2000$	Regional survey (London residents) Cohort study (multi-wave follow-up pre/post-event) 2012–14 (within 24 months of hosting)	Self-reported weekly PA frequency (walking and outdoor PA) measured with the Y-PAQ	Adolescents' perceptions of their neighbourhood environment, and changes in these perceptions due to Olympic urban regeneration, did not consistently predict physical activity.	Nil	Good (22 / 28)
4. Craig and Bauman (2014)	2010 Vancouver Winter Olympics Canada	Children, 5–19 years $N > 19{,}530$	National survey and objective PA measures. Longitudinal (pre-post event) 2007 / 2011 (within 16 months of hosting)	Mean daily step count recorded with pedometer	The 2010 Olympic Games had no measurable impact on objectively measured physical activity or the prevalence of overall sports participation among Canadian children.	Nil	Fair (19 / 28)
5. Perks (2015)	2010 Vancouver Winter Olympics Canada	Youth and adults, 15 years or older $N > 15{,}000$	National time use surveys (self-reported) Longitudinal (pre-post event) 2005 / 2010 (within 10 months of hosting)	Daily sport participation (on an average day)	The Olympics had almost no impact on sport participation in Canada, although there does appear to be a modest bounce in sport participation in the Vancouver area immediately following the Games.	Nil	Fair (17 / 28)
6. Sandercock, Beedie, and Mann (2016)	2012 London Olympics United Kingdom	Children, 10–16 years $N > 900$	Regional survey (London residents) and objective fitness testing. Longitudinal (pre-post event) 2012 / 2013 (within 20 months of hosting)	Cardiorespiratory fitness (VO_2 max testing) Self-reported PA on the PAQ	Children who reported higher levels of inspiration arising from the Olympic Games showed higher levels of fitness and PA behavior compared to other children. No pre-post difference in overall PA or fitness measures.	Nil (overall)	Good (21 / 28)

(Continued)

Table 2. Continued

	Event	Sample	Method	Measure	Findings	Direction of effect	Quality rating
7. Frawley and Cush (2011)	2003 Rugby World Cup (multiple host cities) Australia	Junior (under 18 years) and senior club rugby players N > 30,000	Case study and examination of club rugby registration data pre-post hosting, 2000–2008 (annual follow-up for 5 years post hosting)	Annual percentage change in regional and total club rugby registrations	Rugby witnessed an increase in sport registrations following the staging of the event. The increase, however, was substantially greater for the junior rugby category than the senior rugby category.	Positive	Poor (descriptive, mixed methods) (13 / 28)
8. Veal, Toohey, and Frawley (2012)	2000 Sydney Olympics 2003 Rugby World Cup 2006 Comm Games Australia	Large-scale population and registration data from children and adults. N = varies	Examination of national and regional activity survey and club registration data from 2000–2007 (multiple follow up periods)	Annual percentage change in self-reported PA and club registration data.	Mixed evidence was identified for PA and sport outcomes associated with event hosting: 2000 OG: possible increases in certain sports and age cohorts. 2003 RWC: club registration increases post hosting. 2006 CG: No evidence of PA increases post hosting.	Mixed (nil overall)	Poor (descriptive summary of three events) (14 / 28)
9. Pappous and Hayday (2016)	2012 London Olympics United Kingdom	Children and adult club registrants N > 7000	Examination of national registration data for Judo and Fencing from 2007–2013 (within 11 months of hosting)	Percentage change in annual club registration data.	The data show and overall descriptive increase in participation between 2007 and 2013, in both Judo and Fencing.	Positive	Poor (descriptive, mixed methods) (13 / 28)
10. Potwarka and Leatherdale (2016)	2010 Vancouver Winter Olympics Canada	Females and males aged 12–19 years. N > 1,000,000	National self-reports of daily leisure time PA. Repeated cross-sectional surveys pre-post event, 2007–2012 (within 24 months of hosting)	Self-reported average daily energy expenditure related to leisure time physical activity.	No statistically significant changes were observed in the rate of moderately active/active youth in Canada or the province of British Columbia over a two-year time period. Some regional increase in female participation were identified.	Mixed (nil overall)	Fair (19 / 28)
11. Kokolakakis, Lera-López, and Ramchandani (2019)	2012 London Olympics United Kingdom	English adults aged 16 or older. N > 150,000	National self-reported sport and exercise participation. Repeated cross-sectional survey pre-post event, 2005–2014 (within 24 months of hosting)	Self-reported total minutes of sport and active recreation in a week.	In 2014, the sports participation rates fell relative to 2013 but remained higher than pre-Olympic levels. The sport participation legacy of the Olympic Games appeared to have significant differences between socio-demographic groups.	Positive	Fair (19 / 28)
12. Kokolakakis and Lera-Lopez (2020)	2012 London Olympics United Kingdom	English adults aged 16 or older. N > 150,000	National self-reported sport and exercise participation. Repeated cross-sectional survey pre-post event, 2005–2014 (within 24 months of hosting)	Self-reported total minutes of sport and active recreation in a week.	When focusing the analysis on individual sports, London 2012 has attracted not only regular practitioners but also non-regular participants for the Olympic/Paralympics sports under analysis	Positive	Fair (17 / 28)

Table 3. Mega events and locations included in empirical legacy studies.

Event type	Location / year	Study count[1]
Summer Olympic and Paralympic Games	Tokyo, Japan (1964)[2]	8
	Sydney, Australia (2000)	
	London, UK (2012)	
Winter Olympic and Paralympic Games	Vancouver, Canada (2010)	3
Rugby World Cup	Australia, national (2003)	2
Commonwealth Games	Melbourne, Australia (2006)	1

[1]Note that one study included an evaluation of three mega events hence the study count exceeds the overall number of included studies.
[2]Study published in 2018 based on multi-decade cohort evaluation.

afterwards suggesting that the weight of evidence currently falls on the side of limited mega event impacts. Post-hosting follow-up measures were generally taken over a medium-term period of 10–24 months after hosting, with the exception of one multi-wave cohort study with data gathered over a 50-year period (Aizawa et al. 2018). Summarizing their findings, authors of higher quality studies asserted that without a host government commitment to significant and long-term investment across supportive infrastructure, PA promotion and long-term surveillance, it may not be possible to successfully leverage one-off mega events to sustainably boost public participation (Craig and Bauman 2014; Bauman, Bellew, and Craig 2014; Sandercock, Beedie, and Mann 2016). This sentiment was also supported by positive, though methodologically limited, findings from Aizawa et al. (2018) who surmised that reported cohort increases in PA in the decades following the 1964 Tokyo Olympics were likely related to sustained, multi-sector government investment that aimed to boost social and economic development in post-WW2 Japan (rather than one-off event funding). Among the three higher quality studies that reported positive associations between event hosting and population PA, two were based on evaluations of the same dataset from London 2012 (and could arguably be considered as a single study) (Kokolakakis and Lera-Lopez 2020; Kokolakakis, Lera-López, and Ramchandani 2019), and the third relied on a secondary analysis of historical cohort survey data in Japan as part of a long-term follow-up to the 1964 Tokyo Olympics (Aizawa et al. 2018). While these studies met Downs and Black criteria for a fair-good intervention reports, only one reported effect sizes (odds ratios) (Kokolakakis, Lera-López, and Ramchandani 2019), and all employed problematic definitions of PA (discussed in more detail below).

While the majority of existing evidence suggests limited PA effects associated with hosting the largest sports mega events, it is important to acknowledge that there are significant gaps in what has been measured in recent decades. It is our contention that these issues have not been adequately highlighted in the extant literature – leading to premature judgements about the potential for achieving PA-related legacies. To reinforce this assertion, in the last 20 years less than 15% of the largest international sports mega events have been subjected to any population-level evaluation concerning potential PA legacies (Sports Marketing Intelligence 2017). Even among the 12 largescale studies identified in this review, only four employed valid and reliable measures or standard cut points to differentiate and define PA (Sandercock, Beedie, and Mann 2016; Bauman, Bellew, and Craig 2014; Craig and Bauman 2014; Berger et al. 2019). Notably, all of these measures were associated with assessments of only two event types: the Summer and Winter Olympic and Paralympic Games. The Olympic Games, as a dominant focus of event legacy scholarship, may be problematic as a target for research as such events do not reflect a single sport or activity (the same charge could also be levelled as Commonwealth Games, Asian Games and others), but rather myriad pursuits ranging from physically inactive (e.g., shooting sports) to extremely vigorous (e.g., athletic events). Such complexity could be counterproductive when trying to isolate specific legacy effects on population PA, which may be seen more clearly identified in single-sport events (e.g., Football or Rugby World Cups). Studies that have included comparisons of diverse event types (both single and multi-sport) held within one country have reported a potential advantage for single sport events over multi-sport events in terms of the ability of identify a so-called post-hosting legacy effect (Veal, Toohey, and Frawley 2012), although these studies have been constrained by methodological limitations (discussed below). Beyond the limited number of studies of diverse event types, there are other consistent limitations and gaps that significantly constrain current understanding. These include lack of consideration of potential confounders and covariates, a tendency to make sweeping conclusions based on incomplete information, problematic operationalization and conceptualization of PA, and lack of triangulation of research results with objective measures. These issues are discussed in detail below and a potential way forward is proposed.

Limitations at study level

Among the population studies included in this review, there are limitations that may indicate a bias in the reported results. Firstly, few studies have identified or controlled for the potential influence of confounding, meditating or moderating variables. Variables that are known to influence population PA and which could potentially coincide with event hosting are diverse (though well-articulated in the literature) and include government policy or public health marketing, demographic factors (population aging and density), seasonal effects, urban development, traffic, pollution, crime rate and many others (Annear et al. 2014; Bauman et al. 2012). Among the studies that explicitly attempted to address other potential influences, only factors that were closely related to event hosting were often considered as major covariates in analyses. For example, Aizawa et al. (2018) previously controlled for the effect of hosting non-Olympic sports events in Japan when attempting to track to the cohort-level effects of the 1964 Olympic Games over several decades using historical survey data. Similarly, Berger et al. (2019) included measures of neighbourhood perception in Olympic host areas as a potential moderator when considering the impact of urban regeneration on younger adult PA following the London 2012 Olympics. There is generally a lack of detailed consideration of potential covariates, which is problematic for mega event legacy studies as it ignores or diminishes a wide variety of potential ecological influences that have been reported in the literature that may contribute significantly to explaining study outcomes.

Secondly, several studies make sweeping conclusions based on descriptive analyses of secondary datasets – inferring correlation or causation without appropriate supporting analysis. This is even more concerning considering the prevailing lack of consideration of covariates highlighted above. For example, in their descriptive assessment of participation data among two sports (Fencing and Judo) before and after the London 2012 Olympics, Pappous and Hayday (2016) conclude that, 'Since the Games were awarded to London in 2005, a positive increase in grass-roots participation has been seen' (p.681). Similarly, Veal, Toohey, and Frawley (2012) and Frawley and Cush (2011) both reported increases in

Australian Rugby club participation following World Cup hosting in 2003. Veal et al. concluded that, 'There is a clear indication that the hosting of the event may have boosted both adults' and children's participation in the sport' (p.175). In all three of the aforementioned studies, conclusions were made based on a percentage change in sport registration data with no inferential analyses to confirm that observed participation increases were not attributable to chance or other variables. While caveats and limitations were noted by the study authors (including pre-existing trends for increasing participation), the inclusion of such definitive remarks without corresponding tests of significance and effect size raises questions about the validity of such data and its potential influence on policy makers and researchers. Sweeping conclusions were most commonly identified among research that was reported in event management and leisure studies journals, which currently dominate legacy scholarship. Indeed, following the initial database searches and application of inclusion criteria in the present review, >65% of selected articles were published in these disciplinary areas. A greater diversity of research expertise would undoubtedly help to ensure higher levels of rigor in PA legacy research. Within public health and epidemiology, for example, there are several well-known international guidelines to inform best practice in the analysis and reporting of intervention-type studies (e.g., STROBE, TREND and others) (Des Jarlais, Lyles, and Crepaz 2004; Von Elm et al. 2007) in addition to the availability of robust study evaluation frameworks (e.g., Downs and Black checklist as applied in the present review).

Limitations at outcome level

Limitations at the study outcome level include inconsistencies in concept operationalization and measurement and reliance on PA self-reports. A major challenge when considering PA legacy data is the inconsistency in the phenomenon being measured, despite most researchers using related terminology (e.g., PA, exercise, or sport). Among the 12 studies included in this review, there were seven distinct modes of conceptualizing and measuring PA. In a small number of instances, researchers utilized validated international measures or direct measurement for determining PA level. For example, some studies employed the IPAQ or Y-PAQ self-report measures with analyses reflecting standard cut points for activity and inactivity (e.g., 150 minutes per week or 600 Met-minutes per week as a baseline for moderate activity) (Bauman, Bellew, and Craig 2014; Berger et al. 2019; Potwarka and Leatherdale 2016), while others used direct measures of fitness parameters (e.g., VO_2 max testing and pedometer values) (Sandercock, Beedie, and Mann 2016; Craig and Bauman 2014). Other researchers, however, employed arbitrary measures that have not been scientifically validated or which fail to adequately reflect an evidence-based definition of PA. Problematic conceptualizations and measurements of PA included daily (average) or annual sport participation frequency (Aizawa et al. 2018; Perks 2015), a benchmark value of 3 30-minute exercise bouts per week (Kokolakakis and Lera-Lopez 2020; Kokolakakis, Lera-López, and Ramchandani 2019), and annual changes in sport registration data (Veal, Toohey, and Frawley 2012; Frawley and Cush 2011; Pappous and Hayday 2016). In their use of arbitrary definitions and measures of PA, researchers limited their ability to provide data on the absolute impact of mega event hosting on an important health behaviour.

Due to the large scale of studies included in this review, most measures of PA were necessarily based upon the self-reported data from community volunteers. Indeed, even well-validated and international measures, such as the IPAQ, have been developed and evaluated using self-reported data, rather than objective measures (Bauman et al. 2009). Self-reported PA data are known to often overestimate total activity due to social-desirability and social approval biases, which may result in potentially inaccurate (often higher) PA estimates (Adams et al. 2005; Bauman et al. 2009). To ensure the reliability of their findings and address potential biases, two of the studies in the review included direct measures (VO$_2$ max testing or pedometer values) alongside self-reported data (Sandercock, Beedie, and Mann 2016; Craig and Bauman 2014). Such approaches are useful as they provide a means for triangulating population-level PA data and ruling out significant confounding associated with socially desirability biases. While the use of PA self-reports can often not be avoided in very large studies, there are some reasons why it is not always as problematic as it may seem. For example, if study populations are large enough (e.g., >500 respondents), individual variations can washout during analysis (Motl, McAuley, and DiStefano 2005). Indeed, most measures of population-level PA that use validated self-report measures consistently show low levels (rather than high levels) of participation across a range of typologies (Bauman et al. 2011; Hallal et al. 2012). Additionally, in multiple-time point research designs, behaviour change (or relative effect of an intervention) becomes an equally significant evaluation criterion in addition to absolute activity level (Crutzen and Göritz 2011). Despite some circumstances in which overreporting may not be as problematic as it seems, work is still required to confirm that social desirability biases are not unduly influencing results as a matter of construct and criterion validity.

Hypothesizing a way forward

Population-level studies of mega-event PA legacies that include rigorous designs and analyses are scarce, and the literature is arguably dominated by lower quality and comparatively speculative reports. In the decade ahead, it is recommended that researchers prioritize population-level analyses of PA participation to build a larger evidence base. This may include long-term national PA surveillance efforts, comparative studies at the level of host city/neighbourhood, and more robust evaluations of registration and participation data from representative sports. An example of such widespread surveillance includes the Japanese national fitness tests conducted by the Ministry of Education, Culture, Sports, Science and Technology, which have been undertaken with nationally representative samples for several decades (Tomkinson et al. 2020). Within public health, there are a range of guidelines for best-practice conduct and evaluation of intervention-type studies, and more engagement from researchers in such fields would arguably contribute to resolving current debates by adding a level of rigor that is missing from much of the PA legacy literature. Where possible, population sampling should be achieved across a diversity of age, gender, ethnic, socio-economic, and environmental (e.g., urban/rural) parameters to ensure sufficient contextualization of data based on a range of individual and ecological factors. This is particularly important as population changes accelerate in response to such trends as urbanization, demographic aging and increasing inactivity (Leeson 2018). Relatedly, a diversity of factors needs to be taken into consideration in multi-variate analyses of potential legacy effects due to the multi-dimensional nature of PA influences (Annear et al. 2014; Bauman et al. 2012). Additionally, measurement of potential legacy should include valid and reliable instruments, such as the International Physical Activity Questionnaire (IPAQ) or Global Physical Activity Questionnaire (GPAQ), or the use of standard definitions and cut points for PA (e.g., the WHO guidelines). Beyond this, it is recommended that triangulation is performed with direct PA measurement (e.g., accelerometery, pedometer use or smartphone movement data) to rule out potential measurement biases that are sometimes attributed to self-reported data (Althoff et al. 2017). Finally, it is recommended that a greater diversity of mega-event types are subjected to largescale legacy evaluations as these may provide opportunities to isolate PA-related population changes with more accuracy. For example, Football or Rugby World cups potentially provide fertile ground for researchers as engagement in such pursuits is often undertaken within club and educational settings where participation data may help to corroborate self-reported activity data. Such research, as described above, will be costly and time consuming due to the necessity for scale and repeated measures, yet it is necessary to build a sufficiently robust and objective evidence base. Once there is a larger and consistently higher quality body of literature, a meta-analysis could help to determine the absolute effect of mega event hosting on population PA. Meta-analyses are quantitative and highly structured investigations that utilize statistical methods to estimate the presence and characteristics of an overall effect as part of an examination of a body of higher quality studies (Haidich 2010). Currently, the quantity of higher-quality studies is arguably not sufficient to permit such definitive assessment.

Conclusion

Despite a growing literature, it is important to recognize the relative youth of the sports mega event research field and to clearly distinguish between more and less robust study designs. For example, PA legacy research is far less developed as a field of academic endeavour than studies on the relationship between activity level and health parameters. This is particularly relevant as mega events can be conceptualized as time-bound interventions that have many potential impacts for host cities and nations. Mega events are increasingly promoted for their capacity to contribute to population health objectives, such as encouraging sport and exercise participation via athlete role modelling, festival effects and environmental changes. This systematic review has shown that there is a dearth of high-quality studies that can effectively measure PA-related effects associated with mega-event hosting. Organizers of major sports mega events have only seriously considered wider population goals or post-hosting legacies in the last two decades, and measurable targets (so-called KPIs) are frequently absent from official legacy plans (Tokyo Organizing Committee of the Olympic and Paralympic Games 2016). Following the recent postponement of the 2020 Summer Olympic and Paralympic Games due to the global COVID-19 pandemic and ongoing concerns about the costs of hosting for governments and taxpayers, it is critical that researchers and policy makers accurately quantify the potential impact of such events on KPIs related to population health and activity. Based on the current evidence, it is far from certain that population-level PA improvements are a viable outcome of hosting – although more high-quality data are urgently required.

Disclosure statement

The researchers declare that they have no conflicts of interest.

ORCID

Michael Annear http://orcid.org/0000-0002-9645-3295
Shintaro Sato http://orcid.org/0000-0003-3612-9001

References

Adams, Swann Arp., Charles E. Matthews, Cara B. Ebbeling, Charity G. Moore, Joan E. Cunningham, Jeanette Fulton, and James R. Hebert. 2005. "The Effect of Social Desirability and Social Approval on Self-Reports of Physical Activity." *American Journal of Epidemiology* 161 (4): 389–398. doi:10.1093/aje/kwi054.

Aizawa, Kurumi, Ji Wu, Yuhei Inoue, and Mikihiro Sato. 2018. "Long-Term Impact of the Tokyo 1964 Olympic Games on Sport Participation: A Cohort Analysis." *Sport Management Review* 21 (1): 86–97. doi:10.1016/j.smr.2017.05.001.

Althoff, Tim, Rok Sosič, Jennifer L. Hicks, Abby C. King, Scott L. Delp, and Jure Leskovec. 2017. "Large-Scale Physical Activity Data Reveal Worldwide Activity Inequality." *Nature* 547 (7663): 336–339. doi:10.1038/nature23018.

Annear, M., S. Keeling, T. I. M. Wilkinson, G. Cushman, B. Gidlow, and H. Hopkins. 2014. "Environmental influences on healthy and active ageing: A systematic review." *Ageing & Society* 34 (4): 590–622. doi:10.1017/S0144686X1200116X

Annear, M. J., Y. Shimizu, and T. Kidokoro. 2019. "Sports Mega-Event Legacies andAdult Physical Activity: A Systematic Literature Review and Research Agenda." *European Journal of Sport Science* 19 (5): 671–685. doi:10.1080/17461391.2018.1554002.

Bason, Tom, and Jonathan Grix. 2018. "Planning to Fail? Leveraging the Olympic Bid." *Marketing Intelligence & Planning* 36 (1): 138–151. doi:10.1108/MIP-06-2017-0106.

Bauman, Adrian, Barbara E. Ainsworth, Fiona Bull, Cora L. Craig, Maria Hagströmer, James F. Sallis, Michael Pratt, and Michael Sjöström. 2009. "Progress and Pitfalls in the Use of the International Physical Activity Questionnaire (IPAQ) for Adult Physical Activity Surveillance." *Journal of Physical Activity and Health* 6 (s1): S5–S8. doi:10.1123/jpah.6.s1.s5.

Bauman, Adrian, Barbara E. Ainsworth, James F. Sallis, Maria Hagströmer, Cora L. Craig, Fiona C. Bull, Michael Pratt, Kamalesh Venugopal, Josephine Chau, and Michael Sjöström. 2011. "The Descriptive Epidemiology of sitting. A 20-country comparison using the International Physical Activity Questionnaire (IPAQ)." *American Journal of Preventive Medicine* 41 (2): 228–235. doi:10.1016/j.amepre.2011.05.003.

Bauman, Adrian, Bill Bellew, and Cora L. Craig. 2014. "Did the 2000 Sydney Olympics Increase Physical Activity among Adult Australians?" *British Journal of Sports Medicine* 49 (4): 243–247. doi:10.1136/bjsports-2013-093149.

Bauman, Adrian E., Rodrigo S. Reis, James F. Sallis, Jonathan C. Wells, Ruth J. F. Loos, and Brian W. Martin. 2012. "Correlates of Physical Activity: why Are Some People Physically Active and Others Not?" *The Lancet* 380 (9838): 258–271. doi:10.1016/S0140-6736(12)60735-1.

Beaton, Anthony A., Daniel C. Funk, Lynn Ridinger, and Jeremy Jordan. 2011. "Sport Involvement: A Conceptual and Empirical Analysis." *Sport Management Review* 14 (2): 126–140. doi:10.1016/j.smr.2010.07.002.

Berger, Nicolas, Daniel Lewis, Matteo Quartagno, Edmund Njeru Njagi, and Steven Cummins. 2019. "Longitudinal Associations between Perceptions of the Neighbourhood Environment and Physical Activity in Adolescents: evidence from the Olympic Regeneration in East London (ORiEL) Study." *BMC Public Health* 19 (1): 1760. doi:10.1186/s12889-019-8003-7.

Byers, T., Slack T., and Parent M. 2012. *Key concepts in sport management.* London: Sage.

Carter, R. V., and T. Lorenc. 2015. "A Qualitative Study into the Development of a Physical Activity Legacy from the London 2012 Olympic Games." *Health Promotion International* 30 (3): 793–802. doi:10.1093/heapro/dat066.

Colberg, Sheri R., Ronald J. Sigal, Jane E. Yardley, Michael C. Riddell, David W. Dunstan, Paddy C. Dempsey, Edward S. Horton, Kristin Castorino, and Deborah F. Tate. 2016. "Physical Activity/

Exercise and Diabetes: A Position Statement of the American Diabetes Association." *Diabetes Care* 39 (11): 2065–2079. doi:10.2337/dc16-1728.

Craig, Cora L., and Adrian E. Bauman. 2014. "The Impact of the Vancouver Winter Olympics on Population Level Physical Activity and Sport Participation among Canadian Children and Adolescents: population Based Study." *The International Journal of Behavioral Nutrition and Physical Activity* 11 (1): 107–116. doi:10.1186/s12966-014-0107-y.

Crutzen, Rik, and Anja S. Göritz. 2011. "Does Social Desirability Compromise Self-Reports of Physical Activity in Web-Based Research?" *International Journal of Behavioral Nutrition and Physical Activity* 8 (1): 31–34. doi:10.1186/1479-5868-8-31.

Des Jarlais, Don C., Cynthia Lyles, and Nicole Crepaz. 2004. "Improving the Reporting Quality of Nonrandomized Evaluations of Behavioral and Public Health Interventions: The TREND Statement." *American Journal of Public Health* 94 (3): 361–366. doi:10.2105/ajph.94.3.361.

Downs, S. H., and N. Black. 1998. "The Feasibility of Creating a Checklist for the Assessment of the Methodological Quality Both of Randomised and Non-Randomised Studies of Health Care Interventions." *Journal of Epidemiology and Community Health* 52 (6): 377–384. doi:10.1136/jech.52.6.377.

Frawley, Stephen, and Adam Cush. 2011. "Major Sport Events and Participation Legacy: The Case of the 2003 Rugby World Cup." *Managing Leisure* 16 (1): 65–76. doi:10.1080/13606719.2011.532605.

Garber, Carol Ewing, Bryan Blissmer, Michael R. Deschenes, Barry A. Franklin, Michael J. Lamonte, I-Min Lee, David C. Nieman, and David P. Swain. 2011. "American College of Sports Medicine Position Stand. Quantity and Quality of Exercise for Developing and Maintaining Cardiorespiratory, Musculoskeletal, and Neuromotor Fitness in Apparently Healthy Adults: guidance for Prescribing Exercise." *Medicine and Science in Sports and Exercise* 43 (7): 1334–1359. doi:10.1249/MSS.0b013e318213fefb.

Haidich, Anna-Bettina. 2010. "Meta-Analysis in Medical Research." *Hippokratia* 14 (s1): 29–37.

Hallal, Pedro C., Lars Bo Andersen, Fiona C. Bull, Regina Guthold, William Haskell, and Ulf Ekelund. 2012. "Global Physical Activity Levels: surveillance Progress, Pitfalls, and Prospects." *The Lancet* 380 (9838): 247–257. doi:10.1016/S0140-6736(12)60646-1.

Harden, Angela, and James Thomas. 2005. "Methodological Issues in Combining Diverse Study Types in Systematic Reviews." *International Journal of Social Research Methodology* 8 (3): 257–271. doi:10.1080/13645570500155078.

Heneghan, N. R., S. M. Lokhaug, I. Tyros, S. Longvastøl, and A. Rushton. 2020. "Clinical Reasoning Framework for Thoracic Spine Exercise Prescription in Sport: A Systematic Review and Narrative Synthesis." *BMJ Open Sport & Exercise Medicine* 6 (1): e000713–13. doi:10.1136/bmjsem-2019-000713.

Hiller, Harry H., and Richard A. Wanner. 2015. "The Psycho-Social Impact of the Olympics as Urban Festival: A Leisure Perspective." *Leisure Studies* 34 (6): 672–688. doi:10.1080/02614367.2014.986510.

Hooper, Phil, Jeffrey W. Jutai, Graham Strong, and Elizabeth Russell-Minda. 2008. "Age-Related Macular Degeneration and Low-Vision Rehabilitation: A Systematic Review." *Canadian Journal of Ophthalmology. Journal Canadien D'ophtalmologie* 43 (2): 180–187. doi:10.3129/i08-001.

International Olympic Committee. 2017. *Legacy Strategic Approach: Moving Forward*. Lausanne, Switzerland: International Olympic Committee.

Kokolakakis, Themis, Fernando Lera-López, and Girish Ramchandani. 2019. "Did London 2012 Deliver a Sports Participation Legacy?" *Sport Management Review* 22 (2): 276–287. doi:10.1016/j.smr.2018.04.004.

Kokolakakis, Themistocles, and Fernando Lera-Lopez. 2020. "Sport Promotion through Sport Mega-Events. An Analysis for Types of Olympic Sports in London 2012." *International Journal of Environmental Research and Public Health* 17 (17): 6193–6208. doi:10.3390/ijerph17176193.

Leeson, George W. 2018. "The Growth, Ageing and Urbanisation of Our World." *Journal of Population Ageing* 11 (2): 107–115. doi:10.1007/s12062-018-9225-7.

Liberati, Alessandro, Douglas G. Altman, Jennifer Tetzlaff, Cynthia Mulrow, Peter C. Gøtzsche, John P. A. Ioannidis, Mike Clarke, P. J. Devereaux, Jos Kleijnen, and David Moher. 2009. "The PRISMA Statement for Reporting Systematic Reviews and Meta-Analyses of Studies That

Evaluate Health Care Interventions: explanation and Elaboration." *PLoS Medicine* 6 (7): 1–34. doi:10.1371/journal.pmed.1000100.

Mahtani, Kamal Ram., Joanne Protheroe, Sarah Patricia Slight, Marcelo Marcos Piva Demarzo, Thomas Blakeman, Christopher A. Barton, Bianca Brijnath, and Nia Roberts. 2013. "Can the London 2012 Olympics 'Inspire a Generation' to Do More Physical or Sporting Activities? An Overview of Systematic Reviews." *BMJ Open* 3 (1): 1–8. doi:10.1136/bmjopen-2012-002058.

McCartney, Gerry, Sian Thomas, Hilary Thomson, John Scott, Val Hamilton, Phil Hanlon, David S. Morrison, and Lyndal Bond. 2010. "The Health and Socioeconomic Impacts of Major Multi-Sport Events: systematic Review (1978-2008)." *British Medical Journal* 340: 1–9.

Motl, Robert W., Edward McAuley, and Christine DiStefano. 2005. "Is Social Desirability Associated with Self-Reported Physical Activity?" *Preventive Medicine* 40 (6): 735–739. doi:10.1016/j.ypmed.2004.09.016.

Müller, Martin. 2015. "What Makes an Event a Mega-Event? Definitions and Sizes." *Leisure Studies* 34 (6): 627–642. doi:10.1080/02614367.2014.993333.

Oshimi, Daichi, Munehiko Harada, and Takayuki Fukuhara. 2016. "Residents' Perceptions on the Social Impacts of an International Sport Event: Applying Panel Data Design and a Moderating Variable." *Journal of Convention & Event Tourism* 17 (4): 294–317. doi:10.1080/15470148.2016.1142919.

Pappous, Athanasios, and Emily J. Hayday. 2016. "A Case Study Investigating the Impact of the London 2012 Olympic and Paralympic Games on Participation in Two Non-Traditional English Sports, Judo and Fencing." *Leisure Studies* 35 (5): 668–684. doi:10.1080/02614367.2015.1035314.

Perks, Thomas. 2015. "Exploring an Olympic "Legacy": Sport Participation in Canada before and after the 2010 Vancouver Winter Olympics." *Canadian Review of Sociology = Revue Canadienne de Sociologie* 52 (4): 462–474. doi:10.1111/cars.12087.

Potwarka, Luke R., and Scott T. Leatherdale. 2016. "The Vancouver 2010 Olympics and Leisure-Time Physical Activity Rates among Youth in Canada: Any Evidence of a Trickle-down Effect?" *Leisure Studies* 35 (2): 241–257. doi:10.1080/02614367.2015.1040826.

Rebar, Amanda L., Robert Stanton, David Geard, Camille Short, Mitch J. Duncan, and Corneel Vandelanotte. 2015. "A Meta-Meta-Analysis of the Effect of Physical Activity on Depression and Anxiety in Non-Clinical Adult Populations." *Health Psychology Review* 9 (3): 366–378. doi:10.1080/17437199.2015.1022901.

Rogerson, R. J. 2016. "Re-Defining Temporal Notions of Event Legacy: lessons from Glasgow's Commonwealth Games." *Annals of Leisure Research* 19 (4): 497–518. doi:10.1080/11745398.2016.1151367

Sandercock, Gavin R. H., Chris Beedie, and Steve Mann. 2016. "Is Olympic Inspiration Associated with Fitness and Physical Activity in English Schoolchildren? A Repeated Cross-Sectional Comparison before and 18 Months after London 2012." *BMJ Open* 6 (11): 1–7. doi:10.1136/bmjopen-2016-011670.

Shintaro, S., K. Kinoshita, M. Kim, D. Oshimi, and M. Harada. 2020. "The effect of Rugby World Cup 2019 on residents' psychological well-being: a mediating role of psychological capital." *Current Issues in Tourism*. 1–15. doi:10.1080/13683500.2020.1857713.

Snilstveit, B., S. Oliver, and M. Vojtkova. 2012. "Narrative Approaches to Systematic Review and Synthesis of Evidence for International Development Policy and Practice." *Journal of Development Effectiveness* 4 (3): 409–429. doi:10.1080/19439342.2012.710641.

Sports Marketing Intelligence. 2017. *Global Sports Impact (GSI) Report 2017*. London, UK: Sportcal Global Communications.

Tassignon, B., J. Verschueren, E. Delahunt, M. Smith, B. Vicenzino, E. Verhagen, and R. Meeusen. 2019. "Criteria-Based Return to Sport Decision-Making following Lateral Ankle Sprain Injury: A Systematic Review and Narrative Synthesis." *Sports Medicine (Auckland, N.Z.)* 49 (4): 601–619. doi:10.1007/s40279-019-01071-3.

Tokyo Organizing Committee of the Olympic and Paralympic Games. 2016. *Tokyo 2020 Action and Legacy Plan 2016*. Tokyo, Japan: Japanese Government.

Tomkinson, G. R., T. Kidokoro, T. Dufner, S. Noi, J. S. Fitzgerald, and R. P. Mcgrath. 2020. "Temporal Trends in Handgrip Strength for Older Japanese Adults between 1998 and 2017." *Age and Ageing* 49 (4): 634–639. doi:10.1093/ageing/afaa021.

Veal, A. J., Kristine Toohey, and Stephen Frawley. 2012. "The Sport Participation Legacy of the Sydney 2000 Olympic Games and Other International Sporting Events Hosted in Australia." *Journal of Policy Research in Tourism, Leisure and Events* 4 (2): 155–184. doi:10.1080/19407963.2012.662619.

Veal, A. J., Kristine Toohey, and Stephen Frawley. 2019. "Sport Participation, International Sports Events and the 'Trickle-down Effect.'" *Journal of Policy Research in Tourism, Leisure and Events* 11 (sup1): s3–s7. doi:10.1080/19407963.2018.1556860.

Von Elm, Erik, Douglas G. Altman, Matthias Egger, Stuart J. Pocock, Peter C. Gøtzsche, and Jan P. Vandenbroucke. 2007. "The Strengthening the Reporting of Observational Studies in Epidemiology (STROBE) Statement: guidelines for Reporting Observational Studies." *Annals of Internal Medicine* 147 (8): 573–577. doi:10.7326/0003-4819-147-8-200710160-00010.

Weed, Mike, Esther Coren, Jo Fiore, Ian Wellard, Dikaia Chatziefstathiou, Louise Mansfield, and Suzanne Dowse. 2015. "The Olympic Games and Raising Sport Participation: A Systematic Review of Evidence and an Interrogation of Policy for a Demonstration Effect." *European Sport Management Quarterly* 15 (2): 195–226. doi:10.1080/16184742.2014.998695.

Weed, Mike, Esther Coren, Jo Fiore, Ian Wellard, Louise Mansfield, Dikaia Chatziefstathiou, and Suzanne Dowse. 2012. "Developing a Physical Activity Legacy from the London 2012 Olympic and Paralympic Games: A Policy-Led Systematic Review." *Perspectives in Public Health* 132 (2): 75–80. doi:10.1177/1757913911435758.

Wong, Jen D., Julie S. Son, Stephanie T. West, Jill J. Naar, and Toni Liechty. 2018. "A Life Course Examination of Women's Team Sport Participation in Late Adulthood." *Journal of Aging and Physical Activity* 27 (1): 73–82. doi:10.1123/japa.2017-0193.

World Health Organization. 2019. *Global Action Plan on Physical Activity 2018-2030: more Active People for a Healthier World*. Geneva, Switzerland: World Health Organization.

🔓 OPEN ACCESS

Sport legacy impact on ethnic minority groups: the case of London 2012

Themis Kokolakakis 🆔 and Fernando Lera-López 🆔

ABSTRACT
The sport legacy among ethnic minorities has been neglected despite the positive outcomes of active lifestyle and social inclusion. The current research, applying time series analysis, evaluates evidence of sport legacy among four English ethnic minorities regarding the hosting of Olympic Games (London 2012). A short-term association was found between hosting the Games and sport participation rates among ethnic groups, leading more to increasing frequency of engagement for existing participants than to attracting new participants. The results indicate differences among the ethnic groups and gender, showing that females from Asian ethnicities having the highest engagement. Practical implications for the governance of events in the future relate to improving the festival effect of the Games, to encourage social inclusion for ethnic minorities. Our results might encourage policy makers to maintain a sustained effort in the post-event period to capitalise on sport legacy.

Introduction

In the last ten years, a substantial amount of debate has been conducted about the potential benefits (legacy) of staging sport mega events (SMEs). Such events have delivered economic benefits (Firgo 2021) and positive sport legacies (Castellanos-García et al. 2021) for the hosting countries. Among the SMEs, particularly attention has been paid to the Olympic Games as the most famous SME (see, for example, Annear et al. 2021; Bauman et al. 2021; Scheu, Preuß, and Könecke 2021, for a recent review).

This interest has been closely associated with the global need to increase sport and physical activity (PA) levels and reduce the sedentary behaviour of individuals. International evidence shows that PA levels are falling in many countries and that inactivity is increasing. More than a quarter of the world's adult population (1.4 billion adults) and European adults are insufficiently active (European Commission 2018; World Health Organization 2020),

This is an Open Access article distributed under the terms of the Creative Commons Attribution-NonCommercial-NoDerivatives License (http://creativecommons.org/licenses/by-nc-nd/4.0/), which permits non-commercial re-use, distribution, and reproduction in any medium, provided the original work is properly cited, and is not altered, transformed, or built upon in any way.

having negative effects on health, estimated to be at least $67.5 billion annually (Ding et al. 2020).

In particular, ethnic minorities have shown less engagement in PA and sports than the majority of population (Strandbu, Bakken, and Sletten 2019). For example, data from Sport England's Active Lives Survey reveals significant and persistent differences in PA levels of adults from different ethnic backgrounds in England since 2005 (Sport England 2021). Politically, different voices haver argued against this gap, encouraging, as in the 2007 EU White Paper on Sport, 'a specific focus on access to sport for immigrant women and women from ethnic minorities…' and recognising the potential of sport for the integration of ethnic minorities (European Commission 2007, 8).

Consequently, the Olympic Games have been seen as an opportunity to promote physical activity in the hosting countries and a growing number of studies and reviews have been undertaken to explore the PA-related legacy of the Olympic Games. Recent reviews have shown limited evidence of change in PA participation immediately before or after Olympic Games as well as significant gaps in terms of methodologies used, the conceptualization of PA, long term analysis, and the lack of consideration of potential confounders since the 90s' (Annear et al. 2021; Bauman et al. 2021; Scheu, Preuß, and Könecke 2021).

In recent years, a research focus has been developed to consider sport legacy in some specific population groups. These range from the general perceptions of hosting cities' residents (Ribeiro, Correia, and Biscaia 2021), to a number of recent studies that considered the sport legacy among volunteers (Kim et al. 2019) or people with disabilities (McConkey and Menke 2020). Nevertheless, as far as we know no previous studies have considered the sport legacy of SMEs among ethnic minorities. The traditional smaller level of engagement in sport among ethnic minorities is associated with persistent negative effects on health (Sternfeld et al. 2020) and social inclusion (Dashper, Fletcher, and Long 2019), particularly among women.

Therefore, there is a gap in the analysis of the sport legacy of the Olympic Games among different ethnic backgrounds. This paper attempts to shed light on this potential sport legacy using the information provided by official national statistics about sport participation in England after the 2012 London Olympic Games. The aim of this research is to determine the sport legacy of London Olympic Games among ethnic minorities in England and to check potential differences by gender and ethnic groups. This analysis will contribute towards a better understanding of the SMEs' sport legacies among minority ethnic groups with significant health and social inclusion implications. For policymakers, this research might lead to new insights of social and sport legacy, for a better governance of the upcoming SMEs of the 2020s.

Literature review

Whereas governments and policy-makers emphasise the virtues of hosting the Olympic Games, the academic literature has been, in general, sceptical about the sport event legacy (Annear, Shimizu, and Kidokoro 2019; Annear et al. 2021; Bauman et al. 2021; Scheu, Preuß, and Könecke 2021; Thomson, Kennelly, and Toohey 2020; Weed et al. 2015). The recent increasing number of states hosting different SMEs and the rising costs of bidding for and hosting these SMEs, in particular, the Olympic Games, have increased the number of studies considering this type of legacy and their controversies (Byers, Hayday, and Pappous 2020;

Koenigstorfer et al. 2019; Potwarka and Wicker 2021; Preuss 2019; Thomson, Kennelly, and Toohey 2020). In fact, some poor legacy effects have encouraged opposition 'to large-scale sport event bids, resulting in the withdrawal of active bids for both Summer and Winter Olympic Games' (Thomson, Kennelly, and Toohey 2020, 2).

The Olympic Games account for various legacies in many different areas despite intrinsic difficulties for measuring this legacy (Scheu, Preuß, and Könecke 2021). Preuss (2019) has developed a framework, adopted by the International Olympic Committee, to classify the structural changes due to the Games into six different facets of legacy: urban development, environmental enhancement, policy and governance, human development, intellectual property and social development.[1] Some of these potential legacies could be intangible, such as knowledge and skills for hosting the event, intellectual property, happiness and nation pride, making difficult their evaluation due to their non-pecuniary nature (Schnitzer et al. 2017) Despite this difficulty, Seidl et al. (2021) analysed the intangible impact (perceived satisfaction) of the Innsbruck Youth Olympic Games 2012 among the young people involved in it.

Sport legacy: theoretical perspectives and empirical evidence

Sport legacy incorporates the most important change of habits included into the social development category (as presented in the previous paragraph) and it has been widely analysed in the last two decades. From a theoretical perspective, sport legacy, in general, considers different types of effects (Aizawa et al. 2018; Castellanos-García et al. 2021; Potwarka and Wicker 2021). Firstly, hosting the SMEs could increase the desire of individuals to be involved in an enjoyable sport event, often referred to as festival effect (Cleland et al. 2020; Ramchandani, Coleman, and Christy 2019). Secondly, individuals may be positively inspired by elite athletes as a consequence of their personalities and popularity, often referred to as role model effect (Storm et al. 2018). Two characteristics are relevant to develop the role model effect and influence individuals' behaviour. On the one hand, role models are typically characterised by outstanding sporting achievements. On the other hand, there should be a perception of similarity between the elite athletes and the observing individuals (Potwarka and Wicker 2021). Additionaly, national success in international competitions and SMEs may inspire individuals to be engaged in sport activities (Weed et al. 2015). Finally, hosting an SME implies an improvement in sport infrastructure and transportation (Veal, Toohey, and Frawley 2012) as well as mass media coverage (Misener et al. 2015) that could facilitate changes in behaviour and increase PA levels.

All these effects could generate a positive attitudinal change among spectators or general population towards sport participation. Generally speaking, two different attitudinal changes could take place: inspirational and motivational (Potwarka and Wicker 2021). Inspirational effects are associated to turning inactive and sedentary individuals into sport participants. Motivational effects are associated to behavioural changes within already active individuals by increasing the frequency of participation or by changing the types of sports. According to Weed et al. (2012), sporting success does not inspire individuals who are not emotionally engaged in sport. In other words, it requires already an individual to be a sport participant. From this point of view, it would be better for SMEs to generate a 'festival effect' rooted in local communities, that may have the potential to be harnessed to promote sport engagement among the least active.

From an empirical perspective, there are a growing number of studies and reviews that have been undertaken in the last two decades to analyse the sport legacy of SMEs. The majority of existing evidence and systematic reviews suggests limited PA effects associated with hosting SMEs (Annear, Shimizu, and Kidokoro 2019; Annear et al. 2021; Bauman et al. 2021; Mahtani et al. 2013; McCartney et al. 2010; Scheu, Preuß, and Könecke 2021; Weed et al. 2015). Nevertheless, the evidence is not totally conclusive. For example, some empirical studies have concluded positive short-term (Chen and Henry 2016; Hanstad and Skille 2010; Kokolakakis, Lera-López, and Ramchandani 2019; Potwarka and Leatherdale 2016) and long-term impacts (Aizawa et al. 2018).

Different arguments could be pointed out to explain this controversy of the empirical evidence. Firstly, different reviews, such as Annear et al. (2021) and Scheu, Preuß, and Könecke (2021), have argued that research shortcomings such as the data used (i.e. cross-sectional data and qualitative interviews), small sample sizes, lack of consideration of potential confounders and methods applied (i.e. correlations) have failed to find convincing evidence. Other authors have emphasised that the potential sport SME legacies could be associated with specific sports under consideration (Girginov and Hills 2008; Grix et al. 2017) and there are significant differences among types of sports (Veal, Toohey, and Frawley 2012). If this is the case, it would be more complicated to identify the sport legacy in the Olympic Games than in single-sport events (Annear et al. 2021). A number of studies have shown that these effects might be more pronounced within a youth population (Aizawa et al. 2018; Veal, Toohey, and Frawley 2012), arguing that sporting success and elite athlete role models seem to have a more inspirational effect in children and youth than in adults (Potwarka and Wicker 2020). Finally, a number of researchers have argued that the sport legacy is more likely to materialise in terms of increasing the participation frequency or in activity switching rather than increasing the number of participants (Kokolakakis, Lera-López, and Ramchandani 2019; Kokolakakis and Lera-Lopez 2020; Taks et al. 2014) because the legacy might require people to be engaged in sports, either by being active sport participants (Mutter and Pawlowski 2014) or by being engaged as sport spectators (in live events, through television or social media, etc.) (Hahm, Kang, and Matsuoka 2020). Lovett, Bloyce, and Smith (2020) have offered additional arguments about this lack of conclusive evidence, including the lack of sport infrastructure to absorb more and new participants.

Sport legacy of London 2012

Scheu, Preuß, and Könecke (2021) have accounted for 24 studies dealing with a potential legacy of increased PA in England for the Games in London 2012. Some studies found that the Games have significantly increased motivation to take part in PA (Darko and Mackintosh 2016; Mackintosh, Darko, and May-Wilkins 2016). Considering a medium-term period of 24 months after hosting London 2012, Kokolakakis, Lera-López, and Ramchandani (2019) obtained an increase in regular participation in the year immediately after the Games, with significant differences among socio-demographic groups. Young people, people aged 55–74 and wealthy socio-economic groups experienced greater growth. In contrast, Henry (2016), using a similar time-period, concluded a decrease in sport participation rates after the Games.

Some authors have emphasized that the sport legacy could depend on the type of sport, with significant differences among sports (Grix et al. 2017; Kokolakakis and Lera-Lopez

2020). In the case of specific sports, Brown et al. (2017) and Pappous and Hayday (2016) have shown increases of participation in swimming, and judo and fencing, respectively. Evidence about London 2012 has corroborated previous arguments about the sport legacy being more relevant to increase participation among existing participants than to attract new participants in sports and PA.

Finally, when considering participation in sports by ethnic minority groups after the Games, Sport England (2015) showed that engagement among black and ethnic minority groups had grown more substantially in the period 2006–2015 than was the case for the 'white British' population. Only Kokolakakis, Lera-López, and Ramchandani (2019) have focused on the sport legacy of some specific ethnic minorities (Black and Asian minorities), showing an increase in sport participation after the Games compared with the White British population. Taking into consideration that ethnicity has traditionally been a barrier in sport engagement, hosting the Games was associated with a reduction in the gap between white population and ethnic minorities in England.

Hence, we hypothesise the following:

H1a. London 2012 is positively associated with an increase in sport participations levels for English ethnic minorities.

H1b. Increases in sport participation rates among English ethnic minorities are more relevant for regular than for non-regular participants.

Minority ethnicities and sport participation

Participation in sports has been associated not only with improvement of health status but also with increased social inclusion, mainly because involvement in sport is a powerful way to develop extended social networks and effects on perception and opportunities to socialise (Pawlowski and Schüttoff 2019). This may be true in general, but even more so when considering marginalised or socially excluded groups (Sherry 2010). The 2007 European Union White Paper on Sport has recognised the potential of sport for the integration of ethnic minorities (European Commission 2007).

Consequently, there is wide empirical evidence about the relationship between sport engagement and minor ethnicity communities. Previous studies have indicated that these communities show lower levels of sport engagement than people of white ethnic background for adults, and adolescents (Breuer and Pawlowski 2011; Miller et al. 2019; Strandbu, Bakken, and Sletten 2019) in many European countries and the U.S. In the case of England, empirical evidence has also shown that there are significant differences among Black and Asian ethnic minorities (Long et al. 2009; Sport England 2020, 2021). Further, English data have shown a greater gender disparity among these communities than for white population (Sport England 2020, 2021; Stamatakis and Chaudhury 2008), mainly explained by the different role played by cultural, religious and social class barriers between males and females for these ethnic minorities (Snape and Binks 2008; Strandbu, Bakken, and Sletten 2019). Previous empirical evidence for general population has shown that females are more influenced by hosting the Games than males (Kokolakakis and Lera-Lopez 2020; Wicker and Sotiriadou 2013).

Hence, we hypothesise the following:

H2a. Different associations between London 2012 and engagement among ethnic minorities;

H2b. Different association between London 2012 and gender groups, with females likely to have greater association than males.

Method and materials

Dataset

We have selected the case of the Olympic Games in London 2012 for several reasons. Firstly, Olympic Games is the most worldwide important SME and London 2012 provided one of the first opportunities to examine the results of the planning for sport Olympic legacy (Lovett, Bloyce, and Smith 2020). An integral part of such planning was to increase sport participation among ethnic minority groups. Secondly, previous empirical evidence has shown major variations in the levels of sport participation for different ethnic groups in England (Higgins and Dale 2013; Sport England 2021). Thirdly, an official dataset in England, the Active People Survey (APS), provided detailed information about sport rates in the country.

The research was conducted by analysing the first eight waves of APS between 2005 and 2014, two years after the London Olympic Games. The APS was the largest survey of activity level in Europe: around 165,000 English adults (age 16 and over) were interviewed annually. The sample was randomly stratified, and the results were representative of the English adult population. The subsequent change from APS to Active Lives Survey makes the long-term analysis to the present less reliable and consistent. However, the two years that are included after the Olympic Games are sufficient to draw conclusions about the importance of an SME on the sport participation patterns of ethnic minorities.

We have estimated sport participation rates for four ethnic groups: Black, Mixed, Asian-Muslim, and Asian-other religions. Each of those groups was further subdivided into Males and Females. The classifications of Black, Mixed and Asian are the main headline classifications in the APS. The subdivision of the Asian group into religious grounds was made to take into account the findings of research into sport participation of ethnic groups. A SIRC research report (SIRC (Sport Industry Research Centre) 2021), for example, showed that ethnic minorities in the UK of Indian or Chinese origin are likely to participate more than ethnic minorities of Pakistani or Bangladeshi origin. Further, Higgins and Dale (2013) have pointed out the complex issues Muslim women may face in sport, including dress requirements.

In APS 'Black' is defined as 'Black British or other Black background'; Asian as 'Asian British or other Asian background'; and Mixed as 'other Mixed background'. Examples of Mixed background include: White and Black Caribbean, White and Black African and White and Asian. The Chinese background is identified separately within APS, but for the purpose of this research it is incorporated within the Asian background. Since the fourth wave of APS, religion has been identified explicitly and has been used, in this research, for the construction of required variables.

According to APS, black people are 3.4 percent of the population in England, followed by the Asian group (1.7%), Asian Muslims (1.5%) and Mixed (1.5%), as shown in Table 1 (these proportions are characteristics of the sample and may not reflect the UK proportions from a census). We have a total sample of 12,233 individuals. Finally, the gender distinction introduced in the variables between males and females is justified from the previous empirical evidence about the gender gap among these ethnic groups.

Table 1. Percentage structure of ethnic groups in England (in percentage, %) by overall and gender groups. Year 2012.

Ethnic groups	Total	Males	Females
Mixed	1.5	0.8	0.7
Black	3.4	1.7	1.8
Asian Muslims	1.5	0.7	0.8
Asian Other	1.7	0.9	0.8

Source: APS. Note: A total sample of 12,233 individuals.

The dataset used was constructed using quarterly sport participation rates, rather than months, in order to facilitate the use of seasonally adjusted Gross Domestic Product (GDP) figures from the English National Accounts, which are quarterly published. Since sport participation rates have a strong seasonal pattern with strong peaks during the summer months, they had to be seasonally adjusted to make any evaluation of sport legacy meaningful. This process facilitated comparisons with changes in GDP, which was a parameter affecting sport participation in 2012, as the economy was exiting one of the most important recessions of the post war era.

Measures

Since previous empirical evidence have found significant different legacy effects according to the frequency used in the sport participation definition (Kokolakakis, Lera-López, and Ramchandani 2019; Kokolakakis and Lera-Lopez 2020; Taks et al. 2014; Weed et al. 2015), three different variables were constructed, based on the definition of sport, including all sports and recreational activities around sports and walking for leisure at least 30 minutes long (Sport England 2015):

Regularly Active: The proportion of adults participating in at least 30 minutes of sport, at least moderate intensity, on at least 12 days out of the last 28 days (equivalent to 3 or more days a week).

Moderately Active: The proportion of adults participating in at least 30 minutes of sport, at least moderate intensity, on at least 4 days out of the last 28 days (once a week).

Slightly Active: The proportion of adults participating at least once a month for at least 30 minutes of sport, at least moderate intensity.

All the above definitions are consistent with participating in sport in general (among those aged 16+), including recreational walking, cycling and sport. Although new participants might start with different levels of frequency, we have assumed that new participants would be mainly engaged in sport within the slightly active group, following previous empirical evidence (Kokolakakis, Lera-López, and Ramchandani 2019).

Data analysis

To evaluate changes in sport participation for the minority ethnic groups after London 2012, we are going to compare their real participation rates in the 2012–2014 period with the forecasted participation had the Games not happened, following the trend in sport participation in England since 2005. For this reason, we have seasonally adjusted participation in order to include quarterly participation rates in the time series analysis.

By using regression models, we have forecasted the expected participation rates for the period 2012–2014 using the pre-Olympic participation trend adjusted for seasonality and changes in GDP. Excluding the impact of GDP was important because of the traditional association between income and sport participation (Cabane and Lechner 2015) and the 2009–2010 economic recession which had the strength to potentially change the structure of sport participation in England (Kokolakakis, Lera-López, and Ramchandani 2019).

For forecasting, the regression model applied is the adopted by Sport England from Gratton and Kokolakakis (2012), and it has participation regressed on a constant, a time trend and the percentage change of GDP three quarters before, across all indicators. For example, in the case of the Mixed group and 1 × 30 definition this model becomes:

$$P_t = 44.91 - 0.25xt + 3.10 \times \Delta G_{t-3}$$

(2.12) (0.09) (0.92) R^2 = 39%, standard errors in brackets, (1)

where P and ΔG stand for percentage of sport participation and percentage change in GDP (between successive quarters) respectively.[2]

By applying this model, we obtained a set of regressions from 2005 Q4 to 2011 Q4. This time period creates a model that can help us trace the trend of sport participation in the subsequent period, 2012–2014, after the Games. To check the robustness and the accuracy of the forecast, we estimated the mean absolute percentage error statistic (MAPE), widely used for its intuitive interpretation (De Myttenaere et al. 2016). This measure can only by applied in the pre-Olympic period comparing real and 'forecasted' sport rates. For example, in the recessionary period 2009–2010 the values of MAPE for the regular, moderate, and slight participation definigions of the mixed ethnic group are 7%, 3% and 3% correspondingly. Most values of MAPE for the examined groups are below 5% which is a very good indication of the robustness of the forecasts.

By comparing the real participation rates with the expected/forecasted participation emanating from the pre-Olympic trend (2005–2011), we provide a measure of the Olympic Games association with sport participation, for the examined ethnic groups, in the period 2012–2014. Based on previous literature, if there is a sport legacy, this would be apparent in the full year of the Olympic Games and thereafter. Finally, the results must be interpreted with the caveat that they express associations between participation and the London Olympic Games; they do not, in this form, postulate a causality claim.

Results

Table 2 shows the increases in sport participation for the ethnic groups overall, without any differentiation into genders. The total sport effects column compares the real and expected participation curves for these communities, making a distinction among regular, moderate and slight participation levels. This column shows that across the ethnic groups the effect increases when switching from the regular frequency to moderate frequency and then reduces in size when the slight frequency definition is considered. In only one case (Mixed slightly active) the effect is non-existent. The 'Extra participants in average quarter' column measures the rise in absolute number of participants for each category of frequency, showing some significant differences. The greatest increase occurs in the Asian-others and Black

Table 2. Sport legacy effects by ethnic groups. Overall.

Ethnicity	Frequency of participation	Total sport effect (2012–14)	Extra participants in average quarter (2012–14)	Percentage point sport effect (2012–4),	Percentage point sport effect (2012)	Percentage point sport effect (2013)	Percentage point sport effect (2014, q1–3)
Mixed	Regular	0.93	600	0.30	None	17.60	None
	Moderate	2.27	1400	0.41	None	6.95	None
	Slight	None	None	None	None	5.35	None
Black	Regular	3.09	4200	1.64	None	15.23	None
	Moderate	3.57	4800	0.90	None	8.50	None
	Slight	3.03	4100	0.66	None	7.77	None
Asian Muslim	Regular	1.78	1100	0.93	None	9.27	None
	Moderate	3.44	2100	0.89	None	7.24	2.90
	Slight	0.72	400	0.16	None	9.22	None
Asian other	Regular	5.03	3400	2.55	None	18.77	None
	Moderate	5.03	3400	1.20	None	4.53	0.14
	Slight	3.13	2100	0.64	None	5.14	None

ethnic groups and the least in the Mixed group. Further, the 'percentage point sport effect' column shows the total sport legacy effect compared to the participation rates of the period 2009–11 for each sport frequency. The inclusion of this variable is important as the total sport legacy effect is likely to be greater in the ethnic groups with relatively high participation rates. This column reinforces these differences among the ethnic groups. Therefore, H1a and H2a are accepted.

The last columns in Table 2 shows the 'percentage point sport effect' for the individual years 2012, 2013 and 2014 in order to check the sustainability of the effect during the years following the Olympics. Our interest is to see how the sport legacy appears when the years are examined separately. The most striking result is that at the year of the Olympics (2012) there is no sport legacy effect among the ethnic groups. Almost all the legacy is produced in the next year, 2013, disappearing in 2014. Therefore, the sport legacy associated to London 2012 for the minority ethnic groups in England is a very short-term legacy, mainly based on existing participants increasing their frequent participation. Hence, H1b is accepted.

Tables 3 and 4 present the results for the sport legacy associated to London 2012 for males and females, correspondingly, for the minority ethnic groups. We have included for comparison purposes the figures for English males and females' groups.

From Table 3, we can see that for Asian Muslim and Asian other, there is no sport legacy, showing that for the period 2012–14, sport participation of the Asian males appears to be unaffected by the Olympic Games. Only, in the year 2013 a positive increase is obtained, mainly for existing participants. For the overall period, a legacy effect is shown for the Mixed group in regular and moderate participation and for the Black group in regular involvement. In both cases, the legacy is concentred in the year 2013. Comparing with males for the overall population, we can see two interesting results. Firstly, London 2012 is less associated with an increase in sport participation rates for the males of the ethnic minority groups than for the males of the overall English population. Secondly, for total males, sport legacy is shown for all the years, with a peak in 2013.

In Table 4, we can see the sport legacy of the Females among the examined ethnic groups. Whilst in the case of Males the positive associations with the Olympics were very limited, when considering the period 2012–14, the sport legacy among women is higher and much more widespread. All groups considered are associated with positive effects during the

Table 3. Sport legacy effects by ethnicity-males.

Ethnicity	Frequency of participation	Percentage point sport effect (2012–2014)	Total sport effect (2012–2014)	Percentage point sport effect (2012)	Percentage point sport effect (2013)	Percentage point sport effect (2014, q1–3)
Overall population (males)	Regular	9.97	27.14	5.19	15.39	8.83
	Moderate	None	None	None	1.93	None
	Slight	None	None	None	0.93	None
Mixed	Regular	0.49	1.82	None	26.00	None
	Moderate	0.35	2.29	None	10.78	None
	Slight	None	None	None	6.76	None
Black	Regular	0.22	0.58	None	12.38	None
	Moderate	None	None	None	5.73	0.11
	Slight	None	None	None	5.34	None
Asian Muslim	Regular	None	None	None	7.20	None
	Moderate	None	None	None	3.06	5.31
	Slight	None	None	None	7.25	None
Asian other	Regular	None	None	None	11.65	None
	Moderate	None	None	None	2.90	None
	Slight	None	None	None	3.06	None

Table 4. Sport legacy effects by ethnicity-females.

Ethnicity	Frequency of participation	Percentage point sport effect (2012–2014)	Total sport effect (2012–2014)	Percentage point sport effect (2012)	Percentage point sport effect (2013)	Percentage point sport effect (2014, q1–3)
Overall population (females)	Regular	12.49	25.36	7.66	18.20	10.88
	Moderate	5.32	21.63	2.58	8.99	4.27
	Slight	3.35	16.66	0.52	8.47	0.52
Mixed	Regular	0.54	1.29	None	4.45	6.58
	Moderate	0.76	3.52	None	1.62	6.94
	Slight	0.39	2.03	None	3.38	2.72
Black	Regular	2.98	3.95	None	17.83	7.09
	Moderate	1.72	5.35	None	11.33	None
	Slight	1.43	5.29	None	10.23	None
Asian Muslim	Regular	6.04	6.93	15.25	13.61	None
	Moderate	5.61	14.67	6.12	18.72	None
	Slight	2.24	7.60	1.17	13.09	None
Asian other	Regular	7.62	10.06	3.29	31.08	None
	Moderate	4.85	15.0	4.90	6.69	2.03
	Slight	3.32	12.47	2.35	7.88	None

period 2012–14, showing that the ethnic group Asian-other has the highest increase in sport legacy under all participation definitions. Curiously, the sport legacy is higher among the Asian females than for Mixed and Black females, in contrast with the analysis performed for males. Therefore, H2b is accepted.

However, sport legacy for these ethnic groups among females is below the overall participation effect of females in England as a whole, as it has happened for males. Further, as in the case of males, all ethnic groups show positive effects in the year 2013 under all frequency definitions, strongly indicating the possibility of new sport participants associated with the Olympic Games. In the year 2014, some of the effects disappear, although not to the degree that is happening among males.

In Figure 1, female overall participation is compared with engagement in Asian Muslim women; it is also shown that the Games attract comparatively speaking more new participants among Asian Muslim women.

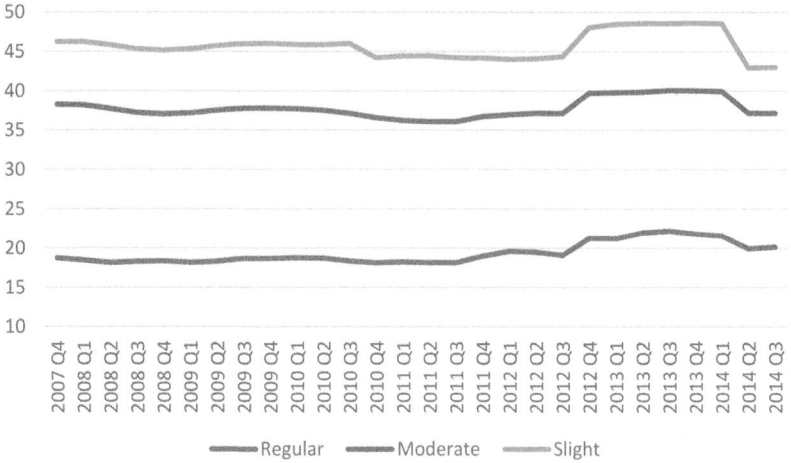

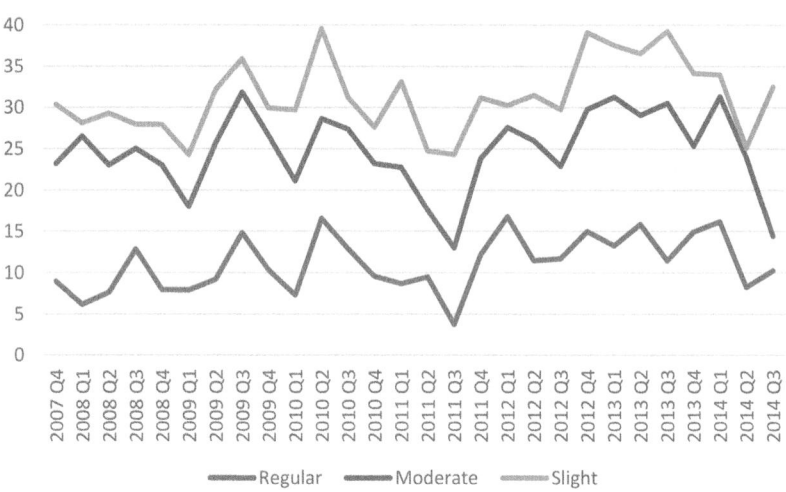

Figure 1. Overall female versus female Asian Muslins participation patterns. (A) Females participation pattern. (B) Asian Muslim Females, participation pattern.

Discussion and conclusions

This study has analysed the sport legacy in England associated to hosting the London 2012 Olympic Games over the period 2012 to 2014 among ethnic minorities. This research must be interpreted with the caveat that it shows associations between participation and the London Olympic Games and cannot suggest a causality claim. Sport legacy has become a recurrent issue in academic discourse about SMEs governance. In the case of London 2012, this sport legacy was a core component of the expected legacy of hosting the Games in England (Thorpe et al 2020). Making a distinction among different frequencies of sport engagement and between males and females, we have obtained significant results for the four ethnic minority groups under study.

Firstly, we have obtained a short-term sport legacy among ethnic minorities, confirming previous empirical evidence about the overall population for London 2012 (Downward, Dawson, and Mills 2013; Kokolakakis, Lera-López, and Ramchandani 2019). In comparative terms, this sport legacy is less intensive than for the overall population, showing that ethnic minorities are less attracted by inspirational and motivational factors associated to hosting the Games in the country. This could be associated to a western image of the Olympic Games, which is occasionally distant from the cultural diversity found in ethnic minorities. In terms of time, we have found that the main sport legacy occurred, mainly in the year after the Games, in 2013, among ethnic groups. This result is also consistent with the literature about sport Olympic legacy that holds that the effect mainly takes place in the year following the Games (e.g. Cashman (2006) for Sydney 2000 and Pappous (2011) for Athens 2004). Nevertheless, in the case of women, the sport legacy lasts during 2013 and 2014, although it is more moderate in 2014.

Secondly, the results show that the sport legacy is more significant in terms of increasing frequency of sport participation than attracting new participants. This is supported by previous studies that argued that SMEs are more likely to increase regular participation than to rise the number of new participants (Cleland et al. 2020; Kokolakakis, Lera-López, and Ramchandani 2019; Ramchandani, Coleman, and Christy 2019). Further, it could suggest, following Weed et al. (2012), that London 2012 has not generated a 'festival effect', bigger than and beyond sport but also rooted in local and cultural communities, that might promote sport engagement among these ethnic minorities, traditionally least active in sport than the overall population (Sport England 2021).

Thirdly, we have obtained differences in terms of sport legacy among the four ethnic minorities under study. Some ethnic minority groups, such as Black and Asian Other, show a higher sport legacy than Asian Muslims. This result is associated with the cultural and religious barriers that have been previously analysed for this group (Strandbu, Bakken, and Sletten 2019) and limit the sport legacy for hosting London 2012 among Asian Muslims.

Fourthly, the differentiated analysis between males and females show interesting differences on sport legacy. Among males, Mixed and Black ethnic groups seem to have the highest sport legacy, which is clearly lower among Asian minorities, particularly in the case of Asian Muslim group. Nevertheless, among females, Asian ethnicities show the highest sport legacy, particularly females of Asian Muslim origin. These results are also aligned with previous empirical evidence (Kokolakakis and Lera-Lopez 2020; Wicker and Sotiriadou 2013) that shows that females are more influenced by hosting the Games than males and emphasise gender differences in inspirational and motivational factors associated to the Games.

To sum up, the results suggest that hosting SMEs might have a positive but limited association with attracting new participants, re-engagement of lapsed sport participants and boosting sport participation frequency among ethnic groups. Further, hosting SMEs could contribute to reverse inequalities in sport participation rates among women and men of ethnic minority groups. The London 2012 sport legacy seems to have higher effect on women than on men. The sport legacy is maximised in the year following the Olympics which creates an opportunity for policy-makers and sport institutions to plan and 'capitalise' upon it.

These results could have some interesting management and practical implications for governance of SMEs in the recent future. Firstly, hosting SMEs, and in particular the

Olympic Games, would not by itself address existing inequalities in diverse ethnic backgrounds, a growing population in many Western countries[3]. Secondly, the sport legacy of hosting SMEs should be more associated to the festival effect, connecting the sport event to cultural and social activities, as a way to favour social inclusion in ethnic minority groups. Thirdly, some ethnic groups deserve special attention to develop sport legacy associated to SMEs. In particular, hosting SMEs could be a great opportunity to attract new sport participants among female Asian Muslims, a group traditionally associated to lower levels of sport engagement (Lenneis and Pfister 2017), but also associated more than Asian Muslim males to the Olympic sport legacy. This might imply that efforts to supply sport facilities for this group that allow them to maintain their embodied respectability (Thorpe et al. 2020) could become critical and should be under consideration for governance of future SMEs. Finally, our results might encourage policy-makers to maintain a sustained effort during the post event period to capitalise on the SME's legacy that is produced immediately after the events and avoid, in this way, a short-term sport legacy.

Limitations of the study and further research

Several limitations about the study need to be noted. The first limitation has to do with the nature of the data. The cross-sectional nature of the survey precludes us from establishing causal chains among the variables. Then, results must be interpreted with the caveat that they express associations between sport participation and the London Olympic Games. In the future, using longitudinal data would allow researchers to track changes over time in sport engagement and to relate them to hosting SMEs. Another limitation is the difficulty to draw definitive conclusions regarding the sport legacy of SMEs because a simple and unique cause cannot be established. For example, it is not possible to isolate the legacy of one SME in a country, in our case the London Olympic Games, with other SMEs hosted in England under the period of analysis. The potential influence of confounders has been limited in our case to the evolution of GDP, but there are other potential variables as government policy, urban development, etc. (Annear et al. 2021). Furthermore, this study has been restricted for methodological reasons[4] to only two years following the Olympic Games. Although a short-term impact has been established, further analysis should be developed to check the longer-term impact of hosting the Olympic Games.

Some research gaps are still open and thus raise interesting research question for further studies. Firstly, would the sport legacy be the same for a general SME, like the Olympic Games, as for a single SME (e.g. Football World Cup) among ethnic minorities? Further research should be focused on single SMEs to measure their legacy among ethnic groups. Another question is related to differences in sport legacy according to age in ethnic minorities. Would the gap shown in this research between males and females in sport legacy be similar through all age groups? Further research on sport legacy in ethnic minorities should consider age intervals. Finally, would the association between a SMEs and sport legacy for ethnic groups be necessary limited to the host nation or could be analysed as a global impact in many countries? These questions would undoubtedly alter SMEs' governance in the future and could offer new insights and opportunities to develop spot legacy among the ethnic minority groups.

Notes

1. See Scheu, Preuß, and Könecke (2021) for a recent review of the empirical evidence about Olympic legacy following the Preuss' framework.
2. The regressions for each ethnic minority group, gender and each variable of sport participation are available upon request.
3. For example, in 2011, 1 in 5 people in England were from Black, Asian, & Minority Ethnic groups; this is projected to increase to 2 in 5 people by 2051 (Sport England 2020).
4. The change from Active People Survey to Active Lives Survey at the end of 2014 in England makes the long-term analysis to the present less reliable and consistent.

Acknowledgments

The authors would like to thank Thanos Panagouleas for his help in data processing and advice.

Disclosure statement

The authors declare that they have no competing interests.

Funding

The study was funded in part with the financial support from the Spanish Ministry of Science and Research and the European Regional Development Fund with the Project ECO2017-86305-C4-4-R (AEI/FEDER, UE).

ORCID

Themis Kokolakakis https://orcid.org/0000-0002-2421-8106
Fernando Lera-López https://orcid.org/0000-0002-9230-9405

References

Aizawa, K., J. Wu, Y. Inoue, and M. Sato. 2018. "Long-Term Impact of the Tokyo 1964 Olympic Games on Sport Participation: A Cohort Analysis." *Sport Management Review* 21 (1): 86–97. doi:10.1016/j.smr.2017.05.001.

Annear, M., S. Sato, T. Kidokoro, and Y. Shimizu. 2021. "Can International Sports Mega Events Be Considered Physical Activity Interventions? A Systematic Review and Quality Assessment of Large-Scale Population Studies." *Sport in Society*: 1–18. doi:10.1080/17430437.2021.1957834.

Annear, M. J., Y. Shimizu, and T. Kidokoro. 2019. "Sports Mega-Event Legacies and Adult Physical Activity: A Systematic Literature Review and Research Agenda." *European Journal of Sport Science* 19 (5): 671–685. doi:10.1080/17461391.2018.1554002.

Bauman, A. E., M. Kamada, R. S. Reis, R. P. Troiano, D. Ding, K. Milton, N. Murphy, and P. C. Hallal. 2021. "An Evidence-Based Assessment of the Impact of the Olympic Games on Population Levels of Physical Activity." *The Lancet* 398 (10298): 456–464. doi:10.1016/S0140-6736(21)01165-X.

Breuer, C., and T. Pawlowski. 2011. "Socioeconomic Perspectives on Physical Activity and Aging." *European Review of Aging and Physical Activity* 8 (2): 53–56. doi:10.1007/s11556-011-0089-6.

Brown, G., S. Essex, G. Assaker, and A. Smith. 2017. "Event Satisfaction and Behavioural Intentions: Examining the Impact of the London 2012 Olympic Games on Participation in Sport." *European Sport Management Quarterly* 17 (3): 331–348. doi:10.1080/16184742.2017.1294193.

Byers, T., E. Hayday, and A. Pappous. 2020. "A New Conceptualization of Mega Sports Event Legacy Delivery: Wicked Problems and Critical Realist Solution." *Sport Management Review* 23 (2): 171–182. doi:10.1016/j.smr.2019.04.001.

Cabane, C., and M. Lechner. 2015. "Physical Activity of Adults: A Survey of Correlates, Determinants, and Effects." *Jahrbücher für Nationalökonomie und Statistik* 235 (4-5): 376–402. doi:10.1515/jbnst-2015-4-504.

Cashman, R. 2006. *The Bitter-Sweet Awakening: The Legacy of the Sydney 2000 Olympic Games*. Sydney: Walla Walla Press.

Castellanos-García, P., T. Kokolakakis, S. Shibli, P. Downward, and J. Bingham. 2021. "Membership of English Sport Clubs : A Dynamic Panel Data Analysis of the Trickle-down Effect." *International Journal of Sport Policy and Politics* 13 (1): 105–122. doi:10.1080/19406940.2021.1877170.

Chen, S., and I. Henry. 2016. "Evaluating the London 2012 Games' Impact on Sport Participation in a Non-Hosting Region: A Practical Application of Realist Evaluation." *Leisure Studies* 35 (5): 685–707. doi:10.1080/02614367.2015.1040827.

Cleland, C. L., A. Ellaway, J. Clark, and A. Kearns. 2020. "Was Glasgow 2014 Inspirational? Exploring the Legacy Impacts of a Mega-Sport Event via the Theorized Demonstration and Festival Effects." *Sport in Society* 23 (5): 810–831. doi:10.1080/17430437.2019.1571044.

Darko, N., and C. Mackintosh. 2016. "'Don't You Feel Bad Watching the Olympics, Watching us?' A Qualitative Analysis of London 2012 Olympics Influence on Family Sports Participation and Physical Activity." *Qualitative Research in Sport, Exercise and Health* 8 (1): 45–60. doi:10.1080/2159676X.2015.1056825.

Dashper, K., T. Fletcher, and J. Long. 2019. "'Intelligent Investment'?" *Leisure Studies* 38 (6): 762–774. doi:10.1080/02614367.2019.1653355.

De Myttenaere, A., B. Golden, B. Le Grand, and F. Rossi. 2016. "Mean Absolute Percentage Error for Regression Models." *Neurocomputing* 192: 38–48. doi:10.1016/j.neucom.2015.12.114.

Ding, D., Ramirez Varela, A. E. Bauman, U. Ekelund, I.-M. Lee, G. Heath, P. T. Katzmarzyk, R. Reis, and M. Pratt. 2020. "Towards Better Evidence-Informed Global Action: Lessons Learnt from the Lancet Series and Recent Developments in Physical Activity and Public Health." *British Journal of Sports Medicine* 54 (8): 462–468. doi:10.1136/bjsports-2019-101001.

Downward, P., P. Dawson, and T. Mills. 2013. *The Impact of the Olympic Games on Sports Participation, Motivation, Health and Well-Being*. Report 5: Post-Games Evaluation. Meta-Evaluation of the Impacts and Legacy of the London 2012 Olympic Games and Paralympic Games. Sport Evidence Base. London: DMCS.

European Commission. 2007. *White Paper on Sport*. Brussels.

European Commission. 2018. *Special Eurobarometer 472. Sport and Physical Activity*. Brussels.

Firgo, M. 2021. "The Causal Economic Effects of Olympic Games on Host Regions." *Journal Regional Science and Urban Economics*. doi:10.1016/j.regsciurbeco.2021.103673.

Girginov, V., and L. Hills. 2008. "A Sustainable Sports Legacy: Creating a Link between the London Olympics and Sports Participation." *The International Journal of the History of Sport* 25 (14): 2091–2116. doi:10.1080/09523360802439015.

Gratton, C., and T. Kokolakakis. 2012. *The Effects of the Current Economic Conditions on Sport Participation. 2012*. London: Sport England. https://www.sportengland.org/media/40196/the-effects-of-economic-conditions-on-sports-participation.pdf.

Grix, J., P. M. Brannagan, H. Wood, and C. Wynne. 2017. "State Strategies for Leveraging Sports Mega-Events: unpacking the Concept of 'Legacy.'" *International Journal of Sport Policy and Politics* 9 (2): 203–218. doi:10.1080/19406940.2017.1316761.

Hahm, J., T.-A. Kang, and H. Matsuoka. 2020. "From Inspiration to Nostalgia: The Football Participation Legacy of the 2002 FIFA World Cup Korea/japan." *Sport in Society* 23 (12): 2055–2077. doi:10.1080/17430437.2020.1807516.

Hanstad, D. V., and E. Å. Skille. 2010. "Does Elite Sport Develop Mass Sport?" *Scandinavian Sport Studies Forum* 1: 51–68.

Henry, I. 2016. "The Meta-Evaluation of the Sports Participation Impact and Legacy of the London 2012 Games : Methodological Implications." *Journal of Global Sport Management* 1 (1-2): 19–33. doi:10.1080/24704067.2016.1177356.

Higgins, V., and A. Dale. 2013. "Ethnic Differences in Sports Participation in England." *European Journal for Sport and Society* 10 (3): 215–239. doi:10.1080/16138171.2013.11687920.

Kim, H., Y. Choe, D. Kim, and J. Kim. 2019. "For Sustainable Benefits and Legacies of Mega-Events: A Case Study of the 2018 PyeongChang Winter Olympics from the Perspective of the Volunteer Co-Creators." *Sustainability*, 11 (9): 2473–2415. doi:10.3390/su11092473.

Koenigstorfer, J., J. N. Bocarro, T. Byers, M. B. Edwards, G. J. Jones, and H. Preuss. 2019. "Mapping Research on Legacy of Mega Sporting Events: Structural Changes, Consequences, and Stakeholder Evaluations in Empirical Studies." *Leisure Studies* 38 (6): 729–745. doi:10.1080/02614367.2019.1662830.

Kokolakakis, T., F. Lera-López, and G. Ramchandani. 2019. "Did London 2012 Deliver a Sports Participation Legacy?" *Sport Management Review* 22 (2): 276–287. doi:10.1016/j.smr.2018.04.004.

Kokolakakis, T., and F. Lera-Lopez. 2020. "Sport Promotion through Sport Mega-Events. An Analysis for Types of Olympic Sports in London 2012." *International Journal of Environmental Research and Public Health* 17 (17): 6193–6117. doi:10.3390/ijerph17176193.

Lenneis, V., and G. Pfister. 2017. "When Girls Have No Opportunities and Women Have Neither Time nor Energy: The Participation of Muslim Female Cleaners in Recreational Physical Activity." *Sport in Society* 20 (9): 1203–1222. doi:10.1080/17430437.2016.1269085.

Long, J., K. Hylton, K. Spracklen, A. Ratna, and S. Bailey. 2009. *Systematic Review of the Literature on Black and Minority Ethnic Communities in Sport and Physical Recreation*. Monograph.

Lovett, E., D. Bloyce, and A. Smith. 2020. "Delivering a Sports Participation Legacy from the London 2012 Olympic and Paralympic Games: evidence from Sport Development Workers in Birmingham and Their Experiences of a Double-Bind." *Leisure Studies* 39 (5): 659–672. doi:10.1080/02614367.2020.1738534.

Mackintosh, C., N. Darko, and H. May-Wilkins. 2016. "Unintended Outcomes of the London 2012 Olympic Games: Local Voices of Resistance and the Challenge for Sport Participation Leverage in England." *Leisure Studies* 35 (4): 454–469. doi:10.1080/02614367.2015.1031269.

Mahtani, K. R., J. Protheroe, S. P. Slight, M. M. P. Demarzo, T. Blakeman, C. A. Barton, B. Brijnath, and N. Roberts. 2013. "Can the London 2012 Olympics "Inspire a Generation" to Do More Physical or Sporting Activities? An Overview of Systematic Reviews." *BMJ Open* 3 (1): e002058. doi:10.1136/bmjopen-2012-002058.

McCartney, G., S. Thomas, H. Thomson, J. Scott, V. Hamilton, P. Hanlon, D. S. Morrison, and L. Bond. 2010. "The Health and Socioeconomic Impacts of Major Multi-Sport Events: Systematic Review (1978-2008)." *BMJ (Clinical Research ed.)* 340 (7758): c2369. doi:10.1136/bmj.c2369.

McConkey, R., and S. Menke. 2020. "The Community Inclusion of Athletes with Intellectual Disability: A Transnational Study of the Impact of Participating in Special Olympics." *Sport in Society* 0 (0): 1–11. doi:10.1080/17430437.2020.1807515.

Miller, J. M., M. A. Pereira, J. Wolfson, M. N. Laska, T. F. Nelson, and D. Neumark-Sztainer. 2019. "Are Correlates of Physical Activity in Adolescents Similar across Ethnicity/Race and Sex: Implications for Interventions." *Journal of Physical Activity & Health* 16 (12): 1163–1174. doi:10.1123/jpah.2018-0600.

Misener, L., M. Taks, L. Chalip, and B. C. Green. 2015. "The Elusive "Trickle-down Effect" of Sport Events : assumptions and Missed Opportunities." *Managing Sport and Leisure* 20: 37–41. doi:10.1080/23750472.2015.1010278.

Mutter, F., and T. Pawlowski. 2014. "Role Models in sports - Can Success in Professional Sports Increase the Demand for Amateur Sport Participation?" *Sport Management Review* 17 (3): 324–336. doi:10.1016/j.smr.2013.07.003.

Pappous, A. 2011. "Do the Olympic Games Lead to a Sustainable Increase in Grassroots Sport Participation?." In *Sustainability and Sport*, edited by K. Savery, 81–87. Champaign, IL: Common Ground.

Pappous, A. S., and E. J. Hayday. 2016. "A Case Study Investigating the Impact of the London 2012 Olympic and Paralympic Games on Participation in Two Non-Traditional English Sports, Judo and Fencing." *Leisure Studies* 35 (5): 668–684. doi:10.1080/02614367.2015.1035314.

Pawlowski, T., and U. Schüttoff. 2019. "Sport and Social Capital Formation." In *The Sage Handbook of Sports Economics*, edited by P. Downward, B. Frick, B. R. Humphreys, T. Pawlowski, J. E. Ruseski, and B. P. Soebbing. 54–63. London: Sage Publications.

Potwarka, L. R., and S. T. Leatherdale. 2016. "The Vancouver 2010 Olympics and Leisure-Time Physical Activity Rates among Youth in Canada: Any Evidence of a Trickle-down Effect?" *Leisure Studies* 35 (2): 241–257. doi:10.1080/02614367.2015.1040826.

Potwarka, L. R., and P. Wicker. 2021. "Conditions under Which Trickle-down Effects Occur: A Realist Synthesis Approach." *Sustainability*, 13 (1): 69–18. doi:10.3390/su13010069.

Preuss, H. 2019. "Event Legacy Framework and Measurement." *International Journal of Sport Policy and Politics* 11 (1): 103–118. doi:10.1080/19406940.2018.1490336.

Ramchandani, G., R. Coleman, and E. Christy. 2019. "The Sport Participation Legacy of Major Events in the UK." *Health Promotion International* 34 (1): 82–94. doi:10.1093/heapro/dax061.

Ribeiro, T., A. Correia, and R. Biscaia. 2021. "The Social Impact of the 2016 Rio Olympic Games: Comparison of Residents' Pre- and Post-Event Perceptions." *Sport, Business and Management: An International Journal* 11 (2): 201–221. doi:10.1108/SBM-02-2020-0014.

Scheu, A., H. Preuß, and T. Könecke. 2021. "The Legacy of the Olympic Games: A Review." *Journal of Global Sport Management* 6 (3): 212–233. doi:10.1080/24704067.2019.1566757.

Schnitzer, M., S. Scheiber, E. Kornexl, and E. Thöni. 2017. "Politicians' Perspective on the Community-Related Impacts of Major Sports Events–A Case Study for Innsbruck-Tyrol." *Sport in Society* 20 (7): 880–904. doi:10.1080/17430437.2016.1274552.

Seidl, M., R. Nagiller, A. Lang, S. Scheiber, and M. Schnitzer. 2021. "Youth Olympic Games (YOG) 2012—Mission Accomplished? A Retrospective Analysis of Intangible Legacies and the Fulfillment of the YOG's Goals." *Journal of Global Sport Management* 6 (3): 292–313. doi:10.1080/24704067.2019.1642122.

Sherry, E. 2010. "(Re)Engaging Marginalized Groups through Sport: The Homeless World Cup." *International Review for the Sociology of Sport* 45 (1): 59–71. doi:10.1177/1012690209356988.

SIRC (Sport Industry Research Centre). 2021. *Tackling Racism and Racial Inequality in Sport, Research Report*. Sheffield Hallam University, Sheffield.

Snape, R., and P. Binks. 2008. "Re-Thinking Sport: Physical Activity and Healthy Living in British South Asian Muslim Communities." *Managing Leisure* 13 (1): 23–35. doi:10.1080/13606710701751377.

Sport England. 2015. *The Active People Survey 7. Questionnaire Content*. London: Sport England.

Sport England. 2020. *Sport for All. Sport for All? Why Ethnicity and Culture Matters in Sport and Physical Activity*. London: Sport England.

Sport England. 2021. *Active Lives Adult Survey November 2019/20 Report. Active Lives Adult Survey November 2019/20 Report*. London: Sport England.

Stamatakis, E., and M. Chaudhury. 2008. "Temporal Trends in Adults' Sports Participation Patterns in England between 1997 and 2006: The Health Survey for England." *British Journal of Sports Medicine* 42 (11): 601–608. doi:10.1136/bjsm.2008.048082.

Sternfeld, B., A. Colvin, A. Stewart, B. M. Appelhans, J. A. Cauley, S. A. Dugan, S. R. El Khoudary, G. A. Greendale, E. Strotmeyer, and C. Karvonen-Gutierrez. 2020. "Understanding Racial/Ethnic Disparities in Physical Performance in Midlife Women: Findings from SWAN (Study of Women's Health across the Nation)." *The Journals of Gerontology. Series B, Psychological Sciences and Social Sciences* 75 (9): 1961–1971. doi:10.1093/geronb/gbz103.

Storm, R. K., C. G. Nielsen, T. G. Jakobsen, R. K. Storm, C. G. Nielsen, and T. O. R. G. Jakobsen. 2018. "Can International Elite Sport Success Trickle down to Mass Sport Participation ? Evidence from Danish Team Handball." *European Journal of Sport Science* 18 (8): 1139–1150. doi:10.1080/17461391.2018.1489000.

Strandbu, Å., A. Bakken, and M. A. Sletten. 2019. "Exploring the Minority–Majority Gap in Sport Participation: Different Patterns for Boys and Girls?" *Sport in Society* 22 (4): 606–624. doi:10.1080/17430437.2017.1389056.

Taks, M., B. C. Green, L. Misener, and L. Chalip. 2014. "Evaluating Sport Development Outcomes: The Case of a Medium-Sized International Sport Event." *European Sport Management Quarterly* 14 (3): 213–237. doi:10.1080/16184742.2014.882370.

Thomson, A., M. Kennelly, and K. Toohey. 2020. "A Systematic Quantitative Literature Review of Empirical Research on Large-Scale Sport Events' Social Legacies." *Leisure Studies* 39 (6): 859–876. doi:10.1080/02614367.2020.1800804.

Thorpe, H., N. Ahmad, Marfell, A., and J. Richards. 2020. "Muslim women's sporting spatialities: navigating culture, religion and moving bodies in Aotearoa New Zealand." *Gender, Place & Culture* 1–39.

Veal, A. J., K. Toohey, and S. Frawley. 2012. "The Sport Participation Legacy of the Sydney 2000 Olympic Games and Other International Sporting Events Hosted in Australia." *Journal of Policy Research in Tourism, Leisure and Events* 4 (2): 155–184. doi:10.1080/19407963.2012.662619.

Weed, M., E. Coren, J. Fiore, L. Mansfield, I. Wellard, D. Chatziefstathiou, and S. Dowse. 2012. "Developing a Physical Activity Legacy from the London 2012 Olympic and Paralympic Games: A Policy-Led Systematic Review." *Perspectives in Public Health* 132 (2): 75–80. doi: 10.1177/1757913911435758

Weed, M., E. Coren, J. Fiore, I. Wellard, D. Chatziefstathiou, L. Mansfield, and S. Dowse. 2015. "The Olympic Games and Raising Sport Participation: A Systematic Review of Evidence and an Interrogation of Policy for a Demonstration Effect." *European Sport Management Quarterly* 15 (2): 195–226. doi:10.1080/16184742.2014.998695.

Wicker, P., and P. Sotiriadou. 2013. "The Trickle-Down Effect: What Population Groups Benefit from Hosting Major Sport Events?" *International Journal of Event Management Research* 8 (2): 25–41.

World Health Organization. 2020. "Physical Activity. Fact Sheet." https://www.who.int/news-room/fact-sheets/detail/physical-activity.

Residents' perceptions of sporting events: a review of the literature

Balázs Polcsik and Szilvia Perényi

ABSTRACT
Increasing attention has been devoted of late to perceptions of sporting events among host city residents. However, a comprehensive literature review that collects and summarizes the content of research in this area lacks scholarly approaches. This study aims to review the literature published between 2000 and 2020 in indexed, peer-reviewed periodicals on perceptions among host city residents. It also analyses the selected 43 papers in the sample with reference to theoretical approaches, methods and findings. It seems that understanding perceived potential social impacts of sporting events in a particular city is essential to the overall success of these events among local communities. Findings from the wide spectrum of studies reviewed can be used in event planning, communication strategies, implementation and reduction of negative impacts, while capitalizing on opportunities. Highlighting key topics and trends in the literature, this analysis also identifies both limitations and possible new research approaches.

Introduction

Although earlier studies focused primarily on the economic impact of sporting events, substantial growth has been observed in the number of studies investigating the social and cultural impacts of sporting events during the past 20 years (Kim et al. 2015; Thomson, Kennelly, and Toohey 2020; Wallstam, Ioannides, and Pettersson 2020), while growing emphasis has also been placed on exploring the perceptions of local residents in cities hosting sporting events (Kaplanidou 2020; Liu 2016).

The global spread of sporting events has made it possible to stage them on nearly every continent (Borgers, Vanreusel, and Scheerder 2013; Graeff and Knijnik 2021). Countries and cities that host mega sporting events (MSEs) must satisfy strict economic requirements, which cannot be met without state funding and a financial commitment from relevant governments (Földesi 2014; Taks, Oshimi, and Agha 2020). The uncertainty of organizing costs and uncertain financial benefits (Mair et al. 2021) additional to possible safety risks (Horne 2015; Ludvigsen 2020) of the events raise numerous concerns among local residents. Between 2013 and 2018, several cities withdrew their bids from hosting the summer or winter Olympic Games due to a referenda or public pressure (Hiller and Wanner 2018; Scheu and Preuss 2018). The views of local residents have become an increasingly important factor in mustering support for events at the community level given the economic, social and environmental anomalies tied to hosting MSEs (Horne 2015; Müller 2012; Prayag et al. 2013). Smaller-scale events are likely to recur within the same community (Kaplanidou 2020; Scholtz 2019; Ouyang, Gursoy, and Chen 2019). In order to maximize the advantages of these events to improve their sustainability, it is crucial to know the perceptions of the local residents, thus making it possible to manage impacts over time (Balduck, Maes, and Buelens 2011; Kaplanidou 2020). Therefore, support from local residents has been stated to become key to the success of sporting events (Kim et al. 2015; Prayag et al. 2013).

The views of local community residents and their attitude to the events represent a central empirical and theoretical topic in the literature reviews on event tourism in the tourism literature (Getz and Page 2016; Sharpley 2014), although sporting events and sport tourism dimensions are not specifically separated in these analyses. Review articles by Thomson et al. (2019) and Scheu, Preuss, and Könecke (2021) deal with sporting event legacies. These articles cover a range of topics from various theoretical questions to different types of legacies and numerous other areas, highlighting the diversity in the legacy literature and demonstrating a multiplicity of research trends. Koenigstorfer et al. (2019) reports on findings from empirical studies on the legacy of MSEs, including research to date on stakeholders, such as host region residents, organizing committees and governments. Thomson, Kennelly, and Toohey (2020) reviewed empirical research on the social legacy of MSEs. Chersulich Tomino, Perić, and Wise (2020) established a system for the wide spectrum of social impacts caused by sport tourism events, including questions of strategic planning, which are necessary to achieve event sustainability. Wallstam, Ioannides, and Pettersson (2020) evaluated the social impacts of sporting and cultural events, while Mair et al. (2021) provided a systematic narrative review and research agenda on the social impacts of mega events. Reviews by Thomson, Kennelly, and Toohey (2020), Chersulich Tomino, Perić, and Wise (2020) and Mair et al. (2021) mention local residents' perceptions in connection with various impacts and legacies within both host and non-host city dimensions; however, the literature search strategies used in these previously noted cases did not target local residents' perceptions, nor provided a review of previous research on this topic. Thus, information on local residents' perception could be considered limited. Although there have been considerable efforts to carry out empirical research that focused on the perceptions of social impacts of sporting events among residents, only a few attempts have been made to provide a theoretical contribution to this field (e.g. Kaplanidou 2020; Kim et al. 2015; Taks, Oshimi, and Agha 2020). A review of existing research on residents' perceptions of sporting events is timely and relevant since the literature indicates that it is critical to understand the needs of residents and how the changes brought about by sporting events have been accepted by the host community (Kaplanidou 2020). Therefore, this present study endeavours to contribute to a more complete understanding of the views of local residents about international sporting events. Specifically, the aim of this paper is to report on empirical studies published in peer-reviewed journals, which examine the perceptions of host city residents in relation to the impacts of sporting events. A further aim is to collate the articles by their focus areas, review methods used for data collection, outline sampling approaches and provide an overview of theoretical backgrounds and main claims. Even though this study deals with the findings of selected publications reviewed, it does not aim to conduct an in-depth analysis or make a comparison of outcomes. Besides a brief summary of findings, this study rather aims to introduce the theoretical frameworks, topics under examination as well as the research methods used.

In the next section, we first define what we mean by sporting events, social impacts and legacies of events. The next section serves to outline our method, which includes the literature search strategy, before we present our results. Thereafter, we introduce residents' perceptions of the events and the theories underpinning their measurement. We provide an overview of the measurement instruments, the data collection methods and the main results of the selected studies. Finally, we offer suggestions, including recommended directions for future research.

Theoretical background

Sporting event typology

The definition of sporting events is not consistent (Horne 2015; Müller 2015; Taks, Chalip, and Green 2015), however, with Taks (2013) distinguishing between two kinds of sporting events, MSEs and non-mega sporting events (NMSEs), while Gratton, Dobson, and Shibli (2000) divides them into four categories based on their nature and chief characteristics of the events. Criteria used to form categories in the literature are visitor drawing power, media attention, audience and impact on economy and tourism (Gratton, Dobson, and Shibli 2000; Müller 2015). According to the international literature, the chief attributes of MSEs are as follows: they attract a significant international audience, they generate considerable economic activity and draw significant media interest, they require major investments in infrastructure and they are accompanied by significant tourist activity (Gratton, Dobson, and Shibli 2000) as well as potentially generating long-term, positive and negative impacts on host communities (Kim, Gursoy, and Lee 2006; Ritchie 1984). NMSEs are smaller-scale, more limited in their economic impact and in the media attention surrounding them (Chen, Gursoy, and Lau 2018; Duan et al. 2020; Gratton, Dobson, and Shibli 2000; Taks 2013), which may also be due to the limited popularity of a particular sport (Oshimi, Harada, and Fukuhara 2016).

Event legacies and impacts

The research on sporting events distinguishes between impact and legacy (Scheu and Preuss 2018). Impact or effect, both often used as synonyms, is generally employed to describe a short-term impulse (Preuss 2007), such as a tendency for tourists to spend during the event and an economic upswing tied directly to that event (Balduck, Maes, and Buelens 2011). On the other hand, legacy is understood to mean a lasting, long-term change (Scheu, Preuss, and Könecke 2021; Thomson et al. 2019), which can be planned and unplanned, positive and negative and with tangible and intangible outcomes (Preuss 2007). Legacies come about in relation to a particular sporting event and remain after the event (Taks, Chalip, and Green 2015; Preuss 2019). Within the category of infrastructure and suprastructure improvements, they include modernized airports and road networks as well as diversified accommodation (Preuss 2015), which are tangible, measurable and 'hard' (Preuss 2007; Thomson, Kennelly, and Toohey 2020). Outcomes which are immaterial, 'soft' and less readily quantifiable than economic impacts and legacies also exist (Taks, Oshimi, and Agha 2020; Thomson, Kennelly, and Toohey 2020), for example, 'psychic income' (i.e. the 'feel good factor') (Kim and Walker 2012), social capital (i.e. community connectedness) (Chalip 2006; Gibson et al. 2014), national pride (Dóczi 2012), happiness (Taks et al. 2016), increased participation in physical activity, international prestige and 'soft power' (Grix et al. 2017) and transfer of knowledge and image or reputation (Kaplanidou and Karadakis 2010). The international literature also features an example of the term impact being used analogously to legacy (Oshimi, Harada, and Fukuhara 2016), but legacy is still generally used to signify a comparatively long-term consequence (Balduck, Maes, and Buelens 2011). However, one should stress the precise interval that determines the classification of the changes that have occurred (Preuss 2007); that is, the period of time within which legacy can or must fall (Scheu, Preuss, and Könecke 2021) is not defined.

Definition of social impacts

Definitions of social impact are mainly found in the tourism research, since attending sporting events is seen as a tourist activity (Balduck, Maes, and Buelens 2011; Fredline, Deery, and Jago 2013; Ohmann, Jones, and Wilkes 2006). The widely accepted definition of social impact, cited, for example, in Balduck, Maes, and Buelens (2011) and in other studies reviewed here, is the one offered by Hall (1992, p. 67), which is understood in the context of sporting events: 'the manner in which tourism and travel effect changes in the collective and individual value systems, behaviour patterns, community structures, lifestyle and quality of life' (Taks 2013). In defining the term, certain researchers also list social aspects of economic and environmental changes (Fredline and Faulkner 2000). For example, (economic) job creation opportunities and (environmental) indicators tied to littering are viewed as social impacts in certain cases, since they exercise an effect on people (Fredline 2005; Ritchie 1984; Wallstam, Ioannides, and Pettersson 2020). Social impact/legacy as a concept is generally tied to 'immaterial impacts' (Kim and Petrick 2005; Scheu and Preuss 2018; Waitt 2003); at the same time, it is often used in studying local residents' perceptions of sporting events (Balduck, Maes, and Buelens 2011; Mair et al. 2021). The literature uses various expressions in this topic area. Some studies examine local residents' perceptions (Kim and Petrick 2005), others explore their reactions to event impacts (Fredline, Deery, and Jago 2013) and still others investigate social impacts (Balduck, Maes, and Buelens 2011; Kaplanidou 2020; Ohmann, Jones, and Wilkes 2006). However, a similar challenging process guides these studies: a survey of positive and negative effects that local residents perceive of sporting events. The expression 'attitude' is used in research on cultural events and local residents' views of tourist destinations (Delamere 2001). The word 'perception' is used in most of the studies reviewed in this present study. Data collection tied to studies among local residents has generally taken place shortly after the events have occurred. Oshimi, Harada, and Fukuhara (2016, p. 3) has thus 'operationally defined social impacts as residents' short-term perceptions of social, economic, cultural and physical/environmental impacts'.

A number of other concepts are also tied to social impacts, including quality of life (QoL), subjective well-being and social capital (Mair et al. 2021; Wallstam, Ioannides, and Pettersson 2020). Some studies endeavour to examine the link between the perceived impacts of sporting events and the QoL of local residents (Al-Emadi et al. 2017; Ma and Kaplanidou 2017; Ouyang, Gursoy, and Chen 2019).

Methods

Literature reviews provide an extensive overview of the current state of publications searched for and categorized in the relevant literature through a synthesis of key findings in a field of study (Pickering and Byrne 2014). They can demonstrate how work in that field has evolved and are useful in identifying main methodologies and data collection approaches, ascertaining what is known about a topic and highlighting areas where further research is needed (Roy, Byrne, and Pickering 2012).

Digital academic databases (Science Direct, TandFonline, Emerald and SAGE) were employed to search for studies published on the topic between 2000 and 2020. Various combinations of key words were used to achieve the most effective search results: 'perceptions of sporting event', 'residents' perceptions', 'social impacts of sporting event' and 'legacy perceptions'. The search was set for titles and abstracts. The publications were reviewed based on their abstracts, with titles accepted or rejected on that basis. Based on the established criteria, publications were further narrowed to those that empirically examined the perceptions of sporting events among residents in host cities directly. The following information was gleaned from the sample: author(s), title of journal, year of publication, location of sporting event, research methods used for the data collection and sample and key findings. A review of the reference lists in the articles also served to ascertain the theoretical frameworks for the topic and to clarify general concepts.

Numerous articles were published on the perceptions of local residents in the previous century. However, this study focuses on publications from the past 20 years, since, as Kaplanidou (2020) indicates, there have been a number of studies starting from the year 2000 that have focused on residents' perceptions of social impacts of sporting events. Temporal and multi-dimensional approaches have been applied to perceptions of tangible and intangible impacts or legacies (Kim et al. 2015; Parra-Camacho et al. 2020). Furthermore, in another literature review, Thomson et al. (2019) chose the starting date of 2000, as it marks the point when conceptual development and debate as regards sporting event legacy accelerated.

The literature search strategy used in this study involved articles registered in four outstanding scholarly databases. However, it is possible that it did not cover the literature in its entirety, which may be viewed as a limitation of the study. Drawing on books and other databases may have yielded additional publications, but these were not included in our analysis. The language of the publications may represent another limitation of the research. Given the nature of the databases selected, only sources in English were included in the review, a limitation which is compensated for by the fact that the search produced a significant portion of the most relevant studies on peer-reviewed, registered international platforms.

Results

Following the predefined systematic search approach, a total of 43 English-language journal articles satisfied the set criteria. Most of the articles were written by multiple authors, with international cooperation and collaboration between institutions being common. Published in 19 different journals, the studies investigated events in different sports on five continents. The research in the sample was conducted in 17 different countries. Enhanced research attention was drawn to sporting events in Asian countries aiming to learn about the perceptions of people living there (see Table 1). Writing on local residents' observations on the impact of sporting events was published in journals within various fields, with Tourism Management ($n=8$) and Journal of Travel Research ($n=4$) being dominant (see Table 2). The findings of this review article are presented following a pre-set structure including the

Table 1. Study location, data collection methods and sample size.

Category	Number of manuscripts
Study location	
Asia	20
Europe	9
America	7
Australia	4
Africa	3
Details of the methods	
Onsite survey	26
Survey by telephone	6
Survey by postal	5
Online survey	3
Door-to-door survey	2
Interviewer-completed questionnaires in house	2
Interview (e.g. individual and group)	3
Participant observation	3
Type of data	
Quantitative	36
Quantitative and Qualitative	7
Data collection	
Cross-sectional (pre-, during, post-event)	27
Repeated cross-sectional	9
Longitudinal	7
Sample size	
0–500	24
500–1000	9
1000<	10

Table 2. Journal and fields.

Journal fields and Journal name	Number of manuscripts
Tourism, Leisure and Event	26
Tourism Management	8
Journal of Travel Research	4
Leisure Studies	3
Annals of Tourism Research	2
Journal of Convention & Event Tourism	2
Tourism Management Perspectives	1
Tourism Planning & Development	1
Tourism and Hospitality Research	1
Tourism Geographies	1
Journal of Destination Marketing & Management	1
International Journal of Event and Festival Management	1
Current Issues in Tourism	1
Sports	16
Sport in Society	3
European Sport Management Quarterly	3
Sport Management Review	3
International Journal of Sports Marketing and Sponsorship	3
Journal of Sport & Tourism	3
Soccer & Society	1
Politics and Space	1
Environment and Planning C: Government and Policy	1
Total manuscripts (Journal = 19)	43

contexts of addressed sporting events; theoretical frameworks used by authors; participants, data collection and instruments; data analysis and key results of the literature reviewed.

Contexts of sporting events addressed

The articles reviewed cover numerous types of sporting events from MSEs to significant annual events within different sports to regular city running races with mass participation (Gratton, Dobson, and Shibli 2000; Müller 2015; Taks 2013). A considerable portion of the studies reviewed concentrate on MSEs, including the Olympic Games (Gursoy et al. 2011; Prayag et al. 2013; Ribeiro et al. 2018; Vetitnev and Bobina 2017), the World Cup (Kim, Gursoy, and Lee 2006; Ohmann, Jones, and Wilkes 2006) and the European UEFA Championship (Garbacz, Cadima Ribeiro, and Mourão 2017). In addition, authors have dealt with impacts perceived by host city communities of popular events in a variety of sports, for example, the Tour de France and Formula 1 (Balduck, Maes, and Buelens 2011; Bull and Lovell 2007; Parra-Camacho et al. 2020; Fredline, Deery, and Jago 2013). A small number of studies examined the perceived impacts of non-mega, mid-sized and small sporting events (Duan et al. 2020; Taks 2013), annual competitions (Fredline, Deery, and Jago 2013) and mass events (Chen, Gursoy, and Lau 2018; Scholtz 2019). Since MSEs – such as the Olympics and World Cup – last approximately 1 month at numerous venues in a city or throughout a country, some studies have spread the sampling over the numerous cities involved in staging the event (Gibson et al. 2014; Gursoy et al. 2017) or collected data nationally (Kim, Gursoy, and Lee 2006). There are very few studies that have investigated the perceptions of non-host city residents (Ritchie, Chien, and Shipway 2020) and then compared them to those living in host cities (Chen and Tian 2015; Karadakis and Kaplanidou 2012).

Theoretical frameworks used

Some of the reviewed studies were not based on an identified theory but were concluded from the conceptual knowledge previously published in sport tourism and event literature, however using different terminologies (see Table 3). The following terms were used: mega sport event impacts, legacies (tangible, intagible) and Crompton's (2004) psychic income paradigm (e.g. Kim and Walker 2012). There was also an example of the widely accepted

Table 3. List of key theoretical frameworks and concepts.

Theoretical frameworks and strategic concepts	Representative studies
Social Exchange Theory	Kim et al. (2015); Kim, Gursoy, and Lee (2006); Oshimi, Harada, and Fukuhara (2016)
Social Representations Theory	Zhou and Ap (2009); Oshimi, Harada, and Fukuhara (2016)
Prospect Theory	Lorde, Greenidge, and Devonish (2011)
Theory of Reasoned Action	Prayag et al. (2013)
Psychic Income	Kim and Walker (2012); Gibson et al. (2014)
Social Capital	Gibson et al. (2014)
Social Leveraging Framework	Balduck, Maes, and Buelens (2011); Bull and Lovell (2007)
Triple bottom line approach	Prayag et al. (2013); Zhang, Byon, et al. (2020); Zhang, Svetina Valdivia, and Byon (2020)
The extrinsic and intrinsic dimension	Mao and Huang (2016); Yao and Schwarz (2018)
Mega sport event impacts	Gursoy et al. (2011); Kim and Petrick (2005)
Non - mega sport event impacts	Chen, Gursoy, and Lau (2018); Duan et al. (2020)
Legacy (tangible, intangible)	Karadakis and Kaplanidou (2012); Ma and Kaplanidou (2017)
Quality of life	Kaplanidou et al. (2013); Ouyang, Gursoy, and Chen (2019)

triple bottom line (TBL) approach in use (Lorde, Greenidge, and Devonish 2011; Prayag et al. 2013; Zhang, Svetina Valdivia, and Byon 2020). TBL integrates three forms of impacts based on economic, environmental and social aspects.

When researchers analyse host city residents' perceptions of sporting events, they rely on such theories that aid them in understanding attitude changes within that same community (Parra-Camacho et al. 2020). Social exchange theory (SET; Emerson 1976; Ap 1992), social representation theory (SRT; Moscovici 1982) and prospect theory (PT; Kahneman and Tversky 1979) are generally employed to explain local residents' perceptions of the social impacts of sporting events (Chen, Gursoy, and Lau 2018; Kim, Gursoy, and Lee 2006; Ma and Kaplanidou 2017; Waitt 2003). Ap (1992) describes SET as 'a general sociological theory concerned with understanding the exchange of resources between individuals and groups in an interaction situation' (p. 668). The theory presumes that people are only willing to enter an exchange if they think that the advantages outweigh the disadvantages (Emerson 1976). The research suggests that SET is an appropriate means to explore local residents' perceptions (Deery, Jago, and Fredline 2012; Gursoy and Kendall 2006). According to this theory – within the context of event impacts – people generally support an event when they feel there are advantages to its impacts (Duan et al. 2020; Prayag et al. 2013). When individuals perceive the impacts as positive, they are willing to make an exchange or exhibit supportive behaviour (Chi, Ouyang, and Xu 2018; Kim et al. 2015). In contrast, when they judge the disadvantages to outweigh the advantages, they do not attempt to engage in any sort of exchange (Kim and Walker 2012). The other dominant theory in the literature is SRT (Zhou and Ap 2009). Social representations are 'systems of preconceptions, images and values which have their own cultural meaning and persist independently of individual experience' (Moscovici 1982, p. 122). Representations are mechanisms with which people endeavour to understand the world around them, for which they use their past experience and knowledge (Yao and Schwarz 2018). SRT focuses on local residents' perceptions, taking into account their direct experience and social interactions as well as the role of the media which may influence their perceptions (Fredline and Faulkner 2000; Zhou 2010; Zhou and Ap 2009). According to PT, initial perceptions provide a mental 'reference point' before the event for future re-evaluations of the impacts (Kahneman and Tversky 1979). After the event has passed, residents are likely to re-evaluate them. In case there is a disparity between pre- and post-event perceptions, the residents' attitude towards hosting a sport event in the future may change (Lorde, Greenidge, and Devonish 2011; Kim, Gursoy, and Lee 2006).

Overall, the majority of the studies in the sample were guided by a particular theoretical framework. SET is the most widespread theory in the research on event impacts and enjoys significant support in the reviewed literature (Scholtz 2019; Wallstam, Ioannides, and Pettersson 2020). Three studies (e.g. Lorde, Greenidge, and Devonish 2011; Oshimi, Harada, and Fukuhara 2016; Prayag et al. 2013) applied the combination of two theories within the same manuscript. Some of the manuscripts cited and provided review on theoretical framework but did not refer to it when explaining the results.

Researchers point to the necessity of new theories and new theoretical frameworks in investigating this area. Kaplanidou (2020) recommends consideration of community development theories as an alternative, while Smith, Ritchie, and Chien (2019) suggests social dilemma theory and calls for it to be integrated with SET.

Measurement instruments used

Although there is no commonly accepted measurement framework for analysing perceived social impacts, a multidimensional integrated approach is generally used with positive and negative elements also being examined (Kim et al. 2015; Liu 2016; Taks, Oshimi, and Agha 2020). Studies by Hall (1992), Higham (1999) and Fredline (2005) are considered fundamental, as these authors analysed the potential impacts of large-scale (sporting) events in detail, lending a theoretical framework to empirical research. Based on the literature, Ritchie (1984), Ohmann, Jones, and Wilkes (2006) and Deery and Jago (2010) synthesized all the social impacts, which may arise as a consequence of an event. Their work describes numerous impacts which may potentially come about with the staging of a (sporting) event. However, it should be stated that the most important claims are based on the authors' judgement, not on statistical analysis (Fredline, Deery, and Jago 2013). The theoretical background of the articles reviewed and the development of the survey instruments described in them have been introduced mainly based on the work of the authors listed above. An in-depth survey of the literature has been conducted involving research findings on assessments of MSEs and on quantifiable findings in particular.

The studies reviewed concentrate on the development of survey instruments (Kim et al. 2015; Kim and Walker 2012) and a comparison of perceived social impacts (Balduck, Maes, and Buelens 2011; Kim, Gursoy, and Lee 2006; Lorde, Greenidge, and Devonish 2011). The research included in the sample has examples of pre-sporting event (Al-Emadi et al. 2017; Bull and Lovell 2007; Prayag et al. 2013) and post-sporting event (Ohmann, Jones, and Wilkes 2006; Gursoy et al. 2017) data collection.

A range of methods have been used to examine resident perceptions of sport events (see Table 1). Every study uses a questionnaire, generally citing existing survey instruments. Among the studies included, Kim, Gursoy, and Lee' (2006) survey instrument appears a number of times (e.g. Gursoy et al. 2011; Lorde, Greenidge, and Devonish 2011). Almost all researchers applied quantitative research designs rather than qualitative ones in the sampled manuscripts. The most frequently applied method was survey involving onsite, telephone and postal or a combination of modes depending on the scale of the study area, demographics of respondents, target and type of sport event. Three of the 43 published papers used a mixed method approach, specifically Inoue et al. (2018), Mackellar (2013) and Vico, Uvinha, and Gustavo (2019) used questionnaire, interview and onsite observation as well.

Data collection by questionnaire used in the majority of the empirical studies involved questionnaires consisting primarily of attitude questions, rounded out by questions of local interest. Attitude scales represent questionnaire processes, with which individual opinions are investigated, measuring attitude to different impacts (Babbie 2008). The respondents are asked to decide the extent to which they agree with the statement. In the studies reviewed, the questionnaires generally consist of closed questions which respondents completed using a five- or seven-point Likert scale. For example, an assessment of opinions of traffic problems would use the statement 'The sporting event caused traffic jams in the city'. Some researchers (e.g. Bull and Lovell 2007; Fredline, Deery, and Jago 2013; Ohmann, Jones, and Wilkes 2006; Waitt 2003) have also incorporated open-ended questions into their questionnaires; by doing so, explanations to replies were allowed.

Generally, positive and negative statements are tied to economic advantages, (sport) infrastructure improvements, community pride, community development, economic costs and traffic problems. In addition, various studies also contain statements on safety risks (Kim et al. 2015), environmental aspects (Gursoy et al. 2011; Karadakis and Kaplanidou 2012) and the political benefits of staging the event (Yao and Schwarz 2018).

Most of the research concentrated on perceptions tied to impacts, while some studies, though only very few, investigated the effect of these impacts on individuals' QoL, including dimensions related to the community, the environment and personal satisfaction (Kaplanidou et al. 2013; Karadakis and Kaplanidou 2012; Ma and Kaplanidou 2017; Ouyang, Gursoy, and Chen 2019). Some authors sought a link between perceptions and support for a particular sporting event or future sporting events (Gursoy et al. 2017; Prayag et al. 2013; Vetitnev and Bobina 2017) and identified variables that influenced them (Yao and Schwarz 2018). Others focused on local residents' judgements of much more limited factors, specifically, psychological and emotional factors (Gibson et al. 2014; Kim and Walker 2012) and those tied to social capital (Gibson et al. 2014).

Therefore, the studies reviewed used primarily quantitative approaches to measure perceived social impacts. In conclusion, the research reviewed used a limited number of data collection techniques, possibly preventing the researchers from a more in-depth understanding of local residents' perceptions and from explaining the underlying reasons.

Participants and data collection

The sample numbers in the studies reviewed are indeed varied, with most of the research involving several hundreds of participants on average (see Table 1). For example, Balduck, Maes, and Buelens (2011) surveyed 235, while Gibson et al. (2014) included 2020 participants. The representativeness of the samples is questionable in most cases, a fact which also demonstrates the difficulty of surveys. Absent an appropriate sampling framework (Lorde, Greenidge, and Devonish 2011), participants in these studies have mostly been selected by convenience sampling. An effort was made to gather respondents with various socio-demographic features and collect data at various locations to minimize distortion (Kim, Gursoy, and Lee 2006; Lorde, Greenidge, and Devonish 2011). Some studies compare local residents' opinions longitudinally (Balduck, Maes, and Buelens 2011; Kim and Petrick 2005), while others do so with a repeated cross-sectional sample (Kim, Gursoy, and Lee 2006; Lorde, Greenidge, and Devonish 2011; see Table 1). As regards longitudinal research, the challenges of a second, follow-up data collection associated with a reduced sample number and the expense of such samples are noted (Balduck, Maes, and Buelens 2011; Kim and Petrick 2005). Post-event data collection was often done within 1 year; for example, Kim, Gursoy, and Lee (2006) conducted theirs after 3 months, and Lorde, Greenidge, and Devonish (2011) did so after 6 months. These time periods seem short if we accept Lorde, Greenidge, and Devonish' (2011) point that changing perceptions of impacts occur among host city residents as a long-term impact of sporting events – referred to as legacies in the literature (Scheu, Preuss, and Könecke 2021). Some authors therefore recommend that data on local residents' perceptions should be collected at no fewer than three points in time: before, during and after an event (Gursoy et al. 2011). They also note that it is worth repeating the sampling 2 or 3 years after an event, when local residents have actually seen all the costs and potential challenges involved in post-event use of the facilities (Chen, Gursoy, and Lau 2018; Gursoy et al. 2011). Changes could be tracked in time, thus improving the capacity to observe long-term impacts. Chen and Tian (2015) studied perceptions 41 months after the Beijing Olympics, but did not conduct a longitudinal study. Fredline, Deery, and Jago (2013) repeated their research on the perceived impacts of the annual Formula 1 Australian Grand Prix 3 years after the event. An important finding of their work – which emerged in the second data collection – was that respondents' concerns had eased, that they had accommodated themselves to the event and that support for the event among the population had also grown; the authors also note that while there had been no significant change in the staging of the event (in terms of venue and time), minor modifications had been made in management style and in making the event more 'family friendly' (Fredline, Deery, and Jago 2013).

Studies that consider perceived social impacts and legacies at a single time point (that is, before, during or after the event) may encounter obstacles, since this does not allow for the identification of potential changes. Given the long-term impact of sporting events (Preuss 2019), the findings in our sample suggest there is still much to be learned before we can understand long-term changes in local residents' perceptions. At the same time, we acknowledge that longitudinal studies are resource-intensive and that they pose a challenge for researchers to fund and implement them.

Most frequent data analysis used

The articles reviewed rely on similar statistical methods. In addition to descriptive statistics, explanatory and confirmatory factor analysis was employed so that the phenomena observed could be structured. Further, MANOVA and ANOVA tests were used to analyse differences in perceptions before and after a particular event. Regression analysis, the t-test and structural equation modelling were also utilized (Prayag et al. 2013). The reliability of statements about the impacts of sporting events was tested with Cronbach's alpha. Some studies rely on methods to find and form homogeneous population groups with similar profiles and common features (Chen and Tian 2015; Fredline, Deery, and Jago 2013; Ma and Rotherham 2016; Mao and Huang 2016; Zhou 2010). Most studies included, however, do not segment the population as key stakeholders. At the same time, host communities are not homogeneous, with members' perceptions frequently diverging from one another. It is possible to understand these differences and handle and address these concerns effectively with a segmental identification among local residents.

Key results of the literature reviewed

The articles reviewed here from a range of international journals investigate sporting events varying in level and size staged in the world's various countries and cities at sites under different economic, social, political and cultural conditions (Pranic, Petric, and Cetinic 2012; Yao and Schwarz 2018). These differences must be taken into account in evaluating the findings. Table 4 provides an overview of the suggested positive and negative perceived impacts of sport events on host local communities.

It is clear from the results in the various studies reviewed that local residents have unanimously positive opinions in a number of areas. These perceived benefits include development of infrastructure and tourism (Kim et al. 2015; Ohmann, Jones, and Wilkes 2006;

Table 4. List of key impacts frequently occurred in the reviewed studies.

Positive impacts	Representative studies
Increased employment opportunities	Chen, Gursoy, and Lau (2018); Prayag et al. (2013)
Increased local business opportunities	Gibson et al. (2014); Fredline, Deery, and Jago (2013); Zhou and Ap (2009)
Economic benefits	Fredline, Deery, and Jago (2013); Mackellar (2013)
Opportunity to meet new people	Vico, Uvinha, and Gustavo (2019); Zhou and Ap (2009)
Improved external image	Balduck, Maes, and Buelens (2011); Bull and Lovell (2007); Müller (2012)
Increased tourism	Al-Emadi et al. (2017); Bull and Lovell (2007)
Community pride	Fredline, Deery, and Jago (2013); Inoue et al. (2018); Ma et al. (2013)
Preservation of local culture/heritage	Karadakis and Kaplanidou (2012); Lorde, Greenidge, and Devonish (2011)
Increased skill base	Karadakis and Kaplanidou (2012); Lorde, Greenidge, and Devonish (2011)
New facilities and infrastructure	Gibson et al. (2014); Kaplanidou et al. (2013); Ohmann, Jones, and Wilkes (2006)
Sport development (activity, participation)	Ohmann, Jones, and Wilkes (2006); Zhang, Byon, et al. (2020)
Symbology, brand and national identity	Al-Emadi et al. (2017); Kaplanidou et al. (2013); Parra-Camacho et al. (2020)
Improvement of residents' quality of life	Ma and Kaplanidou (2017); Karadakis and Kaplanidou (2012)
Social capital/cohesion	Gibson et al. (2014); Prayag et al. (2013)
Negative impacts	
Increased crime levels	Ribeiro et al. (2018); Scholtz (2019); Vetitnev and Bobina (2017)
Economic benefits	Scholtz (2019); Vetitnev and Bobina (2017)
Littering	Gursoy et al. (2017); Vetitnev and Bobina (2017)
Damage to the environment	Gibson et al. (2014); Gursoy et al. (2017); Prayag et al. (2013)
Noise	Al-Emadi et al. (2017); Zhang, Byon, et al. (2020)
Traffic congestion and parking problems	Ribeiro et al. (2018); Ouyang, Gursoy, and Chen (2019)
Disruption of normal way of life	Lorde, Greenidge, and Devonish (2011); Oshimi, Harada, and Fukuhara (2016)
Increased cost of living	Chen and Tian (2015); Kaplanidou et al. (2013); Liu (2016)

Vetitnev and Bobina 2017), the advantages of marketing one's city (Kim, Gursoy, and Lee 2006; Vetitnev and Bobina 2017) and the strengthening of national pride and social cohesion (Chi, Ouyang, and Xu 2018; Gibson et al. 2014; Karadakis and Kaplanidou 2012; Kim and Walker 2012). In the case of studies conducted in China, the perceptions of the positive impact on the country's and host city's brand value stand out the most, even in studies where the authors point to local residents' worries about high organizing costs (Gursoy et al. 2011). As for negative attitudes, a number of researchers highlight price increases and traffic and parking problems (Balduck, Maes, and Buelens 2011; Kim, Gursoy, and Lee 2006; Lorde, Greenidge, and Devonish 2011; Ma et al. 2013), as well as worries about reuse of sports facilities (Kim, Gursoy, and Lee 2006). Further, they also voice concerns about the rising costs of improvements (Gursoy et al. 2011; Kim and Petrick 2005; Ma et al. 2013; Vetitnev and Bobina 2017).

Differences in research findings – which mostly occurred with economic questions – illustrate the differences between MSEs and NMSEs. In the latter case, there is no need for (significant) improvements, construction of stadiums or arenas or a transformation of a city's (sport) infrastructure to stage the event in contrast with the high costs of MSEs (Taks 2013). This is reflected in studies on host city residents' opinions in their relatively positive responses (Chen, Gursoy, and Lau 2018; Duan et al. 2020).

Findings from both the cross-sectional and longitudinal studies are in agreement in the sense that the views of local residents change with time (Chen, Gursoy, and Lau 2018; Kim, Gursoy, and Lee 2006). An important finding in a few studies is that local residents' fears of increased vandalism and crime (e.g. Prayag et al. 2013; Mao and Huang 2016; Ohmann, Jones, and Wilkes 2006) were not confirmed after the events and that prices for services did not rise as much as they had anticipated before the events (Gursoy et al. 2011; Kim, Gursoy, and Lee 2006). Local residents' concerns about noise, traffic jams and overcrowding also dropped (Fredline, Deery, and Jago 2013).

Perceived impacts are affected by numerous factors. Faulkner and Tideswell (1997) place factors influencing social impacts into two categories: intrinsic and extrinsic factors. This was originally developed for the context of tourism, but its relevance for sport tourism and sporting events has been demonstrated as well (Fredline 2005) and has been used to understand social impacts, particularly with regard to intrinsic factors. The extrinsic dimension refers to features of the city staging the sporting event, the type of event, its popularity, its duration and the intensity of the inflow of sport tourists. The intrinsic dimension refers to features of members of the community hosting the sporting event that influence their perception of the impacts of the event within the community. Kim and Petrick (2005) point to differences that emerge in the opinions of various socio-demographic groups. Assessments of impacts often diverged: differences were found in terms of gender, age, educational attainment and income level (Chen, Gursoy, and Lau 2018; Ma et al. 2013; Zhou 2010). Various segments of the population therefore perceived impulses tied to the events in various ways. In addition, according to Vetitnev and Bobina (2017), general familiarity with a particular event, time spent in the city and being affected by tourism are significant factors, the dimensions of which Mao and Huang (2016) supplemented with business involvement in the sporting industry. Gursoy et al. (2017) highlights the extent of the ties to the local community, participation in the planning and decision-making process and local residents' confidence in the organizing committee, while other authors indicate interest in the event (Oshimi, Harada, and Fukuhara 2016), participation in the event as a spectator (Chen, Gursoy, and Lau 2018) and distance between one's residence and the site of the event (Cegielski and Mules 2002; Mackellar 2013; Vico, Uvinha, and Gustavo 2019) as factors that determine perceptions.

Conclusion

Research on the perceived impacts of sporting events has drawn significant scholarly interest, which is consistent with the observation that knowledge and understanding of the opinions of host city residents is key from the perspective of organizing and sustaining events. Therefore, the aim of this research was to review studies on the perceived social impact of sporting events in international journals generally regarded as highly prestigious within their field, with an impact factor based on a recent citation analysis.

The findings can be summarized as follows:

- First, the review demonstrates that studies on the perceived impacts of sporting events examined the perceptions of residents of cities hosting various types of sporting events in various locations. It can be concluded that researchers use various approaches to analyse the views of the local residents on sporting events, in which they frequently cite previous publications, thus demonstrating the interdependence of research concepts and findings. The publications under review place their work into a theoretical framework, are built on research models and provide clear definitions. Having drawn on a large portion of the literature, adjusted to previous research and used those findings, the studies rely on a number of factors in drawing their conclusions. Further, it became clear that the researchers were primarily concentrating on MSEs and, specifically, the summer Olympic Games. Research on these areas is important, since opinions on impacts/legacies are often problematic; in fact, the summer Olympics have been associated with a number of unsuccessful referenda in recent years. Furthermore, the perceived social impacts of small-scale events have rarely been explored in the reviewed manuscripts. Since small-scale sporting events can be found in many communities and have considerable potential (e.g. Gibson, Kaplanidou, and Kang 2012; Taks 2013; Kaplanidou 2020), future research could focus more attention to this issue.

- Second, the research approaches used by the studies in the sample were guided by theoretical framework. At the same time, the research citing the theories is limited to only a few such frameworks. The limitations of SET as a dominant theoretical framework also emerge in the literature on local residents' perceptions. There are recommendations for a revised SET framework, the development of integrated models and use of new theories. Future research may consider alternative theories (e.g. asset-based community development or social dilemma theory), thus further developing research on perceived social impacts (Kaplanidou 2020; Smith, Ritchie, and Chien 2019). For example, social dilemma theory can be used to understand residents' concerns and compromises (Smith, Ritchie, and Chien 2019).

- Third, there is no single theoretical framework or social impact scale for measuring the perceptions of local residents. At the same time, there are certain common, recurring dimensions that are generally examined, for example, economic and tourism development, cultural interest and new opportunities, external image enhancement, consolidation and pride, community spirit, social cohesion, social capital, disorder and conflicts. The vast majority of research concerning host perceptions of sport events employs quantitative methods (questionnaire). Future research may benefit from the use of qualitative and mixed methods to ensure methodological diversity and a more in-depth understanding of the effects. Given that the measurement instruments used were almost exclusively questionnaires, it is important that they should be reliable. Besides the use of Cronbach's alpha, Zhang, Byon, et al. (2020) suggests considering other psychometric features/indicators such as item response theory. The methodological analysis noted above can contribute to knowledge of measurement precision in terms of validity and reliability (Zhang, Byon, et al. 2020).

- Fourth, our analysis has shown that the time frame of the studies under review is often problematic. The studies aimed at measuring the perceived impact of sporting events use data collected not long before and/or after the event. Given that residents' attitudes change over time (Chen, Gursoy, and Lau 2018; Kim, Gursoy, and Lee 2006), this sort of time frame precludes a long-term comparison of the perceptions of local residents in host cities. It should therefore be stressed that long-term studies are necessary.

- Fifth, the research topic is rife with difficulties. Even some of the studies that were included lack methodologically grounded empirical evidence or only analyse a small sample. Consequently, since these surveys lack representative samples, the survey method is recommended with a multi-step, proportionate probability sampling process supplemented by qualitative methods, whose observed effects offer an opportunity for a more in-depth interpretation and an understanding of differences of opinion. Future research should thus lead to more robust empirical findings. Further, the cluster analysis method may make it possible to group local residents by common attributes (Babbie 2008). The clusters from the studies reviewed illustrate that host communities are not homogeneous. Communicative strategies can thus be created based on the needs and interests of individual groups so that every segment of society can be addressed. The studies reviewed identified a number of variables and examined the relations between them which influenced residents' positive and negative opinions of the impacts of sporting events. Beyond the demographic variables, future studies should take into account as many variables as possible for the established cluster membership.

- Sixth, it should be stressed that, according to the literature, the social impacts described above and how they are perceived largely depend on the historical, cultural, economic and environmental features and background of the host cities (Fredline, Deery, and Jago 2013; Gursoy et al. 2011; Yao and Schwarz 2018). The nature, scale, location and duration of the events are among the influencing factors considered (Bull and Lovell 2007; Oshimi, Harada, and Fukuhara 2016). The findings therefore cannot be generalized to include other sporting events and populations, but they offer points of consideration in hosting such events, taking into account particular circumstances and the external environment. An aim of future research could be to be to develop scales with no overlaps in content and with as many standardized indicators as possible to measure the perceptions of local residents with which to compare the perceived social impacts of sporting events. This sort of comparison of sporting events would provide key information for decision-makers in host cities/countries. With this information in hand, individual actors would be more prepared to decide which events to bid for, which events to back and which events to quit. Future studies could confirm findings from previous studies by collecting data in different locations to boost generalizability.
- Finally, it is recommended that future social impact analyses take into account how fear from such risks as the COVID-19 pandemic and terrorism influences (Ludvigsen 2021; Ludvigsen and Hayton 2020; Mair et al. 2021; Parnell et al. 2020) the perceptions of host city residents and the sustainability of sporting events.

This study points to the importance of perceived social impacts, the necessity of a more precise and comprehensive evaluation of the topic and the shortcomings and value of research on all sides involved. The recommendations in the study offer an opportunity for future empirical research to achieve a more in-depth and complete understanding of the perceptions of local residents living in cities that host sporting events. This may make it possible to capitalize on significant drawing power from the perspective of sport and minimize potential negative effects while maximizing existing positives.

In conclusion, to the best of our knowledge, this study is the first comprehensive review and analysis of the research directions, methods and key findings of studies in international, peer-reviewed journals dealing with local residents' perceptions of sporting events hosted in their city, thus providing an opportunity to develop and define new research directions.

Disclosure statement

No potential conflict of interest was reported by the authors.

References

Al-Emadi, A., K. Kaplanidou, A. Diop, M. Sagas, K. T. Le, and S. Al-Ali Mustafa. 2017. "2022 Qatar World Cup: Impact Perceptions among Qatar Residents." *Journal of Travel Research* 56 (5): 678–694. doi:10.1177/0047287516652502.
Ap, J. 1992. "Residents' Perceptions on Tourism Impacts." *Annals of Tourism Research* 9: 665–690.
Babbie, E. 2008. *A Társadalomtudományi Kutatás Gyakorlata*. Budapest: Balassi Kiadó.
Balduck, A. L., M. Maes, and M. Buelens. 2011. "The Social Impact of the Tour de France: Comparisons of Residents' Pre- and Post-Event Perceptions." *European Sport Management Quarterly* 11 (2): 91–113. doi:10.1080/16184742.2011.559134.
Borgers, J., B. Vanreusel, and J. Scheerder. 2013. "The Diffusion of World Sports Events between 1891 and 2010: A Study on Globalisation." *European Journal for Sport and Society* 10 (2): 101–119. doi:10.1080/16138171.2013.11687914.
Bull, C., and J. Lovell. 2007. "The Impact of Hosting Major Sporting Events on Local Residents: An Analysis of the Views and Perceptions of Canterbury Residents in Relation to the Tour de France 2007." *Journal of Sport & Tourism* 12 (3-4): 229–248. doi:10.1080/14775080701736973.
Cegielski, M., and T. Mules. 2002. "Aspects of Residents' Perceptions of the GMC 400-Canberra's V8 Supercar Race." *Current Issues in Tourism* 5 (1): 54–70. doi:10.1080/13683500208667908.
Chalip, L. 2006. "Towards Social Leverage of Sport Events." *Journal of Sport & Tourism* 11 (2): 109–127. doi:10.1080/14775080601155126.
Chen, F., and L. Tian. 2015. "Comparative Study on Residents' Perceptions of Follow-Up Impacts of the 2008 Olympics." *Tourism Management* 51: 263–281. doi:10.1016/j.tourman.2015.05.029.
Chen, K. C., D. Gursoy, and K. L. K. Lau. 2018. "Longitudinal Impacts of a Recurring Sport Event on Local Residents with Different Level of Event Involvement." *Tourism Management Perspectives* 28: 228–238. doi:10.1016/j.tmp.2018.09.005.
Chersulich Tomino, A., M. Perić, and N. Wise. 2020. "Assessing and considering the Wider Impacts of Sport-Tourism Events: A Research Agenda Review of Sustainability and Strategic Planning Elements." *Sustainability* 12 (11): 4473. doi:10.3390/su12114473.
Chi, C. G. Q., Z. Ouyang, and X. Xu. 2018. "Changing Perceptions and Reasoning Process: Comparison of Residents' Pre- and Post-Event Attitudes." *Annals of Tourism Research* 70: 39–53. doi:10.1016/j.annals.2018.02.010.
Crompton, J. 2004. "Beyond economic impact: An alternative rationale for the public subsidy of major league sports facilities." *Journal of sport management*, 18 (1): 40–58.
Deery, M., and L. Jago. 2010. "Social Impacts of Events and the Role of Anti-Social Behaviour." *International Journal of Event and Festival Management* 1 (1): 8–28. doi:10.1108/17852951011029289.
Deery, M., L. Jago, and L. Fredline. 2012. "Rethinking Social Impacts of Tourism Research: A New Research Agenda." *Tourism Management* 33 (1): 64–73. doi:10.1016/j.tourman.2011.01.026.
Delamere, T. A. 2001. "Development of a Scale to Measure Resident Attitudes toward the Social Impacts of Community Festivals, Part II. Verification of the Scale." *Event Management* 7 (1): 25–38. doi:10.3727/152599501108751452.
Dóczi, T. 2012. "Gold Fever (?): "Sport and National Identity–The Hungarian Case." *International Review for the Sociology of Sport* 47 (2): 165–182. doi:10.1177/1012690210393828.
Duan, Y., B. Mastromartino, J. J. Zhang, and B. Liu. 2020. "How Do Perceptions of Non-Mega Sport Events Impact Quality of Life and Support for the Event among Local Residents?" *Sport in Society* 23 (11): 1841–1860. doi:10.1080/17430437.2020.1804113.
Emerson, R. M. 1976. "Social Exchange Theory." *Annual Review of Sociology* 2 (1): 335–362. doi:10.1146/annurev.so.02.080176.002003.
Faulkner, B., and C. Tideswell. 1997. "A Framework for Monitoring Community Impacts of Tourism." *Journal of Sustainable Tourism* 5 (1): 3–28. doi:10.1080/09669589708667273.
Földesi, G. S. 2014. "The Impact of the Global Economic Crisis on Sport." *Physical Culture and Sport. Studies and Research* 63 (1): 22–30.

Fredline, E. 2005. "Host and Guest Relations and Sport Tourism." *Sport in Society* 8 (2): 263–279. doi:10.1080/17430430500087328.

Fredline, E., and B. Faulkner. 2000. "Host Community Reactions: A Cluster Analysis." *Annals of Tourism Research* 27 (3): 763–784. doi:10.1016/S0160-7383(99)00103-6.

Fredline, L., M. Deery, and L. Jago. 2013. "A Longitudinal Study of the Impacts of an Annual Event on Local Residents." *Tourism Planning & Development* 10 (4): 416–432. doi:10.1080/21568316.2013.779314.

Garbacz, J., J. Cadima Ribeiro, and P. R. Mourão. 2017. "Discussing the Post Hosting Evaluation of a Mega Sporting Event: The Perception of Warsaw Residents toward UEFA EURO 2012." *Tourism and Hospitality Research* 17 (4): 392–410. doi:10.1177/1467358416642009.

Getz, D., and S. J. Page. 2016. "Progress and Prospects for Event Tourism Research." *Tourism Management* 52: 593–631. doi:10.1016/j.tourman.2015.03.007.

Gibson, H. J., K. Kaplanidou, and S. J. Kang. 2012. "Small-Scale Event Sport Tourism: A Case Study in Sustainable Tourism." *Sport Management Review* 15 (2): 160–170. doi:10.1016/j.smr.2011.08.013.

Gibson, H. J., M. Walker, B. Thapa, K. Kaplanidou, S. Geldenhuys, and W. Coetzee. 2014. "Psychic Income and Social Capital among Host Nation Residents: A Pre–Post Analysis of the 2010 FIFA World Cup in South Africa." *Tourism Management* 44: 113–122. doi:10.1016/j.tourman.2013.12.013.

Graeff, B., and J. Knijnik. 2021. "If Things Go South: The Renewed Policy of Sport Mega Events Allocation and Its Implications for Future Research." *International Review for the Sociology of Sport* : 1–18.

Gratton, C., N. Dobson, and S. Shibli. 2000. "The Economic Importance of Major Sports Events: A Case-Study of Six Events." *Managing Leisure* 5 (1): 17–28. doi:10.1080/136067100375713.

Grix, J., P. M. Brannagan, H. Wood, and C. Wynne. 2017. "State Strategies for Leveraging Sports Mega-Events: Unpacking the Concept of 'Legacy'." *International Journal of Sport Policy and Politics* 9 (2): 203–218. doi:10.1080/19406940.2017.1316761.

Gursoy, D., and K. W. Kendall. 2006. "Hosting Mega Events: Modeling Locals' Support." *Annals of Tourism Research* 33 (3): 603–623. doi:10.1016/j.annals.2006.01.005.

Gursoy, D., C. G. Chi, J. Ai, and B. T. Chen. 2011. "Temporal Change in Resident Perceptions of a Mega-Event: The Beijing 2008 Olympic Games." *Tourism Geographies* 13 (2): 299–324. doi:10.1080/14616688.2010.529935.

Gursoy, D., M. Yolal, M. A. Ribeiro, and A. Panosso Netto. 2017. "Impact of Trust on Local Residents' Mega-Event Perceptions and Their Support." *Journal of Travel Research* 56 (3): 393–406. doi:10.1177/0047287516643415.

Hall, C. M. 1992. "Adventure, Sport, and Health Tourism." In *Special Interest Tourism*, edited by B. Weiler and C. M. Hall, 141–158. London: Belhaven.

Higham, J. 1999. "Commentary-Sport as an Avenue of Tourism Development: An Analysis of the Positive and Negative Impacts of Sport Tourism." *Current Issues in Tourism* 2 (1): 82–90. doi:10.1080/13683509908667845.

Hiller, H. H., and R. A. Wanner. 2018. "Public Opinion in Olympic Cities: From Bidding to Retrospection." *Urban Affairs Review* 54 (5): 962–993. doi:10.1177/1078087416684036.

Horne, J. 2015. "Assessing the Sociology of Sport: On Sports Mega-Events and Capitalist Modernity." *International Review for the Sociology of Sport* 50 (4-5): 466–471. doi:10.1177/1012690214538861.

Inoue, Y., C. Heffernan, T. Yamaguchi, and K. Filo. 2018. "Social and Charitable Impacts of a Charity-Affiliated Sport Event: A Mixed Methods Study." *Sport Management Review* 21 (2): 202–218. doi:10.1016/j.smr.2017.06.005.

Kahneman, D., and A. Tversky. 1979. "Prospect Theory: An Analysis of Decision under Risk." *Econometrica* 47 (2): 263–291. doi:10.2307/1914185.

Kaplanidou, K. 2020. "Sport Events and Community Development: Resident Considerations and Community Goals." *International Journal of Sports Marketing and Sponsorship* 22 (1): 53–66. doi:10.1108/IJSMS-05-2020-0082.

Kaplanidou, K., and K. Karadakis. 2010. "Understanding the Legacies of a Host Olympic City: The Case of the 2010 Vancouver Olympic Games." *Sport Marketing Quarterly* 19 (2): 110.

Kaplanidou, K., K. Karadakis, H. Gibson, B. Thapa, M. Walker, S. Geldenhuys, and W. Coetzee. 2013. "Quality of Life, Event Impacts, and Mega-Event Support among South African Residents before and after the 2010 FIFA World Cup." *Journal of Travel Research* 52 (5): 631–645. doi:10.1177/0047287513478501.

Karadakis, K., and K. Kaplanidou. 2012. "Legacy Perceptions among Host and Non-Host Olympic Games Residents: A Longitudinal Study of the 2010 Vancouver Olympic Games." *European Sport Management Quarterly* 12 (3): 243–264. doi:10.1080/16184742.2012.680067.

Kim, H. J., D. Gursoy, and S. B. Lee. 2006. "The Impact of the 2002 World Cup on South Korea: Comparisons of Pre- and Post-Games." *Tourism Management* 27 (1): 86–96. doi:10.1016/j.tourman.2004.07.010.

Kim, S. S., and J. F. Petrick. 2005. "Residents' Perceptions on Impacts of the FIFA 2002 World Cup: The Case of Seoul as a Host City." *Tourism Management* 26 (1): 25–38. doi:10.1016/j.tourman.2003.09.013.

Kim, W., and M. Walker. 2012. "Measuring the Social Impacts Associated with Super Bowl XLIII: Preliminary Development of a Psychic Income Scale." *Sport Management Review* 15 (1): 91–108. doi:10.1016/j.smr.2011.05.007.

Kim, W., H. M. Jun, M. Walker, and D. Drane. 2015. "Evaluating the Perceived Social Impacts of Hosting Large-Scale Sport Tourism Events: Scale Development and Validation." *Tourism Management* 48: 21–32. doi:10.1016/j.tourman.2014.10.015.

Koenigstorfer, J., J. N. Bocarro, T. Byers, M. B. Edwards, G. J. Jones, and H. Preuss. 2019. "Mapping Research on Legacy of Mega Sporting Events: Structural Changes, Consequences, and Stakeholder Evaluations in Empirical Studies." *Leisure Studies* 38 (6): 729–745. doi:10.1080/02614367.2019.1662830.

Liu, D. 2016. "Social Impact of Major Sports Events Perceived by Host Community." *International Journal of Sports Marketing and Sponsorship* 17 (1): 78–91. doi:10.1108/IJSMS-02-2016-005.

Lorde, T., D. Greenidge, and D. Devonish. 2011. "Local Residents' Perceptions of the Impacts of the ICC Cricket World Cup 2007 on Barbados: Comparisons of Pre- and Post-Games." *Tourism Management* 32 (2): 349–356. doi:10.1016/j.tourman.2010.03.004.

Ludvigsen, J. A. L. 2020. "The 'Troika of Security': Merging Retrospective and Futuristic 'Risk' and 'Security' assessments before Euro 2020." *Leisure Studies* 39 (6): 844–858. doi:10.1080/02614367.2020.1775872.

Ludvigsen, J. A. L. 2021. "When 'the Show' cannot Go on: An Investigation into Sports Mega-Events and Responses during the Pandemic Crisis." *International Review for the Sociology of Sport* : 1–18.

Ludvigsen, J. A. L., and J. W. Hayton. 2020. "Toward COVID-19 Secure Events: Considerations for Organizing the Safe Resumption of Major Sporting Events." *Managing Sport and Leisure* : 1–11. doi:10.1080/23750472.2020.1782252.

Ma, S. C., and I. D. Rotherham. 2016. "Residents' Changed Perceptions of Sport Event Impacts: The Case of the 2012 Tour de Taiwan." *Leisure Studies* 35 (5): 616–637. doi:10.1080/02614367.2015.1035313.

Ma, S. C., and K. Kaplanidou. 2017. "Legacy Perceptions among Host Tour de Taiwan Residents: The Mediating Effect of Quality of Life." *Leisure Studies* 36 (3): 423–437.

Ma, S. C., S. M. Ma, J. H. Wu, and I. D. Rotherham. 2013. "Host Residents' Perception Changes on Major Sport Events." *European Sport Management Quarterly* 13 (5): 511–536. doi:10.1080/16184742.2013.838980.

Mackellar, J. 2013. "World Rally Championship 2009: Assessing the Community Impacts on a Rural Town in Australia." *Sport in Society* 16 (9): 1149–1163. doi:10.1080/17430437.2013.790893.

Mair, J., M. Chien, S. J. Kelly, and S. Derrington. 2021. "Social Impacts of Mega-Events: A Systematic Narrative Review and Research Agenda." *Journal of Sustainable Tourism* : 1–22. doi:10.1080/09669582.2020.1870989.

Mao, L. L., and H. Huang. 2016. "Social Impact of Formula One Chinese Grand Prix: A Comparison of Local Residents' Perceptions Based on the Intrinsic Dimension." *Sport Management Review* 19 (3): 306–318. doi:10.1016/j.smr.2015.08.007.

Moscovici, S. 1982. "The Coming Era of Social Representations." In *Cognitive Approaches to Social Behaviour*, edited by J. P. Codol and J. P. Leyens, 115–150. The Hague: Nijhoff.

Müller, M. 2012. "Popular Perception of Urban Transformation through Mega Events: Understanding Support for the 2014 Winter Olympics in Sochi." *Environment and Planning C: Government and Policy* 30 (4): 693–711. doi:10.1068/c11185r.

Müller, M. 2015. "What Makes an Event a Mega-Event? Definitions and Sizes." *Leisure Studies* 34 (6): 627–642. doi:10.1080/02614367.2014.993333.

Ohmann, S., I. Jones, and K. Wilkes. 2006. "The Perceived Social Impacts of the 2006 Football World Cup on Munich Residents." *Journal of Sport & Tourism* 11 (2): 129–152. doi:10.1080/14775080601155167.

Oshimi, D., M. Harada, and T. Fukuhara. 2016. "Residents' Perceptions on the Socio-Economic Impacts of an International Sporting Event: Applying Panel Data Design and a Moderate Variable." *Journal of Convention & Event Tourism* 17 (4): 294–317. doi:10.1080/15470148.2016.1142919.

Ouyang, Z., D. Gursoy, and K. C. Chen. 2019. "It's All about Life: Exploring the Role of Residents' Quality of Life Perceptions on Attitudes toward a Recurring Hallmark Event over Time." *Tourism Management* 75: 99–111. doi:10.1016/j.tourman.2019.04.032.

Parnell, D., P. Widdop, A. Bond, and R. Wilson. 2020. "COVID-19, Networks and Sport." *Managing Sport and Leisure* : 1–7. doi:10.1080/23750472.2020.1750100.

Parra-Camacho, D., V. Añó Sanz, D. Ayora Pérez, and R. J. González-García. 2020. "Applying Importance-Performance Analysis to Residents' Perceptions of Large Sporting Events." *Sport in Society* 23 (2): 249–263. doi:10.1080/17430437.2019.1627330.

Pickering, C., and J. Byrne. 2014. "The Benefits of Publishing Systematic Quantitative Literature Reviews for PhD Candidates and Other Early-Career Researchers." *Higher Education Research & Development* 33 (3): 534–548. doi:10.1080/07294360.2013.841651.

Pranic, L., L. Petric, and L. Cetinic. 2012. "Host Population Perceptions of the Social Impacts of Sport Tourism Events in Transition Countries: Evidence from Croatia." *International Journal of Event and Festival Management* 3 (3): 236–256.

Prayag, G., S. Hosany, R. Nunkoo, and T. Alders. 2013. "London Residents' Support for the 2012 Olympic Games: The Mediating Effect of Overall Attitude." *Tourism Management* 36: 629–640. doi:10.1016/j.tourman.2012.08.003.

Preuss, H. 2007. "The Conceptualisation and Measurement of Mega Sport Event Legacies." *Journal of Sport & Tourism* 12 (3-4): 207–228. doi:10.1080/14775080701736957.

Preuss, H. 2015. "A Framework for Identifying the Legacies of a Mega Sport Event." *Leisure Studies* 34 (6): 643–664. doi:10.1080/02614367.2014.994552.

Preuss, H. 2019. "Event Legacy Framework and Measurement." *International Journal of Sport Policy and Politics* 11 (1): 103–118. doi:10.1080/19406940.2018.1490336.

Ribeiro, T. M., A. Correia, R. Biscaia, and C. Figueiredo. 2018. "Examining Service Quality and Social Impact Perceptions of the 2016 Rio De Janeiro Olympic Games." *International Journal of Sports Marketing and Sponsorship* 19 (2): 160–177. doi:10.1108/IJSMS-08-2017-0080.

Ritchie, B. J. R. 1984. "Assessing the Impact of Hallmark Events: Conceptual and Research Issues." *Journal of Travel Research* 23 (1): 2–11.

Ritchie, B. W., P. M. Chien, and R. Shipway. 2020. "A Leg (Acy) to Stand on? A Non-Host Resident Perspective of the London 2012 Olympic Legacies." *Tourism Management* 77: 104031. doi:10.1016/j.tourman.2019.104031.

Roy, S., J. Byrne, and C. Pickering. 2012. "A Systematic Quantitative Review of Urban Tree Benefits, Costs, and Assessment Methods across Cities in Different Climatic Zones." *Urban Forestry & Urban Greening* 11 (4): 351–363. doi:10.1016/j.ufug.2012.06.006.

Scheu, A., and H. Preuss. 2018. "Residents' Perceptions of Mega Sport Event Legacies and Impacts." *German Journal of Exercise and Sport Research* 48 (3): 376–386. doi:10.1007/s12662-018-0499-y.

Scheu, A., H. Preuss, and T. Könecke. 2021. "The Legacy of the Olympic Games: A Review." *Journal of Global Sport Management* 6 (3): 212–233.

Scholtz, M. 2019. "One Ultramarathon, Two Cities: Differences in Social Impact Perceptions." *Journal of Sport & Tourism* 23 (4): 181–202. doi:10.1080/14775085.2019.1654905.

Sharpley, R. 2014. "Host Perceptions of Tourism: A Review of the Research." *Tourism Management* 42: 37–49. doi:10.1016/j.tourman.2013.10.007.

Smith, A., B. W. Ritchie, and P. M. Chien. 2019. "Citizens Attitudes towards Mega-Events: A New Frame-Work." *Annals of Tourism Research* 74: 208–210. doi:10.1016/j.annals.2018.07.006.

Taks, M. 2013. "Social Sustainability of Non-Mega Sport Events in a Global World." *European Journal for Sport and Society* 10 (2): 121–141. doi:10.1080/16138171.2013.11687915.

Taks, M., D. Oshimi, and N. Agha. 2020. "Other-Versus Self-Referenced Social Impacts of Events: Validating a New Scale." *Sustainability* 12 (24): 10281. doi:10.3390/su122410281.

Taks, M., L. Chalip, and B. C. Green. 2015. "Impacts and Strategic Outcomes from Non-Mega Sport Events for Local Communities." *European Sport Management Quarterly* 15 (1): 1–6. doi:10.1080/16184742.2014.995116.

Taks, M., M. Littlejohn, R. Snelgrove, and L. Wood. 2016. "Sport Events and Residential Happiness: The Case of Two Non-Mega Sport Events." *Journal of Global Sport Management* 1 (3-4): 90–109. doi:10.1080/24704067.2016.1231925.

Thomson, A., G. Cuskelly, K. Toohey, M. Kennelly, P. Burton, and L. Fredline. 2019. "Sport Event Legacy: A Systematic Quantitative Review of Literature." *Sport Management Review* 22 (3): 295–321. doi:10.1016/j.smr.2018.06.011.

Thomson, A., M. Kennelly, and K. Toohey. 2020. "A Systematic Quantitative Literature Review of Empirical Research on Large-Scale Sport Events' Social Legacies." *Leisure Studies* 39 (6): 859–876. doi:10.1080/02614367.2020.1800804.

Vetitnev, A. M., and N. Bobina. 2017. "Residents' Perceptions of the 2014 Sochi Olympic Games." *Leisure Studies* 36 (1): 108–118. doi:10.1080/02614367.2015.1105857.

Vico, R. P., R. R. Uvinha, and N. Gustavo. 2019. "Sports Mega-Events in the Perception of the Local Community: The Case of Itaquera Region in São Paulo at the 2014 FIFA World Cup Brazil." *Soccer & Society* 20 (6): 810–823. doi:10.1080/14660970.2017.1419471.

Waitt, G. 2003. "Social Impacts of the Sydney Olympics." *Annals of Tourism Research* 30 (1): 194–215. doi:10.1016/S0160-7383(02)00050-6.

Wallstam, M., D. Ioannides, and R. Pettersson. 2020. "Evaluating the Social Impacts of Events: In Search of Unified Indicators for Effective Policymaking." *Journal of Policy Research in Tourism, Leisure and Events* 12 (2): 122–141. doi:10.1080/19407963.2018.1515214.

Yao, Q., and E. C. Schwarz. 2018. "Impacts and Implications of an Annual Major Sport Event: A Host Community Perspective." *Journal of Destination Marketing & Management* 8: 161–169. doi:10.1016/j.jdmm.2017.02.007.

Zhang, J. C., D. Svetina Valdivia, and K. K. Byon. 2020. "An Item Response Theory Analysis of Residents' Perceived Sporting Event Impacts." *Journal of Global Sport Management* : 1–29. doi:10.1080/24704067.2020.1731701.

Zhang, J. C., K. Byon, K. Xu, and H. Huang. 2020. "Event Impacts Associated with Residents' Satisfaction and Behavioral Intentions: A Pre-Post Study of the Nanjing Youth Olympic Games." *International Journal of Sports Marketing and Sponsorship* 21 (3): 487–511. doi:10.1108/IJSMS-03-2019-0027.

Zhou, J. Y. 2010. "Resident Perceptions toward the Impacts of the Macao Grand Prix." *Journal of Convention & Event Tourism* 11 (2): 138–153. doi:10.1080/15470148.2010.485179.

Zhou, Y., and J. Ap. 2009. "Residents' Perceptions towards the Impacts of the Beijing 2008 Olympic Games." *Journal of Travel Research* 48 (1): 78–91. doi:10.1177/0047287508328792.

"Winning the women's world cup": gender, branding, and the Australia/New Zealand *As One 2023* social media strategy for the FIFA Women's World Cup 2023™

Adam Beissel ⓘ, Verity Postlethwaite ⓘ and Andrew Grainger ⓘ

ABSTRACT
In this article we critically explore the social media strategy of the successful Australia-New Zealand 'As One' joint bid for the FIFA Women's World Cup 2023™. We explore how the As One bid harnessed Twitter to communicate a hosting vision that appealed to multiple audiences while strategically, and successfully, resonating with contemporary FIFA politics. We adopt quantitative and qualitative content analysis methods to develop the constructed presence and narrative patterns from the As One bid's Twitter activity. Our findings suggest content relied on two primary 'legacy' narratives which both conformed to current FIFA strategy and broader social and regional politics: growing football participation among women and girls and strengthening cultural, economic, and political relations in the Asia-Pacific. Ultimately, we argue the use of Twitter was strategic and targeted, deliberately appropriating popular FIFA narratives to build an emotive 'legacy' vision to gain support from voting members of the FIFA Council.

Introduction

The hosting rights for the FIFA Women's World Cup 2023™ (FWWC 2023™) were recently awarded to a joint bid from Australia and Aotearoa/New Zealand.[1] The Trans-Tasman bid, known as 'As One', will be one of several firsts for the tournament: the first to be held in the southern hemisphere; the first to be hosted under an expanded 32-team format; and the first time hosting rights have been shared by two nations. The successful Australia-New Zealand bid is also notable for being the first host for a women's event selected since the 2016 release of 'FIFA 2.0,' the much-hyped 'roadmap' for the 'restructuring' of football and FIFA, and the subsequent launch of FIFA's *Women's Football Strategy* (FIFA 2016, 2018). Released in the wake of a series of high-profile corruption scandals (Sugden and Tomlinson 2017), and only a few months after the election of reform-touting Gianni Infantino as president, FIFA 2.0 sets out a range of strategic measures underpinned by promises of transparency, accountability, and cooperation (FIFA 2016). Also notable in the new vision is FIFA's overt commitment to building the women's game and bringing it into the mainstream; in FIFA's words, to develop the grassroots, sporting, and commercial growth of the women's game and 'enable more women and girls from all backgrounds to play the game or participate in football in a variety of ways' (FIFA 2016, 7). The subsequent release of its *Women's Football Strategy* complements FIFA's publicly-stated goals for the women's game, with promises to increase participation, address 'historic shortfalls in resources and representation' and enhance the commercial value of and commercial benefits for women's football (FIFA 2018, 4).

Likely recognizing the competitive advantage offered by fitting their bid within this wider context, and echoing FIFA's desire to develop and commercialize women's football (Coche 2021), the As One joint bid was based around a concerted strategy of growing the women's game in the Asia-Pacific region and promoting broader social change and gender equality on and off the field. In order to garner public and political support for their bid (and gain the necessary votes from the majority of FIFA's 35-member executive committee), the As One bid launched an aggressive digital-media-focussed public relations and branding campaign that emphasized themes of women's empowerment, regional development, and global partnership. Through the use of popular social media hashtags, stylish web-based videos, and heavy cross-promotion from well-known players, the bid—notably the first spearheaded by a woman—put women's football, and women's sport in general, at the visible heart of its strategy. While the FIFA Council's decision was undoubtedly based on a series of factors, it is notable that the As One bid was unique among its competitors in establishing a social media presence, engaging Twitter in particular as a central plank in its communication and branding strategy.

Within this paper, we critically interrogate the conjunctural politics of the As One bid by contextualizing its strategy and articulating its connections to the various, social, cultural, political, and economic forces currently shaping global sport mega-events (SMEs). Particularly, this paper focuses on the combination of social and commercial political circumstances engaged by and shaping the As One bid and explores how social media became an important—and influential—means through which the bid was able to constitute its identity and interests. Taking As One's tweets as central discursive resources, we seek to analyse how Twitter became a digital space through which the bid was able to construct its preferred vision for FWWC 2023™ and ask how this vision resonated with the socio-cultural and organizational politics currently informing global football and its feature tournaments. Our primary objective is to examine how the successful Australia-New Zealand joint bid mobilized social media to construct and communicate an integrated hosting vision which invoked multiple audiences (e.g., policy makers, the media, and the public) while strategically appealing to key decision-makers and, most importantly, FIFA, the awarding body.

Our analysis seeks to address three primary research aims. First, to investigate how the As One bid campaign used Twitter to strategically engage various audiences. Of particular interest is how the As One campaign used Twitter to conspicuously communicate the bid's legitimacy, including its ability to meet the requirements of FIFA and 'sell' the tangible and intangible benefits of choosing the As One bid over its competitors. Our second aim is to explore the degree to which the As One hosting vision engaged with, and conformed to, preferred FIFA narratives about women's football, women's empowerment, and the potential of the FWWC to grow participation among women and young girls. Third, and relatedly, we track how FIFA's vision of the World Cup as a diplomatic and developmental tool was discursively mobilized in the As One campaign's bidding narratives. It is important to note that we do not seek to analyse the substance of the As One bid's implied benefits for either women's sport or diplomatic relations in the Asia-Pacific; rather, our objective is to discover the degree to which such narratives were harnessed as convenient narratives through which to constitute and promote the As One brand. Our focus is the narrative strategies and tactics—as expressed through Twitter—used to develop the bid's digital identity and how they are emblematic of the need for contemporary bid campaigns to recognize the complex socio-historic conditions in which the current bid processes for SMEs are being contested.

In order to address these aims, we use a mixed-method approach which combines aspects of qualitative and quantitative content analysis to explore the social media strategy of the As One bid, focussing on the narrative themes emerging from the bid's Twitter activity. We analyse more than six weeks of As One-related tweets between May 2019 (the start of the As One Twitter account) and July 2020 (the announcement of the host and end of the As One Twitter account activity). We consider the reach, use, negotiation, and narratives of the bid campaign's social media posts towards constructing a social media presence by contextualizing this strategy in relation to official bid documents, published news media reports, and public statements from key stakeholders (e.g., politicians, bid representatives, commercial partners). While previous research on the use of Twitter in the sport industry has largely focussed on its potential to promote consumer engagement and develop brand relationships, our suggestion is that the As One bid's primary audience was less 'consumers' per se than those 'audiences' who render the bid legitimate and desirable—politicians, governments, corporate partners, and, most importantly, those FIFA Council members holding the power to grant hosting rights. Thus, our interest is less the measurable 'brand impact' of the As One bid's Twitter account or the engagement with and effect of specific messages but, rather, the nature and content of the messaging and what it suggests as the priorities for the winning of hosting rights for SMEs in the contemporary sporting moment. Given the limitations of space and scope, we focus on the primary self-presentation strategies used on Twitter by the As One bid campaign, highlighting and discussing the core narratives while recognizing that other themes may warrant further analysis in future research.

Literature review

As the scale and scope of international SMEs continued to grow, and the economic, social, and ecological costs of hosting them continue to escalate (Tomlinson 2014), international sport organizations (e.g., FIFA and the International Olympic Committee [IOC]) have made major reforms to their bidding processes in order to attend to widespread public criticism of these negative outcomes. In this context of public and political scrutiny and the desire for increased levels of transparency, bidding has become an increasingly complex undertaking. Prospective host cities and countries are now required to produce integrated hosting visions and legacy planning and deploy large-scale public relations and media strategies to maximize the chances of gaining the support of voting members and global audiences (Byun, Ellis, and Leopkey 2021; Byun, Loepkey, and Ellis 2020). More recently, in response to such challenges and requirements, joint event bids, uniting multiple cities or nations in a single proposal, have become more prominent, and increasingly encouraged by governing bodies, as a strategy for hosting international events.

In the case of the IOC, their strategic planning Agenda 2020 includes bidding requirements that allow portions of the Games to be staged outside the host city or country to enhance sustainability, mitigate risks, and share costs. Likewise, World Rugby (WR), the governing body for international rugby, recently announced it would now accept joint bids for its 2025 and 2029 Women's Rugby World Cups (WRWC) and the 2027 and 2031 Men's Rugby World Cups (MRWC). With regard to football, one of the changes ushered in with FIFA 2.0 was to expand the FIFA Men's World Cup (FMWC) from 32 to 48 teams, promising to 'harness football as a common thread to connect the world' (FIFA 2016, 19) while simultaneously optimising the tournament's profitability amid rising costs via the development of new 'event structures' and 'delivery models' (FIFA 2016, 42). This prompted a joint bid from Canada, Mexico, and the United States to share the hosting rights for the FMWC 2026™. Several joint bids have also been announced in the race to secure hosting rights for the FMWC 2030™, with confirmed bids from: Spain and Portugal; Bulgaria, Greece, Romania, and Serbia; Uruguay, Argentina, Chile, and Paraguay; and England, Northern Ireland, Scotland, Wales, and the Republic of Ireland.

Indeed, instances of joint bids for what Roche (2000, 2017) calls 'first-order' SMEs have grown more frequent. This is not to suggest joint bids or joint hosting are wholly novel. The Union of European Football Associationss (UEFA), the administrative body for football in Europe, has used a multi-host model to stage its quadrennial Men's European Football Championships ('Euros') on three out of the last four occasions: UEFA Men's Euro 2008 (Austria and Switzerland); UEFA Men's Euro 2012 (Poland and Ukraine); and UEFA Men's Euro 2020 (12 cities in 12 countries) (see Stura et al. 2018; Ludvigsen 2019, 2020). However, while joint bids may not be a new phenomenon, they are becoming increasingly common. Moreover, as Byun, Leopkey, and Ellis (2020) point out, instances of successful joint SMEs bids have also grown in the case of 'second order SMEs' (Roche 2000, 2017). Recent examples include: the 2018 Fédération Internationale de Volleyball (FIVB) Men's World Championships in Italy and Bulgaria; the 2019 International Handball Federation (IHF) World Men's Handball Championship in Denmark and Germany; the 2023 IHF World Men's Handball Championship in Poland and Sweden; the 2023 IHF World Women's Handball Championship in Denmark, Norway, and Sweden; and the 2023 Fédération Internationale de Basketball (FIBA) Men's Basketball World Cup in Indonesia, Japan, and the Philippines. Since this is a relatively recent trend, there is little research examining the contextual forces necessitating joint bids and deconstructing strategic hosting visions, event legacies, and the 'unified partnership' narratives that are leveraged during the competitive bid process.

Literature on the competitive bidding process for first order international SMEs is well established (see Black 2007, 2008; Chalip, 2014; Cornelissen 2004, 2010; Grix 2012). This body of literature serves as a collection of individual case studies that examine bidding strategies that are diverse, multifaceted, and contextually specific. Many studies examining the competitive bid process focus on the economic promises of SMEs (see Baade, Baumann, and Matheson 2008; Porter 1999; Zimbalist 2015). Event legacies are frequent sources of analysis for scholars (see Chappelet 2006; Preuss 2007). Still other work focuses on the strategic decision-making of, and image projection by, host cities and countries involved in the competitive bid process. Chalip's work on the leveraging of SMEs (Chalip 2014) focuses on both the economic and social leveraging of SMEs (Chalip 2004, 2006). However, cities and states have increasingly leveraged SMEs as a strategic means through which to enhance civic or national 'brand image' (Grix 2012). Indeed, *image leveraging* is concerned with how the bid processes and the events themselves have been used to communicate key messages to the national populace and improve perceptions among foreign publics. Rehearsing Cornelissen's (2004) 'ideas of the state' and Redeker's (2008) 'imaginary power of the state,' Black (2007, 262) notes this as a pursuit of symbolic politics: 'a chance to signal important changes of direction, 'reframe dominant narratives about the host, and/or reinforce key messages about what the host has become/is becoming.'

Due to the relatively recent nature of the joint/multi-host SME format, however, there is a limited body of literature that examines their strategic hosting visions, event legacies, and the geopolitical implications therein. Stura et al. (2018) critically appraise UEFA's decision to share the 2020 Men's Euros among 12 European nations, identifying positive and negative effects of the new event model. These include potential benefits (e.g. new hosting opportunities and shared financial costs) as well as important barriers and constraints (e.g. a fragmented sense of community or sponsorship difficulties). Building on Stura et al. (2018), Ludvigsen (2019) views the emergence and growing frequency of the multi-host SME format as a call to arms, imploring further research to be conducted on: tourist perceptions; individual consumer-citizen experiences; and the media discourses that frame these events through well-branded event slogans. Heeding his own call, Ludvigsen (2020) examines the Euro 2020 multi-host event by focussing on the challenges and opportunities for hosts, which he sees as including: logistical and financial concerns for travelling supporters; the opportunity for less experienced SME hosts to learn from others; and the establishment of shared hosting practices.

Recent work by Byun, Leopkey, and Ellis (2020) examines joint bids for hosting international SMEs as 'strategic alliances' in order to understand why joint event bids are formed and how they gain a unique position over other candidates within the bidding process. In their systematic review of joint bids for first- and second-order SMEs, they explore the motivations and drivers of joint bids, identifying a narrow range of reasons for these strategic alliances: an attempt to win the competitive bid process; gaining access to partner resources; differentiating and adding value to the bid; leveraging opportunities; and reducing the potential threat of competition. Byun, Ellis, and Leopkey (2021) make similar arguments about the underpinnings of joint bids but posit further that joint bids are a means through which to create different types of 'legitimacy', each encompassing different 'audiences.' As they argue, 'joint bidding alliances could help provide practices and structures that bring about its legitimacy in the eyes of those holding the power to grant hosting rights' (Byun, Ellis, and Leopkey 2021, 2).

In the context of football, FIFA has previously signalled a move towards new models for sharing in the benefits and dispersing the costs of hosting across several nations with its historic decision to award joint hosting rights for the finals to South Korea and Japan in 2002. The primary purpose of awarding the FMWC 2002™ hosting rights to South Korea and Japan was to bring the world's largest and most popular football tournament to the Asia-Pacific region and, thus, develop a potentially lucrative commercial football market (see Horne and Manzenreiter 2013). The FMWC 2002™ was the biggest single-sport, first-order SME in Asia to that point, with the 64-game tournament and its 32 participating teams watched by an unprecedented 2,705,197 spectators in both countries and an accumulated worldwide TV audience of nearly 50 billion (Dolles and Söderman 2008). However, while notable as the first joint bid in FMWC history, it is important to point out that the bid was not strategically integrated nor were any overt strategic alliances established to leverage the bid; instead, each country submitted their own bid with separate development plans and projected legacy outcomes. The result was sometimes divergent approaches to strategy and leveraging; the Korean bid positioned the tournament as a 'catalyst for peace' on the Korean peninsula (Sugden and Tomlinson 1998, 118) while the Japanese portion of the bid focussed on Japan's ability to promote political stability, the country's infrastructure, and its history as a leader in technology and technological innovation (Dolles and Soderman 2008).

With regard to joint bids for the football's most prestigious tournament, recent research by Beissel and Kohe (2020) examines the conjunctural politics of the hosting vision and event legacies of the FMWC 2026™, which will be jointly hosted by the United States, Mexico, and Canada. The North American effort, known as the 'United Bid', promoted an integrated hosting vision and strategy of 'United as One,' promising to strengthen continental partnership and use FIFA's signature event as a platform to unite the international (football) community by leveraging the tournament to promote global unity (Beissel and Kohe 2020). Not only was the United Bid the most commercially lucrative and financially certain for FIFA, but there were three interrelated contextual factors that saw the United States partner with its North American neighbours in the joint bid formation: the *practical* (the expanded tournament needed a scale of infrastructure that helped and mitigate hosting costs); the *strategic* (the U.S. Department of Justice was, at the time, investigating FIFA for fraud and corruption); and the *political* (the joint bid was a clear attempt by organizers to shift the focus away from then-U.S. President Donald Trump and his racist immigration policies) (see also Beissel and Andrews, 2021).

Pertinent to our analysis that follows is the distinct lack of research on joint bids for, or co-hosting of, major women's sport events. Obviously, this is in large part due to the fact that few such bids or events exist. This, in turn, likely reflects the scale and appeal of—and, thus, resources and capacity required for—major women's sports events (of course, this itself is an outcome of a long history of the under-resourcing and under-exposure of women's sport). The historical underappreciation for, and analysis of, major women's sports events perhaps also reflects a (misguided) perception among those seeking to harness sport events as a tool of civic, national, or regional development that women's sports events lack the 'value' (both symbolic and economic) of their male counterparts. Ultimately, in relation to joint bids or co-hosting major women's sporting events, examples are few and far between. Outside of the women's football tournament at the 2012 London Olympics (which took place in England, Wales, and Scotland), the 2022 FIVB Women's Volleyball World Championship (due to be co-hosted by the Netherlands and Poland), the 2022 Women's FIH Hockey World Cup (to be played across Terrassa, Spain and Amstelveen, Netherlands), and the 2010 and 2018 ICC Women's T20 World Cups (technically 'multi-national,' though ultimately organized by single governing body in Cricket West Indies), one is hard-pressed to find instances of two or more countries coming together in an effort to host a major women's sport event. The FWWC 2023™ in Australia and New Zealand is therefore a unique opportunity to explore the nature and politics of a joint bid for a major women's sport event. Moreover, with the possible exception of the aforementioned case of London 2012, cases of joint-hosted major women's tournaments have been limited to *international*, rather than global, events, with their scale and relatively limited global popular appeal making them unlikely to fulfil the generally agreed criteria of a 'mega' or even 'major' event (Roche 2000). Whereas it could be argued that past joint-hosted women's events lack the size and appeal to be considered SMEs, the same cannot be said of the FWWC 2023™, which—if the interest and impact of the most recent iteration in France in 2019 is anything to go by—will undoubtedly be a 'major,' and truly global, event (Coche 2021).

In a more specific sense, the bidding context of women's SMEs is a neglected aspect of scholarship. As discussed in the literature review above, the bidding process is shaped by a range of contextual factors and a conjuncture of circumstances—practical, strategic and political—which impact on the leveraging objectives and strategic positioning of the bidding parties. Where there has been a gendered lens or focus on SME contexts, it has often been to problematize the male domination or decision-making of the respective international federation. For instance, numerous scholars have considered the historically patriarchal nature of international sport governance. Black and Peacock (2013), for instance, describe the gatekeepers (the IOC) to the largest SME (the Olympic Games) as an 'old boys' club' (711). Similarly, Chatziefstahiou and Henry (2013) and Tomlinson (2014) trace the leadership of Pierre de Coubertin and Sepp Blatter for significant periods of the IOC's and FIFA's history, and how the inclusion and recognition of women in leadership positions, women as athletes, or women in general were marginalized within the organization's priorities. While not wishing to deny the importance of such work, our article seeks to explore a different aspect relating to the gendered nature of SME organization and delivery: that of the bidding process itself and, more specifically, how narratives of gender and gender empowerment were effectively mobilized in As One's successful bid for the FWWC 2023™.

Theoretical framework

Our philosophical standpoint is informed by interpretivist scholars and tenants who view the process of bidding and hosting as a mixture of practical and strategic contextual factors and conjunctural political circumstances, thus arguing that there is no exact science or repeatable circumstances in which a bid committee functions or executes a strategy. This standpoint is reflected in the three aims of this paper where we seek to critically explore the construction of a Twitter presence, the tendency to conform with FIFA narratives about women's football, and the ability to achieve diplomatic and developmental objectives through a SME. This paper focuses on the bid committee's use of social media, type of communication, and creates multifaceted dynamics of presentation and interaction between the bid committee and its intended audiences. Considering our standpoint aims, the theoretical framework adopts aspects of institutional, gendered media, and social media framings to create a way for the researcher to look across the As One bid brand, social media usage, and vision for hosting. As this paper focuses on the development of the bid between the announcement to bid and the announcement of the bid success, there are a variety of dimensions of the As One bid to capture, thus theoretically we adopt multiple theoretical approaches to considering social media, gender and joint hosting. What stabilizes our theoretical engagement is the focus on social media and the use of Twitter by the bid committee. Our theoretical engagement, therefore, seeks to capture the intricacies of a bid committee and Twitter campaign for a jointly-hosted women SME as these ways to bid will be utilized by future sporting bid or organizing committees.

At present, research examining major jointly-hosted women events is somewhat disparate in terms of both topic and approach. While due in part to a lack of events to study, this diversity has much to do with scholars from different disciplines utilizing a variety of theoretical and empirical angles to understand the power and politics involved in the varying sites and spaces of these types of SMEs. A prominent theoretical framing is around institutional theory and notions of nation building. Indeed, such a framework was employed by Byun, Leopkey, and Ellis (2020) in their study of joint bids and the building of bid legitimacy. While useful for aspects of our own analysis, the framework does not fully capture the gendered elements and narrative strategies of the As One joint bid. Legitimacy does feature in our analysis and theoretically we engage with the notion that SMEs provide a powerful platform through which actors both internationally and domestically can engage in brand-building and the politics of persuasion through varying means (diplomacy) and actors (e.g., FIFA, bidding committee or spectators) (Postlethwaite and Grix 2016). We focus on the bidding committee (a non-state actor) and their use of social media (Twitter) as a means to manufacture support and develop narratives from their bid vision (i.e., a form of building bid legitimacy). The bid committee's Twitter usage, as it is for a women's event and a jointhosted bid, encompasses varying concepts connected to gender, and conjunctural politics of FIFA, Australia, New Zealand, and the Asia-Pacific region.

Considering a gendered theoretical framework, the Desjardins (2021) study on all the bids (Brazil, Colombia, Japan, and Australia and New Zealand) for the FWWC 2023™ utilized a feminist critical discourse analysis to problematise both the bids and FIFA's agenda around women and sport. Again, while relevant to part of our analysis herein, Desjardins' study did not attempt to bring in substantive media discourse, social media strategy, or national socio-political context elements of one specific bid and the conjunctural political events surrounding the context of a particular bid. While useful for aspects of our own analysis, the approach and framework did not consider the modes of communication or the depth of a particular bid or bidding contexts. As this paper seeks to focus specifically on the As One bid and its development of a hosting vision through social media, there is a need to theoretically consider the mode of communication and how this engaged both organizational legitimacy as discussed by Byun, Leopkey, and Ellis (2020) and gender equality discourses as discussed by Desjardins (2021).

With regard to our approach, we seek to extend scholarship on gender, media representation, and SMEs with the ideas of organizational legitimacy and gender equality discourses. To date, the vast majority of work in this area has focused on the portrayal of athletes in the media or, more recently, the self-presentation of athletes on social media during an event. For example, and in direct relation to women's football, the 2015 edition of the FWWC in Canada has generated a series of articles and studies about the framing of players or teams by traditional media as well as how players are framed by fans on social media (e.g. Burch, Billings, and Zimmerman 2018). Petty and Pope (2019) and Black and Fielding-Lloyd (2019) both focus on the English print media coverage of the FWWC 2015™ to put forward evidence and arguments that there was a growth in media coverage of the event by print media and that this coverage was largely positive. Black and Fielding-Lloyd (2019) further this by stating that, while temporarily challenging gender boundaries, the success of the English team served to (re)establish a traditional representational order which positions men's football as superior. The role of print media and the framing of gender theories to uncover positive and negative aspects of media coverage is a productive way to approach the research, especially as print media is one-directional and produced by a set of journalists who target particular consumers (i.e., the masses and popular culture).

Moving into popular culture further, Pegoraro, Comeau, and Frederick (2018) and Toffoletti, Pegoraro, and Comeau (2019) continue the argument put forward by these other studies but focus on the self-representation of fandom using visual media and the social media platform Instagram. Both studies use event-related hashtags to identify social media usage and analyse the framing of the event via social media, focussing on how social media both reproduces and challenges stereotypes of female athletes and fans. For the purposes of our analysis, it is worth noting that the pieces highlighted here used, in varying ways, narrative-based theoretical frameworks to retrospectively demonstrate media coverage, content and discursive ordering in comparison with other events. While such approaches all productively contribute to our understanding of the framing of the event, they did not consider the bid itself nor explore the official or organizational media strategies for the event. Our interest is the role of gender in the bidding process and strategic mobilization of 'equality' and 'empowerment' narratives in building a positive 'bid image' through social media. Taking a theoretical cue from Desjardins' (2021) neoliberal feminist analysis of the bid books for FWWC 2023™, we explore how the As One Twitter campaign strategically mobilized discourses of gender equality and empowerment as a means of 'selling' the bid to FIFA and other key decision-makers.

Beyond media representations of gender, there is a broader scholarship around use of social media by sport organizations. While not focussing on major women's sporting events per se, the organizational use of social media is, of course, a topic of growing scholarly interest. A significant argument to emerge from recent scholarship is that there is an increasingly fragmented sport-media environment (Sherwood et al. 2019). The implications of this fragmentation are multi-fold, including changes to the media's agenda-building function, changes to the engagement and consumption of media by fans and athletes, and, most pertinent to this article, changes to the communication strategies by organizations to influence international federations and other stakeholders. Over the last decade a growing body of research, across a variety of disciplines, has explored how Facebook, Twitter, Instagram inter alia have enabled sports organizations ('producers') to reach out to consumers or corporate partners. Our theoretical framing of social media is underpinned by the position that 'stakeholders' in the social media sport space range from athletes to governing bodies, through to fans and sponsors, and that 'content' is variously top-down, provider-generated, bottom-up, user-generated, and co-produced (Bowman and Cranmer 2014).

To date, studies of digital and social media use within the sport industry have largely focussed on their potential as a communication and/or marketing tool and how social media platforms are used variously to share information with constituents or encourage audiences to take action (e.g., to buy a product or watch and event) (Naraine and Parent 2016; Burch, Billings, and Zimmerman 2018). More recently, scholars have explored how sport organizations and marketers use social media as a means for 'engaging' audiences and building relationships between the organization and their 'stakeholders' (e.g., Naraine and Parent 2016). While contributing to these discussions, our primary interest is less the degree of engagement, whether messages were 'effective,' or the measurable 'impact' of the As One bid's Twitter use than how Twitter was used to construct preferential narratives, build support for the bid, display competence, and establish organizational legitimacy. In this regard and to link back to the studies cited around institutional theory, our article builds on previous research exploring the use of social media for organizational communication, but focuses more specifically on social media's role in a communication strategy primarily directed towards establishing organizational legitimacy among stakeholders. Theoretically, this aspect of our analysis is heavily informed by previous research which sees organizational legitimacy as a central objective and influence of the SME bidding process (e.g., Byun, Ellis and Leopkey 2021). However, while taking into account the politics of legitimacy—particularly its role in shaping social media use—we do not seek to distinguish the different types of legitimacy at play or who or what provides legitimacy; our goal instead is to explore the use of social media within the context of a complex event bidding process in which the desire to be seen as legitimate is one of a number of objectives. It is possible to achieve this goal as our theoretical framework reflects the dynamic engagement the As One bid committee had with social media and their ambitions to construct, project and interact with a particular host vision and different audiences. As we discuss below, capturing Twitter usage and other bid-related materials complements the adoption of institutional, gendered media, and social media theoretical framings outlined in this section.

Methodology

Drawing on the literature and theoretical underpinnings outlined above, and with regard to the aims of this piece, it is important to ground the methodology in relation to the competitive bidding process for SMEs, the history and politics of SMEs in Australia and New Zealand, and the use of social media in women's sport. In terms of social use with the sport industry generally, over the past decade a growing number of studies have explored topics as varied as women's sport, representation, and Instagram (Pegoraro, Comeau, and Frederick 2018; Toffoletti, Pegoraro, and Comeau 2019) to how sport organizations engage sponsors and other stakeholders through Twitter and other forms of social media (Naraine and Parent 2017; Winand et al. 2019; Wang 2021). Our methodology borrows from various aspects of collection and analysis from this extant research; however, the methodological decisions we present here represent one part of a larger study where social and print media sources will be traced across the life course of the bidding for, hosting, and legacy of FWWC 2023™. The following paragraphs outline the influence of previous studies in sport studies which use social media as a data source, the process we used to collect and analyse the data, and, finally, some remarks about limitations. Before doing so, we wish to highlight an important point implied, though not explicitly stated, in the literature review and discussion of our theoretical framework above, and underpinning our aforementioned research aims. Our objective is not to use Twitter activity as a data source through which to a question or (dis)prove a hypothesis; instead, our methodology is shaped by our research aims and evolved over the course of the research (Shapiro and Markoff 1997; Duriau, Reger, and Pfarrer 2007). We agree with other scholars who have noted how social media is a contested site of analysis and raises complex questions concerning interpretation given the difficulties of establishing authorship and intent; therefore, our analysis and interpretation represents *our* contextually-informed reading of the As One social media campaign rather than a comprehensive conclusion on the intentions behind, and ultimate effect of, the bid's Twitter strategy. Our primary aim is to open up further lines of inquiry and discussion (Patton 2015; Corbett and Edwards 2018).

In their review of scholarship on sport and social media, Filo, Lock, and Karg (2015) and Corbett and Edwards (2018) both suggest there has been a rapid increase in academic engagement with social media. This work has borrowed tools from print media studies and has embraced the use of theory and method from the distinct emerging field of social media studies. Of particular relevance is the development of mixed methodologies where both quantitative and qualitative methods are used to collect and analyse the social media data. A continued debate is around the manual or automatic techniques for collection and analysis, in particular the merits of using an automatic digital programme to collect, code and/or process large quantities of social media data (e.g., NVivo, Gephi or Leximancer). Although, beyond the scope of this article to discuss the advantages of manual over automatic approaches, or vice versa, we have chosen to utilize both manual and automatic techniques to identify, access, collect, and analyse social media data via Twitter—an approach which Murthy (2017) maintains provides a more balanced means of analysis and one which accounts for the advantages of both automatic and manual (interpretive, contextually-grounded) methods.

In terms of automated data collection, social media content extracted from Twitter was collected via NCapture, a web-browser extension, three weeks prior to the host announcement, the week of the host announcement, and two weeks after Australia and New Zealand were announced as joint hosts. Tweets were gathered based on hashtags (#AsOne or #asone2023, #fifawwc2023 and #GetOnside) then through searches of phrases and accounts connected to FIFA (@FIFAWWC, FIFA Women's World Cup). While the account connected to the bid (@AsOne2023) was live between May 2019 and July 2020 (total 812 tweets), the main data gathering phase for this article lasted for six weeks between June and July 2020, to consider the reach, use, and negotiation of the As One bid and success.

The data collection methods produced quantitative and qualitative data which were then subjected to a collaborative content analysis. As an approach, content analysis is 'any methodological measurement applied to text…for social science purposes' (Shapiro and Markoff 1997, 14). Consequently, content analysis provides a great deal of autonomy when gathering and analysing data. However, most studies utilizing content analysis are similar in their belief that language provides insights into authorial intentions and has important consequences for human perception (Duriau, Reger, and Pfarrer 2007). In this case, the use and display of certain information by official organizations can give insight about what is important to the organizations in question and the way they want to be viewed and perceived by the public (Abrahamson and Hambrick 1997). Specifically, a Twitter content analysis was chosen as the methodology for this study because of its nonintrusive nature, its ability to uncover latent meanings within text, and its robustness against research demand bias (Hsieh and Shannon 2005). Furthermore, it provided a strong fit with the research aims guiding this study.

Quantitively, we analysed the social media data using NVivo, a data management application which allows for: textual and network content analysis (e.g. author of tweet and dialogue); numerical content analysis (e.g. number retweets of significant tweets or number or usage of a hashtag); and geographical analysis (e.g. visual display of the geography of Twitter communication). The quantitative data informed the authors of the general social media strategies used by the bid committee and what type of Twitter content received the most engagement and reach (i.e. significant social media 'moments') during the bid and announcement. Complementing this quantitive analysis, and building on the themes emerging from the NVivo coding, we examined the content and rhetoric of significant Twitter posts. This qualitative portion of the analysis was complemented and contextualized by analysing these tweets in relation to official bid documentation and media coverage from major news publications from Australia, New Zealand, and around the world. We analysed several official bid documents utilized during the selection process in order to fully contextualize the As One bid social media and foreground our qualitative and quantitative Twitter findings. These included: the official 'Bid Book' produced by the AsOne campaign organizers; FIFA's Overview of the 2023 Bidding Process; FIFA's Bid Evaluation Report; FIFA's 2.0 Vision for the Future; FIFA's Women's Football Strategy; and official FWWC 2023™ press releases on FIFA.com. We further contextualized these findings with public statements from politicians, athletes, sport administrators, local organizers, corporate partners, and sport governing bodies; all of whom were quoted in news media reports of the AsOne bid campaign. This allowed for triangulation of the social media data and provided a form of member checking in relation to initial quantitative findings. The mechanisms of analytical triangulation and member checking were informed by Patton's (2015) guidelines around using different data sources and having multiple members of a research team. In this case, we utilized the quantitative and qualitative aspects of the Twitter and As One bid campaign to inform and develop our three main research aims. As presented below, we turn to each of these aims and demonstrate how the empirical and conceptual aspects of our paper demonstrate varying aspects of the bid committee's use of social media and the overall bid campaign.

Analysis

The research findings, conceptual underpinnings, and data analysis are presented here in three sections with the empirical focus being on the As One bid team's social media campaign. We begin by considering the construction of a social media 'presence' by the bid committee and the role of Twitter therein. We then explore the Twitter data to unpack the nature and content of tweets gathered throughout the bidding period. Next, we consider the promotion of women and girls through social media messaging and through Twitter engagement throughout the bidding process. Finally, we explore the use of social media to complement broader bid narratives relating to cultural, economic, and political relations between Australia, New Zealand, and the wider Asia-Pacific Region in general. These narratives are obviously not unrelated. The idea that the tournament will be a boost to the rights and access of women and girls to sport, and the overt commitment to growing participation rates for women and girls in sport, can also be seen as a form of political symbolism (a useful signifier of a socially-progressive society) and a rhetorical mechanism of soft-power diplomacy (a means to both catalyze engagement and proactively manage image and reputation). We therefore acknowledge the inter-relatedness and overlaps of these themes. We further recognize that there is a need for future research which critically explores how Western ideals of gender and sport are mobilized within the As One bid and the problematic use of women's football in the service of diplomacy (see McDonald, 2015; Desjardins, 2021). Our analysis below is therefore less a comprehensive analysis of the bid than a starting point for discussing the dominant representational politics and unstated assumptions that underlie the As One social media strategy and exploring how social media was used as a space to construct preferential bid narratives which helped to build support for the bid campaign among its constituent audiences.

Constructing a social media presence

In December 2019, Football Federation Australia[2] (FFA) and New Zealand Football (NZF) declared their intent to submit a joint bid to host the FWWC 2023™. The FFA had long planned on submitting its own bid, with the Australian government pledging A$5 million in hosting support, and was joined by its trans-Tasman neighbours, New Zealand, in an announcement mere hours before the official *FWWC 2023™ Bid Book* was to be submitted to FIFA. The decision for a joint bid was driven in large part by the belief of both football governing bodies that a joint bid had more chance of success given tough competition and strong interest from other nations for hosting rights. It is also important to note that the FFA had already been unsuccessful in previous attempts to host the quadrennial tournament (including disastrous bids for the men's 2018 and 2022 FWCs) and, when the women's tournament was expanded from 24 to 32 teams for 2023, there were serious reservations whether New Zealand would meet the hosting requirements established by FIFA.

Upon its announcement, the As One bid was heralded by both football federations as a truly historic moment for the commercialization of the women's game and a crucial moment in growing womens' and girls' involvement in sport. FFA chairman Chris Nikou said the event would promote a healthier, more equal society, both inside and outside the sport: 'The decision to host the FIFA Women's World Cup in 2023 in Australia and New Zealand, two leading nations in the promotion of women's football and gender equality, will accelerate the game at both the grassroots and professional levels, lighting a path for future generations of footballers, administrators, and fans in Asia-Pacific' (quoted in 'Australia and New Zealand Join Forces' 2019). Grant Robertson, New Zealand's Minister for Sport and Recreation, said the countries,

> 'can work as a team to deliver something unique and world class, while also creating a legacy for women and for football in our countries and across Asia and Oceania' (quoted in 'Australia New Zealand Confirm Joint Bid' 2019).

Similarly, Matildas[3] forward and captain Samantha Kerr maintained: 'There is so much untapped potential, not just in Australia but right across Asia and the Pacific region, that I really do believe we would offer something incredibly special' (quoted in 'Australia New Zealand Confirm Joint Bid' 2019).

The announcement of the As One bid partnership was also celebrated as a demonstration of how sport can unite and strengthen the shared heritage, socio-economic relations, and diplomatic ties of the two neighbouring countries. According to NZF President Johanna Wood, the cross-confederation bid 'represent[ed] a new level of cooperation for football,' with the cooperation of the countries to develop the joint bid submission 'highlight[ing] the excellent way in which the nations would work to host the tournament proper (quoted in 'Australia NZ Confirm Joint Bid' 2019). Australian Sports Minister Richard Colbeck cited historical precedent for sport event partnerships between the two countries: 'We've got a reputation for it and we've done joint events before, in both cricket [the 1992 and 2015 world cups] and rugby league [2017 world cup] and they've both been hugely successful' (quoted in 'Australia and New Zealand enter Joint FIFA Women's World Cup™ bid' 2019).

Immediately following the joint bid announcement, the bid committee launched an extensive digital marketing/branding campaign, including a strategic social media presence, designed to articulate the As One strategic hosting vision and legitimate the trans-Tasman partnership to stakeholders. The bid website, initially AusBid2023.com, was quickly transformed into AsOne2023.com, and introduced the event AUNZ2023 logo, the #AsOne hashtag, and the iconic colour scheme of navy blue, Cambridge blue, and mint green that would be the trademark of its entire digital media presence over the forthcoming year (see Figure 1). Notably, and as described above, previous FIFA bid processes have only allowed joint bids to be formed as separate projects, developed and submitted individually by each of the prospective joint hosts. An illustrative example is the South Korea-Japan bid for, and co-hosting of, the FMWC 2002™—an arrangement that was less strategic than a solution to a political stalemate. As Manzenreiter's (2008) description of the tournament suggests, joint bids may sometimes be politically expedient but can be organizationally incohesive, logistically complicated, and diplomatically fraught. According to Manzenreiter, while some of the primary legacy outcomes were realized (e.g., economic growth and infrastructural development), many of the benefits for both countries (e.g., 'levelling up' in international consciousness, improving bilateral relations, and shifting public perceptions of Asia) were less the result of an integrated and cohesive partnership between the two host nations than the latent outcome of the type of reproachment required to bring the tournament together. In contrast, the As One campaign sought to conspicuously demonstrate the joint nature of the bid from the outset through a coordinated brand and integrated social media presence. Seen within the context of FIFA's recent changes to the bidding process and its encouragement of joint or regional bids (see Homewood 2016), the prominence of a single, unified 'bid brand' can be seen as an important means through which to strengthen the legitimacy of the As One bid.

The official bid website featured quick access links to official As One bid information including the official bid book as well as information aimed at informing audiences about the bid process and strategic vision including: a list of bid champions such as Kerr and Football Ferns[4] captain Ali Riley (see Figure 1); a timeline of the bid selection process;[5] and the As One strategic hosting vision. Significantly, the vision in the bid book was articulated through 'four key areas' defined by benefits for: 1) Football, 2) Women and Girls, 3) FIFA, and 4) Players and Fans (AsOne.com, 2019). The bid book and strategy, as noted by Desjardins (2021), employed themes of women's sport, gender equality, and the phrases from the *FIFA Women's Football Strategy* (FIFA 2018). Pertinent for this piece is the

Figure 1. Examples of website, hashtag, and logo from the As One bid campaign. Source: Football Australia.

mobilization of *social* elements aimed at constituents of the bid; that is, the sport, a particular gender group, the gatekeeper sport organisation, and the event participants/spectators. The nuance to this vision demonstrates that the bid book and website were designed to showcase a vision and space for hosting that go beyond merely commercially-viable aspects and economic benefits.

Although the As One website generated a lot of interest and web traffic in the aftermath the bid announcement, it remained largely unchanged, and failed to generate much engagement, throughout the competitive bid process that would unfold until the hosting rights announcement on June 22, 2020. The bid's Twitter account, initially created in May 2019 to coincide with the launch of the Australian bid, provided the bid committee with a social media and online presence that was truly unprecedented in the history of a SME bids. Similar to the website, the bid's Twitter account and handle was updated to incorporate the As One logo and branding following the December 2019 announcement of the joint bid (see Figure 2). The Twitter account was subcontracted by FFA to Red Agency, an Australian public relations and advertising company, who were given the remit of 'leading and executing an integrated communications strategy that builds national awareness and encourages Australia to #GetOnside by registering their support for the bid at AusBid2023.com' ('Red Agency to Handle PR & Social' 2019). Over the next six months, the As One Twitter account became the *primary source* of bid information during the competitive bid process. In order to build and sustain momentum following the official launch, Red Agency 'engaged with a number of high-profile Australians via an unpaid Twitter campaign which asked

Figure 2. Examples of the As One Twitter campaign. Source: Football Australia.

them to post their own #GetOnside message and encourage their followers to register their support' ('Red Agency to Handle PR & Social', 2019). The Twitter account shared images of vocal supporters, current and former players, local and national politicians, and prominent business leaders holding 3-dimensional #GetOnside and #AsOne hashtag emblems, often photographed adorned in Matildas or Football Ferns' merchandise and/or in front of iconic Australian or New Zealand landmarks (see Figure 2).

As we argue below, the primary purpose of the Twitter account was for the bid committee to utilize social media to leverage for hosting rights and legitimate the bid in the view of key stakeholders. A key element therein was the collection of the 'signatures' of FWWC 2023™ supporters who would #GetOnside in support of the bid. The Twitter account encouraged supporters of the bid to visit the AsOne.com website to sign up and register their support; updated running totals were then provided on Twitter throughout the competitive bid process. By the time of the bid announcement on June 22, 2020, the As One bid had collected 803,436 'signatures' from those pledging their support for Australia and New Zealand to co-host the FWWC 2023™. In May 2020, just one month before FIFA would award the hosting rights, the As One Twitter account proudly celebrated the results of the *FIFA Bid Evaluation Report* that rated the As One bid the highest of all submissions (an overall score of 4.1/5.0), over its two competitors Japan (3.9/5.0) and Colombia (2.8/5.0) (Brazil had dropped out by this stage). By comparison, in the entire six month build-up to the awarding of the FWWC 2023™ in June 2020, none of the As One bid competitors had a website, a Twitter account, nor any integrated social media presence which may have provided further leveraging for their bids.

A quantitative analysis of the As One Twitter account reveals a sustained and integrated social media strategy aimed at generating high levels of supporter engagement. Our analysis of social media data collected on the As One Twitter account demonstrates a strategic and successful use of digital spaces to produce content and increase engagement opportunities around an SME bid campaign. The As One Twitter account had sustained engagement from May 2019 to July 2020 with 812 total tweets. Of the 812 total As One Tweets, 42.6 percent were original tweets by the As One account and 57.4 percent were retweets (see Figure 3). The As One Twitter account's peak period occurred from June 10th-July 5th 2020, a period coinciding with the immediate lead-up to, and celebration of, FIFA's announcement of the 2023 FWWC hosting rights on June 22 (see Figures 3 and 4). Similarly, as demonstrated by Figure 4 below, the #AsOne and #GetOnside hashtags peaked in engagement during the bid announcement months of June. Concurrent to a significant increase in As One account Twitter activity, the Twitter mentions by week of the hashtags spike during the week of the bid announcement and the hashtag #AsOne had the most mentions with 13,600 tweets using this hashtag the week of the bid announcement (see Figure 4). The data presented here shows a distinct use of Twitter and digital space by the Australia-New Zealand bid committee to manufacture support and engagement for their bid through the official bid account and through the use of preferable hashtags. Compared to rival bids, of which none had a social media presence or website, the As One bid had a pronounced advantage in the competitive bid process by being able to craft its own narrative and mobilize stakeholder support for the bid.

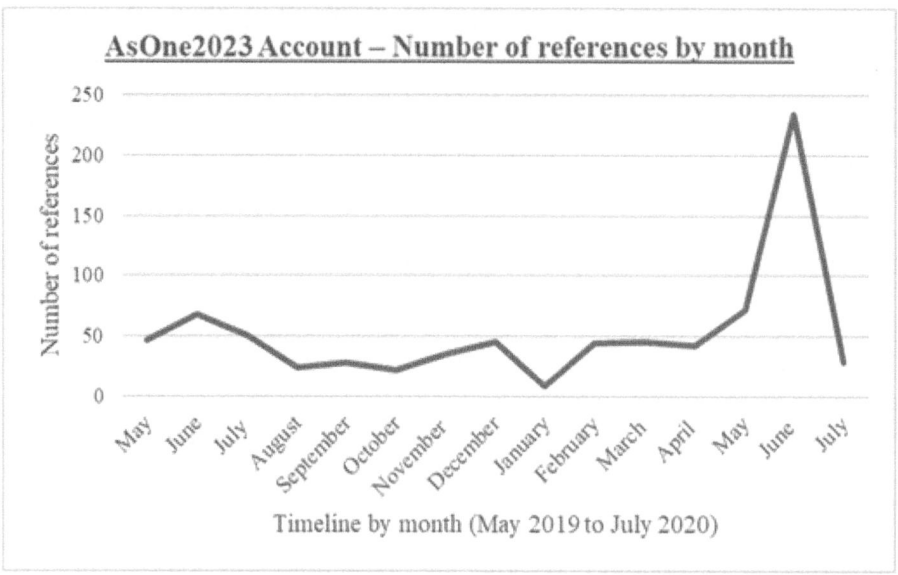

Figure 3. Duration of tweets by month of the @AsOne2023 Twitter account.

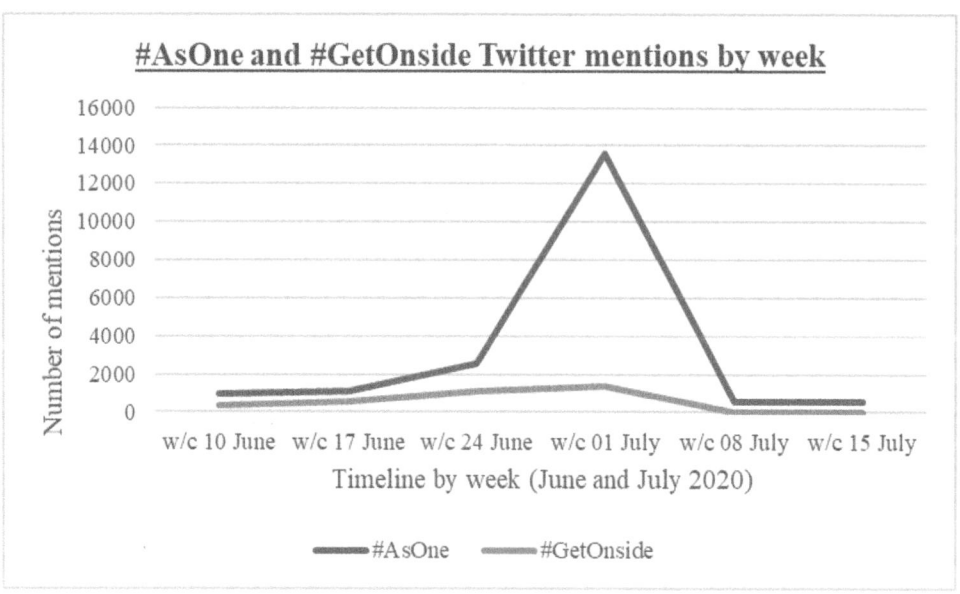

Figure 4. Duration of tweets per week of the #AsOne and #GetOnside Twitter mentions.

Promoting active involvement of women and girls in football

Perhaps the most prominent theme of As One campaign was the promise that the FWWC 2023™ would increase the active involvement of women and girls in football throughout Australia, New Zealand, and the Asia-Pacific region more generally. The official As One website included reference to the As One strategic hosting vision and event legacies with the objectives of: getting more women and girls playing and loving football; creating greater pathway opportunities for women and girls; increasing facility investment for women's football; and improving the public visibility and commercial viability of the women's game. According to the website, the Australia-New Zealand bid would be an opportunity to 'leverage the FIFA Women's World Cup 2023 to accelerate the advancement of women's football and utilize its potential to act as a social game-changer for women' (AsOne.com 2019, para. 3). The idea of using an event to promote women's participation in sport is obviously not novel; nor is using social media to promote such event-related aspirations. For example, in their analysis of the representation of female athletes on Twitter during the 2018 Gold Coast Commonwealth Games, Yang et al. (2020) use Framing Theory to highlight gender marginalization, using the same findings to inform stakeholders of how the strategic use of social media during SMEs provides possibilities for advancing a more inclusive sport culture. Arguably, the As One website, bid book, and Twitter account attempted to do exactly that—however, in this case, years in advance of the event and as part of building support for the bid, rather than as a part of the event leveraging per se.

The frequency with which the terms 'women' and 'girls' feature in the As One bid's Twitter activity is revealing of the core role played by gender in the bid's social media strategy. Of the 812 tweets from the As One account (original and retweets), the term 'women' is used 230 times, the term 'girls' is used 33 times. These were often used in conjunction with the term 'growth', which featured 12 times and develops the link between the bid's vision and the social media space by promoting the participation legacies of the event. By way of example:

'A player-centric tournament, Australia-New Zealand promises to deliver record-breaking crowds and long-term participation growth, bringing football together As One to celebrate the most amazing athletes in the women's game. @FFA @NZ_Football #AsOne'

'A @FIFAWWC would accelerate the growth of women's football across New Zealand and the entire Asia-Pacific region @rosiewhite13 #AsOne'

'Football has risen to record numbers across Australia. In the national football census released by @FFA, females playing the most popular club-based participation sport in the country rose by 11 per cent. A @FIFAWWC in 2023 would turbo charge that growth! #OneFuture #AsOne'

'Promoting women's football sends a clear message to young girls around the world: you can be anything you want. We strongly believe in harnessing the power of sport to promote #GenderEquality on and off the pitch. #GetOnside to show your support at https://t.co/EDlmBJetyW'

The narratives displayed here, and the consistency of these tweets during the bid campaign, demonstrate a deliberate and strategic use of 'women' and 'girls' by the bid committee to showcase the bid's vision. It also uses language and evidence which links this gendered narrative to Australia, New Zealand, FIFA, and other vested parties. Desjardins (2021) also noted the use of this type of gender empowerment narrative in the FIFA *Women's Football Strategy* and found the mobilization of gender equality to be a common feature of all of the FWWC 2023™ bids books, including that submitted by As One. Desjardins suggests, in line with our findings here, that the rhetoric of gender 'equality' and 'empowerment' was used by the bid committees to position their bid favourably with FIFA. In direct reference to the As One bid, Desjardins also noted how Australia and New Zealand went beyond conjecture and aspiration to showcase how both nations have seen growing public support for women's sport and how both have also already shown themselves to have a history of commitment to, and investment in, women's sport. The latter is, of course, a point of conjecture (as Desjardins argues), but, as the tweet examples above highlight, there is obviously enormous strategic and symbolic value in being able to make use of current participation 'evidence' and the growing international reputation of Australia and New Zealand as committed to equality, both on and off the sports field. Thus, the social media space, as evidenced by the tweets above, strategically enacted the vision laid out in the bid book, building an emotional narrative of gender development and growth at both the national and regional levels. While one could be critical of the commercial motivations here (see Desjardins 2021), the As One bid shows how social media can be harnessed to promote engagement with and support for a more inclusive sport culture. The narrative strategy, while obviously not correlating to actually achieving the aims, goes some way to showcasing how a strategic social media space can garner support, credibility and legitimacy to ambitions around participations and legacies for particular groups.

There is a need for some caution in suggesting that the strategic use of social media can contribute towards positive cultural change and support initiatives to maximize the participation legacies of SMEs. For instance, Desjardins (2021, 1) expresses reservations about the authenticity of the FWWC 2023™ bids, noting that while built around narratives of women's equality, there was lack of acknowledgement in the bidding nations' accountability for policies and practices 'that disenfranchized women's football in the first place.' Also of note is the way the construction and presence of visions and narratives on social media, such as that offered by As One, can perpetuate problematic and homogenized notions of women and girls (Ahmad and Thorpe 2020). As other studies of the FWWC have argued (Black and Fielding-Lloyd 2019; Pegoraro, Comeau and Frederick 2018; Petty and Pope 2019; Toffoletti, Pegoraro and Comeau 2019), and with regard to both traditional and social media, the representation of women and girls is a contested space; moreover, the As One Twitter account was a manufactured and strategic digital space rather than a space designed to create or enhance community. As further evidence of this view, it is worth pointing out the superficiality of the As One Twitter account and the rather cursory and non-specific nature of its messaging. While it is obviously difficult to convey complex policy or concrete initiatives in 280 characters or less, analysis of the tweets highlights how there was little or no explanation of the mechanisms by which the bid would seek to harness the FWWC 2023™ to increase the number of women and girls participating in football or improve diplomatic relations between the two host nations and the Asia-Pacific. The mechanisms and strategies that would be used to deliver these aspirational and transformative event legacies were if not absent, then decidedly ambiguous. Reproducing the common rhetoric of SMEs as unambiguously positive, the As One social media campaign instead relies on the taken-for-granted assumption that hosting the FWWC 2023™ would inevitably have a 'trickle-down effect' on various aspects of sporting and social development within Australia, New Zealand, and the Asia-Pacific. Indeed, precisely how the FWWC 2023™ would, to use the words of the As One bid itself, 'contribute the development of women's sport' or 'create new opportunities for participation, coaching, and leadership' was not discussed on any social media platforms.

As demonstrated by our analysis of the website, Twitter, and bid vision, the As One bid attempted to create authentic and substantive narratives around gender equality and increasing participation; however, beyond hashtags, percentages, and vision, there needs to be more understanding to how 'young girls around the world' will receive messages via an event and its supporting media. Moreover, and in line with Desjardins (2021) suggestion that any political significance of such narratives can be undermined by commercial purposes, we suggest that the As One campaign's mobilization of gender was less symbolic of present commitments to gender equality than about building support for the bid among key audiences. That is, the social media presence of the As One bid, combined with the method and rhetoric of its social media messaging, was central to manufacturing consent and support for the FWWC 2023™ hosting rights from relevant stakeholders—and FIFA most importantly. The As One bid committee's use of social media can be characterized as a sustained, integrated strategy that sought to leverage a strategic hosting vision which was informed by the contextual politics of FIFA 'reforms' and gender 'empowerment'; that is, social media was deliberately harnessed by the As One bid as a means of bolstering its credibility and 'legitimacy' in the eyes of FIFA and other key decision-makers. Considering that the competing bids of Japan and Colombia had no website, no Twitter account, and no social media presence, we argue the As One social media strategy was a competitive advantage in the SME bid process and arguably *the* principle reason why the FWWC 2023™ hosting rights were awarded to the Australia-New Zealand joint bid. We suggest this to be the case on the basis that the As One bid strategy appropriated and reproduced messaging from the FIFA 'playbook,' mimicking in particular a central principle of FIFA 2.0 and FIFA's *Women's Football Strategy*: namely, FIFA's stated commitment to promote women's and girls' involvement in football and commercializing the women's game.

Strengthening between Australia and New Zealand

A key strategic element of the As One bid was the 'regionality' of their social media campaign. Analysis of the tweets turned up numerous mentions of not only bilateral relations but the potential role of the FWWC 2023™ in promoting football—and, by association, *development*—throughout the Asia-Pacific. By way of example:

> 'Given the geographic proximity of South-East Asia to Australia and New Zealand, a @FIFAWWC in our region would help develop women's football throughout AFF in the lead up to 2023 and beyond';

> 'A @FIFAWWC in 2023 would accelerate our plans to grow the women's game across the Asia-Pacific';

> 'Our nations sit in the geographical centre of two Confederations that have huge untapped potential - unlocking it is the heart of our #AsOne vision.'

Such a strategy is perhaps unsurprising. In the first instance, the politico-economic 'regionalisation of the world' is one of the most important developments in global governance in the past two decades (Castle 2018, 151). We see this generally in the dramatic growth of multi-lateral, regional organizations and unions, preferential trade agreements, and (frequently contentious) multi-national 'mega-deals' like the Trans-Pacific Partnership and Transatlantic Trade and Investment Partnership. Such shifts bear similarities to more long-standing examples in sport; for example, the establishment of regional or continental confederations during the mid-twentieth century is a feature of the modernization of sport and its administration, and they continue to act a key bridge between the national and the global (Maguire 1999; Guilianotti 2007). In this case of football in the Asia-Pacific, the politics of sporting governance and aspiration reflect broader contextual politico-economic shifts in the region. In particular, while Australia has had a somewhat ambiguous relationship with Asia as a region, recent years have seen more concerted efforts to forge greater links with Asia across the political, economic, and cultural domains (Rowe 2018). Australian football mirrors this trend. Long a reluctant member of the Oceania Football Confederation (see Carniel 2012), the FFA's move to the much larger Asian Football Conference aligns with Australia's broader geopolitical shift towards Asia and its desire to broaden diplomatic and economic ties beyond the South Pacific.

Just as the shifting geopolitics of the Asia-Pacific are reflected in the membership and governance of the Asia-Pacific's sports confederations, they are echoed in the rhetoric and politics of the As One bid—a point most visible in the frequent references to the wider regional benefits of the Australia-New Zealand bid. As we have suggested, the As One Twitter campaign is suggestive of Australia and New Zealand using social media as a strategic resource through which to pursue legitimacy in the eyes of FIFA. Highlighting the broader, region-wide benefits of the As One bid can be seen as an appeal to FIFA's stated desire to 'leverage its showcase competitions' as a means of 'driv[ing] women's football development' at the host, regional, and global level (FIFA 2018, 19). Moreover, allusions to the (potential) regional impacts of the tournament overtly addresses a key metric of the 'hosting vision and strategy' component of a candidate's FIFA Bid Book; in particular, the need for prospective host cities to provide information on 'the manner in which the competition is intended to contribute to the development of women's football both locally and regionally' (FIFA 2019, 8).

Evidence of the regionality of the As One bid can be seen in the geography of Twitter engagement with the As One campaign. The map presented (see Figure 5) showcases a pattern in Twitter engagement with the As One Twitter account which is decidedly regional, if not Oceania dominant. Unsurprisingly, the Twitter engagement is most prominent in Australia and New Zealand; however, while the FWWC 2023™ is a global affair there is little engagement outside of the 'geographic neighborhood' (Ratuva and Brady 2019) of the host nations. The Twitter engagement suggests the intention of social media use is less the promotion of the 'global game' or the 'improvement of women's football globally' (FIFA 2019, 21) than it is about building support from Twitter users in the Oceania region, in particular Australia, New Zealand and immediate 'neighbors' in the Pacific and South East Asia; an important metric when seeking legitimacy from voting members of the FIFA Council (see FIFA 2019).

The image of unity and harmony that permeates the As One bid is also a means by which to build—or, at least, *signify*—other forms of organizational legitimacy, structural legitimacy (e.g. Australia and New Zealand harmony and concurrence) and linkage legitimacy (connections to key decision-makers and important stakeholders) in particular (Byun, Ellis, and Leopkey 2021). In contrast to previous joint bids, the bid campaign and projected legacy are presented in a cohesive and integrated manner. Joint bids are often 'marriages of convenience' formed by pragmatic motives such as meeting infrastructure requirements (e.g. the joint bid between Scotland and Ireland for Euro 2008 was forged to meet UEFA's requisite eight stadium minimum) or commercial imperatives (such as expanding the potential market for audiences, fans, tourists, and sponsors). Very often the difficulties of managing these international alliances can be overlooked resulting in 'parallel,' rather than integrated, bids which fail to capitalize on the advantages of strategic alliances (Byun, Ellis, and Leopkey 2021). In contrast to examples such as the FMWC 2002™ discussed above, the bid for the

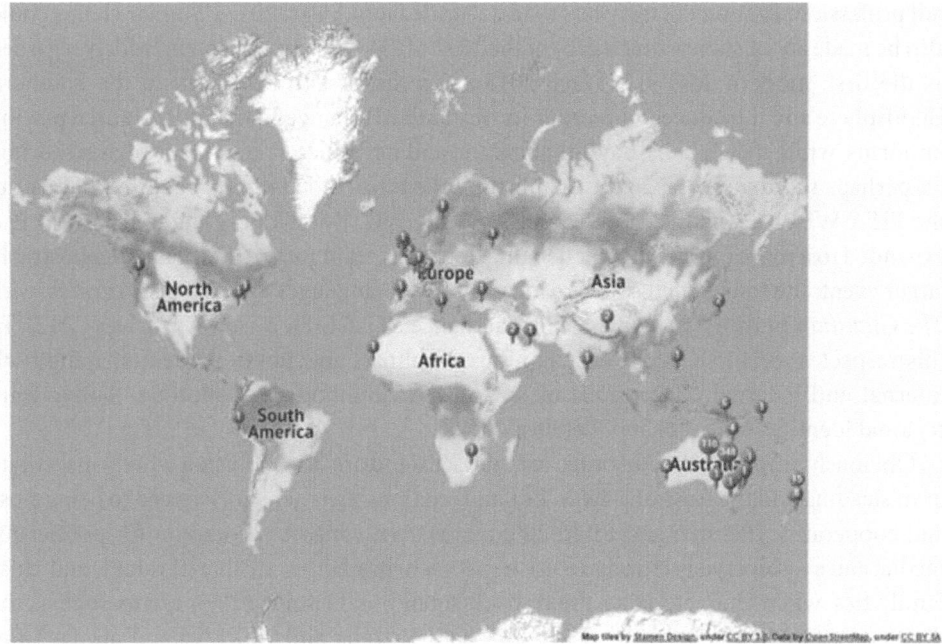

Figure 5. Map of the @AsOne2023 Twitter account geographical engagement. Source: FIFA Women's World Cup 2023 Website: https://www.footballaustralia.com.au/fwwc2023

FWWC 2023™ takes a distinctly different approach which stresses cooperative regionalism, inter-national and inter-organizational cohesion, and the desire to maximize the *shared* social and sporting legacies of hosting. As seen in tweets below, the As One Twitter account produces content where the partnership and strategy of co-hosting is positioned as both deliberate and pioneering. Of particular importance is the co-confederation angle of the bid; something stressed as not only historic but a possible 'game changer' and potential 'blueprint' for future bids:

> 'With a long history of true partnership, Australia and New Zealand share more than simply our passion for sport and the world game';

> '@FFA and @NZ_Football's innovative two-country model to co-host the @FIFAWWC 2023 is a game-changer and provides the opportunity for other nations to combine to host the tournament in the future'

Highlighting the historically close ties between Australia and New Zealand is a particularly prominent theme of the tweets captured over the course of the bid period. This type of rhetoric is not uncommon in Australasia and is obviously important for securing the public and political support of two nations with close ties but sometimes divergent interests (Rolfe, 2019). It is also worth noting that FWWC 2023™ will not be the first time that Australia and New Zealand have co-hosted a major sporting event. Of particular note are the MRWC in 1987 and the 1992 and 2015 Men's Cricket World Cups (MCWC). Although the inaugural MRWC in 1987 lacked the kind of global participation and television audiences typical of a modern SME, the success of the tournament has been credited by some for proving the long-term viability of the MRWC as well as playing a part in the eventual full professionalization of rugby less than a decade later (Swart 2017). Similar claims could also be made about success and legacy of the 1992 MCWC. The tournament, widely regarded as the first 'modern' MCWC (Wagg 2018), was the first to be played in the Southern Hemisphere and introduced numerous (now standard) changes including coloured playing uniforms, white match balls, day/night games, and new rules to encourage higher scoring. Of perhaps more importance for establishing the types of legitimacy required of hosting the FIFA WFWC, was the more recent 2015 MCWC. By this time the tournament had expanded to a more logistically-challenging, fourteen-team format and was a demonstrably larger event: the tournament was broadcast in seven languages across 220 territories, with *The Guardian* putting the estimated TV audience as 2.5 billion viewers (Selvey 2015). In this respect, the 2015 CWC was a significant cultural and political event shaping both internal and external conceptions of not only nationhood but collective, Antipodean, regional identity (Malcolm and Fletcher, 2017).

Obviously, implying the Australia and New Zealand are 'As One' is not wholly inaccurate or misleading and the Australia-New-Zealand relationship is generally agreed to being close and cooperative (Patman and Rudd 2005). However, while it is common for politicians, media, and even everyday citizens to use terms such 'brotherhood', 'shared values', and 'close family ties' when characterizing the trans-Tasman bond (Rolfe 2019), events such as the ill-fated 2003 MRWC bid are a reminder that Australia and New Zealand are far from homogenous and remain sovereign countries with interests that do not always coincide. Notably, there is also a long-standing asymmetry to the trans-Tasman bond. In particular, Australia often perceives New Zealand as a 'junior partner'. McPhee (1988) has aptly captured the prevailing Australian view of New Zealand in his contention that New Zealanders tend to know far more about Australia than Australians of New Zealand. Relatedly, Australia in sport, as in other areas of Australian ambition, Australia tends to be more interested in establishing itself among the world's sporting superpowers (Horton 2010).

An important caveat to the trans-Tasman sporting harmony that these events may imply is the 2003 MWRC. The International Rugby Board (IRB, the previous name of WR) originally issued an invitation to tender for the tournament in April 1997 and the Australian Rugby Union (ARU) and New Zealand Rugby Football Union (NZRFU) agreed on a joint bid a few months later. However, not long after the IRB confirmed Australia as hosts and New Zealand as sub-hosts, debates between the host unions began to emerge. A major point of contention was the rising costs of the tournament since the initial bid. When it was subsequently found that New Zealand was likely to face substantial financial losses, the IRB refused to subsidize tournament costs or provide financial guarantees to the NZRFU. Australia also refused to agree to New Zealand's demands to share tournament profits. After a series of acrimonious meetings taking place over a near three-year period, Australia took back its invitation for New Zealand to sub-host the tournament and shortly after, following a successful bid to the IRB, was awarded sole hosting rights (Frawley and Cush 2011). New Zealanders reacted to losing the tournament with a mixture of embarrassment and trans-Tasman resentment (McIlraith 2020); embarrassment at having lost out to its larger neighbour (thus reinforcing its national inferiority complex (James 2015), and resentment of what was perceived to be bullying tactics and arrogance on the part of Australia (thus reinforcing what many New Zealanders see as Australia's long-standing 'paternalistic, even patronising, attitude towards New Zealand' (Smith 2004, 177). Thus, the 2003 MRWC serves as an important reminder of how jointly hosted SMEs between Australia and New Zealand can be fraught with tensions, and can possibly lead to acrimonious – rather than harmonious – geopolitical relations.

It is perhaps worth noting that an emergent theme of the As One account—and bid campaign more generally—was the presence and greater suggested legitimacy of the Australian aspects of the bid; that is, the Matildas, FFA, and Australian organizations, politicians, celebrities, and athletes had a considerably greater presence in tweets and across the digital aspects of the campaign more broadly. In the word cloud presented below (see Figure 6), the words in the largest font demonstrate the most used phrases in the As One Twitter content. Notably, the phrases 'Australia' and '@thematildas' are as prominent as 'football,' 'women,' '#getonside,' and '2023,' while their New Zealand equivalents (i.e., 'Football, Ferns,' 'New Zealand') are only as large as mentions as prominent Australia players (e.g., @samkerr1') or the (largely Australian-focused) mentions of 'home soil.'

Overall, there is an obvious imbalance in the socially-mediated representation of the trans-Tasman 'team,' with New Zealand athletes, politicians, and celebrities considerably less prominently featured or positioned in the digital space. For example, of the 346 original tweets from the As One account there are 83 mentions of NZF and no mentions of the Football Ferns while there 112 mentions of the FA and 197 mentions of The Matildas. Without wanting to overstate the significance of New Zealand's underrepresentation in As One tweets, it nevertheless raises questions about the power balance in the bid strategy and

Figure 6. Word frequency from the @AsOne2023 Twitter account word cloud.

Australia's motivation for incorporating New Zealand into a joint bid—especially when Australia would likely have met most, if not all, of the FIFA bid criteria on its own (FIFA 2019). Future research exploring whether the asymmetries of the Twitter space reflect the realities of the As One bid or the nature of the current co-hosting relationship are therefore warranted.

Conclusion

In this paper, we have critically examined how the As One, Australia-New Zealand, joint bid to host the FWWC 2023™ used social media as a means through which to communicate a hosting vision which resonated with FIFA voters at the same time as it appealed to, and built support among, multiple audiences. In contrast to rival bids, social media was a central and significant element of the As One bid campaign, thus providing a potential competitive advantage and a strategic means through which to supplement its professional-technical capabilities through emotional appeals to the transformative potential of the FWWC 2023™. At a 'local' level, the As One bid appealed to key audiences in Australia and New Zealand, playing to long-standing—and politically expedient—discourses of trans-Tasman cooperation and harmony. At a broader level, Twitter was used to conspicuously demonstrate the As One bid's conformity to FIFA's new 'vision' for the future of football—something which FIFA itself highlighted as a fundamental consideration when evaluating bids. Tweets echoed FIFA's 2018 goals with regard to the growth and development of women's football and mirrored FIFA narratives as to the potential of the FWWC to be a vehicle for social development and enhanced international relations. While generating public awareness of, and support for, the bid were undoubtedly elements of the Twitter strategy, we argue that the *primary* audience of the As One tweets—those who were being encouraged to '#GetOnside'— were local politicians and FIFA voters (with the conspicuous support of the former key to gaining the support of the latter). Moreover, although interpellating 'citizen stakeholders' was undoubtedly a motivation behind the tweets, the thousands who signed up to the As One account, and the more than 800,000 'signatures' of support collected by bid cheerleaders, were important for the bid only in as much as they provided 'evidence' of public support for the bid; that is, growing the online audience was less about selling the tournament to fans than it was about establishing a measure of symbolic proof to FIFA and the Australian and New Zealand governments of public approval for the As One bid. In this way, social media was harnessed not as a means of marketing to 'consumers' but as a strategic tool to 'market' the bid to an audience of key decision-makers; that is, As One's social media was less a promotional campaign aimed at consumer awareness or relationship marketing than a strategically-produced, mediated space for satisfying the contrasting interests of disparate audiences.

We suggest that, when viewed through a *social* development prism, the FWWC 2023™ potentially speaks to a collective moment of *genuine* commitment to women's football and women's sport more generally; however, such views must always be tempered by the fact that, however noble these pursuits may be, they are nonetheless inextricably linked to commercial logics and the desire for market growth (Sherwood et al. 2019; Desjardins 2021). That the As One bid was ultimately successful points to the success of the social media strategy while also raising the possibility that *social*, as opposed to solely *commercial*, criteria have taken on a greater priority in the support for, and awarding of, SMEs. Our analysis finds that the As One bid campaign's harnessing of these themes was ultimately a strategic and overt means of signalling appreciation of, and conformity to, both current FIFA strategy and the broader cultural politics of the Asia-Pacific region.

It is worth noting that the As One bid has been dormant on Twitter since July 2020 and has not attempted to build on the momentum and interest created by the bid's success. The ephemerality of the As One Twitter account is perhaps the clearest suggestion of the specificity of its purpose: if it was truly about informing the public of the substantive legacies (and costs) of the bid, it would likely still be actively producing relevant, informative, and meaningful content. Instead, the strategic value of social media here is the way it was harnessed as a means of creating an ephemeral groundswell of support that could be leveraged to build 'bid legitimacy' and, thus, convince FIFA that Australia and New Zealand were the countries most suited to host the 2023 tournament. While evidently superficial, and thus open to criticism on a number of grounds, the As One social media campaign was, of course, ultimately a contributor to the bid's success. In this regard, the As One campaign's strategic use of social media may become the archetype for future SME bids. Indeed, given rival bids failed to engage the digital campaign space, the type of strategic, integrated, and sustained digital branding campaign developed by As One may now become an *essential* aspect of the SME competitive bid process. Such branding will be even more pivotal for jointly-hosted SMEs which are required to articulate a unified and united hosting vision among geographically, culturally, and economically disparate partners. Potentially, this may accelerate another trend noted by a number of scholars (e.g., Chalip 2014; McGillivray and Turner 2017; Byun, Leopkey, and Ellis 2020; Beissel and Ternes 2019): the growing use of 'intermediaries' in the planning and delivery of bid campaigns. This includes companies set up at arm's length to either or both sporting bodies and government to bid for events and/or bring public–private coalitions together. It also extends to a range of *cultural* intermediaries, public relations firms, marketers, and private information corporations hired to influence public opinion. It will therefore be more difficult to parse the well-managed and heavily-branded SME promises from their truly aspired to, and ultimately realized, social, economic, and political impacts on host countries. It will thus be critical for governments and other key decision-makers to critically evaluate the substance of social media messaging lest they be enticed by the allure of bids that seem to have more support than they actually do.

By way of conclusion, we acknowledge the risk of overstating the role played by social media in the As One bid's success. A clear limitation of our research is that it only considers the role of social media in building support for the As One bid, and further research would obviously be required to accurately gauge its influence on the FIFA Council. Moreover, we have no *direct* information on the intentions behind and development of As One's Twitter activity (e.g., internal documents or evidence indicating why certain words or images were chosen or how the use and content of the Twitter accounts was managed and governed). Our analysis assumes that the content of tweets reflects the aims and values of the organization and further research would help to substantiate the explicit objectives of the Twitter account and specific organizational structures, cultures, relationships, and resources which shaped the production of Twitter messaging. Another limitation is the specific timeframe of our data collection. The duration of our Twitter analysis began with the bid announcement in May 2019 and ended shortly after Australia and New Zealand were awarded the FWWC 2023™ just over a year later. The three-year period in the build-up to the event itself will be a telling measure of whether the benefits touted on social media are constructively and substantively pursued—and whether they are ultimately realized. In order to address these shortcomings, future research should consider the role of other forms of media (e.g., print media, television, radio) in mobilizing support for bid campaigns from their inception through build-up and preparation and throughout the tournament itself. Furthermore, in the case of FWWC 2023™ in particular, a bid document analysis should be conducted, both as a basis for comparing the social media strategy and critically appraising the substantive aspects of the bid itself, the strategic hosting vision, and the event legacies. Finally, and most significantly, future research needs to consider the mobilization of gender and gender empowerment narratives in bidding for women's SMEs. Further questions need to be asked as to whether the rhetoric of bidding and the ostensible commitment to promoting the inclusion of women and girls in sport is backed up via practical initiatives and investment in infrastructure and support, from grassroots through to the elite level.

Notes

1. Aotearoa is the Māori name for New Zealand. Aotearoa/New Zealand is often used in combination to signify the country's official commitment to biculturalism and the bicultural nature of the country's identity. We have chosen to use simply 'New Zealand' throughout for the purposes of clarity and in keeping with the predominant conventions of the As One bid; however, we recognize the cultural politics of using or not using te reo (the Māori language) and suggest this itself is worthy of exploring in future analyses of FWWC 2023™.
2. FFA was officially rebranded as Football Australia (FA) in December, 2020, a change first mooted in principle two, "Reset the Australian football narrative" of the FFA 'XI Principles' document (see: Rugari 2020).
3. The Matildas is the nickname given to the Australian Women's national football team.
4. The Football Ferns is the nickname given to the New Zealand women's national football team.
5. This timeline was later revised due to the COVID-19 pandemic.

Disclosure statement

No potential conflict of interest was reported by the authors.

ORCID

Adam Beissel ⓘ https://orcid.org/0000-0003-2024-0629
Verity Postlethwaite ⓘ https://orcid.org/0000-0003-3246-4611
Andrew Grainger ⓘ https://orcid.org/0000-0001-8960-4000

References

Abrahamson, Eric, and Donald C. Hambrick. 1997. "Attentional Homogeneity in Industries: The Effect of Discretion." *Journal of Organizational Behavior* 18 (S1): 513–532. doi:10.1002/(SICI)1099-1379(199711)18:1+<513::AID-JOB905>3.3.CO;2-#.

Ahmad, Nida, and Holly Thorpe. 2020. "Muslim Sportswomen as Digital Space Invaders: Hashtag Politics and Everyday Visibilities." *Communication & Sport* 8 (4-5): 668–691. doi:10.1177/2167479519898447.

Australia and New Zealand Enter Joint FIFA Women's World Cup Bid. 2019. "Australia and New Zealand Enter Joint FIFA Women's World Cup Bid." *ABCNews.com*, December 12. https://www.abc.net.au/news/2019-12-13/fifa-world-cup-australia-new-zealand-joint-bid-for-womens-cup/11796388

Australia and New Zealand Join Forces for 2023 Women's World Cup Bid. 2019. "Australia and New Zealand Join Forces for 2023 Women's World Cup Bid." *The Guardian*, December 12. https://www.theguardian.com/football/2019/dec/13/australia-and-new-zealand-join-forces-for-2023-womens-world-cup-bid

Australia New Zealand Confirm Joint Bid. 2019. "Australia New Zealand Confirm Joint Bid." *FoxSports.com*, December 12. https://www.foxsports.com/stories/soccer/australia-nz-confirm-joint-bid-for-2023-womens-world-cup

Australia NZ Confirm Joint Bid. 2019. "Australia NZ Confirm Joint Bid." *USAToday.com*, December 12. https://www.usatoday.com/story/sports/soccer/2019/12/12/australia-nz-confirm-joint-bid-for-2023-womens-world-cup/40809675/

Baade, Robert A., Robert Baumann, and Victor A. Matheson. 2008. "Selling the Big Game: Estimating the Economic Impact of Professional Sports through Taxable Sales." *Southern Economic Journal* 74 (3): 794–810. doi:10.2307/20111996.

Beissel, Adam, and Neal Ternes. 2019. United as one: FIFA, soft power, and the 2026 FIFA men's world cup united bid. Paper presented at The Football Collective Annual Conference Sheffield, England, United Kingdom, November.

Beissel, Adam, and David L. Andrews. 2021. "Art of the Deal: Donald Trump, Soft Power, and Winning the 2026 FIFA Men's World Cup Bid." In *Populism and the Sport and Leisure Spectacle*, edited by Bryan Clift and Alan Tomlinson, 234–253. Abingdon: Routledge.

Beissel, Adam, and Geoffrey Z. Kohe. 2020. "United as One: The 2026 FIFA Men's World Cup Hosting Vision and the Symbolic Politics of Legacy." *Managing Sport and Leisure* 25 (5). Advance online publication. doi:10.1080/23750472.2020.1846138.

Black, David, and Byron Peacock. 2013. "Sport and Diplomacy." In *The Oxford Handbook of Modern Diplomacy*, edited by Andrew F. Cooper, Jorge Heine, and Ramesh Thakur, 708–725. Oxford: Oxford University Press

Black, David. 2007. "The Symbolic Politics of Sport Mega-Events: 2010 in Comparative Perspective." *Politikon* 34 (3): 261–276. doi:10.1080/02589340801962536.

Black, David. 2008. "Dreaming Big: The Pursuit of 'Second Order' Games as a Strategic Response to Globalization." *Sport in Society* 11 (4): 467–480. doi:10.1080/17430430802019441.

Black, Jack, and Beth Fielding-Lloyd. 2019. "Re-Establishing the 'Outsiders': English Press Coverage of the 2015 FIFA Women's World Cup." *International Review for the Sociology of Sport* 54 (3): 282–301. doi:10.1177/1012690217706192.

Bowman, Nicholas David, and Gregory A. Cranmer. 2014. "SocialMediaSport: The Fan as a (Mediated) Participant in Spectator Sports." In *Routledge Handbook of Sport and New Media*, edited by Andrew C. Billings and Marie Hardin, 213–224. Abingdon: Routledge.

Burch, Lauren M., Andrew C. Billings, and Matthew H. Zimmerman. 2018. "Comparing American Soccer Dialogues: Social Media Commentary Surrounding the 2014 US Men's and 2015 US Women's World Cup Teams." *Sport in Society* 21 (7): 1047–1062. doi:10.1080/17430437.2017.1284811.

Byun, Jinsu, Becca Leopkey, and Dawn Ellis. 2020. "Understanding Joint Bids for International Large-Scale Sport Events as Strategic Alliances." *Sport, Business and Management: An International Journal* 10 (1): 39–57. doi:10.1108/SBM-09-2018-0074.

Byun, Jinsu, Dawn Ellis, and Becca Leopkey. 2021. "The Pursuit of Legitimacy through Strategic Alliances: The Examination of International Joint Sport Event Bidding." *European Sport Management Quarterly* 21 (4): 544–563. Advance online publication. doi:10.1080/16184742.2020.1759668.

Carniel, Jessica. 2012. "Reflections on Race, Regionalism and Geopolitical Trends via Australian Soccer." *The International Journal of the History of Sport* 29 (17): 2405–2420. doi:10.1080/09523367.2012.746832.

Castle, Matthew. 2018. "Embedding Regional Actors in Social and Historical Context: Australia-New Zealand Integration and Asian-Pacific Regionalism." *Review of International Studies* 44 (1): 151–173. doi:10.1017/S0260210517000316.

Chalip, Lawrence. 2004. "Beyond Impact: A General Model for Sport Event Leverage." In *Sport Tourism: Interrelationships, Impacts and Issues*, edited by Brent W. Ritchie and Daryl Adair, 226–252. Clevedon, UK: Channel View Publications.

Chalip, Lawrence. 2006. "Towards Social Leverage of Sport Events." *Journal of Sport & Tourism* 11 (2): 109–127. doi:10.1080/14775080601155126.

Chalip, Lawrence. 2014. "From Legacy to Leverage." In *Leveraging Legacies from Sports Mega-Events: Concepts and Cases*, edited by Jonathan Grix, 2–12. New York: Palgrave Macmillan.

Chappelet, Jean-Loup. 2006. "The Tale of Three Olympic Cities: Forecast for Torino on Basis of Grenoble and Innsbruck." Paper presented at the *Torino 2006 XX Winter Games Symposium*, Turin, February 9.

Chatziefstahiou, D., and I. Henry. 2013. *Discourses of Olympism: From the Sorbonne 1894 to London 2012*. New York: Palgrave Macmillan.

Coche, Roxane. 2021. "A New Era? How the European ESPN Covered the 2019 Women's World Cup Online." *International Review for the Sociology of Sport* 56 (2). doi:10.1177/1012690221992242.

Corbett, Ben, and Allan Edwards. 2018. "A Case Study of Twitter as a Research Tool." *Sport in Society* 21 (2): 394–412. doi:10.1080/17430437.2017.1342622.

Cornelissen, Scarlett. 2004. "'It's Africa's Turn!' the Narratives and Legitimations Surrounding the Moroccan and South African Bids for the 2006 and 2010 FIFA Finals." *Third World Quarterly* 25 (7): 1293–1309. doi:10.1080/014365904200281285.

Cornelissen, Scarlett. 2010. "The Geopolitics of Global Aspiration: Sport Mega-Events and Emerging Powers." *The International Journal of the History of Sport* 27 (16-18): 3008–3025. doi:10.1080/09523367.2010.508306.

Desjardins, Bridgette M. 2021. "Mobilising Gender Equality: A Discourse Analysis of Bids to Host the FIFA Women's World Cup 2023™." *International Review for the Sociology of Sport*, 1–17. Advance online publication. doi:10.1177/1012690221998131.

Dolles, Harald, and Sten Söderman. 2008. "Mega-Sporting Events in Asia-Impacts on Society, Business and Management: An Introduction." *Asian Business & Management* 7 (2): 147–162. doi:10.1057/abm.2008.7.

Duriau, Vincent J., Rhonda K. Reger, and Michael D. Pfarrer. 2007. "A Content Analysis of the Content Analysis Literature in Organization Studies: Research Themes, Data Sources, and Methodological Refinements." *Organizational Research Methods* 10 (1): 5–34. doi:10.1177/1094428106289252.

FIFA. 2016. "FIFA 2.0: Vision for the Future." https://resources.fifa.com/image/upload/fifa-2-0-the-vision-for-the-future.pdf?cloudid=drnd5smfl6dhhxgiyqmx.

FIFA. 2018. "FIFA Women's Football Strategy." https://resources.fifa.com/image/upload/women-s-football-strategy.pdf?cloudid=z7w21ghir8jb9tguvbcq.

FIFA. 2019. "Bidding Process for the FIFA Women's World Cup 2023™." https://resources.fifa.com/image/upload/overview-of-scoring-system-for-the-technical-evaluation-of-bids.pdf?cloudid=dxohjnzw2apxfri10pir.

Filo, Kevin, Daniel Lock, and Adam Karg. 2015. "Sport and Social Media Research: A Review." *Sport Management Review* 18 (2): 166–181. doi:10.1016/j.smr.2014.11.001.

Frawley, Stephen, and Adam Cush. 2011. "Major Sport Events and Participation Legacy: The Case of the 2003 Rugby World Cup." *Managing Leisure* 16 (1): 65–76. doi:10.1080/13606719.2011.532605.

Grix, Jonathan. 2012. "'Image' Leveraging and Sports Mega-Events: Germany and the 2006 FIFA World Cup." *Journal of Sport & Tourism* 17 (4): 289–312. doi:10.1080/14775085.2012.760934.

Guilianotti, Richard. 2007. *Football: A Sociology of the Global Game*. Cambridge, UK: Polity Press.

Homewood, Brian. 2016. "FIFA Unveil 2026 World Cup Bidding Process," May 11. *Reuters*. https://www.reuters.com/article/us-soccer-fifa-2026-idUSKCN0Y12UJ

Horne, John, and Wolfram Manzenreiter, eds. 2013. *Japan, Korea and the 2002 World Cup*. Abingdon: Routledge.

Horton, Peter. 2010. "The Geopolitical Balance of the Asia-Pacific Region Post-Beijing 2008: An Australian Perspective." *The International Journal of the History of Sport* 27 (14-15): 2530–2566. doi:10.1080/09523367.2010.504589.

Hsieh, Hsiu-Fang, and Sarah E. Shannon. 2005. "Three Approaches to Qualitative Content Analysis." *Qualitative Health Research* 15 (9): 1277–1288. doi:10.1177/1049732305276687.

James, Colin. 2015. *The Quiet Revolution: Turbulence and Transition in Contemporary New Zealand*. Auckland: Bridget Williams Books.

Ludvigsen, Jan Andre. 2019. "'Continent-Wide' Sports Spectacles: The 'Multiple Host Format' of Euro 2020 and United 2026 and Its Implications." *Journal of Convention & Event Tourism* 20 (2): 163–181. doi:10.1080/15470148.2019.1589609.

Ludvigsen, Jan Andre. 2020. "The More, the Merrier?' Euro 2020, Transnational Collaboration, Opportunities and Challenges." *Leisure/Loisir* 44 (1): 127–150. doi:10.1080/14927713.2020.1745673.

Maguire, Joseph. 1999. *Global Sport: Identities, Societies, Civilisations.* Cambridge, UK: Polity Press.

Malcolm, Dominic, and Thomas Fletcher. 2017. "The International Cricket Council World Cup: A 'Second Class' Megamediasport Event?." In *Sport, Media and Mega-Events*, edited by Lawrence A. Wenner and Andrew C. Billings, 85–99. Abingdon: Routledge.

Manzenreiter, Wolfram. 2008. "Football Diplomacy, Post-Colonialism and Japan's Quest for Normal State Status." *Sport in Society* 11 (4): 414–428. doi:10.1080/17430430802019359.

McGillivray, D., and D. Turner. 2017. *Event bidding: Politics, persuasion and resistance.* Routledge.

McIlraith, Matt. 2020. "New Zealand's Strong Arm Tactics Evoke Memories of 2003 Rugby World Cup Debacle." *The Guardian*, August 11. https://www.theguardian.com/sport/2020/aug/11/new-zealands-strong-arm-tactics-evoke-memories-of-2003-rugby-world-cup-debacle.

McPhee, P. 1988. "An Australian View of New Zealand." In *Tasman Relations*, edited by K. Sinclair, 277–297. Auckland: Auckland University Press.

Murthy, Dhiraj. 2017. "The Ontology of Tweets: Mixed Methods Approaches to the Study of Twitter." In The SAGE Handbook of Social Media Research Methods, edited by Luke Sloan & Anabel Quan-Haase, 559–572. London: Sage.

Naraine, Michael L., and Milena M. Parent. 2017. "The Evolution of Twitter Communication by Youth Olympic Games Organising Committees." *International Journal of Sport Management and Marketing* 17 (4/5/6): 403–425. doi:10.1504/IJSMM.2017.087439.

Patman, Robert G., and Chris Rudd. 2005. "Introduction: New Zealand Sovereignty in the Era of Globalization." In *Sovereignty under Siege? Globalisation and New Zealand*, edited by Robert G. Patman and Chris Rudd, 1–19. Abingdon: Routledge.

Patton, M. Q. 2015. *Qualitative Research & Evaluation Methods: Integrating Theory and Practice.* Thousand Oaks: SAGE Publications.

Pegoraro, Ann, Gina S. Comeau, and Evan L. Frederick. 2018. "#SheBelieves: The Use of Instagram to Frame the US Women's Soccer Team during #FIFAWWC." *Sport in Society* 21 (7): 1063–1077. doi:10.1080/17430437.2017.1310198.

Petty, Kate, and Stacey Pope. 2019. "A New Age for Media Coverage of Women's Sport? An Analysis of English Media Coverage of the 2015 FIFA Women's World Cup." *Sociology* 53 (3): 486–502. doi:10.1177/0038038518797505.

Porter, P. K. 1999. "Mega-Sports Events as Municipal Investments: A Critique of Impact Analysis." In *Sport Economics: Current Research*, edited by J. Fizel, E. Gustafson, and L. Hadley, 61–73. Westport, CT: Praeger Publishers.

Postlethwaite, V., and J. Grix. 2016. "Beyond the Acronyms: Sport Diplomacy and the Classification of the International Olympic Committee." *Diplomacy & Statecraft* 27 (2): 295–313. doi:10.1080/09592296.2016.1169796.

Preuss, Holger. 2007. "The Conceptualisation and Measurement of Mega Sport Event Legacies." *Journal of Sport & Tourism* 12 (3-4): 207–228. doi:10.1080/14775080701736957.

Ratuva, Steven, and Anne-Marie Brady. 2019. "Neighbours and Cousins: Aotearoa-New Zealand's Relationship with the Pacific." In *Small States and the Changing Global Order: New Zealand Faces the Future*, edited by Anne-Marie Brady, 145–164. Cham, Switzerland: Springer.

Red Agency to Handle PR & Social for FFA's 2023 Women's World Cup Bid. 2019. "Red Agency to Handle PR & Social for FFA's 2023 Women's World Cup Bid." *B&T Magazine*. https://www.bandt.com.au/red-agency-handle-pr-social-ffas-2023-womens-world-cup-bid/

Redeker, Robert. 2008. "Sport as an Opiate of International Relations: The Myth and Illusion of Sport as a Tool of Foreign Diplomacy." *Sport in Society* 11 (4): 494–500. doi:10.1080/17430430802019482.

Roche, Maurice. 2000. *Mega-Events and Modernity: Olympics and Expos in the Growth of Global Culture.* London: Routledge.

Roche, Maurice. 2017. *Mega-Events and Social Change: Spectacle, Legacy and Public Culture*. Manchester: Manchester University Press.

Rolfe, Jim. 2019. "Pragmatic Optimisation: Australia-New Zealand Relations in the 21st-Century." In *Small States and the Changing Global Order: New Zealand Faces the Future*, edited by Anne-Marie Brady, 93–110. Cham, Switzerland: Springer.

Rugari, Vince. 2020. "'A More United Football': FFA to Rebrand as 'Football Australia.'" *The Sydney Morning Herald*, November 25. https://www.smh.com.au/sport/soccer/ffa-to-rebrand-as-football-australia-20201125-p56hty.html.

Selvey, Mike. 2015. "More Money, More Viewers and Fewer Runs in Prospect for Intriguing World Cup." *The Guardian*, February 12. https://www.theguardian.com/sport/blog/2015/feb/12/cricket-world-cup-icc-50-overs.

Shapiro, Gilbert, and John Markoff. 1997. "A Matter of Definition." In *Text Analysis for the Social Sciences: Methods for Drawing Statistical Inferences from Texts and Transcripts*, edited by Carl W. Roberts, 9–31. Mahwah, NJ: Lawrence Erlbaum Associates, Inc.

Sherwood, Merryn, Marissa Lordanic, Tharindu Bandaragoda, Emma Sherry, and Damminda Alahakoon. 2019. "A New League, New Coverage? Comparing Tweets and Media Coverage from the First Season of AFLW." *Media International Australia* 172 (1): 114–130. doi:10.1177/1329878X19852495.

Smith, Adrian. 2004. "Black against Gold: New Zealand-Australia Sporting Rivalry in the Modern Era." In *Sport and National Identity in the Post-War World*, edited by Dilwyn Porter and Adrian Smith, 168–193. Abingdon: Routledge.

Stura, Claudia, Christina Aicher, Robert Kaspar, Carina Klein, Susanne Schulz, and Stefan Unterlechner. 2018. "The UEFA Euro Championship 2020: A Path to Success or a Mistake in the Making?." In *Routledge Handbook of International Sport Business*, edited by Mark Dodds, Kevin Heisey, and Aila Ahonen, 26–36. Abingdon: Routledge.

Sugden, J., and Alan Tomlinson. 1998. *FIFA and the Contest for World Football: Who Rules the Peoples' Game?* Eastbourne, UK: Polity Press.

Sugden, J., and Alan Tomlinson. 2017. *Football, Corruption and Lies: Revisiting "Badfellas", the Book FIFA Tried to Ban*. Abingdon: Routledge.

Swart, Kamilla. 2017. "The Rugby World Cup as a Global Mega-Event." In *The Rugby World in the Professional Era*, edited by John Nauright and Tony Collins, 108–117. Abingdon: Routledge.

Toffoletti, Kim, Ann Pegoraro, and Gina S. Comeau. 2019. "Self-Representations of Women's Sport Fandom on Instagram at the 2015 FIFA Women's World Cup." *Communication & Sport* 9 (5): 695–717. doi:10.1177/2167479519893332.

Tomlinson, Alan. 2014. *FIFA (Fédération Internationale de Football Association): the Men, the Myths and the Money*. Abingdon: Routledge.

Wagg, Stephen. 2018. *Cricket: A Political History of the Global Game, 1945-2017*. Abingdon: Routledge.

Wang, Yuan. 2021. "Building Relationships with Fans: How Sports Organizations Used Twitter as a Communication Tool." *Sport in Society* 24 (7): 1055–1069. Advance online publication. doi:10.1080/17430437.2020.1725475.

Winand, Mathieu, Matthew Belot, Sebastian Merten, and Dimitrios Kolyperas. 2019. "International Sport Federations' Social Media Communication: A Content Analysis of FIFA's Twitter Account." *International Journal of Sport Communication* 12 (2): 209–233. doi:10.1123/ijsc.2018-0173.

Yang, Elaine Chiao Ling, Michelle Hayes, Jinyan Chen, Caroline Riot, and Catheryn Khoo-Lattimore. 2020. "A Social Media Analysis of the Gendered Representations of Female and Male Athletes during the 2018 Commonwealth Games." *International Journal of Sport Communication* 13 (4): 670–695. doi:10.1123/ijsc.2020-0045.

Zimbalist, Andrew. 2015. *Circus Maximus: The Economic Gamble behind Hosting the Olympics and the World Cup*. Washington, D.C.: Brookings Institution Press.

Media coverage and public opinion of hosting a women's football mega-event: the English bid for UEFA Women's Euro 2022

Jonathan Rocha de Oliveira, Maria Thereza de Oliveira Souza and André Mendes Capraro

ABSTRACT

For the second time in history, England was announced as the host for the 13th edition of the *UEFA Women's Euro* by the Union of European Football Associations (UEFA). This study aims to analyse media coverage and public opinion of England's host bid and the country's choice as hosts of the *UEFA Women's Euro 2022*. This research was based on a content analysis of the English newspapers The Guardian, The Sun, and The Times regarding the media, and the social media Twitter to analyse public opinion. After applying filters, we analysed 65 news reports and 480 Twitter interactions. Thus, investigating these two different views on the same subject, we noted a relative consonance of positions: expectations for the organisation of the tournament, the success of the English team and the development of women's football, and criticism of the regional distribution of the games and the use of modest stadiums.

1. Introduction

On 3 December 2018, England[1] was elected to host the 13th edition of the *UEFA Women's Euro*, a few months after being the only country to submit an official candidacy to the Union of European Football Associations (UEFA) (BBC 2018a; UEFA 2018). To host the main football championship among the national teams of Europe, England announced the use of ten stadiums, spread over nine cities in different regions around the country. The competition will be played by 16 teams over 25 days (UEFA, 2020a). Initially, the *UEFA Women's Euro* was scheduled to start on 7 July 2021. However, it was postponed to the same time the following year (2022) due to the COVID-19 pandemic (UEFA, 2020b). This was only possible because the men's World Cup, which will be held in Qatar in 2022, will take place in November due to the country's climatic conditions.

This was the second time England was chosen to host *UEFA Women's Euro*; the country hosted the tournament for the first time in 2005. At the period, the championship received significant audiences in stadiums and relatively expressive media attention, representing a watershed for developing women's football in the country (Bell 2012, 2019). However, there are still barriers regarding public interest, including among women who are fans of men's football (Pope 2018).

Studies showed that the *UEFA Women's Euro 2005* registered stadium audiences (predominantly youth) and television audiences exceeded the organisers' expectations. In addition, it captured sponsorships from famous commercial brands and provided positive changes in short and long-term visibility, public and commercial interest, marketing and promotion, television broadcasts, and investments in the women's game (Bell 2012, 2019; Bell and Blakey 2010). Petty and Pope (2019) argue that media coverage of women's football in England has gradually transformed in a more representative and positive way, ushering in a new era for the sport in the country. Although the event significantly supported to accentuate the recent and significant growth of women's football in England as well as remarkable campaigns of the women's English national team (semi-finalist in the last continental and world championships) and global development of women's football as a whole (Clarkson et al. 2020).

Overall, English women's football has significantly gained more attention, awareness, structure, and investments since (and supported by) the *UEFA Women's Euro 2005*, despite still facing engagement, organisational, and inequality issues (Bell 2019; Clarkson et al. 2020). The event itself has also increased to the extent of becoming a major sporting event (see the next section) and a potential tool to foster economic and tourism sectors (Clarkson et al. 2020). However, scholars have debated whether large scale sports events benefit the host (country/city/community) or not.

On the one hand, decision-makers (i.e. government and organisers) have argued economic growth and infrastructure transformation to advocate bidding support for hosting such sports events, especially after Barcelona's Olympic Games in 1992 (Calavita and Ferrer 2000). On the other hand, the negative impacts have already been observed, and some nations "[…] spend decades repaying debt incurred to stage the event" (Agha, Fairley, and Gibson 2012, 217). Likewise, studies focused on London 2012 Olympic Games revealed significant conflicts and opposition among local residents to host the mega-event in the English context. The most prominent complaints and criticism were over the high costs, disruption of civic life, the gentrification of low-income residents, corruption allegations, environmental damage, and previous failures to deliver long-term benefits (i.e. lack of jobs and business infra-structural improvements) to the host people (Giulianotti et al. 2015; Giulianotti and Langseth 2016; Watt 2013).

Notably, England already has some of the best social, urban, transport, and sports infrastructure in the world, as well as high tourist demand related to football [(e.g. 800,0000 international tourists attend matches in the country annually (VisitBritain, 2015)]. Even though this demand is likely to be linked to men's football rather than women's football. Therefore, what were the possible reasons for England's interest in hosting the *UEFA Women's Euro* for a second time? It might be argued that it was intended to leverage further the development of the women's game in England and enhance the country's image as one of the main hubs of women's football. As such, it would be necessary to obtain media support and public acceptance, which leads us to the following research question: How did the public opinion (observed on social media) and the local press receive England's application to host the tournament?

This study aims to analyse media coverage and public opinion in the online environment about England's candidacy and choice as the host of the *UEFA Women's Euro 2022*. According to Pfister (2015), media coverage is a crucial element in women's football growth, contributing to legitimising players' achievements and promoting their public acceptance. Hence, we chose to analyse the mega-event reverberation in the media and the broader social context of public opinion. As pointed by scholars (Corbett and Edwards 2018; Fan et al. 2020; Kirilenko and Stepchenkova 2017), the rapid spread of social media use has turned online platforms (e.g. Twitter and Facebook) into prolific tools to analyse public discourses and reactions about a social phenomenon as sports. Lastly, the present study seeks to distance itself from comparisons/correlations with men's football, as the literature presents a broad gendered approach to women's football (Bell 2012; Bell and Blakey 2010; Pfister 2010, 2015; Pope 2018; Williams 2003a), which already has conditions that must be addressed to overcome such discussions.

2. Women's football development: Growing towards a new era

Women's football has historically been neglected and even banned in several European countries (Williams 2011; Williams and Hess 2015). However, this does not mean that women did not practice the sport. There are records of football matches between national teams from England and Scotland in the 1880s, composed exclusively of women (Williams and Hess 2015). Nevertheless, such a practice did not have the attention of communication vehicles and an appreciative public, nor was it socially accepted. However, it is possible to identify gradual advances in its popularisation and (semi) professionalisation.

The first steps forward for the evolution of this sport took place gradually from the 1970s, with greater prominence in developed countries in Europe (such as Germany, France, England, Italy, the Netherlands, Norway, Sweden, etc.), South America, and North America (Canada and the USA), which officially allowed the practice of sports by women (with some restrictions/constraints in some countries), created national leagues, and institutionalised the management of the sport in their national football federations (Pfister 2015; Williams 2011). Another crucial factor was the role of the top entity in world football, the *Fédération Internationale de Football Association* (FIFA), and the UEFA, both taking control of women's world and European football, respectively, in 1969 (Williams 2011). This may be related to student demonstrations in 1968, with greater force in France, but that had significant effects later in the Western world's social context, primarily in the fight against conservatism (Judt 2016).

Consequently, the favourable European scenario of the 1960s accentuated the development of women's football. Two characteristics were the most striking, namely, attention and competitiveness. Both influenced demand, public interest, levels of media coverage, and sponsorship opportunities (Valenti, Scelles, and Morrow 2018). First, international championships between national teams were created, organised, structured, and even sponsored, such as the first edition of the *UEFA Women's Euro*, held between 1982 and 1984 in a longer format and without a fixed host; the realisation of the first FIFA Women's World Cup (FIFA WWC), the main championship among national teams in the world, in China in 1991, and the inclusion of women's football in the Summer Olympic Games in Atlanta (USA), in 1996 (Pfister 2015; Williams 2003b, 2011). Second, there was a growing demand for the sport from the public and audiences/spectators, and commercial interest, mainly in the FIFA WWC and the *UEFA Women's Euro* mega-events (FIFA 2019a; Hallmann 2012; Petty and Pope 2019; UEFA 2017). Third, there was greater female involvement in sport on the global stage. It is estimated that 29 million women were actively involved in football in 2020; FIFA plans to reach 60 million by 2026 (FIFA 2020). For example, according to official FIFA data (FIFA 2019b), in 2019, there were 13.36 million female practitioners of organised football (professional or amateur) in the world, with another 63,000 acting as coaches and 80,000 as referees. Furthermore, the number of academic studies of women's football has increased, particularly in the past two decades (Valenti, Scelles, and Morrow 2018).

Indeed, recent sports events indicate an increasing and positive change in the level of women's football, especially regarding its visibility, prestige, coverage, organisation, promotion, and investment. For instance, the latest FIFA WWC, held in France in 2019, showed a 30% increase in television audiences than the previous edition, held in 2015 in Canada (FIFA 2019a). The mega-event was watched by 1.12 billion viewers in 2019, and the final match of the tournament had approximately 82 million viewers (FIFA 2019a). Another significant example occurred in the last edition of the *UEFA Women's Euro*, held in 2017 in the Netherlands. The championship presented expressive transmission, audience, and stadium spectator results, as well as boasting the largest organisational structure in tournament history. According to organisers (UEFA 2017), 1,500 volunteers (professionals and students) helped organise the event. Nine global brands (Adidas, Carlsberg, Coca-Cola, Continental, Hisense, McDonald's, Kia, SOCAR, and Turkish Airlines) and five other national brands acted as sponsors. Approximately 240,000 people watched all 31 matches of the tournament in loco, a record for the tournament, while approximately 72,000 people, including international tourists, followed the games in the fan zones spread around the eight host cities. Furthermore, 33 TV channels broadcast matches to 154 territories/countries, reaching 178 million viewers around the world.

These numbers reinforce that the women's game is experiencing unprecedented popularity. Sport in general is experiencing a period of large-scale events. The number and magnitude of this type of event are also growing (Horne 2007; Maennig and Zimbalist 2012; Müller 2015). The authors of this article chose to treat the *UEFA Women's Euro* as a sport mega-event because the tournament has crucial characteristics for such a classification: it attracts a significant number of visitors (Getz 2008; Müller 2015); it has international relevance and popular appeal (Horne 2007); it provides opportunities to promote tourist attractions, facilities, and local culture, and seeks to ensure the safety of participants (Lee Ludvigsen 2018); it enables the development of a positive image (Getz 2008); it has a transformative impact on the built environment and media reach (Müller 2015); it is a strong revenue generator (economic impact) (Maennig and Zimbalist 2012); and it has a short duration and long-term effects (Roche 1994). It is emphasised that there are difficulties in establishing simplified criteria to classify the magnitude of an event due to its subjectivity (see examples in Maennig and Zimbalist 2012).

Finally, it is worth noting that, despite this positive development, women's football still faces challenges that slow its progress, especially concerning the sport's social and economic aspects. The women's game has a broad amateur nature, indicated by players' remuneration, underdeveloped infrastructure, low commercialisation, and limited financial investment (Williams 2011). According to Pfister (2015), championships, matches, and players still have secondary or marginalised importance in the media and broader public. In fact, women's football is still underrepresented, underestimated, or insufficiently addressed in media coverage, even in main hubs, such as in England (Petty and Pope 2019). In addition, Valenti, Scelles, and Morrow (2018) warn that we should take care when diagnosing a general state of women's football, since there are significant variations in the different cultural contexts of sport worldwide. For these authors, only England, France, Germany, and Sweden have leagues and matches that have gained the attention of the media and audiences in Europe (Valenti, Scelles, and Morrow 2018).

3. The landscape of the growing English women's football

In England, women's football took a long road until reach its recent growth. For instance, women were officially banned from football for 50 years (1921–1971) due to a regulation imposed by the FA on its affiliated clubs (Williams 2003b). After the end of the ban, the FA took more than two decades to take over English women's football administration and governance in 1993 (Bell 2012; Clarkson et al. 2020). Since then, there has been an increase in women's English football participation and development (Bell 2019; Williams 2003b).

In 2011, the Football Association (FA) created one of the top national leagues of women's football in the world, the FA Women's Super League (FA WSL), only six years after hosting the *UEFA Women's Euro* for the first time. Currently, the FA WSL is the only wholly professional championship in Europe. In the season 2021–2022, the league consists of 12 clubs, with all players having full-time contracts (a minimum of 20 hours per week) (BBC 2018b; The FA 2018). Noteworthy, the FA also created the FA Women's Championship[2] in 2014, the equivalent to the second division of English women's football, consisting of 11 teams. However, this league's structure is still semi-professional, as most clubs do not have full-time footballers (BBC 2018b; The FA 2018).

Following the recent women's football development, the Barclays Bank announced a millionaire investment in FA WSL, considered 'the largest commercial investment in women's sport in the United Kingdom,' and estimated at £10,000,000. The brand entered into a three-year agreement with the FA to sponsor the championship and create strategies to develop it, such as an unprecedented £500,000 winner's award, renaming the championship to the Barclays FA Women's Super League during the term of the agreement, and the creation of 100 football schools to train 6,000 girls (Barclays 2019; BBC 2019; The FA 2019).

There is also evidence of fan growth, even though the average audience in most women's games is less than 2,000 people per game in the FA WSL (Pope 2018). Conversely, the league's decisive matches, the English team's games, and the national cup finals at Wembley stadium tend to receive a high number of fans (e.g., 52,000 tickets were sold for the 2019 Women's FA Cup final (Wrack 2019a)].

4. Methods

The present research takes the form of a case study, as the *UEFA Women's Euro 2022* is a contemporary phenomenon, which authors analysed in-depth and within its context. Furthermore, this paper sought evidence from multiple sources using prior theoretical propositions to guide data collection and analysis, triangulating and analysing the data together in the following step (Yin 2014). Guided by the study's scope, the data collection and analysis were based on virtual environments of two distinct perspectives of *UEFA Women's Euro 2022*: media coverage and public opinion. Importantly, all data collection procedures were discussed and decided by the three authors. Due to the authors' backgrounds, the second author led data collection for media coverage, whereas the first author led data collection for public opinion (on social media). Together, these two authors codified the materials gathered. All three authors then analysed media coverage and public opinion data at various online meetings.

Data collection for media coverage was conducted in three leading English newspapers: The Sun, The Times, and The Guardian. These three newspapers are constantly cited in the top 10 newspapers read monthly in the UK (Watson 2021). Thus, they were chosen for their national prominence, scope, and extensive sports coverage. Such aspects about these newspapers were also previously defended by other authors in similar studies (Villeneuve and Aquilina 2016; Vincent et al. 2019).

Initially, newspapers were consulted in their online versions, and we used the search tool of each platform to gather data. The research was carried out with the terms *Women's Euro 2021* and *Women's Euro 2022*, comparing the results and excluding duplicated materials. Then, we applied the following inclusion criteria to collect data: (1) news that had one of the two chosen terms or their variations summarised in the title, subtitle, or text were selected; (2) the time frame used was from August 2017 to 2020, after the previous edition of the *UEFA Women's Euro* and when news of England's application for the 2021 edition first appeared, until the end of the last year before this survey was carried out; (3) reports that focused on women's competition were maintained and were not, for example, simply treated as a branch of matters related to the *UEFA Men's Euro* or the rescheduling of events due to the COVID-19 pandemic; and (4) news related to the preparation or performance of athletes or teams that will participate in the *UEFA Women's Euro 2022* was included, without the competition necessarily being the focus of the story.

We gathered a total of 65 news and exported them to an electronic spreadsheet. After that, we applied a Content Analysis into the selected material using Geoff Payne and Judy Payne's (2004) methodological premises. The authors stated this methodology '[…] seeks to demonstrate the meaning of written or visual sources (like newspapers and advertisements) by systematically allocating their content to pre-determined, detailed categories, and then both quantifying and interpreting the outcomes' (Payne and Payne 2004, 51). In this research, this process and the creation of categories were done after two of the authors reading the news in full. The reading was done independently and later compared. As a result, eight themes were identified (See Table 2) in this process and discussed in the findings section.

Regarding the public opinion on social media, we analysed participation on Twitter, which has approximately 353 million active users worldwide. We chose this digital platform because it is a widely utilised site characterised as microblogging, allowing only short posts and interactions (i.e. through hyper-links, hashtags, public messages, and retweets, see Wang 2021), meaning that interactions tend to be more direct (Price, Farrington, and Hall 2013). Moreover, the posts and profiles available on Twitter are publicly accessible and do not require authorisation nor fees for use (Corbett and Edwards 2018). Twitter is a social media more focused on the message (in the form of news and/or opinion) than other related virtual platforms such as Facebook (Corbett and Edwards 2018).

We ran a Python code of programming language that used Twitter API v2 to extract data from Twitter. We collected tweets and retweets posted until 31 December 2020. The terms used for gathering data were '#Weuro2021 AND host' and '#UEFAWomensEuro2021 AND host'. A total of 683 interactions were found among tweets and retweets. The following exclusion criteria were applied: (1) non-English tweets and retweets; (2) duplicate or tripled messages during extraction. As a result, a total of 480 Twitter interactions were analysed through a Sentiment Analysis as successfully adopted by previous studies using Twitter to analyse sentiments in the sports event's literature (Kirilenko and Stepchenkova 2017; Yu and Wang 2015).

Sentiment Analysis is a less time-consuming approach that has been increasingly used to analyse people's emotions, attitudes, or opinions regarding an issue in virtual settings (Yu and Wang 2015). For sentiment analysis and data coding, we used the *Nvivo 12 plus* software. First, all the 480 messages were exported to the software and reviewed by the authors. Then, six categories were created to represent better the feelings' intensity of people: very positive, moderately positive, neutral, mixed, moderately negative, and very negative. Noteworthy, two word-clouds were created in *Nvivo 12 plus*. One with positive interactions (very positive and moderately positive) and the other with negative interactions (very negative and moderately negative). Additionally, both also contemplated 'mixed' interactions. For this construction, all figures or emojis were excluded, as well as the terms '#Weuro2021' and '@uefawomensEuro'.

5. English media coverage: *the Guardian*, *the Sun*, and *the Times*

The English Women's national team (also known as Lionesses) performed well at the *UEFA Women's Euro 2017* and the FIFA WWC 2019. In both competitions, the Lionesses was defeated in the semi-finals by the Netherlands in the European competition and by the United States in the world championship. After years of banning women's football in England and the subsequent period of low development (Williams and Hess 2015), these achievements seem to have ushered in a new era of women's football in the country. The country applied to host the *UEFA Women's Euro* 2022 in August 2018. However, before that, the FA had already preliminarily applied to host the FIFA WWC 2019. However, it withdrew the application before the official application period, believing that its recent disagreements with FIFA would be detrimental to England's chances (Dickinson 2014).

This new context, driven by the English team's recent performance, seems to have elevated women's football in the country. For example, the media coverage focused on the *UEFA Women's Euro 2022* extends beyond specific reports about the organisation itself, and includes articles about coaches, athletes, and professionals involved in the competition. This grants visibility to local clubs.

In this study, findings revealed that 65 news items found and framed in the filters. Table 1 shows the distribution of the results by newspaper.

Regarding the total news items, two were published in 2017, eight in 2018, 21 in 2019, and 34 in 2020. A division by thematic category was then created in order to group together news items with similar themes, as detailed in Table 2.

We emphasise that media coverage was related to the other component teams of the United Kingdom (Scotland, Wales, and Northern Ireland), and not only England. The news's main theme category was these countries' national coaches, totalling 22 items; it was the

Table 1. Number of results by newspaper.

Newspaper	News Frequency	%
The Guardian	20	30.76%
The Sun	14	21.53%
The Times	31	47.69%

Table 2. News themes and frequency.

Themes	Frequency
Coaches	22
Preparation of national teams from the UK for the tournament	13
Bid and organisation of the event	11
Football players	7
Tournament postponement	5
World Cup results seeking to the *UEFA Women's Euro*	3
Comparisons with men's football/visibility/salaries	3
Television broadcasting rights	1

category with the largest number of items. There is a high appreciation of tactical and collective plans and, consequently, of the coaches' interviews, explanations, and ideas. England coach Phill Neville was the main focus of 15 of the news items. This can be justified by both the greater attention that the English team has received, and the coach's importance, since he was also a football player. An example of this perspective is the news "If Phil Neville stays on as England manager than he has to be bold," published in The Guardian and written by Suzanne Wrack. The journalist made a retrospective about the competitive year of the Lionesses team and defended that Neville needed to make his team more consistent (Wrack 2019b).

Another 13 news articles were focused on selections. They differed from the previous category due to their focus on the teams' preparations from a more general perspective without emphasising the coaches. Again, greater attention was paid to the English team's preparation, which was the focus of eight such news items. Scotland was the focus of two items, with Wales and Northern Ireland with one each; the other news items discussed the national teams of Scotland, Northern Ireland, and Wales together.

Beyond linking news from the competition, the newspapers started to publish stories related to players who were likely to participate in the *UEFA Women's Euro 2022* for their national teams. This demonstrates how the competition may have had reflexes that surpassed the tournament itself in increasing the visibility of women's football. There were seven articles in this category. It is interesting to notice that, as demonstrated by Carrie Dunn (2016), since the London Olympics edition in 2012, there has been an attempt to give more visibility to female athletes through local, regional, and national policies in the UK. According to the researcher, in this context, female footballers gained an image of "role models" to young women, and the athletes see it as "[…] an opportunity to encourage young people to play football" (Dunn 2016, 11). It was deemed as a change in the gendered vision about this sport, which maintained women away from the institutionalised football for so long in the country (Williams and Hess 2015).

In 2020, as mentioned earlier, the *UEFA Women's Euro* was postponed from 2021 to 2022. This meant that five news items related to the UEFA decision were linked in the newspapers.

Another category chosen was 'World Cup results seeking to the UEFA Women's Euro'. The 2019 edition of the tournament, held in France, was covered in the articles. In that period, England had already been chosen as the host for the *UEFA Women's Euro 2022*. Thus, three news items related to the world championship included mentions of the sequence of national teams for the next significant tournament.

Only three out of the 65 news items made comparisons with men's football or addressed gender-related issues in some way when reporting on the women's game. For instance, Molly Hudson critics to the fact that England Women fly in the premium economy to *SheBelieves Cup* in 2020, while Male Team always uses private fly in competitions (Hudson 2020b); and, the news assigned by Brian Mahon, which demonstrated that Irelands women footballers get 20 per cent of the men's fee by the appearance in the national team (Mahon 2020). In general, there was no attempt to treat women's football based on analyses of the personal and often stereotyped identities of players—woman/mother/wife—to the detriment of technical and tactical analyses, something that was common in the past. An example of the previous coverage model is the first world championship with ample media visibility, FIFA WWC 1999 (Christopherson, Janning, and McConnel 2002).

In the 'Television broadcasting rights' category, one news item was isolated because its theme was quite different. In 2019, Martin Ziegler reported in The Times that the BBC had purchased the broadcast rights for the *UEFA Women's Euro 2022*. The journalist said that such interest was justified by the large audience who watched the FIFA WWC 2019 semifinal between England and the United States, considered to be the largest audience of any TV program in the year at that time with 11.7 million viewers. He also interviewed Barbara Slater, the BBC's director of sport, who discussed the expectation that the FA WSL matches could also be televised if the *UEFA Women's Euro 2022* is successful (Ziegler 2019).

Finally, the category regarding the English bid and the organisation of the *UEFA Women's Euro 2022* was composed of 11 news items. The newspapers highlighted that England was the only host candidate, the moment of the host confirmation, and match division trends by territory and English stadium. This category was more detailed, precisely because it is the main focus of this research.

The Guardian, through a report by Martha Kelner, announced in 2017 that England would launch a bid for the *UEFA Women's Euro 2022*, after '[…] the most successful ever tournament in the Netherlands', referring to the final result among the four semi-finalists in the championship. Kelner also reported a speech by Martin Glenn, the FA chief executive, in which he shows enthusiasm and makes a promise regarding the tournament: 'We will fill big stadia for women's games', he said. 'This is an important tournament in its own right and we want to give it prestige' (Kelner 2017). The Times also echoed Martin Glenn's speech and focused on analysing the possibility that Manchester United, the only English Premier League club that did not yet have a women's team, would set up its own squad inspired by the moment of visibility of women's football (Ziegler 2017); this finally happened in 2018.

On the official bid day, in August 2018, The Guardian returned to detailing the FA proposal regarding the cities that would host games (Guardian Sport 2018). The Sun also reported on the official bidding and emphasised that this FA initiative occurred due to the English team's excellent campaign in the 2017 edition of the championship. They also transcribed the speeches of Martin Glenn and Sue Campbell, the FA's director of women's football, on the importance of the competition for the development of women's football in the country (Downes Jr. 2018). The Times provided fewer details regarding England's candidacy. In July 2018, this was cited as a secondary part of a story about Wembley (Northcroft 2018), and at the end of August, shortly after the official candidacy, Molly Hudson emphasised the preparation of the English team under the command of Phill Neville for the qualifying games for the FIFA WWC 2019 (Hudson 2018).

On 6 September, shortly after the bidding deadline, The Sun reported that the FA had been the only national football body to have submitted an official candidacy to UEFA, even though Hungary and Austria had previously waved proposals. Joe Miles, who signed the report, also stated great confidence in the English team for winning their first title at home and highlighted that the final was scheduled for Wembley (Miles 2018).

Louise Taylor reported in The Guardian on 3 December 2018, the day of England's official choice as host, that the organisation had broken some promises. Smaller and lesser-known stadiums were part of the official bid, and Wembley was only included to host the final. Another point of critique was that no city in the country's northeast would not host any games. The newspaper also cited Sue Campbell's speech, resuming the development discourse:

> Tournaments of the scale and profile of Euro 2021 have the power to inspire a new generation of young girls, and women of all ages, to get involved in the sport – as well as the opportunity to grow support for the women's game at both a club and national level. A home Euro in 2021 has the potential to be a pivotal moment in the development of the women's game in England (Taylor 2018).

In The Sun, Joshua Jones emphasised that England was the only country to submit a candidacy and recalled that they had hosted the 2005 edition. He also emphasised the England women's team's goal of winning their first title after being defeated in two finals, in 1984 and 2009 (Jones 2018).

In 2020, the news related to the championship in England was that the Old Trafford Stadium would be used for the competition's opening game. According to The Times, the FA and UEFA want to host the game in a stadium with 76,000 seats to break the tournament audience record, which happened in 2013 in Sweden (41,301 spectators). The choice had a positive impact and Nadine Kessler, UEFA's head of women's football, defended it by stating, 'To kick off at the Theatre of Dreams in Manchester and to have the final at the iconic Wembley Stadium shows just how far the game has come. This is what women's football deserves' (Wrack 2020). The report also showed other numbers that indicated the growth of expectations for the competition: 70,000 tickets would be available for the 31 tournament games, while in the previous edition, only 480,000 were available, with an occupation rate of 50% of the seats on that occasion (240,000 people attended the championship in loco). The Times also echoed the decision and noted that it was made due to the institutional perception that the popularity of women's football in Europe had increased considerably after the 2019 FIFA WWC (Hudson 2020a). Thus, it seems that hosting the *UEFA Women's Euro 2022* is part of a growth project of women's football in England. The project also aims to develop the England Women's Super League in a spectacularised way, as demonstrated by Fielding-Lloyd, Woodhouse, and Sequerra (2020).

6. Public opinion on social media: Twitter

Twitter has increasingly been used as a space for interactions between sports fans and people involved in football (e.g., fans, players, journalists, managers, etc.). This social media is often used to obtain and spread news or as a mean to express feelings and emotions (Price, Farrington, and Hall 2013). Clubs and sports organisations also have accounts on social media, looking to interact with fans and promote their brands. To date, the official profile of the *UEFA Women's Euro* on Twitter (@UEFAWomensEURO) has 84,164 followers and has posted 10,300 tweets. Among the 480 posts collected, it was possible to identify and categorise the public's feelings about the event on social media.

Figure 1 shows that public opinion on Twitter was significantly positive and receptive to the mega-event, as seen in the expressive superiority of the 343 positive comments ('very' and 'moderately'), which totalled 71.45% of the analysed interactions. The 55 negative comments ('very' and 'moderately') added up to a significantly smaller share: only 11.45% of the sample. Figures 3 and 4 discuss in detail the content of positive and negative interactions, respectively. Regarding neutral comments, that is, those of a more informative nature and without emotions, 74 posts were identified. These neutral interactions generally reported confirmation from England or a specific city or stadium as a venue for the tournament and contained information about registering for ticket purchases or qualifying matches. Eight interactions were categorised as 'mixed', as they presented positive and negative meanings.

The first four tweets collected were posted on 8 August 2017 and the last two on 23 April 2020, indicating a difference of two years and nine months. Whereas Figure 2 illustrates the interactions' timeline, it also contains the type of feeling and the proportion of these in this same period.

This timeline indicates three distinct moments highlighted in terms of the number of interactions. They were December 2018 (256 tweets), August 2019 (87 tweets), and February 2020 (83 tweets). In all these periods, the proportion of 'very positive' tweets was significantly higher than all other sentiment categories.

First, more than half of the interactions were posted in the same month (December) when England was selected as host of the mega-event. This suggests that the news generated a positive sentiment of public receptivity on Twitter, since most of the comments during this period were 'very positive' with 181 tweets (70.70%), followed by 'moderately positive'

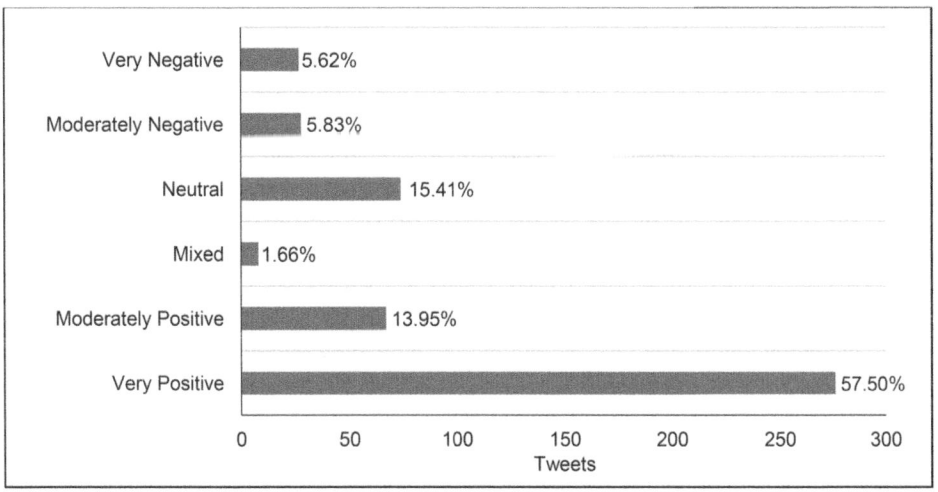

Figure 1. Quantity and proportion of tweets by sentiment type.

with 26 tweets (10.15%). Kassens-Noor and colleagues (2019) found that, generally, people still deem positive to host large scale sports events, although there is an increasing acknowledgement of the significant downside previously mentioned. Conversely, English candidacy was officially submitted three months earlier (at the end of August 2018), and only one (informative) tweet was found. This suggests that there was no public interest and awareness in the tournament at that time; however, following England's winning bid of the *UEFA Women's Euro 2022* being made official, the mega-event became a relevant and highly positive topic on Twitter.

The second moment was identified in August 2019, when the organisers announced the official list of cities and stadiums that would host the 31 games of the tournament. One

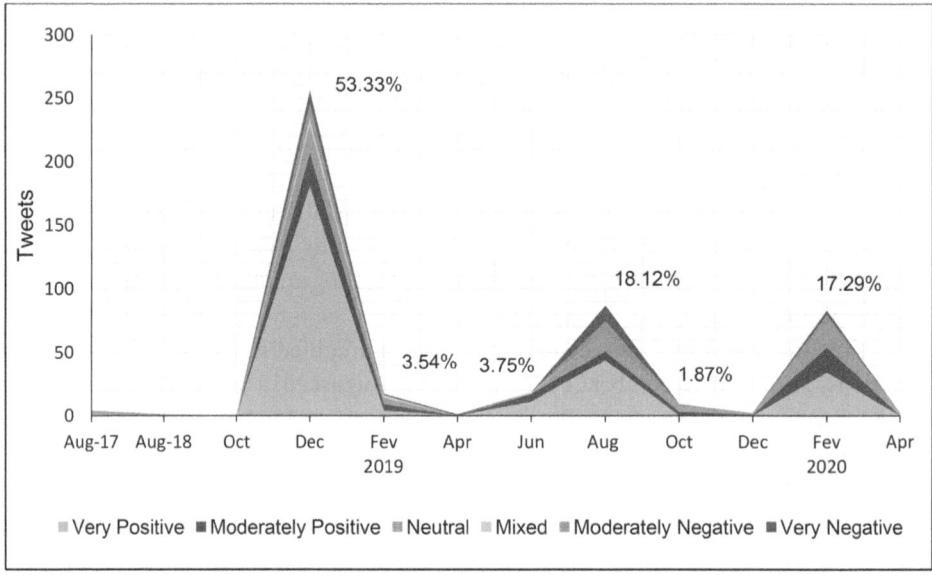

Figure 2. Tweets timeline and sentiment types.

Figure 3. Word cloud of positive and mixed sentiments on Twitter.

Figure 4. Word cloud of negative and mixed sentiments on Twitter.

month earlier, the Lionesses team remarkably reached the semi-final FIFA WWC – losing to the championship winner, the United States. Both factors may have contributed to these positive feelings. Findings on this study expanded Fan et al. (2020) results, which contend that people on social media (Twitter) express their sentiments of pride and identification with the Men's national English team. Significantly, we revealed people's engagement and pride sentiments connected to the Women's English team on Twitter. On the other hand, not only an expressive number of positive comments (see Figure 3) were generated in this topic but was also the target of criticism and feelings of indignation and discontent (see Figure 4).

The third most expressive period occurred in February 2020, due to the release of the official tournament calendar and a countdown of 500 days to the start of the championship. The tweets related to this represented a significant part of the interactions in that month. The announcement showed the stadium that would host the opening match (Old Trafford, with a capacity of 76,000 people), since Wembley Stadium (with a capacity of 89,000 people) had already been confirmed to host the final (UEFA 2020a). Thus, the choice of the opening venue for the first match of the *UEFA Women's Euro* was received with satisfaction and positive expectations from the public on Twitter.

In the word cloud presented below (Figure 3), the highlighted terms (in the centre and larger) were found most frequently in comments deemed positive and demonstrated the main topics and guidelines in these interactions.

We observed the mega-event generated a feeling of receptivity in the population. Several interactions celebrated the news and showed a high expectation to host the English women's team matches.

First, 'very positive' terms such as 'brilliant', 'excited', 'fantastic', 'great', 'amazing', 'buzzing', 'love', 'proud', 'well done', 'delighted', 'involved', and 'inspire' were posted following the mega-event's confirmation. Likewise, 'very positive' sentiments regarding the expectations for the championship's start were identified (e.g. some tweets counted down to the start of the tournament). Phrases such as 'It is coming home' and 'I cannot wait' were significantly used in the sense of optimism, celebration, and even anxiety. A smaller but still relevant part of the tweets referred to the news as an opportunity to promote and develop local women's football or sports in general and saw it as a step in that direction.

Confirmation of a specific city and stadium was analysed next. Figure 3 highlights terms related to the cities of Wigan and Leigh and the Leigh Sports Village Stadium, the cities of Nottingham and Rotherham, the city of Manchester and Manchester City Academy Stadium, and the city of Sheffield and the Bramall Lane Stadium. We noted that the public interacted with pride and happiness regarding these choices, showing satisfaction in having a venue in their region which foster the sentiment of national identity on social media linked to the Lionesses as revealed before. Furthermore, a considerable part of these interactions confirmed interest in attending as many games as possible.

Third, the terms 'register', 'tickets', and 'matches' have also been identified in interactions about registering to purchase tickets for matches, becoming a volunteer, or about people saying that they will attend matches on the spot. Noteworthy, a significant amount of these tweets was informative, containing external links for more detailed information; however, all contained user sentiments. According to Wang (2021), sports organisations can use Twitter to foster marketing strategies, and the *UEFA Women's Euro 2022* organisers achieved considerable engagement on that social media.

Comments that presented negative feelings can be seen in Figure 4. From this, it may be possible to establish relationships between the terms and the subjects that are more frequently used and discussed.

Negative sentiments were significantly lower than other categories. The period in which these feelings stood out most was in August 2019. Such tweets were not a negative reaction towards women's football but to the announcement of the host cities and stadiums. Although the chosen cities were highly celebrated, the regions not chosen resulted in tweets of dissatisfaction and severe criticism (some with profanity). Specifically, cities' distribution was the most prominent point criticised, since the southwest, southeast, and mostly the northeast regions were not considered to host matches. Notably, Bell's study (2019) pointed out that *UEFA Women's Euro 2005* contributed significantly to developing women's football in its venues' regions (i.e. England's northwest). Therefore, spreading venues across England could lead to growth in underdeveloped areas such as those regions missed by the organisers of *UEFA Women's Euro 2022*.

This triggered a series of negative manifestations on Twitter. Figure 4 shows how the mentioned fact is related to 'very negative' terms, such as 'shame', 'disappointing', 'missed', 'ignored', 'nothing', 'difficult', 'poor', and 'shit'. These terms were found frequently related to the words 'venues', 'host', 'stadium', 'places', and 'region', which corroborates the dissatisfaction about this aspect revealed in the research. Negative perceptions have gained space on social media due to the lack of control over the platform's tweets, as pointed out by Kassens-Noor, Vertalka, and Wilson (2019). When reviewing the tweets, we also observed that several interactions contained positive, yet ironic, words. Some of them appear in Figure 4. Middlesbrough, Sunderland, and Newcastle were the cities that generated the most negative feelings (frustration, indignation, and revolt), because they were not chosen as championship venues. These three cities are in the northeast of the country, a region that has a football culture, being one of the first to develop women's football in England with the appearance of several clubs in the region, even in the early twentieth century (before the FA ban) (Ben Porat 2020).

Another issue was the choice of Manchester City Academy Stadium and Leigh Sports Village as the venues for some matches, as these stadiums have a relatively small attendance capacity—4,700 and 7,000 fans, respectively (Williams 2011)—and are located close to each other (18 miles) and to Old Trafford, which is in the same region. In contrast, we agreed with Clarkson et al. (2020) that suggested organisers should prioritise hosts venues in places with potential tourism demand, especially to surpass the challenges from Covid-19.

7. Conclusion

Newspapers and Twitter are different communication channels. While the former presents facts and opinions unilaterally and with a greater need to follow certain rules, the latter presents itself as a wider space for public manifestations and, consequently, is less controllable. Despite this, a relative consonance of positions was noticed when we investigated these two different means on the same subject, the *UEFA Women's Euro 2022*. The more media press released confirmation of cities, stadiums, and match schedules, the more people's interactions on Twitter with the mega-event increased. Therefore, we contend that media coverage influenced the public engagement increase on Twitter.

In short, the analysed newspapers indicated that among athletes, coaches, and organisers, there is an expectation that this iteration of the *UEFA Women's Euro 2022* would be the biggest in the event's history. There is also enthusiasm for the performance of the English national team, with the bid to host the tournament itself influenced by team's campaign at the *UEFA Women's Euro 2017*. There was typical news related to the candidacy that brought photos of players celebrating the national team's goals. Very positive terms were widely used in public interactions. They were aligned with the FA leaders' speeches, as reported in newspapers by Sue Campbell and Martin Glenn.

In addition to hosting the championship itself, we identified that the newspapers addressed the FA's general interest in developing English women's football in other spheres. The fact that Manchester United created its women's team after England was confirmed as a host, and that the BBC is considering transmitting the FA WSL after the *UEFA Women's Euro 2022*, can already be viewed as possible effects. However, the tournament was also targeted by criticism on both platforms. Media coverage showed that certain venue choices were considered controversial and seemingly contrary to the organisers' main goal. Public opinion on Twitter, negative reactions followed the same tone, mostly complaining about the uneven distribution of the host venues.

To conclude, this study theoretically advances the literature of women's football and sports events in many ways. Focusing on the English context, we found three aspects seen as encouraging signs of the changes taking place in women's football. Firstly, there was no significant frequency of comparative comments made by journalists, editorials, or the public about men's football or opinions based on gender frameworks. We advocate that women's football sport is starting to forge its own path based on its technical, tactical, and administrative characteristics, as Petty and Pope (2019) had also linked to the FIFA WWC 2015. Second, 38 of the 65 news items published in newspapers were written by women (approximately 58%). This demonstrates that these women writers and reporters have positioned themselves in another historically masculine domain that frequently receive criticism for following a logic that is mostly linked to the patriarchy (Hardin, Shain, and Shultz-Poniatowski 2008). Third, findings support that women's football is growing towards a new era due to the significant public engagement and media coverage of the *UEFA Women's Euro 2022*. As the analysed event has taken place among the large-scale sports events, this study expanded the discussion of the events' magnitude in women's football.

8. Limitations

We acknowledge limitations in this study. First, using three newspapers (The Sun, The Times, and The Guardian) is not a total representation of the English media press as well as Twitter does not represent the entire virtual environment of social platforms, even though both source types used are relevant. Second, we did not analyse media coverage and public opinion during and after the event. Then, we recommend that future research should explore the sentiment of fans and media coverage during the UEFA Women's Euro 2022 to understand in real-time as well as focused on other sources and events (i.e. FIFA WWC 2023). Methodologically, the adopted approach to collect newspaper material could be limited by the key words chosen as well as on Twitter with the two used hashtags.

Notes

1. Each British nation has distinct football identities. Thus, they all have their national team of men's and women's football to compete in international championships. The only exception occurs at the Olympic Games, an event in which there is a union representing the United Kingdom. We chose to cite these nations separately when necessary
2. Each British nation has distinct football identities. Thus, they all have their national team of men's and women's football to compete in international championships. The only exception occurs at the Olympic Games, an event in which there is a union representing the United Kingdom). We chose to cite these nations separately when necessary

Acknowledgements

This study was funded by the Higher Education Personnel Improvement Coordination (CAPES). We also would like to thank Editage (www.editage.com) for English language editing.

Disclosure statement

No potential conflict of interest was reported by the authors.

ORCID

Jonathan Rocha de Oliveira ⓘ http://orcid.org/0000-0002-3704-8169
Maria Thereza de Oliveira Souza ⓘ http://orcid.org/0000-0002-1636-6969
André Mendes Capraro ⓘ http://orcid.org/0000-0003-3496-3131

References

Agha, N., S. Fairley, and H. Gibson. 2012. "Considering Legacy as a Multi-Dimensional Construct: The Legacy of the Olympic Games." *Sport Management Review* 15 (1): 125–139. doi:10.1016/j.smr.2011.08.004.
Barclays. 2019. "Barclays has announced its sponsorship of the Football Association Women's Super League, the largest ever commercial investment in women's sport in the UK." https://home.barclays/news/2019/3/barclays–record-breaking-investment-in-the-fa-women-s-super-lea/
BBC. 2018a. "England only applicant to host European Women's Championship in 2021." https://www.bbc.com/sport/football/45374721
BBC. 2018b. "Women's Super League: New Full-Time, Professional Era – All You Need to Know." https://www.bbc.com/sport/football/45355268
BBC. 2019. "Women's Super League: Barclays Agree Multi-million Sponsorship Deal." https://www.bbc.com/sport/football/47605807
Bell, B. 2012. "Levelling the Playing Field? Post-Euro 2005 Development of Women's Football in the North-West of England." *Sport in Society* 15 (3): 349–368. doi:10.1080/17430437.2012.653205.
Bell, B. 2019. "Women's Euro 2005 a 'Watershed' for Women's Football in England and a New Era for the Game?" *Sport in History* 39 (4): 445–461. doi:10.1080/17460263.2019.1684985.
Bell, B., and P. Blakey. 2010. "Do Boys and Girls Go Out to Play? Women's Football and Social Marketing at Euro 2005." *International Journal of Sport Management and Marketing* 7 (3/4): 156–172. doi:10.1504/IJSMM.2010.032548.
Ben Porat, A. 2020. "Cosi (Non) Fan Tutte: Women's Football 'Made in Israel.'" *Soccer & Society* 21 (1): 39–49. doi:10.1080/14660970.2018.1487842.
Calavita, N., and A. Ferrer. 2000. "Behind Barcelona's Success Story." *Journal of Urban History* 26 (6): 793–807. doi:10.1177/009614420002600604.
Christopherson, N., M. Janning, and E. D. McConnel. 2002. "Two Kicks Forward, One Kick Back: A Content Analysis of Media Discourses on the 1999 Womens World Cup Soccer Championship." *Sociology of Sport Journal* 19 (2): 170–188. doi:10.1123/ssj.19.2.170.
Clarkson, B. G., A. Culvin, S. Pope, and K. D. Parry. 2020. "Covid-19: Reflections on Threat and Uncertainty for the Future of Elite Women's Football in England." *Managing Sport and Leisure*: 1–12. doi:10.1080/23750472.2020.1766377.
Corbett, B., and A. Edwards. 2018. "A Case Study of Twitter as a Research Tool." *Sport in Society* 21 (2): 394–412. doi:10.1080/17430437.2017.1342622.
Dickinson, M. 2014, June 23. "FA's Poor Relations with Fifa Spell the End for 2019 Women's bid." The Times. https://www.thetimes.co.uk/article/tas-poor-relations-with-fifa-spell-the-end-for-2019-womens-bid-vhfnwzgw79h
Downes, Jr., W. 2018, August 28. "England Launch Bid to host Women's Euro 2021 Championships with Plans to Host Final at Wembley." The Sun. https://www.thesun.co.uk/sport/football/7125317/england-womens-euro-2021/
Dunn, C. 2016. "Elite Footballers as Role Models: Promoting Young Women's Football Participation." *Soccer & Society* 17 (6): 843–855. doi:10.1080/14660970.2015.1100893.
Fan, M., A. Billings, X. Zhu, and P. Yu. 2020. "Twitter-Based BIRGing: Big Data Analysis of English National Team Fans during the 2018 FIFA World Cup." *Communication & Sport* 8 (3): 317–345. doi:10.1177/2167479519834348.
Fielding-Lloyd, B., D. Woodhouse, and R. Sequerra. 2020. "More than Just a Game': family and Spectacle in Marketing the England Women's Super League." *Soccer & Society* 21 (2): 166–179. doi:10.1080/14660970.2018.1541799.

FIFA. 2019a. "FIFA Women's World Cup France 2019 – Global broadcast and audience report." https://img.fifa.com/image/upload/rvgxekduqpeo1ptbgcng.pdf

FIFA. 2019b. "Women's football – Member associations survey report." https://img.fifa.com/image/upload/nq3ensohyxpuxovcovj0.pdf

FIFA. 2020. "Women's Football Strategy." https://resources.fifa.com/image/upload/women-s-football-strategy.pdf?cloudid=z7w21ghir8jb9tguvbcq

Getz, D. 2008. "Event Tourism: Definition, Evolution, and Research." *Tourism Management* 29 (3): 403–428. doi:10.1016/j.tourman.2007.07.017.

Giulianotti, R., G. Armstrong, G. Hales, and D. Hobbs. 2015. "Sport Mega-Events and Public Opposition: A Sociological Study of the London 2012." *Journal of Sport and Social Issues* 39 (2): 99–119. doi:10.1177/0193723514530565.

Giulianotti, R., and T. Langseth. 2016. "Justifying the Civic Interest in Sport: Boltanski and Thévenot, the Six Worlds of Justification, and Hosting the Olympic Games." *European Journal for Sport and Society* 13 (2): 133–153. doi:10.1080/16138171.2016.1183930.

Guardian Sport. 2018. August 28. "England 2021? FA Bids to Host Women's Euros with Wembley Final." https://www.theguardian.com/football/2018/aug/29/fa-bids-2021-womens-euros-england-wembley-final

Hallmann, K. 2012. "Women's 2011 Football World Cup: The Impact of Perceived Images of Women's Soccer and the World Cup 2011 on Interest in Attending Matches." *Sport Management Review* 15 (1): 33–42. doi:10.1016/j.smr.2011.05.002.

Hardin, Marie, Stacie Shain, and Kelly Shultz-Poniatowski. 2008. "There's No Sex Attached to Your Occupation": The Revolving Door for Young Women in Sports Journalism." *Women in Sport and Physical Activity Journal* 17 (1): 68–79. doi:10.1123/wspaj.17.1.68.

Horne, J. 2007. "The Four "Knowns" of Sports Mega-Events." *Leisure Studies* 26 (1): 81–96. doi:10.1080/02614360500504628.

Hudson, M. 2018. August 30. "Phil Neville's Old-School Approach Starting to Pay Off for England Women." The Times. https://www.thetimes.co.uk/article/phil-neville-instilling-pride-in-lionesses-before-crucial-world-cup-qualifier-against-wales-3gmst6b6p

Hudson, M. 2020a. February 3. "Old Trafford Hosts England's First Game at Women's Euro 2021." The Times. https://www.thetimes.co.uk/article/old-trafford-hosts-englands-first-game-at-womens-euro-2021-6dbjv6p36

Hudson, M. 2020b. February 27. "England Women Fly Premium Economy to SheBelieves Cup." *The Times*. https://www.thetimes.co.uk/article/england-women-flying-economy-to-shebelieves-cup-p0nct859w

Jones, J. 2018, December 3. "IT'S COMING HOME England to Host Women's Euro 2021 Championships After Approval from Uefa." The Sun. https://www.thesun.co.uk/sport/football/7886548/england-host-womens-euro-2021-championships/

Judt, T. 2016. *Postwar: A History of Europe since 1945*. New York: Penguin Books.

Kassens-Noor, E., J. Vertalka, and M. Wilson. 2019. "Good Games, Bad Host? Using Big Data to Measure Public Attention and Imagery of the Olympic Games." *Cities* 90: 229–236. doi:10.1016/j.cities.2019.02.009.

Kelner, M. 2017, August 9. "England Prepare Bid for Euro 2021 to Chip Away at "Nasty Prejudice"." The Guardian. https://www.theguardian.com/football/2017/aug/09/fa-european-women-championship-2021-bid

Kirilenko, A. P., and S. O. Stepchenkova. 2017. "Sochi 2014 Olympics on Twitter: Perspectives of Hosts and Guests." *Tourism Management* 63: 54–65. doi:10.1016/j.tourman.2017.06.007.

Lee Ludvigsen, J. A. 2018. "Sport Mega-Events and Security: The 2018 World Cup as an Extraordinarily Securitized Event." *Soccer & Society* 19 (7): 1–1071. doi:10.1080/14660970.2018.1487841.

Maennig, W., and A. Zimbalist. 2012. "What is a Mega Sporting Event?" In *International Handbook on the Economics of Mega Sporting Events*, edited by W. Maennig and A. Zimbalist, 9–14. Cheltenham: Edward Elgar Publishing.

Mahon, B. 2020, December 8. "Ireland's Women Footballers Still Waiting for Equal Pay." *The Times*. https://www.thetimes.co.uk/article/irelands-women-footballers-still-waiting-for-equal-pay-sj29kf0dr

Miles, J. 2018, September 6. "England set to host women's Euro 2021 after FA was ONLY association to submit bid." The Sun. https://www.thesun.co.uk/sport/7193461/england-host-womens-euro-2021-fa-bid/

Müller, M. 2015. "What Makes an Event a Mega-Event? Definitions and Sizes." *Leisure Studies* 34 (6): 627–642. doi:10.1080/02614367.2014.993333.

Northcroft, J. 2018, July 15. "The FA can keep good times coming by Selling Wembley for starters." The Times. https://www.thetimes.co.uk/article/the-fa-can-keep-good-times-coming-by-selling-wembley-forstarters-mkr7qz98r

Payne, G., and J. Payne. 2004. *Key Concepts in Social Research*. Thousand Oaks: SAGE Publications.

Petty, K., and S. Pope. 2019. "A New Age for Media Coverage of Women's Sport? An Analysis of English Media Coverage of the 2015 FIFA Women's World Cup." *Sociology* 53 (3): 486–502. doi:10.1177/0038038518797505.

Pfister, G. 2010. "Women in Sport-Gender Relations and Future Perspectives." *Sport in Society* 13 (2): 234–248. doi:10.1080/17430430903522954.

Pfister, G. 2015. "Assessing the Sociology of Sport: On Women and Football." *International Review for the Sociology of Sport* 50 (4–5): 563–569. doi:10.1177/1012690214566646.

Pope, S. 2018. "Who Could Name an England Women's Footballer?': Female Fans of Men's Football and Their Views of Women's Football in England." In *Female Football Players and Fans: Intruding in a Man's World*, edited by G. Pfister and S. Pope, 125–153. London: Palgrave Macmillan. doi:10.1057/978-1-137-59025-1_7.

Price, J., N. Farrington, and L. Hall. 2013. "Changing the Game? The Impact of Twitter on Relationships between Football Clubs, Supporters and the Sports Media." *Soccer & Society* 14 (4): 446–461. doi:10.1080/14660970.2013.810431.

Roche, M. 1994. "Mega-Events and Urban Policy." *Annals of Tourism Research* 21 (1): 1–19. doi:10.1016/0160-7383(94)90002-7.

Taylor, L. 2018. December 3. "England to Host Women's Euro 2021 But Venue Choices Prove Controversial." The Guardian. https://www.theguardian.com/football/2018/dec/03/england-host-womens-european-championship-2021

The FA. 2019. "Barclays Unveiled as Title Sponsor of FA women's Super League." https://www.thefa.com/news/2019/mar/20/barclays-fa-wsl-lead-sponsor-200319

The FA. 2018. "Naming of Restructured Women's League Pyramid Confirmed." https://www.thefa.com/news/2018/feb/26/womens-league-pyramid-restructure-260218

UEFA. 2017. "UEFA Women's Euro 2017 – Tournament Review." https://www.uefa.com/MultimediaFiles/Download/TechnicalReport/competitions/WOCO/02/51/72/60/2517260_DOWNLOAD.pdf

UEFA. 2020a. "Women's EURO in England: All You Need to Know." https://www.uefa.com/womenseuro/news/0258-0e2c4c13b77a-1553560769ae-1000–uefa-women-s-euro-2021-england/

UEFA. 2020b. "UEFA Women's EURO Moved to July 2022." https://www.uefa.com/womenseuro/news/025c-0f3d8be5c46b-a606252552ee-1000–women-s-euro-moved-to-july-2022/

UEFA. 2018. "England to Host Women's EURO 2021." https://www.uefa.com/womenseuro/news/024c-0e1774824d07-89710029dcc5-1000-england-to-host-uefa-women-s-euro-2021/

Valenti, M., N. Scelles, and S. Morrow. 2018. "Women's Football Studies: An Integrative Review." *Sport, Business and Management: An International Journal* 8 (5): 511–528. doi:10.1108/SBM-09-2017-0048.

Villeneuve, J.-P., and D. Aquilina. 2016. "Who's Fault is It? An Analysis of the Press Coverage of Football Betting Scandals in France and the United Kingdom." *Sport in Society* 19 (2): 187–200. doi:10.1080/17430437.2015.1067772.

Vincent, J., J. Harris, E. (Ted). Kian, and A. Billings. 2019. "The Isles of Wonder—A New Jerusalem? British Newspaper Narratives about the Opening Ceremony of the XXXth Olympiad." *Sport in Society* 22 (7): 1275–1296. doi:10.1080/17430437.2018.1515203.

VisitBritain. 2015. "Football Tourism Scores for Britain: Inbound Visitors that Watch Live Football." In *Foresight*. (Issue 141, pp. 1–6). https://www.visitbritain.org/sites/default/files/vb-corporate/Documents-Library/documents/2015-9%20VisitBritain%20Report_Football%20tourism%20scores%20for%20Britain.pdf

Wang, Y. 2021. "Building Relationships with Fans: How Sports Organizations Used Twitter as a Communication Tool." *Sport in Society* 24 (7): 1055–1069. doi:10.1080/17430437.2020.1725475.

Watson, A. 2021. July 2. Monthly Reach of Leading Newspapers in the United Kingdom from April 2019 to March 2020. *Statista*. https://www.statista.com/statistics/246077/reach-of-selected-national-newspapers-in-the-uk/

Watt, P. 2013. "It's Not for Us": Regeneration, the 2012 Olympics and the Gentrification of East London." *City* 17 (1): 99–118. . doi:10.1080/13604813.2012.754190.

Williams, J. 2003a. *A Game for Rough Girls? A History of Women's Football in Britain*. London: Routledge.

Williams, J. 2003b. "The Fastest Growing Sport? Women's Football in England." *Soccer & Society* 4 (2–3): 112–127. doi:10.1080/14660970512331390865.

Williams, J. 2011. "Women's football, Europe and Professionalization 1971–2011." https://uefaacademy.com/wp-content/uploads/sites/2/2019/05/20110622_Williams-Jean_Final-Report.pdf

Williams, J., and R. Hess. 2015. "Women, Football and History: International Perspectives." *The International Journal of the History of Sport* 32 (18): 2115–2122. doi:10.1080/09523367.2015.1172877.

Wrack, S. 2019a. "Record attendance for Women's FA Cup final expected at Wembley." The Guardian. https://www.theguardian.com/football/2019/may/01/record-attendance-womens-football-expected-fa-cup-final

Wrack, S. 2019b. November 14. "If Phil Neville Stays on as England Manager then He Has to be Bold." *The Guardian*. https://www.theguardian.com/football/blog/2019/nov/14/phil-neville-stays-on-england-womens-manager-bold

Wrack, S. 2020. February 23. "Old Trafford Picked to Stage Grand Opening of Women's Euro 2021." The Guardian. https://www.theguardian.com/football/2020/feb/23/old-trafford-stage-grand-opening-2021-women-euros-england-phil-neville

Yin, R. K. 2014. *Case Study Research Design and Methods*. 5th ed. Thousand Oaks: Sage Publications.

Yu, Y., and X. Wang. 2015. "World Cup 2014 in the Twitter World: A Big Data Analysis of Sentiments in U.S. sports Fans' Tweets." *Computers in Human Behavior* 48: 392–400. doi:10.1016/j.chb.2015.01.075.

Ziegler, M. 2017. August 10. "Manchester United Urged to Launch a Women's Side." The Times. https://www.thetimes.co.uk/article/fa-want-england-to-host-womens-euros-in-2021-glb-3wdxq7

Ziegler, M. 2019. July 12. "BBC secures Women's Euro 2021 Rights and Is Keen to Televise Super League." The Times. https://www.thetimes.co.uk/article/bbc-secures-women-s-euro-2021-rights-and-keen-to-televise-super-league-w5xj9nxwl

Anti-bribery and corruption in sport mega-events: stakeholder perspectives

Christina Philippou

ABSTRACT
Sport mega-events are often accompanied by allegations of bribery and corruption, with concerns around corruption opportunities expected to continue into the 2020s. Research on anti-corruption around sport mega-events is important for understanding how these risks can be mitigated. This paper addresses the gap in knowledge surrounding anti-corruption issues associated with the organisation of sport mega-events. 39 interviews were conducted with anti-corruption specialists, sport governance officials, and stakeholders working in sport to gain their perspective on bribery and corruption issues and prevention in relation to sport mega-events. Thematic analysis was then conducted on the data. The results showed a consistency in perception with regards to the main issues and areas of concern for national and international sport governing bodies involved in organising sport mega-events, as well as providing a number of suggestions for addressing these through specific policies for implementation.

Introduction

Large sporting events, later growing into sport mega-events (SMEs), such as the Olympics, have been around since ancient times, often accompanied by allegations of bribery and corruption (Spivey 2012). There are multiple and diverse examples of corruption, including bribery, abuse of power, embezzlement, fraud, and vote-rigging (Brooks, Aleem, and Button 2013). The early 21st century saw a number of scandals engulfing large national (SGBs) and international sport governing bodies (ISGBs) in relation to SMEs, particularly with regards to corruption within these organisations (Conn 2018; Jennings 1996). As a result of these, some governance reforms took place, including around decision-making, official election and retention, financial monitoring, and accountability, such as FIFA and the International Tennis Federation investment in reform around corruption (ITIA 2021; FIFA 2020b).

SMEs normally come under the jurisdiction of their respective ISGBs and are often their largest source of revenue (FIFA 2020a; IOC 2020). There is a known link between large sums of money controlled by small numbers of individuals and corruption (Klitgaard 1998; Rose-Ackerman 1999), so is not surprising that SMEs are linked to scandals nor that concerns around corruption opportunities associated with SMEs remain, and are expected to continue into the 2020s. Further reforms are thus required at most levels of the sport organisation hierarchy to ensure that previous SMEs scandals do not repeat going forward.

Given the limited empirical literature on anti-bribery and corruption (ABC) in sport (Philippou 2019), this paper addresses some of the gap in knowledge by exploring diverse stakeholder perspectives on ABC surrounding organisation of SMEs by SGBs and ISGBs. The paper explores perceptions of three specialist groups through their narratives on, and solutions to, ABC problems in SMEs, and analyses this data within the constructs of existing conceptual ABC and corruption frameworks. This paper's contribution to knowledge is a qualitative exploration of the ABC issues as considered by both stakeholders within the sport industry (governance officials and others) and those external but with a relevant expertise (ABC specialists), and a comparison of their narratives against conceptual financial corruption literature.

This paper is structured as follows: the literature review around ABC in sport and SMEs is considered, before the method is discussed. The results of the analysis are evaluated both in relation to governance and SME participants and beneficiaries in the discussion section, before concluding.

Literature review

While there is a wealth of literature defining corruption (Ashforth and Anand 2003; Den Nieuwenboer and Kaptein 2008; Transparency International 2016), definitions vary in scope (Rose 2017), with researchers agreeing that effects on stakeholders are largely negative (Rose-Ackerman 1999). Consequently, corruption in the awarding of, organising of, and participation in SMEs affects a large number of stakeholders.

While there is a wealth of literature on corruption scandals (occurrence), there is limited empirical research conducted in the area of ABC (prevention) in sport, with most corruption literature being either fully conceptual in nature, or focused on general governance concerns (Alm 2019; Chappelet 2011; Geeraert 2016) or potential for reform within SGBs and ISGBs (Sugden and Tomlinson 2017).

Conceptual research on corruption has tried to make sense of the intricate relationships underpinning ISGBs and their hierarchy, and the issues arising thereon. Gardiner, Parry, and Robinson (2017) conceptualise corruption from an integrity standpoint, arguing that responsibility, accountability, and concern for reputation are key to both the concept and solutions. Gardiner's (2018) model of sport-related corruption distinguishes between a core of certainty (including major financial corruption) and a penumbra of uncertainty (including gamesmanship and cheating). Kihl (2018) focuses on the multidimensional aspects of sport corruption contextualising the issue within concepts of rationalisation, moral disengagement, social networks, and abuse of power.

Some literature takes an ISGB-specific approach. For example, Mason, Thibault, and Misener (2006) conceptualise the corruption problem within the IOC from a corporate governance agency theory perspective, where solutions include monitoring for the bidding process, and 'secondary residual claimants' in control functions within the ISGB. This is in line with Chappelet (2011), whose suggestions for reform of the IOC include a rigorous overview of the accountability issues including transparency, evaluation, and dealing with complaints. Accountability is also the topic of Numerato's (2009) research on both the microsocial and macrosocial dimensions in the media's relationship with sport corruptors. Pielke (2013) concentrates on the different forms of accountability (hierarchical, fiscal, legal, reputational and so on) and their applicability to curbing corruption within FIFA, further developed in the work of Sugden and Tomlinson (2017).

Empirical studies on corruption are few, and include a number of research outputs from an ethnographic study of Greek football clubs which analysed financial crimes (including fake tax certificates, players' salary payments, match-fixing, and ticket sale concerns) (Manoli, Antonopoulos, and Levi 2016) and the inevitability of endemic corruption in football (Manoli, Antonopoulos, and Bairner 2019). Thematic analyses of legal regulations (Thorpe 2014) and political organisations' recommendations (Næss 2019) add further weight to the need for regulation, as do studies of attitudes to SME host nation corruption (Kulczycki and Koenigstorfer 2016) and motivation for sharing sport insider information via social media (Onwumechili 2018).

Maennig (2005) made the distinction between competition (on-field) corruption and management (governance) corruption. The empirical and exploratory sport corruption literature focuses on the former, with consideration of actions and events rather than controls, often predominantly around match-fixing (Hill 2016; Manoli, Antonopoulos, and Bairner 2019). However, these elements of corruption are arguably minimal for SMEs (some match-fixing allegations around the start of SME competitions aside) due to the strong controls in place internally, as well as the external scrutiny, both of which enhance accountability and, in turn, decrease the propensity for corruption (Klitgaard 1998). On the other hand, controls around SME governance have been and continue to be weaker (Geeraert 2016; Sugden and Tomlinson 2017). These include voting for SME host nations (Youd 2014; Jennings 1996), control around sponsors (Smit 2006; Kulczycki and Koenigstorfer 2016), allocation of tickets (Tighe and Rowan 2020), and allocation and procurement of construction and other related services (Conn 2018).

On the governance side, Masters' (2015) TASP (type, activity, sector, place) sport corruption typology allows sport corruption case study analysis, including for particular SMEs. For assessing ABC as a whole within ISGBs, the framework proposed by Philippou (2019) relates exclusively to ABC controls (as opposed to general prevention or poor governance) in sport corruption literature, and covers three elements: clarifying concepts (including definitions), assessing risk factors (including economic rent and culture), and assessing governance (including accountability, monitoring, and enforcement). Stakeholders are key to applying the framework to SMEs, as the definitional aspect of clarifying the concept of 'corruption' will very much depend on this. Table 1 is therefore a (non-exhaustive) list of stakeholders (adapted from Chadwick, Roberts, and Cowley (2018)) linked to corruption in SMEs.

Table 1. Stakeholders in SMEs.

Athletes	Sponsors
Fans	Advertising companies
Media	Construction companies
Sport governance officials	Concession and service providers
ISGBs/ SGBs	Betting companies
Residents in host cities	
Politicians	
Law enforcement in host cities	

The stakeholders in the left-hand column in Table 1 relate to those long-term affected by the SME, while those on the right relate to recipients of short-term benefits. Taking the left-hand side first, the top five should not, in theory, be overly affected by SME location, while the bottom three (alongside those working in the tourist industry) and those in the right-hand column would. This is important when considering the process surrounding host nation selection from an ABC perspective.

Other issues relating to ABC relevant to SMEs include monitoring and investigation, similar to those applied to fraud (Albrecht et al. 2018; Schuchter and Levi 2016). There is also the importance of transparency in the ABC process, both within organisations (Geeraert 2016) and externally via media and public scrutiny (Ionescu 2015).

Overall, monitoring (Lipicer and Lajh 2013), benchmarking (Geeraert 2016), reporting on sport governance measures (Chappelet and Mrkonjic 2013), reporting procedures (Erickson, Patterson, and Backhouse 2019), and ethics audits (McNamee and Fleming 2007) all form part of the compliance agenda when it comes to SMEs. Compliance considerations are often linked to rational choice theory (Becker 1968), adapted to corruption by Nichols (2012), but there are other forms of regulation that don't (Croall 2004).

This paper therefore positions itself in addressing the literature gap on ABC controls to prevent SME corruption. It does this through an exploratory study of perceptions of three key distinct stakeholder groups to provide data in support of some of the conceptual literature discussed above.

Method

The lack of in-depth and rich data to compare against the conceptual corruption literature on ABC led to this qualitative analysis of SME stakeholder perspectives undertaken through interviews, unencumbered by conforming pressure often associated with sensitive-topic focus groups. To do this, semi-structured one-hour interviews were conducted by the researcher with individuals from three internationally-dispersed (across 6 continents) distinct groups in the period 2018–2020: ABC specialist practitioners, sport governance officials, and stakeholders working in sport, to gain both internal (governance and other) and external expert perspectives on bribery and corruption prevention in relation to SMEs. Table 2 provides an overview of the groups' sample populations and motivations in relation to bias. Interviewees were selected using purposive snowball sampling and interviews were conducted (in English) to the point where in-depth inquiry could be attained (Crouch and McKenzie 2006) and saturation achieved (Guest, Bunce, and Johnson 2006).

Definitions of both corruption and SMEs differ across the literature, so this study allowed participants their own definitions, although examples of the latter provided by interviewees included the Olympics, a variety of World Cups (football, rugby, cricket), and league finals (Superbowl, UEFA Champions League final).

Participants were asked whether there were any specific ABC measures they would expect around hosting of SMEs. Thematic analysis was then conducted by the researcher using NVivo software on the transcripted data following the approach of Braun and Clarke (2006). Two strands emerged from the coded data in line with Maennig (2005): governance and competition corruption. Following an abductive approach, analysis on the former themes

Table 2. Interviewees.

Group	Prefix designation	Number of interviewees	Population description	Motivations
ABC specialists	F	16	ABC experts and forensic accountants working in ABC investigations	Professional, financial
Sport governance officials	G	14	Those that currently were or had previously held a non-sporting position with an ISGB or SGB	Position in relation to colleagues
Other stakeholders	S	9	Individuals working within sport, including members of the media, club officials, coaches, and athletes from sports including football, rugby, athletics, and cricket	Wide ranging

was structured in relation to the Philippou (2019) ABC framework (which considers ABC controls in relation to sport corruption), while the competition theme lent itself to the types and activities elements on the Masters (2015) corruption typology (see Table 3). Within these themes, the data was compared to the ABC conceptual literature.

The limitations of this method include the concerns around neutrality of information arising from the interviewees, which was to a degree tapered by use of three different groups within the sample.

Snowball sampling also limits the study to the researcher's wider network (and with it potential bias), as does the need for English (at least as a second language) by the interviewees. The anti-corruption positionality of the participants would not threaten the validity of research undertaken on ABC, as prevention would not necessarily be broached by those denying its need.

Finally, thematic analysis suffers from being intrinsically embedded with the researcher's contextual interpretation and positionality. However, data triangulation (through use of both interviews and ISGB documents) and theory triangulation (through the use of both multiple theories and perspectives) was applied to ensure rigour, as appropriate to flexible designs in qualitative research (Robson and McCartan 2016).

Results and discussion

The study's resulting themes, discussed in this section, are summarised in Table 3.

Stakeholders are key to setting an ABC agenda, and this was recognised by participants as the '*whole process [being] impacted by so many stakeholders*' (F1). One participant highlighted the importance of '*creat[ing] a relationship between as many stakeholders as you can when you're running a major sport event. So for the World Cup it will be the police, there will be government…*' (G8). There were also references to partnerships and networks, although these were concentrated within the first two groups (not including the other stakeholders), in support of the work of Chadwick, Roberts, and Cowley (2018).

Clarifying concepts

A key aspect of ABC is defining concepts (Philippou 2019), including definitions of corruption (Rose 2017). Participants across all three groups agreed SME corruption focused on awarding of both the host event (in line with Mason, Thibault, and Misener (2006) and

Table 3. Key corruption and ABC themes.

Corruption type (Maennig 2005)	Framework element (Masters 2015; Philippou 2019)	Themes
Governance	Clarifying concepts	Defining corruption within SMEs
	Assessing Risk Factors	Governance official involvement in SMEs: o Due diligence o Transparency

	Assessing Governance	• Accountability:
		  o Networks
		  o Media
		  o Bidding process
		• Independence
		• Economic rent

	Monitoring and Control	• Monitoring • Controls
	Enforcement	Enforcement
Competition	Host Nations	Legacy
	Auxiliary Businesses	Procurement
	SME Competition	• Athlete involvement • Match-fixing

Chappelet (2011)) and subsequent contracts attached. An ABC specialist summarised the issues as:

> *The process for awarding major events, the construction and delivery spend for those major events, the way that their funds are spent by local subsidiary organisations, and the allocation of those funds and then the spend of those funds.* (F11)

The groups differed in their focus within these areas, as would be expected. The ABC specialist group focused on methods of corrupt behaviour, similar to those found by Manoli, Antonopoulos, and Levi (2016)). The consensus was that corrupt behaviour took the form of '*a very simplistic scheme, I don't think there's anything complicated about it*' (F3), in line with Sugden and Tomlinson's (2017) treatment of corruption by FIFA governance officials.

In contrast, governance officials focused on the broader aspects of corruption, similar to those found in Brooks, Aleem, and Button (2013), discussing types of corruption such as '*awarding ... sponsoring, broadcasting, contracts and so on*' (G15).

The other stakeholders group's main focus was on corruption within ISGBs and SGBs themselves, such as SMEs '*help[ing] attract that sort of investment coming into a country, and it just looks like Monopoly, people are just moving money around*' (S3). Overall, the stakeholder group outlook concentrated on the problem of money leaving the game or '*where there's a middleman there's a prone for money to go missing in the middle*' (S4), through social networks and abuse of power (Kihl 2018).

Assessing risk factors

All three groups covered issues relating to governance officials' involvement in corruption. The ABC specialist group offered a number of suggestions around mitigation, most around having similar internal controls for sport governance officials to those used for politicians by '*just saying what is acceptable*' (F2). Another suggestion was having registers, similar to those '*you find ... in some parliaments, that government officials have to register the lobbyists that they meet ... and even travel arrangements*' (F5). Others discussed due diligence and a focus on transparency from the start, in line with common industry ABC controls (Chappelet 2011). One governance official suggested that hierarchical accountability (Pielke 2013) should exist through monitoring of '*your bank accounts, looking at your lifestyle*' (G11).

In fact, transparency (Chappelet 2011) was the most commonly coded ABC control for SMEs amongst participants in all three groups. For example, one participant covered the business interest control requirements for '*financial disclosure by the individuals involved, disclosure of their conflicts of interest, it's oversight by a third party, so an audit of the process, and transparency around the awards, so people shouldn't be allowed to vote anonymously*' (F5), which shows a need to focus on monitoring (Mason, Thibault, and Misener 2006) and abuse of power (Kihl 2018). Another participant argued that '*transparency's the way forward, however much you can generate it or engineer it just to show me that things are being made for the right reasons or the right considerations*' (G14) reinforces financial implications (Kulczycki and Koenigstorfer 2016) of corruption, as well as reputational ones (Gardiner, Parry, and Robinson 2017). While the idea of transparency is a key part of ABC literature (Geeraert 2016), it also translates directly to practical considerations in the case of SMEs. For example, to avoid issues raised by Sugden and Tomlinson (2017) and Jennings (1996) around SME organising, '*you have a transparent bidding process ... [and] better standard compliance guidelines for everyone who's in that local organising committee, or on the decision-making board*' (S10).

This theme also went beyond the bidding process to '*making it clear when those deadlines have hit or missed, and if they've missed why they missed and how they're going to mitigate for that*' (G13), in support of the idea of audited and monitored long-term accountability (Chappelet 2011; Gardiner, Parry, and Robinson 2017).

Assessing governance

Transparency overlaps with the idea of public scrutiny as a cornerstone of ABC (Klitgaard 1998; Rose-Ackerman 1999). Accountability created by public scrutiny (Numerato 2009) or '*having the power to publically name and shame*' (F17) negatively affects the propensity for corruption in most sectors (Lipicer and Lajh 2013). One stakeholder compared ISGBs, stating, '*look at [other sports] and they are just information overload with how things run, but FIFA it's like a mystery*' (S8), in line with Pielke's (2013) and Sugden and Tomlinson (2017) suggestions for reform, although there is evidence that this is changing (Philippou and Hines 2021).

The importance of networks (Bond, Widdop, and Parnell 2019; Chadwick, Widdop, and Burton 2020) and social media for dissemination of information was also evident, especially amongst the other stakeholder group. However, it was an ABC specialist that considered social activism: '*there's never been a better time for public opinion to influence the way in which these big companies think. Literally unprecedented. And I'm surprised that actually we're not seeing more on social media about people campaigning, urging boycott of companies due to corruption*' (F10), of which there is little in the literature. However, there is mixed evidence on whether corrupt behaviour amongst monopolies actually affects consumers, or the effects of social media on corruption (Hölzen and Meier 2019), but it is clear that corruption affects risks taken by organisations (Bruinsma and Bernasco 2004).

Research on media accountability, where the interrelationship between sport corruptors and the media sees causation run from both actors at different times, with the media occasionally enabling corruption through their reporting (Numerato 2009) was also covered. For example, one participant stated how *'we've heard so many things in the media when something happens and a country's been accused of this, that or the other ... and they say oh it's just because of the World Cup that's coming up, they don't want us to host it'* (F4). This also touches on issues of insider information (Onwumechili 2018) and concern for reputation as conceptualised by Gardiner, Parry, and Robinson (2017).

All three groups also discussed the bidding process within the prism of transparency (Chappelet 2011). A number of governance officials shared personal experiences: *'you just see lots of different, should I say influencing strategies when it comes to voting, and I think some will be downright illegal, corrupt, and others will be technically within the rules but probably morally questionable'* (G11). It was highlighted how *'you can buy a vote by paying for the federation official to go to the congress ... and that might be enough for them to make sure they vote the way you want them to vote'* (G1). This is as contextualised within both Gardiner's (2018) core of certainty and Kihl's (2018) abuse of power maxim.

Within this theme, problems around robust bidding processes for SMEs were acknowledged to avoid concerns highlighted by Jennings (1996) and Conn (2018). For example: *'it's a difficult thing for [ISGB] cos they have to keep the balance and they have to go to new markets as well, I think it's hard to keep that transparency and the augmentation for these decisions'* (S10) acknowledges the commercial concerns of ISGBs in relation to SMEs, while also heeding the need for accountability (Klitgaard 1988). A number of solutions were suggested, with simple changes to improve the ABC process through transparency, such as *'a bidding system that is 100% transparent, that ... build[s] in criteria that favour bids from people who have not hosted for a particular period'* (G9), which ties into agency theory (Mason, Thibault, and Misener 2006).

As with the rest of the themes, ABC specialists focused on the controls aspects of bidding. One suggested likening governance officials to *'a corporate ... entertaining a government official, put strict criteria in place and make sure it's being appropriately audited and scrutinised'* (F2). Some focused on transparency within the bidding process to avoid vote-rigging as *'if they have a set of particular criteria that they need to meet then it's harder to exchange getting tournaments for privileges'* (F9), in line with solutions to the agency theory conceptualisation proposal by Mason, Thibault, and Misener (2006).

Finally within this theme, while all three groups discussed vote-rigging, one participant's suggestion overlapped with another well-trodden theme, where there *'should be more independent oversight of the selection process'* (F10), also well-covered in the literature (Chappelet and Mrkonjic 2013).

When applied to SMEs, independence as a form of control was considered in relation to the bidding process by participants across all three groups. The problem was summarised as *'lack of independence is significant on the global stage'* (F1) and affecting the overall process for SME hosting as *'There should be an audit, a regular audit of your contracts, of your bidding process, done by an external body'* (F17), linking the concept of moral disengagement (Kihl 2018) with monitoring (Lipicer and Lajh 2013).

Corporate governance business processes, where independent NEDs are often skilled individuals from other industries, was a solution offered to the responsibility problem set out by Mason, Thibault, and Misener (2006) by *'put[ting] another independent body to follow the processes and to analyse how this whole thing is done, and who does it, and who okays it'* (F4).

Taking the sporting and other interests out of the bidding equation were considered across groups, even if the independent members were not necessarily external to the industry, as this would *'cut out all of the nonsense that goes with the actual bidding process'* (G3) and focus on official's core responsibilities (Gardiner, Parry, and Robinson 2017). This solution also applies to all aspects of SME service-provision, where *'it should be like in sports that the best one should win'* (S10), where McNamee and Fleming (2007) ethics focus on corruption is applied to ABC.

The biggest impediment to integrating independence within ISGBs and SGBs was considered to be the decision-makers: *'I think it's down to the country and then that in itself comes with bribery cos then you feel encouraged because you have to also suck up to basically every other country'* (S8), which would negate the influence of social networks on corruption (Kihl 2018). The definition of independence is also important here, as there have been allegations of independent advisors at the same luxury hotels at SMEs as the governance officials that they are monitoring (Rushden, Auclair, and Panja 2021). One solution to this is *'to do it on an event-to-event basis, appoint a different consultant'* (F17).

This then links into the idea of culture (Philippou 2019), summarised by one participant as *'probably business as usual'* (F3). One suggested solution to the culture problem, in line with proponents of regulation (Næss 2019; Thorpe 2014), was the installation of *'an independent governing body or regulator that's got absolutely nothing to do with organising the competition'* (S4), and once again links into the social networks concept (Kihl 2018). There are arguments that most ISGBs are involved in direct competition with their regional and national federations, especially when it comes to SMEs. This then creates issues around self-regulation, as covered in ample literature on autonomy (Geeraert, Mrkonjic, and Chappelet 2015).

Another participant discussed the proposed regulator's potential position within the current structure of sport governance and law:

> G11: Yeah, and it's fascinating isn't it that organisations like the Court of Arbitration for Sport are there to listen to it when it's gone wrong, what if we decided to create an equivalent ... organisation like that you could create for tier one events
>
> Interviewer: Yeah cos CAS ultimately is there to wrangle the legal points rather than...
>
> G11: Regulatory.

Another theme arising was how economic rent derived from the importance of the SME affects corruption (Klitgaard 1998; Rose-Ackerman 1999). This was mainly covered by ABC specialists and governance officials, with one participant referring to the effects of economic rent on corruption as *'the one that people get, people kill for. Because every country or whatever, anyone that hosts, everyone thinks that when they host a sports event that it's about economic gain isn't it, and financial gain, so they don't mind spending to get it'* (F4), although does not take account of the negative effects of perceived corruption on host country attitudes to sponsors raised by Kulczycki and Koenigstorfer (2016).

Another participant explained why particular SMEs were more susceptible to management corruption (Maennig 2005) than other, smaller-scale events:

> *If you take the World Cup and you take the Olympics, there's a real clamber by some brands to have to be involved in that. Whereas if you look at [other] world cups having to fight to get a brand in, so there's is little or no chance of someone being corrupt in [...] place because it's [them] doing the asking.* (G11)

This is in line with economic rent effects on corruption (Klitgaard 1998; Nichols 2012). The comparison with small events was made by a number of participants in the ABC specialist and governance officials groups, particularly as *'the public has no idea who sits on the committees, what is the approval process, what is the vetting process that these events can actually take place'* (F1), confirming rationalisation (Kihl 2018) as part of the SME corruption context.

This ties into the ABC monitoring process as part of assessing governance (Philippou 2019), summarised by one governance official as: *'if you want to launder money, you're not going to the World Cup, you're going to the small competitions and events where you could get a chance of actually doing something'* (G6), which would require Gardiner's (2018) model to adjust its core of certainty in order to reflect size of sporting event.

Monitoring and control

Considering the corruption opportunities highlighted above, and the ABC possibilities to mitigate for these, it is unsurprising that another well-covered theme was around monitoring and controls (Mason, Thibault, and Misener 2006), or *'people shouldn't mark their own homework'* (F4). It was the ABC specialists and governance officials that focused on this topic, hardly touched upon by the stakeholder group (only one of a single interview was coded to this theme), which emphasises the different motivations in play and links soft power (Chadwick, Widdop, and Burton 2020) with concepts of social networks (Kihl 2018) in corruption.

Areas to consider in the ABC process included *'vetting of contracts or a project'* (F15) and having *'a whistleblower hotline, a possibility to report any wrongdoing, any suspicion, and then have the right procedures in place to deal with any information you receive to investigate'* (G15), where good governance encouragement of reporting (Erickson, Patterson, and Backhouse 2019) cut through responsibility concepts affecting corruption (Gardiner 2018). Other participants focused on the idea of registers, comparing to corporate procedures common in other industries such as *'I know everything ... offered or gifted over [X currency amount] has to go on the register. I'd love to see how many times that register is independently audited. You're laughing'* (G11).

One ABC specialist focused on the ability to investigate wrongdoing through transparent investigation policies, such as *'audited declarations of income by decision-makers ... pre-decision-making, post-decision-making'* (F17), similar to the idea of hierarchical accountability (Pielke 2013).

Another consideration, in line with Lipicer and Lajh (2013) calls for monitoring, was the need to implement bespoke controls depending on location, with '*general policies and procedures in place, and then you look to have something in place that fits in with that particular sporting event*' (G8). Alternatively, considering individuals' networks in the form of conflicts of interest such as '*the person you went to school together and you want to give them the business*' (F4) or '*government officials or individuals with ties to government in a particular geographic locale*' (F7) would prevent abuse of power and social networks for corrupt purposes (Kihl 2018). This theme was only addressed by the ABC specialist group, with solutions offered including '*end[ing] up with quite extensive due diligence on the major parties, so the suppliers, the construction companies*' (F11), or agency problems influencing corruption (Mason, Thibault, and Misener 2006).

Collusion was also addressed in the conflicts of interest theme, bringing issues related to autonomy (Geeraert, Mrkonjic, and Chappelet 2015). One stakeholder participant considered the '*political restraints cos some confederations support each other in these votes …. So there's lots of political restraints and relationships which obviously have an impact on these processes*' (S10), circling back to preventing corrupt social networks (Kihl 2018) in robust ABC.

The link between politics and sport is another contentious issue, covered by ample literature elsewhere (Chadwick, Widdop, and Burton 2020). While governance officials didn't touch upon this, the other two groups discussed the political element and its impact on corruption and ABC quite extensively, with a lot of cynicism on display: '*funding, you talk about that as a very legitimate and very good way, very good initiative to help develop football, ultimately ways of throwing money at associations to get votes*' (S1), which also links to the fiscal elements of Pielke's (2013) work.

There was, however, a concession among participants that the link between politics and sport helps foster some of the corruption as '*it's difficult because the governments are involved as well and certain governments do not follow compliance guidelines*' (S10) or regulation (Thorpe 2014). They also considered that there is '*a whole lot of soft power that's coming into play and countries would like to show themselves in a different light*' (S14), in line with Gorse and Chadwick (2010) contextualization of the topic.

Enforcement

The theme of enforcement (Philippou 2019) was explicitly covered by a number of ABC specialist participants linked to economic rent (Klitgaard 1998). One participant likened this to the risk-reward problem in economic literature (Nichols 2012): '*because they're such big contracts, there's a small payment one way or the other in order to get those contracts there's certainly incentive to do that*' (F3).

The importance of enforcement as a control tool (Croall 2004), where '*there need to be very steep consequences when anything … untoward is found out*' (F4), was also evident in the data. While there were few participants discussing this theme, coding occurred across all three groups.

There were a few suggestions around how to mitigate the problem, the main one relating to cooperation, where '*what you want to do is create a relationship with the local law enforcement, but that's not straightforward*' (G8). This also turns the concept of social networks linked to corruption (Kihl 2018) on its head, utilising networks in a positive manner for ABC.

This concluded the themes linked to the management corruption (Maennig 2005) side of the SME process (left-hand column of Table 1), relating to corruption and ABC. The following section considers the remaining stakeholders and the issues relevant to those.

Competition corruption

Corruption related to SME events themselves form a number of strands in the thematic analysis: effects on host nation(s), on business leading up to and/or participating in the SME, and of the competition itself, all linked to elements of Masters (2015) corruption typology.

Legacy

Although not explicitly a form of competition corruption (Maennig 2005), this was part of staging a SME, and thus more suited to analysis in line with Masters (2015). The idea of legacy as part of SME corruption (Jennings 1996) was considered by all three groups, but was most prominent in the stakeholder group, where all but one made reference to it. The overall view was a negative one, supporting Kulczycki and Koenigstorfer's (2016) findings on CSR as a tempering mechanism for SME perception in light of corruption, summarised by one participant as:

> *It's not that the legacy should be the stadium, the legacy should be fundamental building blocks for your society there. Big nice stadium, lovely thing to look at, absolutely useless if your kids can't go to school.* (G6)

Issues of abuse of power (one of the definitions of corruption (Transparency International 2017) and a key tenet of Kihl (2018)) were considered by some of the participants, with some links to colonialisation: '*I always think of the World Cup as financially raping the country that it's actually being in … it's a big foreign gentrification I feel*' (S3). This linked in with introspective ethical considerations (McNamee and Fleming 2007), particularly by members of the governance officials group who had been involved in SMEs:

> *I felt morally conflicted [about Rio], because you're looking at what has been built, and you're looking at the favelas and you're hearing stories about the people who come from them, how the hell can we be spending this amount of money, or allowing for this amount of money to be spent on a three weeks sports event for a majority of people who are elite athletes who have a very high standard of living, and you have all these VIPs coming in being chauffeured around the city and staying in amazing hotels, and you have people who are destitute.* (G6)

One suggested solution was to include sustainability in the criteria for bidding but also to ensure that the aftermath is included in the monitoring and control process, also suggested by Mason, Thibault, and Misener (2006). For example, SME nations being assessed on '*what have you achieved in relation to each element of what you have proposed and prove the sustainability of it at the time*' (F10) points to the need for conceptual corruption models to include sustainability, leaning more on governance assessment frameworks (Alm 2019).

Procurement

Another of the themes concerned corruption in the lead-up to the SME taking place, particularly around construction and other contracts (Jennings 1996; Conn 2018), as *'criminals or administrators ...see an opportunity either to ...get a kickback, or cream something off the top'* (G4).

The risk of corruption around construction of stadia and procurement was considered across all groups, as *'of course there's enormous amounts of construction happening around these events, and that's an area that's notorious for more corruption as well. And graft'* (F5), and is less well-covered in the sport than in the general corruption literature.

The ABC specialist group provided a range of solutions to the concession contract problem, mirroring agency theory (Mason, Thibault, and Misener 2006). Some have already been covered in the governance section above, including treating the ISGB/SGB leading the SME as *'a government organisation'* (F3), or transparency in the form of *'an open ... regular procurement process where multiple companies submit bids through some sort of online procurement portal ...that's blind as to who the participants are'* (F3).

Other examples included *'demonstrable compliance ...– supplier checks – mystery shopping'* (F18), and other forms of hierarchical and supervisory accountability (Pielke 2013) to prevent abuse of power (Kihl 2018).

Finally, there were some links to discretionary powers, an element of both the Philippou (2019) framework and the Klitgaard (1998) corruption equation, with one participant stating that *'as soon as you have a decision-making power you are potentially at the risk of that person can definitely take a kick-back'* (F17). This is not amply covered in the literature beyond match-fixing (Manoli, Antonopoulos, and Bairner 2019, Hill 2016), and is therefore ripe for further research.

Another theme often coded in relation to SME corruption is ticketing (Conn 2018), which was raised primarily by the governance officials group, mainly as an aside, such as alluding to it in a list of general problems faced in organising SMEs, including *'counterfeiting, merchandise, tickets'* (G4). This has also been found at league level (Manoli, Antonopoulos, and Levi 2016).

In relation to the event itself, similar issues to procurement arose in relation to sponsors and advertising by the ABC specialist group: *'I've never understood why all these state-owned enterprises seem to get the advertising at all the big sporting events, well I do understand why ...and I think there's a myriad of issues.'* (F8). This mirrors the corruption concerns raised by Kulczycki and Koenigstorfer (2016) on attitudes of host nations, resulting from conflicts of interest and social networks (Kihl 2018).

On-field competition

Concerning the SME itself, athletes were the stakeholders discussed by all groups, albeit in slightly different ways. ABC specialists focused on their involvement in governance, reflected in Gardiner's (2018) model:

> Being a good sportsperson doesn't make you necessarily the right person to be running a major international organisation ...so if you've got the wrong people in positions of power it doesn't really matter what your governance structures are going to look like, you're going to end up with problems. (F11)

Conversely, governance officials and other stakeholders concentrated on on-field corruption (Maennig 2005) involving athletes within the penumbra of uncertainty in Gardiner's (2018) corruption model. One such example was around bribery for personal advancement where '*you have it even in some countries, in Africa for example, players bribing the national coach to be part of the national team to get into the focus of Europe team clubs to have the chance for a career in Europe*' (G15). Another example of on-field corruption provided was '*doping*' (S4). Not only is doping considered a form of corruption (Brooks, Aleem, and Button 2013), but '*you could also put doping into the match-fixing category because clearly doping is there to try and gain an unfair advantage, and to try and get ahead, and again money is a big driver there…*' (G16), a view also in line with Gardiner's (2018) model.

Match-fixing was a theme involving few participants from each group, but it was not a much-discussed theme, despite its importance in the literature. This is probably as result of it being '*too expensive with major sporting events, you couldn't fix the World Cup final or something like this is just not possible*' (S5), or the high levels of scrutiny diminishing the probability of corruption (Klitgaard 1988) and therefore need for ABC.

However, match-fixing was often linked to unregulated gambling and corruption (McNamee 2013), as '*match fixing, manipulation of competitions, that's usually linked to corruption, sometimes blackmailing and other things, but usually it's linked to corruption connected with sports betting*' (G15). One solution to this problem is the idea of partnership or, as one official stated, '*you've got the betting operators, so you get them on board, people that monitor betting markets*' (G8).

Finally, the rules themselves need consideration as there have been allegations of rules manipulation by governing bodies (Donaghy 2010). This theme was only covered by a single participant, who nevertheless stated that '*bribery could potentially be for sporting benefits, so it could be for example, in relation to rules changes that might favour a country or a discipline or something like that*' (G1). This supports some of the issues around regulation and legislation raised by Thorpe (2014) and Næss (2019), and showcases how they could be applied within ABC policies.

Conclusion

Overall, despite diversity of roles and geographical location, there was a large amount of consistency on the perceived concerns and solutions for SGBs and ISGBs around SME corruption amongst the groups in this study, and most aligned with the conceptual literature. For most themes, all stakeholder groups provided a number of suggestions for addressing the issues through specific policies and recommendations for practical implementation, mirroring the literature.

Table 4 provides a summary of some of the key ABC themes covered, and solutions provided by participants.

Overall, the analysis highlighted that the perception of the issues were consistent across groups, and these also tied in with relevant literature on sport corruption (Maennig 2005; Masters 2015) and ABC (Philippou 2019). The most frequently coded themes related to governance of sports by SGBs and ISGBs (Pielke 2013), with problems of accountability (Kihl 2018), transparency (Chappelet 2011), and lack of compliance (Mason, Thibault, and Misener 2006) particularly common, in line with media reporting (Conn 2018; Jennings

Table 4. Proposed solutions for SME corruption.

Themes	Proposed solutions
Defining corruption within SMEs	–
Governance official involvement in SMEs: • Due diligence • Transparency	• Registers of interests/ gifts/ expenses • Independent third party oversight • Transparent bidding
Accountability: Networks	• Independent third party oversight • Conflicts of interest registers • Independent NEDs • External regulator
Accountability: Media	Public scrutiny
Accountability: Bidding process	• External bidding system • Clear bidding criteria • Independent third party oversight
Independence	Independent third party oversight
Economic rent	–
Monitoring	• Whistleblowing lines
Controls	• Transparent investigations
Enforcement	Cooperation with law enforcement
Legacy	Sustainability in legacy criteria
Procurement	• Transparency in procurement • Demonstrable compliance • Monitoring
Athlete involvement	–
Match-fixing	Work with betting companies

1996). This highlighted the key ABC issues in relation to SMEs but also how they tied into the current conceptual literature.

However, as shown in Table 4, there were solutions offered for SME corruption problems faced by SGBs and ISGBs looking to host SMEs, and forms part of the practical contributions of this paper. There are examples of positive change: the International Tennis Federation's independent body deals with corruption issues (ITIA), and FIFA's compliance handbook details numerous ABC measures (including some suggested in the interviews conducted for this study) for regional and national football associations to follow (FIFA 2020b). The suggested solutions to the various contextual SME corruption problems could be implemented by these and other ISGBs in the future.

There is, however, room to grow. Further research can be conducted around impediments and implementation of recommendations, whether culture or regulation (through stronger enforcement powers, independent monitoring, or a regulator) have the strongest effect on SME corruption, and how stakeholders outside the sport (fans, governments, and others) view and react to corruption surrounding SMEs. It is vital for the integrity of sport to ensure that the SMEs of the 2020s are less tarred by the brush of corruption than some of their predecessors.

Disclosure statement

No potential conflict of interest was reported by the author.

References

Albrecht, W. S., C. O. Albrecht, C. C. Albrecht, and Mark Zimbleman. 2018. *Fraud Examination*. 6th ed. Boston, MA: Cengage Learning.

Alm, Jens. 2019. *Sports Governance Observer 2019: An Assessment of Good Governance in Six International Sports Federations*. Aarhus C: Play the Game.

Ashforth, B. E., and Vikas Anand. 2003. "The Normalization of Corruption in Organizations." *Research in Organizational Behavior* 25: 1–52. doi:10.1016/S0191-3085(03)25001-2.

Becker, Gary. 1968. "Crime and Punishment: An Economic Approach." *Journal of Political Economy* 76 (2): 169–217. doi:10.1086/259394.

Bond, Alexander, Paul Widdop, and Daniel Parnell. 2019. "Topological Network Properties of the European Football Loan System." *European Sport Management Quarterly* 20 (5): 624–655. doi:10.1080/16184742.2019.1673460.

Braun, Virginia, and Victoria Clarke. 2006. "Using Thematic Analysis in Psychology." *Qualitative Research in Psychology* 3 (2): 77–101. doi:10.1191/1478088706qp063oa.

Brooks, Graham, Azeem Aleem, and Mark Button. 2013. *Fraud, Corruption and Sport, Global Culture and Sport*. Basingstoke: Palgrave Macmillan.

Bruinsma, Gerben, and Wim Bernasco. 2004. "Criminal Groups and Transnational Illegal Markets." *Crime, Law & Social Change* 41 (1): 79–94. doi:10.1023/B:CRIS.0000015283.13923.aa.

Chadwick, S., Samantha Roberts, and R. Cowley. 2018. "The Impact of Sports Corruption on Organisational Stakeholders." In *Corruption in Sport: Causes, Consequences, and Reform*, edited by Lisa A. Kihl, 110–125. Abingdon, Oxon: Routledge.

Chadwick, Simon, Paul Widdop, and Nicholas Burton. 2020. "Soft Power Sports Sponsorship – a Social Network Analysis of a New Sponsorship Form." *Journal of Political Marketing* 1–22. doi:10.1080/15377857.2020.1723781.

Chappelet, Jean-Loup. 2011. "Towards Better Olympic Accountability." *Sport in Society* 14 (3): 319–331. doi:10.1080/17430437.2011.557268.

Chappelet, Jean-Loup, and M. Mrkonjic. 2013. Existing Governance Principles in Sport: A Review of the Published Literature. *Action for good governance in international sports organisations*. Danish Institute for Sports Studies.

Conn, D. 2018. *The Fall of the House of FIFA*. London: Yellow Jersey Press.

Croall, Hazel. 2004. "Combating Financial Crime: regulatory versus Crime Control Approaches." *Journal of Financial Crime* 11 (1): 45–55. doi:10.1108/13590790410809031.

Crouch, Mira, and Heather McKenzie. 2006. "The Logic of Small Samples in Interview-Based Qualitative Research." *Social Science Information* 45 (4): 483–499. doi:10.1177/0539018406069584.

Den Nieuwenboer, N. A., and Muel Kaptein. 2008. "Spiraling down into Corruption: A Dynamic Analysis of the Social Identity Processes That Cause Corruption in Organizations to Grow." *Journal of Business Ethics* 83 (2): 133–146. doi:10.1007/s10551-007-9617-8.

Donaghy, Tim. 2010. *Personal Foul: A First-Person account of the Scandal That Rocked the NBA*. Covington, KY: Clerisy Press.

Erickson, Kelsey, Laurie Patterson, and Susan Backhouse. 2019. "The Process Isn't a Case of Report It and Stop": Athletes' Lived Experience of Whistleblowing on Doping in Sport." *Sport Management Review* 22 (5): 724–735. doi:10.1016/j.smr.2018.12.001.

FIFA. 2020a. *Annual Report 2019*. Zurich: FIFA.

FIFA. 2020b. "Compliance Handbook." https://digitalhub.fifa.com/m/4a1daee06e72f0c6/original/lp015yxfdqesvrleo6ii-pdf.pdf

Gardiner, Simon. 2018. "Concptualising Corruption in Sport." In *Corruption in Sport: Causes, Consequences, and Reform*, edited by Lisa A. Kihl, 10–29. Abingdon, Oxon: Routledge.

Gardiner, Simon, Jim Parry, and Simon Robinson. 2017. "Integrity and the Corruption Debate in Sport: where is the Integrity?" *European Sport Management Quarterly* 17 (1): 6–23. doi:10.1080/16184742.2016.1259246.

Geeraert, Arnout. 2016. "Indicators and Benchmarking Tools for Sports Governance." In *Global Corruption Report: Sport*, edited by Transparency International, 76–84. Abingdon, Oxon: Routledge.

Geeraert, A., M. Mrkonjic, and Jean-Loup Chappelet. 2015. "A Rationalist Perspective on the Autonomy of International Sport Governing Bodies: Towards a Pragmatic Autonomy in the Steering of Sports." *International Journal of Sport Policy and Politics* 7 (4): 473–488. doi:10.1080/19406940.2014.925953.

Gorse, S., and S. Chadwick. 2010. "CONCEPTUALISING Corruption in Sport: Implications for Sponsorship Programmes." *The European Business Review* 4: 40–45.

Guest, Greg, Arwen Bunce, and Laura Johnson. 2006. "How Many Interviews Are Enough? An Experiment with Data Saturation and Variability." *Field Methods* 18 (1): 59–82. doi:10.1177/1525822X05279903.

Hill, D. 2016. "Why Sport is Losing the War to Match-Fixers." In *Global Corruption Report: Sport*. Transparency International.

Hölzen, Martin, and Henk Erik Meier. 2019. "Do Football Consumers Care about Sport Governance? An Analysis of Social Media Responses to the Recent FIFA Scandal." *Journal of Global Sport Management* 4 (1): 97–120. doi:10.1080/24704067.2018.1432983.

IOC. 2020. "IOC Annual Report 2019." IOC.

Ionescu, Luminita. 2015. "The Economics of Corruption in Professional Sport." *Economics, Management, and Financial Markets* 10 (2): 109–114.

ITIA. 2021. "International Tennis Integrity Agency." Accessed February 17, 2021. https://itia.tennis/.

Jennings, Andrew. 1996. *The New Lords of the Rings: Olympic Corruption and How to Buy Gold Medals*. New York, NY: Pocket Books.

Kihl, Lisa. 2018. "Individual and Group Explanations of Sport Corruption." In *Corruption in Sport: Causes, Consequences, and Reform*, edited by Lisa A. Kihl, 30–44. Abingdon, Oxon: Routledge.

Klitgaard, Robert. 1988. *Controlling Corruption*: Berkeley, CA; London: University of California.

Klitgaard, Robert. 1998. "International Cooperation against Corruption." *Finance and Development* 35 (1): 3–6.

Kulczycki, Wojciech, and Joerg Koenigstorfer. 2016. "Why Sponsors Should Worry about Corruption as a Mega Sport Event Syndrome." *European Sport Management Quarterly* 16 (5): 545–574. doi:10.1080/16184742.2016.1188839.

Lipicer, Simona, and Damjan Lajh. 2013. "Monitoring Systems of Governance in Sport: Looking for Best Practices from the European Union and beyond." *Kinesiologia Slovenica* 19 (3): 43–59.

Maennig, Wolfgang. 2005. "Corruption in International Sports and Sport Management: Forms, Tendencies, Extent and Countermeasures." *European Sport Management Quarterly* 5 (2): 187–225. doi:10.1080/16184740500188821.

Manoli, Argyro Elisavet, Georgios A. Antonopoulos, and Alan Bairner. 2019. "The Inevitability of Corruption in Greek Football." *Soccer & Society* 20 (2): 199–215. doi:10.1080/14660970.2017.1302936.

Manoli, Argyro Elisavet, Georgios A. Antonopoulos, and Michael Levi. 2016. "Football Clubs and Financial Crimes in Greece." *Journal of Financial Crime* 23 (3): 559–573. doi:10.1108/JFC-06-2015-0030.

Mason, Daniel S., Lucie Thibault, and Laura Misener. 2006. "An Agency Theory Perspective on Corruption in Sport: The Case of the International Olympic Committee." *Journal of Sport Management* 20 (1): 52–73. doi:10.1123/jsm.20.1.52.

Masters, Adam. 2015. "Corruption in Sport: From the Playing Field to the Field of Policy." *Policy and Society* 34 (2): 111–123. doi:10.1016/j.polsoc.2015.04.002.

McNamee, Mike. 2013. "The Integrity of Sport: Unregulated Gambling, Match Fixing and Corruption." *Sport, Ethics & Philosophy* 7 (2): 173–174. doi:10.1080/17511321.2013.791159.

McNamee, M. J., and Scott Fleming. 2007. "Ethics Audits and Corporate Governance: The Case of Public Sector Sports Organizations." *Journal of Business Ethics* 73 (4): 425–437. doi:10.1007/s10551-006-9216-0.

Næss, Hans Erik. 2019. "Good Intentions, Vague Policies: A Thematic Analysis of Recommendations by the United Nations, the European Commission and the OECD on Sporting Events and Human Rights." *Journal of Global Sport Management* 4 (1): 25–37. doi:10.1080/24704067.2018.1531245.

Nichols, P. M. 2012. "The Psychic Costs of Violating Corruption Laws." *Vanderbilt Journal of Transnational Law* 45 (1): 145–210.

Numerato, Dino. 2009. "The Media and Sports Corruption: An Outline of Sociological Understanding." *International Journal of Sport Communication* 2 (3): 261–273. doi:10.1123/ijsc.2.3.261.

Onwumechili, Chuka. 2018. "Nigerian Football: A Case of Social Media and Sport Insider Information." *Soccer & Society* 19 (7): 1038.

Philippou, Christina. 2019. "Towards a Unified Framework for anti-Bribery in Sport Governance." *International Journal of Disclosure and Governance* 16 (2–3): 83–99. doi:10.1057/s41310-019-00058-w.

Philippou, Christina, and Tony Hines. 2021. "Anti-Bribery and Corruption Policies in International Sports Governing Bodies." *Frontiers in Sports and Active Living* 3 (93): 649889. doi:10.3389/fspor.2021.649889.

Pielke, Roger.Jr. 2013. "How Can FIFA Be Held Accountable?" *Sport Management Review* 16 (3): 255–267. doi:10.1016/j.smr.2012.12.007.

Robson, Colin, and Kieran McCartan. 2016. *Real World Research: A Resource for Users of Social Research Methods in Applied Settings*. 4th ed. Chichester, UK: Wiley.

Rose, Jonathan. 2017. "The Meaning of Corruption: Testing the Coherence and Adequacy of Corruption Definitions." *Public Integrity* 20 (3): 214–220. doi:10.1080/10999922.2017.1397999.

Rose-Ackerman, Susan. 1999. *Corruption and Government: causes, Consequences, and Reform*: Cambridge: Cambridge Unversity Press.

Rushden, Max, Philippe Auclair, and Tariq Panja. 2021. *The Psychology of Doping and Whistleblowing in Sport with Dr Kelsey Erickson*, edited by Joel Grove. The Guardian.

Schuchter, Alexander, and Michael Levi. 2016. "The Fraud Triangle Revisited." *Security Journal* 29 (2): 107–121. doi:10.1057/sj.2013.1.

Smit, Barbara. 2006. *Pitch Invasion: Three Stripes, Two Brothers, One Feud: Adidas and the Making of Modern Sport*. London, England: Allen Lane, Penguin Group.

Spivey, Nigel. 2012. *The Ancient Olympics*. Oxford, UK: Oxford University Press.

Sugden, John, and Alan Tomlinson. 2017. *Football, Corruption and Lies: revisiting "Badfellas," the Book FIFA Tried to Ban*. Abingdon, Oxon: Routledge, Taylor & Francis Group.

Thorpe, David. 2014. "The Efficacy (and Otherwise) of the 'New' Sport anti-Corruption Legislation." *Victoria University Law and Justice Journal* 4 (1): 102–116. doi:10.15209/vulj.v4i1.55.

Tighe, Mark, and Paul Rowan. 2020. *Champagne Football*. UK: Penguin Random House.

Transparency International. 2016. *Global Corruption Report: Sport*, edited by Gareth Sweeney. Abingdon, Oxon: Routledge.

Transparency International. 2017. "Anti-corruption Glossary." Accessed July 26, 2017. https://www.transparency.org/glossary/term/bribery.

Youd, Kate. 2014. "Winter's Tale of Corruption: The 2022 FIFA World Cup in Qatar, the Impending Shift to Winter, and Potential Legal Actions against FIFA, The [comments]." In, 167.

Uniting, disuniting and reuniting: towards a 'United' 2026

Nicholas Wise and Jan Andre Lee Ludvigsen

ABSTRACT
Co-hosting mega-events is not a new concept. It has been viewed as a strategic endeavour among nations to not only ease the cost of hosting, but to work on multi-national collaborations that go beyond underlying political and economic agreements. United 2026 is a successful FIFA World Cup bid led by the United States to co-host the event with Canada and Mexico. This commentary offers a cultural and political geographical discussion of this bid and the future mega-event. Some of the governance challenges include critically discussing the uniting of these three nations (based on the role of NAFTA and neoliberalism), contested points of disuniting (through the rise of right-wing political movements) through to an intended reuniting (through a shared mega-event hosting). This political and cultural journey of working towards a United 2026 event began in the early-1990s with the NAFTA agreement initially negotiated by George H.W. Bush and signed by Bill Clinton (as the economic binding of the USA, Canada and Mexico) through to Donald Trump's threats of a US withdrawal and what would ultimately be renegotiated as the new USMCA Agreement. This context provides some geographical/geo-political underpinnings for understanding the potential and perceived governance of a United 2026, following the longitudinal political history of uniting, disuniting and reuniting. With the geopolitical climate in North America, a united effort is (somewhat) contradictory to the apartness that framed the recent relationship between the USA and Mexico in the past years. But alternatively, a co-hosting approach can be viewed as working towards a new North American togetherness, at least in the sense of an event spectacle and imaginary. From a political geography standpoint, power relations will likely exist in a matter similar to that of NAFTA, but as events are promotion oriented opposed to production focused, it is expected that a newfound cultural connection could emerge amid evolving political disruptions using sport as a cultural driver.

Introduction

On 13 June 2018 it was announced that the hosting rights for the 2026 FIFA men's World Cup were awarded to the Canada, Mexico and the United States. In the FIFA congress, the bid – promoted as 'United 2026' – received 134 votes, whereas the other bid by Morocco, received 65 votes (The Guardian 2018). The successful bid has, indeed, already revealed a political and cultural frame attached to it. The now former US President, Donald Trump, known for relying on 'Twitter-diplomacy' (Panke and Petersohn 2017), endorsed the United 2026 bid and tweeted the following on 27 April 2018: 'It would be a shame if countries that we always support were to lobby against the U.S. bid. Why should we be supporting these countries when they don't support us (including at the United Nations)?' (quoted in The Independent 2018). Meanwhile, reacting to the successful bid in June 2018, United States Soccer Federation President, Carlos Cordeiro, declared that: 'Football is the only victor. We are all united in football' (quoted in BBC 2018).

The two Tweeted perspectives showcase the complexities of being 'United'. Corderio considers the unitedness of sport, which is widely acknowledged (e.g. Dolan and Connolly 2016; Ein 2018), whereas Trump's quote seems to position the bid as being a 'US bid', that needed support, opposed to identifying the bid as a united one with its neighbours to the north and south. While it is beyond this paper to debate perspectives of Tweets, these do set the tone of the paper given the geo-political complexities of uniting, disuniting and reuniting that US, Canada and Mexico in the past three decades. As such, we look at how this may impact a United 2026 hosting amid debates and new agreements.

Ultimately, what is unique about this hosting from a sport and events perspective is that this will be the first time that a World Cup is hosted by more than two countries. United 2026 will be the third time Mexico hosts a World Cup (having previously hosted the tournament in 1970 and 1986) and the second time for the US (having previously hosted the 1994 World Cup). Meanwhile, it is the first time Canada hosts the men's World Cup. Moreover, United 2026 will be the first World Cup for which 48 teams will qualify. In terms of the assigned games, at the time of writing, the US will stage 60 matches (including the final), Canada ten and Mexico ten. The mega-event is therefore marked by an inherent novelty in its tournament and geographical formats, making it an important case study for scholarly investigation.

Sport, geography and the history/politics of co-hosting mega-events

Since the work by published by Wagner (1981) and Bale (2003), there is an ever-growing and expanding focus on sport research that considers critical geographical perspectives (see Koch 2017; Wise 2015; Wise and Kohe 2020). Research on 'sport' and 'politics' has been addressed for some time (Vinokur 1988) and has a dedicated journal to the thematic area: *Journal of Sport Policy and Politics*. The scope of research on sport with a dedicated political geography has considered contested geo-political spaces (e.g. Shobe 2008), urban cultural realms (e.g. Sam and Hughson 2010), scale (e.g. Harris and Wise 2011), nation building (e.g. Koch 2013), geographical imaginations (e.g. Shears and Fekete 2014), fandom identities (e.g. Lawrence 2016) to recent work on relocations (e.g. Wise and Kirby 2020) and national allegiances (e.g. Storey 2020), as some examples. From this base, as even more defined focus of literature that considers, sport, politics and events has also been addressed (see Conner 2014; Lee 2019; Overton, Murray, and Heitger 2013; Wise 2017; Wise and Harris 2019; Won and Chiu 2020), and is an area where more work needs considered even beyond this commentary that addresses the complexities and geo-political connections across future host-countries who united for a bid.

While work around this broader area has now been acknowledged, this section provides a socio-historical account of the co-hosting of mega-events. It will also unpack the politics of mega-events and co-hosting in the twenty-first century. As this commentary article argues, co-hosting must be critically approached as a strategic endeavour among nations to work on multi-national collaborations. Furthermore, the co-hosting of mega-events can also be seen in light of the enormous costs and organizational demands that are related to mega-event hosting, as captured by Müller's (2015) 'mega-event syndrome', which explains why mega-event planning rarely proceeds as planned. Co-hosting therefore allows nations and cities to bid for (and potentially win) hosting rights and thereby stage events, though at a lower cost and with less responsibilities than by acting as a single host.

In order to fully understand co-hosting, it is first necessary to contextualize the socio-political realities of mega-events within broader globalization discourses. For Roche (2000), mega-event hosting rights have, since the late nineteenth century, been pursued by cities or regions. Cities or countries, attracted by mega-events' global media coverage, have thereby sought to exhibit their cultural attributes and identities on a global scene. Simultaneously, mega-events have worked as vessels that push economic impacts, flows of investment and tourism. Furthermore, Roche (2000) argues that mega-events, historically and presently, are used on the international scene to promote dominant ideologies and to present global images of progress. It is also clear that, mega-events are staged for leaving a set of what broadly is defined as post-event legacies (Preuss 2007). This gives insight into the multi-faceted nature and origins of mega-events.

More recently, scholars have examined how sport mega-events are used as tools for 'soft power' and brand building (Brannagan and Giulianotti 2015; Chadwick, Widdop, and Burton 2020). In the realm of international politics, 'soft power', coined by Joseph Nye, refers to the 'ability to get what you want through attraction rather than coercion or payments' (Nye 2004, 256). 'Soft power' has subsequently been used to make sense of recent mega-events, including the 2006 FIFA World Cup, London 2012 Olympics (Grix and Houlihan 2014) and Qatar's 2022 World Cup (Brannagan and Giulianotti 2015; Rookwood 2019). In this context, Brannagan and Giulianotti (2015, 705) also introduce the concept of 'glocal consciousness'. This explains,

> [H]ow nation-states imagine themselves within the global context and position themselves vis-à-vis processes of globalization. Glocal consciousness underpins, for example, how national governments engage with global sport, most obviously when bidding to host sport mega events such as the FIFA World Cup or Olympic Games. Such events provide host cities and nations with exceptional opportunities to construct new, authorised brand identities before both their own citizens and global audiences (ibid.)

Additionally, sport mega-events can enable governmental and nongovernmental diplomacy in the pre-bidding and event planning (Lee 2019). Further, mega-events' security operations require significant transnational efforts and knowledge exchange (Klauser 2011; Ludvigsen 2019). Thus, it is prudent to argue that sport mega-event hosting is 'never only about sports (Kowalska 2017, 81) and that '[g]lobal sport mega-events and world politics often intersect' (Lee 2019, 2). Broadly, mega-events can work as 'means of improving a nation's image, credibility, stature, economic competitiveness and (they hope) ability to exercise agency on the international stage' (Grix and Lee 2013, 522). As such, mega-event bidding and hosting are commonly tied firmly to economic ambitions and neoliberal processes (Andrews and Silk 2012). These processes are also highly politicized since mega-events can work as a political tool or strategy for nation states in the international system (Brannagan and Giulianotti 2015; Grix and Houlihan 2014; Grix and Lee 2013). The intersection between mega-events and international politics remains highly integral as our paper proceeds to examine the politics and history of co-hosting.

Traditionally, mega-events have been hosted by one country (i.e. in the case of football World Cups or European Championships) or one city (most common for the Olympic Games). However, since the turn of the millennium, it has become increasingly usual that two nations – often sharing borders or located in close geographic proximity to each other – have co-hosted events. This means that the relevant event's hosting rights are shared between a set of nations. In 2000, the European Championship (Euro 2000) in men's football was co-hosted by Belgium and the Netherlands (Stott 2003). Two years later, the 2002 Men's World Cup was the 'the first ever to [...] be co-hosted by two countries' (Horne and Manzenreiter 2004, 187) when South Korea and Japan shared the historical event's hosting rights. To date, this is also the only FIFA World Cup that has been staged in more than one country.

Six years later, Euro 2008 was co-hosted by Switzerland and Austria (Klauser 2011) whereas Poland and Ukraine hosted Euro 2012 together (Kowalska 2017). Notwithstanding, the meaning of 'co-hosting' took another turn when UEFA announced in 2012 that Euro 2020 would be hosted by no less than 12 co-hosting countries spread across the European continent (Ludvigsen 2019). Euro 2020, which was postponed for 12 months in light of the global COVID-19 pandemic (Parnell et al. 2020), clearly had a political frame attached to it. It was branded as a 'Euro for Europe' and the official logo of the event consisted of European bridges that symbolically connected, or bridged, the European cities (UEFA 2016). In addition, there has been a number of unsuccessful bids from potential co-hosts. That includes 'Nordic 2008' (Denmark, Finland, Norway and Sweden's bid for Euro 2008) and Spain and Portugal's joint bid for the 2018 World Cup (BBC 2010).

An argument can be made maintaining that co-hosting of (or the plans/desire to co-host) mega-events has become a common and attractive concept in the realm of international sporting events in the twenty-first century. Yet, it still remains necessary to unpack in more detail exactly why nations may decide to co-host and how this links up to the aforementioned political or economic ambitions of mega-event staging. Additionally, co-hosting must not merely be seen as a process that occurs in the relatively short time period in which an event is actually staged; often between three weeks and a month. Co-hosting journeys begin years in advance and before an official bid for event hosting rights is formally submitted. We align some of these points here with evolving agreements between the US, Mexico and Canada, and with what happened between Japan and the Republic of Korea, we are perhaps reminded that what we are seeing unfold in not in fact new.

Co-hosting may be viewed in the context of a growing scepticism towards mega-event bidding and staging (Talbot 2021). This again is highly connected with the sheer economic cost of mega-events (Dowse and Fletcher 2018), their associated construction projects and the issue of 'white elephants' and stadia that are not sufficiently maintained post-event (Horne 2007). As Horne (2007, 91) writes, 'one of the persistent public concerns is whether [mega-event] monuments can turn into 'white elephants' and end up costing considerably more than they are worth'. This is something observed in both Brazil and South Africa where host cities saw venues constructed that had limited use after the event (see Maharaj 2015; Wise and Hall 2017).

Evidently, cost concerns have deterred some nations from entering the bidding stage for mega-event hosting rights. Oslo (Norway), for example, pulled out of a bid for the 2022 Winter Olympics following concerns over high costs, after the Norwegian government voted against providing IOC with the necessary guarantees (Reuters 2014). Meanwhile, whilst the aforementioned Euro 2020 was both praised and criticised for its novel format, the decision to award the event to 12 hosts was also related to the 'the difficulty of finding countries with about 12 stadiums capable of hosting a competition of this size, which involve 24 teams' (Parent and Chappelet 2015, 11). This again implies a lack of interested hosts and may reveal a wider trend. Thus, co-hosting becomes one way to be a mega-event host whilst concurrently sharing the associated costs and responsibilities in a time of growing scepticism towards, and interest in mega events and their hosting rights.

Furthermore, there are some clear cultural and political dimensions that are tightly knitted to co-hosting or co-hosting bids. Essentially, co-hosting can be seen as a vessel to improve – or at least convey images of improved international relations and unifying efforts. For example, in the context of the 2002 World Cup, it was argued that the decision to award the hosting rights to South Korea and Japan was complex and 'provoked the formation of a fragile alliance' between two nations that had an uneasy relationship 'still deeply tainted by memories of the Japanese annexation of the Korean peninsula in 1910 and the colonial oppression during greater part of the first half of the 20th century' (Horne and Manzenreiter 2004, 189). In this sense, Butler (2002, 55) contended that co-hosting 'encouraged the two countries to realise strengthened cultural ties' were necessary prior to the event.

Whereas this case demonstrates that a sense of collective connection or togetherness may have been worked towards, it also encapsulates how mega-event co-hosting – somewhat paradoxically – may take place amid uneasy, complex and tense international relations and geopolitical contexts (McLauchlan 2001). Against this backdrop, the concept of mega-event co-hosting raises a series of important questions in relation to the geographies and politics of mega-events. These speak, *inter alia*, to power relations and dynamics, unifying efforts and the broader political aims or ambitions that are pursued through the hosting of mega-events (Brannagan and Giulianotti 2015; Grix and Lee 2013).

Towards a United 2026

A number of these questions re-emerged on 13 June 2018. It was then officially announced by FIFA that Canada, the US and Mexico had won the rights to host the 2026 World Cup (BBC 2018). The North American 2026 World Cup will be the second time that a FIFA Men's World Cup is hosted in more than one country. Meanwhile, it is the first time that a World Cup will have more than two hosts and a 48-team format. Arguably, this highly politicized case provides an opportunity to critically examine the cultural, political and geographical aspects of the United 2026 bid and further, to produce an outlook of the forthcoming World Cup. Fundamentally, the World Cup, as a tournament, is one of the largest and most mediated mega-events worldwide and each edition is regarded as a global occasion (Horne and Manzenreiter 2004). United 2026 provides not only a completely novel context for this mega-event, but a context that requests further scholarly examination.

The shadow of the North American Free Trade Agreement (NAFTA) is perhaps the underlying geopolitical motivation for three nations endeavouring on a joint-bid to host one of the worlds most celebrated mega-events, the Men's FIFA World Cup. Some of the governance challenges include the complexities of NAFTA which was signed in the early-1990s, an agreement initially negotiated by George H.W. Bush and signed by Bill Clinton (as the economic binding of the USA, Canada and Mexico). As countries enter a joint bid or host venture, economic and political disputes are not uncommon, especially considering that Japan and South Korea entered talks over disagreements and disputes in 1998, just a few years prior to co-hosting FIFA 2002, but after the bid to co-host was successful. That joint bid was also forged in the political shadow of an agreement between the nations signed in 1965, knows as the Treaty on Basic Relations between Japan and the Republic of Korea. The mounting tensions in the lead up to the event (four year prior) saw a new Japan-South Korea Joint Declaration signed between the nations.

A similar story is unfolding between the US, Mexico and Canada here, as joint economic declarations that unite these nations have experienced turbulence. The making of the would-be NAFTA agreement is credited with discussions between the late US President George H. W. Bush and Mexico's president Carlos Salinas de Gortari. The late Ronald Regan, who preceded Bush as US President, had focused on an agreement with Canada entered into the Canada-United States Free Trade Agreement in 1988. As talks between the US and Mexico began shortly after the US and Canada agreement, Canada's then Prime Minister Brian Mulroney was concerned about what a US-Mexico agreement would do to the newly signed US-Canada agreement. So, Mulroney decided to seek involvement in the talks to consider the wider economic relations and impacts that would ultimately connect the three nations with the signing of NAFTA by Mulroney, Salinas and Bush and signed into law by Bill Clinton in December 1993.

The agreement would be the world's largest free trade agreement and would define the next wave of neoliberal ideology associated with economical liberalism and free-market capitalism. This agreement saw trade barriers and the ability to invest eliminated between the nations, and such a presence through economic liberalisation and mutual collaboration between nations led to a joint bid to host the FIFA 2026 World Cup, unveiled in April 2017 by the three nations football/soccer federations. Like the South Korea-Japan joint bid, a longstanding economic agreement in place for decades arguable cemented the desires to co-host, adding the element of spectacle to decades long agreements. Amid the geopolitical disruptions, sport and hosting did not absorb this narrative and instead focused on a new narrative of integration among nations for the good of promoting sport and concentrating efforts on play over politics (at least during the staging of the event).

Likewise, as we saw with Japan and the Republic of Korea, who won a joint hosting bid and then entered re-negotiations of their joint economic decelerations, the same narrative unfolded between the US, Mexico and Canada. NAFTA, which was widely criticized by then current US President Donald Trump, is no longer in effect following a renegotiating of the agreement's terms. Trump's election was seen as a pivotable transition point in the unmaking of a decades long NAFTA agreement as it stood. While the initial phases of NAFTA renegotiations were met with criticism and concern over the binding future of the agreement, this along with threats that the US would 'walk away' and the months in mid-2018 when the US and Mexico entered bilateral talks with Canada not at the negotiating table. Similar to Japan and the Republic of Korea in the years leading up to their joint hosting, the US, Mexico and Canada reached the United States–Mexico–Canada Agreement (USMCA) which would again cement the trilateral ties as of July 2020. The signing of the agreement between Trump, Mexico's President Enrique Peña Nieto and Canada's Prime Minister Justin Trudeau is the redefining of an agreement between the three nations that will set the tone in future elections in each country as abrupt change and uncertainty defines our contemporary times.

Future considerations

Free trade agreements are founded on neoliberalism, with agreements sought between nations to seek an economic advantage. Such agreements as we see in the examples in this paper, can set the precedence for co-bidding and ultimately co-hosting mega-events. However, unlike the agreements and renegotiated agreement between Japan and the Republic of Korea, tensions, uncertainty and rapidly evolving and changing politics are contesting agreements, almost on a day-by-day or week-by-week basis. With concerns (and sometimes fears) over disuniting and the impact and rise of right-wing political movements around the world, sport and the hosting of events can be, at least conceptually, observed as an intended reuniting of nations whereby sport is a cultural coalescent that can transcend contemporary politics. This political and cultural journey of working towards a 'United 2026' event began in the early-1990s with the NAFTA agreement initially negotiated by George H.W. Bush and signed by Bill Clinton (as the economic binding of the USA, Canada and Mexico). The politics and 'Twitter-diplomacy' of Donald Trump was seen as a potential disintegration of a new hosting union between the three nations. His threats of a US withdrawal, after a relatively short period of time would ultimately be renegotiated as the new USMCA Agreement.

It is too early to undertake a full empirical analysis of the impact of United 2026, but Beissel and Kohe (2020) have begun to look at how visions are a step towards shaping an event legacy. This commentary – with its background, discussion and future considerations – set some precedence and context for what will come in 2026 in the years leading up to and the realisation of this mega-event. This context provides some geographical/geo-political underpinnings for understanding the potential and perceived governance of a United 2026, following the longitudinal political history of uniting, disuniting and reuniting, which could be seen again before the event is hosted and will depend on the outcome of elections and political majority views in each nation. And so, the United 2026 case may demonstrate *exactly* why global mega-events and (geo)politics are so intertwined (Lee 2019; Rowe 2019) and why, as Rowe (2019) recently argued, there is a pressing need to persistently and critically examine sport mega-events academically.

Currently, given the geopolitical climate in North America, a united effort is (somewhat) contradictory to the apartness that framed the relationship between the USA and Mexico in recent years. But alternatively, a co-hosting approach can be viewed as working towards a new North American togetherness, at least in the sense of an event spectacle and imaginary if political agreements and disagreement were to arise again in the next 5 to 6 years. A key consideration is from a political geography standpoint, power relations will likely (and continue to) exist in a matter similar to that of NAFTA or USMCA, given the role of the US steering current agreement demands, and given in the event the US will host the vast majority of matches, including the finals. A key take-away here is whether uniting forged by events can be viewed as promotion oriented opposed to production focused. Therefore, one might expect a newfound cultural connection should emerge amid evolving political disruptions using sport as a cultural driver for uniting nations.

References

Andrews, D., and M. Silk, eds. 2012. *Sport and Neoliberalism: Politics, Consumption, and Culture*. Philadelphia: Temple University Press.

Bale, J. 2003. *Sports Geography*. London: Routledge.

BBC. 2010. "Spain-Portugal 2018 World Cup: Football, Sun and Fun." *BBC*. https://www.bbc.co.uk/news/world-europe-11890994.

BBC. 2018. "World Cup 2026: Canada, US & Mexico Joint Bid Wins Right to Host Tournament." *BBC*. https://www.bbc.co.uk/sport/football/44464913.

Beissel, A. S., and G. Z. Kohe. 2020. "United as one: the 2026 FIFA Men's World Cup hosting vision and the symbolic politics of legacy." *Managing Sport and Leisure*. https://doi.org/10.1080/23750472.2020.1846138.

Brannagan, P. M., and R. Giulianotti. 2015. "Soft Power and Soft Disempowerment: Qatar, Global Sport and Football's 2022 World Cup Finals." *Leisure Studies* 34 (6): 703–719. doi:10.1080/02614367.2014.964291.

Butler, O. 2002. "Getting the Games: Japan, South Korea and the co-Hosted World Cup." In *Japan, Korea and the 2002 World Cup*, edited by J. Horne and W. Manzenreiter, 43–55. London: Routledge.

Chadwick, S., P. Widdop, and N. Burton. 2020. "Soft Power Sports Sponsorship – A Social Network Analysis of a New Sponsorship Form." *Journal of Political Marketing* : 1–22. doi:10.1080/15377857.2020.1723781.

Conner, N. 2014. "Global Cultural Flows and the Routes of Identity: The Imagined Worlds of Celtic FC." *Social & Cultural Geography* 15 (5): 525–546. doi:10.1080/14649365.2014.908233.

Dolan, P., and J. Connolly. 2016. "Sport, Unity and Conflict: An Enduring Social Dynamic." *European Journal for Sport and Society* 13 (3): 189–196. doi:10.1080/16138171.2016.1229836.

Dowse, S., and T. Fletcher. 2018. "Sport Mega-Events, the 'Non-West' and the Ethics of Event Hosting." *Sport in Society* 21 (5): 745–761. doi:10.1080/17430437.2018.1401359.

Ein, M. 2018. "The Uniquely Unifying Power of Sports, and Why It Matters." *World Economic Forum*, February 9. https://www.weforum.org/agenda/2018/02/north-and-south-korea-have-shown-us-the-unifying-power-of-sport/.

Grix, J., and B. Houlihan. 2014. "Sports Mega Events as Part of a Nation's Soft Power Strategy: The Cases of Germany (2006) and the UK (2012)." *The British Journal of Politics and International Relations* 16 (4): 572–596. doi:10.1111/1467-856X.12017.

Grix, J., and D. Lee. 2013. "Soft Power, Sports Mega-Events and Emerging States: The Lure of the Politics of Attraction." *Global Society* 27 (4): 521–536. doi:10.1080/13600826.2013.827632.

Harris, J., and N. Wise. 2011. "Geographies of Scale in International Rugby Union – The Case of Argentina." *Geographical Research* 49 (4): 375–383. doi:10.1111/j.1745-5871.2011.00714.x.

Horne, J. 2007. "The Four 'Knowns' of Sports Mega-Events." *Leisure Studies* 26 (1): 81–96. doi:10.1080/02614360500504628.

Horne, J. D., and W. Manzenreiter. 2004. "Accounting for Mega-Events: forecast and Actual Impacts of the 2002 Football World Cup Finals on the Host Countries Japan/Korea." *International Review for the Sociology of Sport* 39 (2): 187–203. doi:10.1177/1012690204043462.

Klauser, F. 2011. "The Exemplification of 'Fan Zones' Mediating Mechanisms in the Reproduction of Best Practices for Security and Branding at Euro 2008." *Urban Studies* 48 (15): 3203–3219. doi:10.1177/0042098011422390.

Koch, N. 2013. "Sport and Soft Authoritarian Nation-Building." *Political Geography* 32: 42–51. doi:10.1016/j.polgeo.2012.11.006.

Koch, N., ed. 2017. *Critical Geographies of Sport: Space, Power and Sport in Global Perspective*. London: Routledge.

Kowalska, M. Z. 2017. *Urban Politics of a Sporting Mega Event: Legitimacy and Legacy of Euro 2012 in Anthropological Perspective*. Cham: Palgrave Macmillan.

Lawrence, S. 2016. "We Are the Boys from the Black Country'! (Re)Imagining Local, Regional and Spectator Identities through Fandom at Walsall Football Club." *Social & Cultural Geography* 17 (2): 282–299. doi:10.1080/14649365.2015.1059481.

Lee, J. W. 2019. "Olympic Ceremony and Diplomacy: South Korean, North Korean, and British Media Coverage of the 2018 Olympic Winter Games' Opening and Closing Ceremonies." *Communication & Sport* : 1–24. doi:10.1177/2167479519886544.

Ludvigsen, J. A. 2019. ""Continent-wide" sports spectacles: The "multiple host format" of Euro 2020 and United 2026 and its implications." *Journal of Convention & Event Tourism* 20(2): 163–181. doi:10.1080/15470148.2019.1589609.

Maharaj, B. 2015. "The Turn of the South? Social and Economic Impacts of Mega-Events in India, Brazil and South Africa." *Local Economy: The Journal of the Local Economy Policy Unit* 30 (8): 983–999. doi:10.1177/0269094215604318.

McLauchlan, A. 2001. "Korea/Japan or Japan/Korea? The Saga of Co-Hosting the 2002 Soccer World Cup." *Journal of Historical Sociology* 14 (4): 481–507.

Müller, M. 2015. "The Mega-Event Syndrome: Why so Much Goes Wrong in Mega-Event Planning and What to Do about It." *Journal of the American Planning Association* 81 (1): 6–17. doi:10.1080/01944363.2015.1038292.

Nye, J. S. 2004. "Soft Power and American Foreign Policy." *Political Science Quarterly* 119 (2): 255–270. doi:10.2307/20202345.

Overton, J., W. E. Murray, and J. Heitger. 2013. "Pass the Passport! Geographies of the Rugby World Cup 2011." *New Zealand Geographer* 69 (2): 94–107. doi:10.1111/nzg.12013.

Panke, D., and U. Petersohn. 2017. "President Donald J. Trump: An Agent of Norm Death?" *International Journal: Canada's Journal of Global Policy Analysis* 72 (4): 572–579. doi:10.1177/0020702017740159.

Parent, M. M., and J. L. Chappelet, eds. 2015. *Routledge Handbook of Sports Event Management*. London: Routledge.

Parnell, D., P. Widdop, A. Bond, and R. Wilson. 2020. "COVID-19, Networks and Sport." *Managing Sport and Leisure* : 1–7. doi:10.1080/23750472.2020.1750100.

Preuss, H. 2007. "The Conceptualisation and Measurement of Mega Sport Event Legacies." *Journal of Sport & Tourism* 12 (3-4): 207–228. doi:10.1080/14775080701736957.

Reuters. 2014. "Norway Withdraws Oslo Bid for 2022 Winter Games." Reuters. https://www.reuters.com/article/us-olympics-winter-norway/norway-withdraws-oslo-bid-for-2022-winter-games-idUSKCN0HQ4QE20141001.

Roche, M. 2000. *Mega-Events and Modernity: Olympics and Expos in the Growth of Global Culture*. London: Routledge.

Rookwood, J. 2019. "Access, Security and Diplomacy: Perceptions of Soft Power, Nation Branding and the Organisational Challenges Facing Qatar's 2022 FIFA World Cup." *Sport, Business and Management. An International Journal* 9 (1): 26–44. doi:10.1108/SBM-02-2018-0016.

Rowe, D. 2019. "The Worlds That Are Watching: Media, Politics, Diplomacy, and the 2018 PyeongChang Winter Olympics." *Communication & Sport* 7 (1): 3–22. doi:10.1177/2167479518804483.

Sam, M. P., and J. Hughson. 2010. "Sport in the City: Cultural and Political Connections." *Sport in Society* 13 (10): 1417–1422. doi:10.1080/17430437.2010.520933.

Shears, A., and E. Fekete. 2014. "Re-Constructing the Map: NBC's Geographic Imagination and the Opening Ceremony for the 2012 London Olympics." *Sociological Research Online* 19 (1): 121–128. http://www.socresonline.org.uk/19/1/7.html. doi:10.5153/sro.3249.

Shobe, H. 2008. "Football and the Politics of Place: Football Club Barcelona and Catalonia." *Journal of Cultural Geography* 25 (1): 87–105. doi:10.1080/08873630701822661.

Storey, D. 2020. "National Allegiance and Sporting Citizenship: Identity Choices of 'African' Footballers." *Sport in Society* 23 (1): 129–141. doi:10.1080/17430437.2018.1555228.

Stott, C. 2003. "Police Expectations and the Control of English Soccer Fans at 'Euro 2000.'" *Policing: An International Journal of Police Strategies & Management* 26 (4): 640–655. doi:10.1108/13639510310503550.

Talbot, A. 2021. "Talking about the 'Rotten Fruits' of Rio 2016: Framing Mega-Event Legacies." *International Review for the Sociology of Sport* 56 (1): 20–35. doi:10.1177/1012690219878842.

The Guardian. 2018. "US, Canada and Mexico Beat Morocco in Vote to Host 2026 World Cup." https://www.theguardian.com/football/2018/jun/13/world-cup-2026-vote-north-america-morocco.

The Independent. 2018. "Donald Trump Issues Warning to Other Countries over Voting against US 2026 World Cup Bid." *Independent*. https://www.independent.co.uk/sport/football/world-cup/donald-trump-twitter-tweets-world-cup-2026-bid-usa-morocco-date-announcement-a8324766.html.

UEFA. 2016. "EURO 2020 Logo Unveiled." UEFA. https://www.uefa.com/insideuefa/mediaservices/mediareleases/newsid=2406605.html?redirectFromOrg=true.

Vinokur, M. B. 1988. *More than a Game: Sports and Politics*. Westport, CT: Greenwood Press.

Wagner, P. 1981. "Sport: Culture and Geography." In *Space and Time in Geography*, edited by A. Pred, 85–108. Lund: Gleerup.

Wise, N. 2015. "Geographical Approaches and the Sociology of Sport." In *Routledge Handbook of the Sociology of Sport*, edited by R. Giulianotti, 142–152. London: Routledge.

Wise, N. 2017. "Rugby World Cup: New Directions or More of the Same?" *Sport in Society* 20 (3): 341–354. doi:10.1080/17430437.2015.1088717.

Wise, N., and G. Hall. 2017. "Transforming Brazil: Sporting Mega-Events, Tourism, Geography and the Need for Sustainable Regeneration in Host Cities." In *Sport, Events, Tourism and Regeneration*, edited by N. Wise and J. Harris, 24–39. London: Routledge.

Wise, N., and J. Harris. 2019. *Events, Places and Societies*. London: Routledge.

Wise, N., and S. Kirby. 2020. "A 'Home Away from Home': The (London) Jaguars and the NFL's Established International Presence—A Semi-Deterritorialization Approach." *Sport in Society* 23 (1): 72–87. doi:10.1080/17430437.2018.1555220.

Wise, N., and G. Kohe. 2020. "Sports Geography: New Approaches, Perspectives and Directions." *Sport in Society* 23 (1): 1–10. doi:10.1080/17430437.2018.1555209.

Won, D., and W. Chiu. 2020. "Politics, Place and Nation: Comparing the Hosting of Sport Events in Korea and Taiwan." *Sport in Society* 23 (1): 142–158. doi:10.1080/17430437.2018.1555911.

ə OPEN ACCESS

From sport-for-development to sports mega-events: conflict, authoritarian modernisation and statecraft in Azerbaijan

Joel Rookwood

ABSTRACT
Azerbaijan has considerable energy resources and exports oil across the world. Some of the resultant wealth has been reinvested, primarily centralised in Baku and concentrated on specific projects. This has shaped ambitious nation-building efforts including staging major events. Baku hosted the 2019 men's UEFA Europa League final and four UEFA Euro 2020 matches. This article analyses these sporting events in relation to Azerbaijan's political system, providing a lens through which Azerbaijani statecraft and authoritarian modernisation is examined. It also explores a 2004 sport-for-development project implemented 320 kilometres from Baku. This juxtaposition and frame of reference emphasises some key issues facing Azerbaijan and contextualises the subsequent modernisation and impact of hosting events. Data are examined from interviews conducted in 2004, 2019 and 2021 comprising international aid workers, civilians, translators and event spectators. This longitudinal study investigates Azerbaijan's political context and conflicts, sport-for-development, energy wealth, modernisation projects, sports event hosting and statecraft.

Introduction

The Republic of Azerbaijan is one of six independent Turkic states. It is located in the Caucasus, a geo-political region at the intersection of Europe and Asia, occupying an important geopolitical space as a land buffer between Russia and Iran. Azerbaijan was part of the Soviet Union but became independent in October 1991, shortly before the dissolution of the USSR. In 1993, Azerbaijan's president Abulfaz Elchibey was overthrown by a military insurrection. His successor Heydar Aliyev promised social order and territorial integrity, ruling the independent state for ten years. Shortly before his death, he appointed his son Ilham as his party's sole presidential candidate, who has served as president since 2003 (Sjoberg 2014). The country has been tainted by fraud, corruption, conflict and inequality (Öge 2014). It has also faced an ongoing nation-building dilemma, in search of a distinct national identity (Garagozov 2012).

This is an Open Access article distributed under the terms of the Creative Commons Attribution-NonCommercial-NoDerivatives License (http://creativecommons.org/licenses/by-nc-nd/4.0/), which permits non-commercial re-use, distribution, and reproduction in any medium, provided the original work is properly cited, and is not altered, transformed, or built upon in any way.

Azerbaijan has also experienced societal problems and ongoing political and militaristic struggles, involving multiple territorial disputes. The established pattern of antagonism between Azerbaijan and neighbouring Armenia in particular has fostered strained relations, notably regarding Nagorno-Karabakh (Cornell 2017). The struggle for the political and military control of this territory which lies within Azerbaijani borders came to define aspects of its national identity and remains heavily disputed (Askerov 2020). Beyond Baku, many Azerbaijani citizens have lived in relative poverty, whilst those residing in and near Nagorno-Karabakh have experienced sustained, fractious instability. Various international agencies have intervened, seeking to protect, relocate and promote the development of Azerbaijan's affected civilians. For instance, in 2004, an international, inter-agency programme was implemented aiming to support a rehoused community of approximately 10,000 internally displaced persons (IDPs). I worked on this project, which involved installing a playground facility and implementing a football initiative in a newly constructed IDP camp in Mingachevir, 320 kilometres from the capital.

During this period, the Azerbaijani state also engaged in extensive mining of its energy resources, as an oil boom in Azerbaijan-controlled areas of the Caspian Sea saw a notable upturn in state wealth. The transition to concentrated oil production yielded remarkable economic development. Azerbaijan's GDP growth rose sharply after 2004, reaching 34.6 per cent in 2006 – the highest in the world – before subsiding from 2008 (Kalyoncu, Gürsoy, and Göcen 2013). Whilst this energy wealth fostered dependency on and vulnerability to fluctuating oil prices (demonstrated during their collapse in 2015 and 2016), there has been considerable if selective investment in Azerbaijan since 2005, facilitated by the profits secured from the oil boom (Rojo-Labaien 2020). Under Ilham Aliyev's leadership, Baku commenced a process of grand modernisation and event hosting projects, symbolised by the iconic Flame Towers and the Chrystal Hall, the latter becoming the venue for the 2012 Eurovision Song Contest. Inspired notably by the examples of UAE and Qatar, Azerbaijan has undertaken considerable state sponsorship and investment in sport and related events. Between 2013 and 2015 'Azerbaijan: Land of Fire' (the country's adopted motto) was the shirt sponsor of Spanish football club Atlético Madrid, coinciding with the club securing the 2014 La Liga title. This agreement was financed by Hafiz Mammadov, an Azeri oligarch and founder of the energy, transportation and infrastructure company the Baghlan Group, who has close ties to the Azerbaijani government. The partnership was designed to strengthen the branding of the club and 'promote the image of Azerbaijan' as 'a tool to achieve important goals. In other words, it was about public diplomacy and soft power' (Krzyzaniak 2018, 504).

The co-existence of conflict and poverty within Azerbaijan's interior and the extensive modernising and state building projects and event hosting activities in the capital render this a significant case study of twenty-first century statecraft, and the associated role of sport. This research builds upon the empirical investigations of authoritarian states who have invested significant resources to stage sports events, published in the recent edited collection on 'Sport, Statehood and Transition'. This includes Horák's (2020) study of Turkmenistan, Rodríguez-Díaz's research on Belarus, and particularly Rojo-Labaien (2020) examination of Azerbaijan. This article investigates Azerbaijan's portfolio of hosting sporting events and its state-building initiatives. It also explores the preceding lived experience of an Azeri community subjected to poverty and conflict, providing a juxtaposing frame of reference. 11 semi-structured interviews were conducted (via translators when required) with international aid workers, civilians and translators during the IDP sport-for-development (SfD) project in 2004. Six further interviews were conducted with spectators who attended men's football events in Baku, namely the 2019 UEFA Europa League (UEL) final between Chelsea and Arsenal, and Wales' Euro 2020 matches against Switzerland and Turkey in 2021. Select extracts are presented here. The remainder of this article is structured around a political contextualisation of Azerbaijan, followed by an overview of the Nagorno-Karabakh conflict and an examination of the 2004 SfD programme in Mingachevir. The work then addresses Azerbaijan's energy wealth and key modernisation projects, before examining the state's event hosting profile and its use of sport in relation to statecraft.

The political context of Azerbaijan

Azerbaijan is a sovereign Eurasian state bordered by Russia, Georgia, Armenia, Turkey and Iran, with a 713-kilometre Caspian Sea coastline. The territory was under Iranian control until the Russo-Persian War of 1804–1813, before being ruled by the Russian Empire. In 1918 the Azerbaijan Democratic Republic proclaimed its independence, becoming the first secular democratic Muslim-majority state, but was incorporated into the Soviet Union in 1920 as the Azerbaijan Soviet Socialist Republic. The USSR was a centralised state that brought together multiple internal nationalities and ethnic groups under a common culture based on Marxism-Leninism (MacClancy 1996). Until 1991 it covered nearly one-sixth of the world's land surface, as the largest country on earth. More than 100 distinct nationalities lived within its borders, and its population numbered more than 290 million. The Soviet's strategic control of Azerbaijan was partly motivated by Azerbaijan's energy resources, which had seen it become one of the world's largest oil producers and a key provider for imperial Russia and the Soviet Union (Rojo-Labaien 2020). Economic stagnation, calls for reform and growing political unrest helped trigger a legislative conflict between the central Soviet government and several of its constituent republics in 1991, culminating in a declaration that the USSR no longer existed (Rodríguez-Díaz, Rookwood, and Rojo-Labaien 2020).

After the Cold War some former Soviet republics became part of the European Union and joined the NATO military alliance, others retained close links with Russia, forming part of newly formed multilateral organisations such as the Commonwealth of Independent States and the Eurasian Economic Community, in the interests of military and economic cooperation (Rojo-Labaien 2020). Some post-communist governments focused their national projects according to Western criteria, transferring the power of the state to the market and democratising their political system. Many former Soviet republics also moved to socialise citizens with a specific national identity, as statecraft rooted in society. The 1990s proved a challenging and transitional decade for these governments, attempting to direct their economy towards capitalism and their political system towards democracy (Chatzigianni 2018). For newly formed post-Communist states like Azerbaijan, the first decade following independence was marked by extensive political, social and economic challenges and the absence of established order, giving rise in the twenty-first century to an expansion of 'single pyramid' autarchic power structures (Hale 2012, 127).

In 1993 Azerbaijan's democratically elected president Abulfaz Elchibey was overthrown by a military insurrection and succeeded by Heydar Aliyev. This was the fifth change of leadership in the first two years of the fledgling state – in contrast to the stable albeit troubled political continuity experienced since (Rojo-Labaien 2020). Aliyev promised social order and territorial integrity, ruling for ten years before being succeeded by his son (Rasizade 2004). This transfer of power became the first top-level succession in the former Soviet Union (Sjoberg 2014). Ilham Aliyev has served as president since 2003, effectively eliminating all forms of pluralism. He was elected for a third term in 2018, allegedly receiving 86 per cent of votes, although Azerbaijan's electoral legitimacy and transparency has been questioned (Doyle 2019). The country has been tainted by various election frauds, rampant corruption, personality cults, ongoing conflict and economic inequality (Öge 2014). It also faces a persistent nation-building dilemma, in search of a national identity, in opposition to Armenia, aligned with Turkey and distinct from the politically articulated construct under the USSR (Garagozov 2012).

Azerbaijan is technically a secular country with a diverse ethnic composition, although approximately 97 per cent of the 10 million population identify as Muslim (Mammadov 2021). It also exports crude oil from the Caspian Sea to countries across the world, notably via the Baku-Tbilisi-Ceyhan (BTC) pipeline that connects to Turkey's Mediterranean port of Ceyhan. This 1,768-kilometre pipeline was completed in 2005 and runs via Georgia, rather than the more direct route through Armenia. This reflects the strained relations between Azerbaijan and Armenia (German and Bayramov 2019). The recent history and politics of these states are intricately linked, often centred on the Nagorno-Karabakh region and war which continues to overshadow both countries. Azerbaijan has experienced multiple territorial disputes throughout its short independence. The Azerbaijani Lezghins and Talyshs failed in their respective attempts to create independent countries (Ter-Abrahamian 2005), but the struggle for Nagorno-Karabakh defines aspects of Azerbaijan's national identity and international relations. Armenia also gained recognised independence in 1991. Unlike neighbouring Turkey, Iran and Azerbaijan however, Armenia is a Christian country, and international divisions are evident on ethno-religious as well as socio-cultural lines. The pattern of antagonism between Azerbaijan and Armenia is shaped by Nagorno-Karabakh, where territorial ethnic violence has caused widespread death and displacement, and political and military control remains heavily disputed (Askerov 2020).

'Descending into the third world': the Nagorno-Karabakh conflict and sport-for-development in Azerbaijan

The month before a SfD project was implemented for displaced Azeris from Nagorno-Karabakh in 2004, Rasizade published an article entitled 'Azerbaijan descending into the Third World after a decade of independence'. It references the 'non-petroleum anxieties of downtrodden masses… the pervasive bitterness and growing sense of deprivation that most citizens feel about their deteriorating lives', claiming 'Azerbaijan has been relegated to the category of a Third World nation… most Azeris live below the poverty line' (2004, 191). Azerbaijan's subsequent extensive if concentrated modernisation and its commitment to statecraft and international event hosting require contextualisation beyond beneficiaries in Baku. To that end, this section outlines the conflict, the affected IDP community and the SfD project.

Armenians suffered genocidal violence at the hands of the Ottoman Empire from 1915, with mass murder and ethnic cleansing resulting in approximately one million deaths (Kévorkian 2011), the recognition, impact, reparation and commemoration of which remains contested (Gzoyan and Galustyan 2021). For 36 days in 1918, Armenia and

Azerbaijan formed part of the short-lived Transcaucasian Democratic Federative Republic. Following its disintegration, Azerbaijan and Armenia both declared independence, laying claim to specific territories. Related disputes led to the Armenian-Azerbaijani War between 1918 and 1920, which concluded when both countries were annexed by the Soviet Union. During the majority of the Soviet period, relations remained generally peaceful (Broers 2021). In 1988, Armenians petitioned for 'miatsum', meaning unification and integration, as Armenians in Nagorno-Karabakh voted to secede and join Soviet Armenia. This resulted in pogroms, notably in Baku, Sumgait and Kirovabad (now Ganja). In the early 1990s, independent Armenia changed its stance, claiming the right of self-determination for Armenians in Nagorno-Karabakh (Askerov 2020).

The subsequent conflict escalated into full-scale warfare, producing more than 30,000 casualties and a million refugees and IDPs (Askerov 2020). After the dissolution of the Soviet Union, Azerbaijan gained internationally recognised territorial control of Nagorno-Karabakh according to the principle of international law known as *uti possidetis juris*, which preserves the boundaries of colonies emerging as independent states. This principle was developed to help avoid territorial disputes by establishing a new state's territorial heritage at the time of independence and transforming existing lines into internationally recognised borders (Shaw 1997). When Azerbaijan gained independence therefore, the boundaries it had within the Soviet Union became international borders. Armenians typically refer to the territory as Artsakh, usually preceded by 'the republic of' to infer its declared (but unrecognised) independence. It is technically an enclave within Azerbaijan, the only overland access to which is via the Lachin Corridor, a five-kilometre-wide mountain pass controlled by Russian peacemakers (Freizer 2014).

Askerov notes that 'Armenia and Azerbaijan have no diplomatic ties and continue to view each other as archenemies. The mediated talks… have not been successful, and many ceasefire violations have occurred in the conflict zone' (2020, 55). Thousands died and tens of thousands were displaced between September and November 2020 alone, and the Nagorno-Karabakh conflict remains ongoing at the time of writing (Open Society Foundations Armenia 2021). In 2020, ballistic missiles, drones and other heavy artillery were used, resulting in multiple civilian deaths and injuries. Hospitals, churches, kindergartens and schools were hit during the bombardment and missile attacks, which included the use of internationally banned cluster bombs (Amnesty International 2020). As a result of the intensive bombardment of Nagorno-Karabakh by the Azerbaijani armed forces, by October 2020 half of the Karabakh population, mainly women, children, and the elderly, had been displaced to Armenia, further exacerbating the humanitarian catastrophe caused by the COVID-19 pandemic in this region (Kazaryan et al. 2021).

Similarly, during the project in 2004 there were no diplomatic relations between Armenia and Azerbaijan, and Nagorno-Karabakh was disputed, despite international mediation efforts. Azerbaijan had therefore begun relocating ethnically Azeri communities, initially in temporary housing situated in existing Azerbaijani settlements. This included the approximately 10,000 IDPs who were moved to Mingachevir, then a city of 95,000 people located 40 kilometres from and equidistant between Georgia and Nagorno-Karabakh. An IDP can refer to a person who is forced to leave their home but who remains within their country's borders; technically, they continue under the protection of their government, even if that government is the reason for their displacement. IDPs are sometimes referred to as refugees, although they do not fall within the legal definition of a refugee as they do not cross international borders (Janmyr 2017).

Various non-governmental organisations (NGOs) have provided Azerbaijan's IDPs with humanitarian aid, shelter and social development programmes aiming to stabilise social order (Rookwood 2012). For instance, World Vision constructed 'temporary' IDP housing in Mingachevir in 2004. During this process, staff observed violence between locals and IDPs, partly fuelled by competition for resources. Many IDPs interviewed in 2004 were traumatised by the experience of living in and then being forced to leave Nagorno-Karabakh. One stated: 'We came from war, but it was home. We are desperate here. Azerbaijan is very poor. We have nothing.' World Vision partnered with Samaritan's Purse, who installed a playpark in the IDP camp, collaborating with local and IDP community members. Involving residents in such projects can help upskill those individuals, offering valuable experience, knowledge and an enhanced sense of purpose and confidence (Al Adem et al. 2018). Youth participation was encouraged as such groups can feel marginalised from development initiatives (Sommers 2003). The approach intended to promote social integration and cultural assimilation, although the activities this facility enabled could be framed more as 'play-for-development' (PfD) than SfD (Sterchele and Saint-Blancat 2015, 97). 'Playful' interactions can potentially help young people develop social, physical, cognitive, moral and emotional competencies (Lillard, Pinkham, and Smith 2011). This can positively affect self-esteem, self-worth and social integration, especially for those affected by conflict and discrimination (Hughes 2009). One resident said it was '…great to see children play together… in a park they have helped build. Makes them feel this is home.'

After the construction of the playpark at the IDP camp, a value-driven SfD football project was also implemented in a Mingachevir sports complex. Members of both communities were invited to participate in both initiatives. Cultivating shared and safe spaces can prove significant ingredients of effective SfD provision (Spaaij and Schulenkorf 2014). The local community leaders grouped the football players according to age and gender, but deliberately mixed them in terms of cultural background, in order to promote inter-community interaction (see Rookwood 2012). These community leaders helped oversee the promotion, registration and management of the programme and a subsequently established cross-community football project (Rookwood 2012). One of those interviewed stated: 'Football can bring people together and show these kids that we're all the same.' Numerous scholars have stressed the potential interpersonal benefits of SfD and PfD, such as promoting integration, community orientation and leadership skills (Stidder and Haasner 2007). Importantly, this depends on how such projects are devised, implemented, promoted and engaged in.

Several scholars have also critiqued such initiatives as top-down interventions informed by widespread but uncritical, under-researched ideas about the 'nature' of sport and its positive causal relationship with 'development'. The spectrum of impacts and interpretations of such sporting interactions can range from beneficial, inclusive engagement to potentially harmful activities that promote exclusion (Rookwood and Palmer 2011). The point here is not to overstate or even critique the approach, value and impact of such projects, but to outline that Azerbaijan in 2004 was a nation in which an ongoing conflict had caused deaths and displacement; that interventive humanitarian aid was deemed to be required, and development efforts were encouraged by government agencies. As one aid worker noted: 'Most of Azerbaijan is really poor. Some areas are pretty desperate. Meanwhile, they're drilling for oil in the Caspian Sea. This country is about to get rich, *really* rich. what happens with the money? Will it benefit Mingachevir, Karabakh? Or will it all just stay in Baku?'

Authoritarian modernisation and the formation of a petro-state

Azerbaijan's petroleum resources have strongly influenced its development. This is particularly the case post-2004, although the state's oil industry has a long history. The world's first oil-drilled well was constructed near Baku in 1848. Following independence in the 1990s, Azerbaijan's political leaders perceived the most viable means of building the economy to involve revitalising the petroleum industry, which had declined during the Soviet period. By the turn of the century, Azerbaijan produced almost half of the world's oil (Heradstveit 2001). The government and the Azerbaijan International Operating Consortium signed the first production-sharing agreement in 1994. By 2009, more than 25 such agreements had been undertaken to develop onshore and offshore oil and gas deposits (Guliyev 2009). The BTC and South Caucasus pipelines facilitated extensive profitability. With all contracts negotiated with the president, many governments and foreign companies afforded the enriched regime considerable legitimacy, allowing public support to be purchased, undermining civil society institutions (Ciarreta and Nasirov 2012). Increased oil production rendered the emerging petro-state one of the world's fastest growing economies by 2009. However, Azerbaijan's overreliance on a single resource highlighted its vulnerability to boom-and-bust cycles of oil prices (Rojo-Labaien 2020).

An influx of foreign capital into enlarged public sectors of an economy can develop state capacities, although with private businesses dependent on government contracts, in Azerbaijan these were distributed to regime collaborators in return for political loyalty and support (Bedford 2014). Crony capitalism flourished, as the system which can involve politicians distributing economic favours to their personal connections (Reinsberg, Kentikelenis, and Stubbs 2021). Azerbaijan's petroleum revenues have been used to undermine its democratic institutions and free market structures, protecting authoritarian rule whilst leading to considerable patronage spending. This system distributes rents from oil exports through a patronage network, ensuring the support of allies and clientelist groups (Guliyev 2009). Leaders of oil-abundant states often use mineral riches to prolong political regimes (Vasilyeva and Libman 2020), and in Azerbaijan: 'Since the parliament has only a marginal political and oversight role, the president faces no constraints in spending the country's national wealth… Personalistic regimes are not the best candidates for democratization' (Guliyev 2009, 4). Revenues were re-invested, primarily funding Baku's extravagant modernisation.

Oil and natural gas resources produced 75 per cent of Azerbaijan's state revenues and 50 per cent of its GDP, but the decline in oil prices from 2014 yielded a 100 per cent currency devaluation in 2015 (Khalilzada 2019). Industrialization was heavily concentrated in oil-related sectors as others remain under-developed. Likewise, with most of the energy-driven modernisation projects concentrated in Baku, much of the country's interior was marginalised in the process (Ibadoghlu 2019a). Various ambitious building projects were undertaken, symbolised by Baku's iconic Flame Towers and the $350 million Chrystal Hall, the latter becoming the venue for the 2012 Eurovision Song Contest. Some projects are yet to be realised, notably Azerbaijan Tower, a visionary skyscraper intended to be the tallest building on earth, at a projected height of 1,051 metres with 189 floors. Azerbaijan has prioritised sport event hosting, constructing various facilitates. Despite failed bids to host the 2016 and 2020 Olympiads, an 'Olympic Stadium' was constructed in Baku, providing the main venue for the 2015 European Games, and staging UEFA football matches in 2019 and 2021.

Some commentators frame Azerbaijan's stability and continuity as stagnation, others suggest there are signs of political modernisation (De Wall 2019). The president recently promoted a series of younger technocratic figures to his cabinet, and for the first time in twenty-five years, the country now has a prime minister, Ali Asadov. Yet what some consider steps towards progress, others frame as authoritarian modernisation (De Wall 2019). Attacks on democracy and liberty have strengthened Azerbaijan's oppressive political regime. Transparency International ranks the state 120th from 168 countries (Khalilzada 2019). It is also by far Europe's most restrictive country, with access to international broadcasting services strictly controlled. The 2021 Reporters Without Borders annual Press Freedom Index positioned Azerbaijan 167th from 180 countries globally. Kunti (2021) interviewed a Human Rights Watch representative, who stated: 'Almost a decade ago, Azerbaijan had one of the most vibrant civil societies in the region. It is almost completely decimated now. The laws it has adopted make the environment for NGOs restrictive. The country is closed for international scrutiny.' Furthermore: 'Azerbaijan has arrested government critics on various bogus and spurious charges. It has an issue of political prisoners. Freedom of expression, freedom of assembly, freedom of media, freedom of association – those are all rights that are routinely violated in the country.'

Sports mega-events in Baku

The staging, investment, participation and consumption of sports mega-events (SMEs) have become increasingly significant components of the economic, political and cultural landscape of countries across the world (Rookwood 2021). The specific status of SMEs is often determined by their prominent scale, dramatic character, periodicity and widespread importance (Roche 2003). Global interest and impacts can be conveyed through attendance figures, viewer ratings and lucrative commercial and broadcasting contracts, fuelled by mass media exposure and social media engagements (Rookwood 2019). Depending on existing infrastructure, hosting SMEs can incur extensive investment including sports stadia, training facilities, hotels and transportation networks. Political support for such expenditure can be influenced by popular perceptions of sport and engagement in major events. Hosting SMEs can showcase infrastructure, culture and heritage, promote trade and investment, and shape international perceptions. Often envisioned as vehicles for nation branding, public diplomacy and/or soft power, the unintended negative impacts of contemporary event hosting can instead prove disempowering. The range of such outcomes may depend on how such events are presented, received, engaged in and represented by mass media outlets and on social media (Rookwood and Adeosun 2021).

Increases in national levels of sports participation and elite performance, sustained usage of purpose-built facilities and infrastructural investments and enhanced trade are often emphasised as intended SME legacies (Horák 2020). Quantitative projections of such benefits can underestimate costs whilst overstating potential advantages. Determining the details of investments can also prove challenging, particularly in states that lack reliably transparent accountability mechanisms. According to Rojo-Labaien (2018) Baku's staging of the inaugural multi-sport European Games in 2015 incurred costs of $10 billion, with the opening and closing ceremonies alone costing a combined $235 million. By comparison, Belarus invested $180 million in hosting the 2019 European Games, for which its president was roundly criticized internationally (Rodríguez-Díaz 2020). Baku's sport facility construction included gymnastics, shooting and water sports centres. Azerbaijan also paid transportation and living expenses for the 6000 international athletes who competed from 50 European states. Azerbaijan's Ministry of Youth and Sports invested a further $1.2 billion hosting the fourth Islamic Solidarity Games in 2017 (Rojo-Labaien 2020).

Adopting Roche's framework, it is questionable whether such competitions constitute the status of 'mega-events'. However, Azerbaijan has also invested in high profile SMEs, staging the Formula One Grand Prix from 2016. Baku's Olympic Stadium has also hosted prestigious men's UEFA football events, namely the 2019 UEL final between Chelsea and Arsenal, and four Euro 2020 matches. The latter tournament was delayed until 2021 due to the COVID-19 pandemic, and restrictions were imposed on international visitors and stadium attendances, limiting prospects for impact and income generation. Such limitations affected most of the 11 eventual host cities of the collaboratively staged event, as well as other SMEs, notably the Tokyo Olympics in 2021 (Rookwood and Adeosun 2021). As examined in the next section, some scholars frame Baku's SME hosting profile in relation to statecraft, including attempts to acquire soft power and engage in sport diplomacy. Others highlight Azerbaijan's economic misappropriation, endemic corruption and low transparency and accountability standards; framing these events as attempts to whitewash a tarnished public image under the guise of modernisation by creating connections with global leaders in political, sporting and cultural spheres (Ibadoghlu 2019a). Reports of human rights violations continue to undermine diplomatic endeavours, revealing the absence of democratic processes in Azerbaijan (Rojo-Labaien 2020).

SOCAR (State Oil Company of the Azerbaijan Republic) was a major UEFA sponsor for eight years prior to Euro 2020. Azerbaijan had limited previous exposure in football and SOCAR had no track record of football sponsorship (Kunti 2021). SOCAR secured the UEFA contract in 2013, after the expanded, multi-city, transnational tournament format was announced in 2012. In 2014 Baku was declared one of the successful host city bids (Rojo-Labaien 2020). Under scrutiny from pressure groups, UEFA formalised specific human rights criteria for tournament host nations in 2017, but to be applicable only from Euro 2024 (Kunti 2021). Articles 1 and 2(a) of the UEFA Statutes emphasise UEFA's political and religious neutrality, promoting football in Europe in a 'spirit of peace, understanding and fair play, without any discrimination on account of politics, gender, religion, race or any other reason' (UEFA 2018, 1). Some Azerbaijani clubs and personnel have ignored such stated rules and principles. After September 2020, when a military offensive against Armenians in Nagorno-Karabakh was launched, war propaganda became a feature of matchdays and the social media output of some football clubs. Following a Europa League game against Legia Warsaw in October 2020, Azerbaijani champions FK Qarabağ posted a photograph of 27 players and staff giving a military salute with the national flag. Qarabağ's head of Public Relations Nurlan Ibrahimov also published a Facebook post calling for Armenian men, women and children to be killed. UEFA issued a warning to Qarabağ and a lifetime ban to Ibrahimov (O'Conner 2021).

Six football supporters were interviewed for this research following UEFA matches in Baku. This comprised four English attendees of the pre-pandemic 2019 UEL final and two

Welsh interviewees who travelled to Azerbaijan for the COVID-19 era Euro 2020 tournament. These were male supporters each with considerable experience of having attended at least 20 away matches in European football competitions and were selected from the author's networks. UEFA's inflexible policy of refusing to relocate finals when domestic rivals qualify drew criticism in the British media in 2019. The stadiums of Arsenal and Chelsea are 13 kilometres apart, but fans had to travel 4,653 kilometres to Baku for the final. However, as one fan said: 'It's happened before when we [Chelsea] played Man United in Moscow, and then Bayern Dortmund in 2013. The Madrid teams in 2014 too. That's a UEFA thing. But loads of preparation and money goes into these events. You can't just switch venues last minute.' Another respondent stated: 'You want finals in places fans can get to.' Criticism directed at UEFA for holding the contest in Baku, a city the same fan labelled as 'a bit isolated', might seem West-Eurocentric. However, of the 60 UEFA men's Champions League and Europa League finals since the rebranding of the European Cup (i.e. from 1992–2021), only five teams from Eastern Europe have reached a final, and nine of these contests have been staged in Eastern Europe.

Before the postponement of Euro 2020 and the replacement of some host cities partly due to the COVID-19 pandemic, 13 locations were originally selected to host matches from as many countries. Environmental groups were critical of this organisational model, and the extensive travel involved. A single attendance at all 36 group games would have yielded 13.3 tonnes of CO^2 from travel alone, the equivalent to charging 1.7 million smartphones (Croke 2020). The schedule of the Swiss team ultimately incurred the most travel in the tournament, totalling 21,226 kilometres. UEFA partnered with global sustainability solutions provider South Pole, prioritising smart mobility and flight carbon compensation by pledging to plant 50,000 trees in each host nation to offset the effects of the estimated 280,000 tonnes of CO^2 emitted during the tournament (Croke 2020). When asked about environmental issues in the context of Euro 2020 one fan responded: 'The ones who really have a problem with pollution probably just don't go. We didn't choose Baku, UEFA did… If the whole tournament was in Baku, they'd have built more stadiums which wouldn't be used after, like [2022 World Cup hosts] Qatar… Co-hosting makes sense for smaller countries like Azerbaijan… they could have shared it with Turkey.'

A more central concern for fans at the 2019 UEL final however was the infrastructure and accessibility of international transport. Baku's Heydar Aliyev Airport was declared inadequate to receive the number of visitors expected for major European finals (Rojo-Labaien 2020). Unable to source flights, many supporters returned tickets or declined opportunities to travel. The state of the stadium and pitch was criticised, whilst Arsenal's defeat was compounded by the absence of Henrikh Mkhitaryan, their playmaker and Armenian national team captain, who refused to travel to Baku despite Azerbaijani and UEFA authorities making assurances about his safety (Lawrence and Ingle 2019). As one supporter stated however, with 'Qarabağ, who Chelsea have played in the Champions League, and now Baku getting finals, it's put Azerbaijan on the map… I knew nothing about them before.' Another respondent declared: 'We heard horror stories about human rights and restrictions in Azerbaijan. Maybe they're true, who knows? But the locals were friendly, police were ok. It was Chelsea [fans] you had to watch out for!'

Both interviewees who travelled to Euro 2020 expressed perspectives relating to COVID-19. One participant stated: 'Going to Baku wasn't just the first time to Azerbaijan. It was the first time I'd left Wales in fifteen months… It was surreal. You couldn't really go anywhere in Baku, but it was great to get away.' Another Welsh supporter stated: 'Beating Turkey in Baku was immense. It was like a home game for them, as Azerbaijan and Turkey are like allies. But it wasn't really hostile, like Istanbul can be for football.' Wales' match against Switzerland had an attendance of 8,782 despite allowances for 31,000 spectators to attend Euro 2020 contests in Baku. The international media representation of the staging of matches in Azerbaijan focused primarily on attendances, accessibility and pandemic protocols. In other host cities coverage was partly consumed by controversies surrounding the Rainbow campaign and Black Lives Matters (BLM) protests. One supporter stated: 'The tournament will be remembered for COVID, but also the protests, and it kind of divided East and West. Fans in Hungary and Russia seemed to oppose the protests. Western Europe mostly supported them. Baku was a bit different.'

Exploring these particular host nations in such contexts yields useful insight into Azerbaijan's case. Russia decriminalised homosexuality in 2012 but passed a law in 2013 forbidding 'propaganda of non-traditional sexual relationships' among minors (Kondakov and Shtorn 2021, 38). Reports of extrajudicial arrests, torture and killings of gay men in Russia's Chechen republic drew international condemnations in 2017 (Scicchitano 2021), and in 2020 voters backed constitutional amendments stating marriage is only between a man and a woman (Kondakov and Shtorn 2021). In Hungary an 'Anti-Paedophilia Act' was passed during Euro 2020 outlawing the promotion of homosexuality to minors, which critics claim conflates homosexuality with paedophilia (März 2021). Rainbow flags and colours have become international symbols of support for discriminated LGBTQIA + communities. UEFA prohibited the Euro 2020 venue in Munich from being floodlit in rainbow colours, declaring that as a 'neutral' organisation it was obliged to decline such a 'political' request (Evans 2021). This inspired various protests from supporters at matches and on social media. Several sponsors utilised rainbow colours at contests in June to coincide with LGBTQIA + Pride Month. Some advertisers discontinued the approach at matches in July, but other companies including UEFA partner Volkswagen continued, in solidarity with affected communities and in light of the emerging opposition. UEFA declared its support for the 'display of such messages of tolerance and respect for diversity' but stated that it 'requires its sponsors to ensure that their artwork is compliant with local legislation' (ESPN 2021, no page). UEFA banned advertising using the LGBTQIA + rainbow colours at the quarter-final matches in Russia and Azerbaijan, citing local laws.

Marketing professionals have long realised the significance and psychology of colour in advertisements, and the rainbow colours effectively served as both a marketing tool and point of cultural divergence at Euro 2020 (see Melton and MacCharles 2021). Partner agreements and regulations are typically established well in advance of SMEs, but such events are usually simplified by confining them to one or two countries, thus imposing a fixed, consistent legal and cultural framework. Given the fluid pandemic context, the final list of eventual host cities was not confirmed until seven weeks before the tournament, which then took place across eleven diverse countries. The currency of Pride Month, the volume of support and opposition for expressions of LGBTQIA + rights, the associated politicisation and controversy, the involvement of multiple national partners, the development of and opposition to related legislation and the adoption of different positions and means of expression rendered this a complex and changeable situation. A supporter who attended matches in Baku stated:

'We didn't see or hear any problems. Azerbaijan's a Muslim country. A bit like going to Dubai, you know there's laws on homosexuality. It wasn't really talked about… If Baku had more games and more fans went it might have shined more of a spotlight on them. But all the noise was about Hungary because their fans were so vocal, and with their prime minister passing laws during the tournament, no one was talking about oppression in Azerbaijan.'

Revealing legislative detail and exposing the extent of such 'oppression' in Azerbaijan can prove challenging, especially for outsiders. Azerbaijan's government has waged an 'increasingly vicious crackdown on critics and dissenting voices. The space for independent activism, critical journalism, and opposition political activity has been virtually extinguished by the arrests and convictions of many activists, human rights defenders, and journalists, as well as by laws and regulations restricting the activities of independent groups and their ability to secure funding' (Human Rights Watch 2017, no page). Azerbaijan decriminalized same-sex conduct in 2000, but its police have since conducted a 'violent campaign, arresting and torturing men presumed to be gay or bisexual, as well as transgender women' (ibid). This report referrers to an Internal Affairs ministry spokesman who confirmed that police had detained 83 people 'who do not fit our nation, our state, our mentality', arguing that such responses were justified, citing 'citizens' concerns' and employing public health scare tactics, claiming some detainees tested positive for HIV and that the measures were to 'prevent dangerous contagious diseases from spreading' (ibid).

Euro 2020 also saw support for, disengagement from and opposition to athlete activism through the BLM protests. Some teams adopted a collective, consistent approach, communicating a rationale for players who decided to or refrained from 'taking the knee'. Other teams knelt but only before selected matches and warmups, or if their opponents did, or if they were requested to do so. Some players stood as teammates knelt with some spectacles descending into political incidents. One fan interviewed argued: 'It sent out mixed messages. A bit of a PR mess for some. It kind of diluted it… But you could tell which teams definitely supported [taking the knee] and who definitely weren't going to. The further east you went the less likely they'd kneel. Some fans booed it, especially in Eastern Europe.' England, Wales, Belgium and Denmark knelt before all of their matches. Italy, France, Spain, Sweden, Netherlands and Austria declined to do so or did so selectively. Hungary, Croatia, Russia, North Macedonia, Ukraine, Czech Republic, Poland and Slovakia did not kneel at all. Some of these teams, such as the Czechs, pointed to the UEFA 'Respect' inscription on their shirts instead, communicated as generic support for antidiscrimination. Others were more disparaging of the protests. Hungary's Prime Minister Viktor Orbán said the fight against racism 'has no place on a sports field', claiming 'it is not a solution' to impose a moral and historical 'burden' in a country like Hungary which 'has never been concerned with the slave trade', adding: 'If you are invited to a country, make the effort to understand its culture and do not provoke local residents' (Euronews 2021, no page). In keeping with such 'diplomacy', Hungary fans marched with an anti-kneeling banner and displayed such flags during matches. Some also booed players for kneeling, a response evident in other stadiums.

Wales beat Turkey in a crucial group game in Baku in front of more than 30,000 supporters. Relations between Turkey and Azerbaijan are often encapsulated by the term 'two states but one nation' (Beilinson 2019, 137), and a Welsh supporter interviewed stated: 'With so few Wales fans and Turkey being like brothers with Azerbaijan I was worried about it being hostile. But it was great. And both teams took the knee before the match. No sign of any racism like other host cities.' Azerbaijan and Romania were the only countries who hosted matches yet whose national teams failed to qualify, but as the same respondent argued: 'All the grounds mostly had fans from that country… with so many Azerbaijanis in the ground, they were on show, their attitudes. And they didn't boo the knee, or boo players like [Ethan] Ampadu… If I was black, I'd feel safer watching football in Baku than Budapest.' The extensive range of diverse tournament locations provided frames of reference for supporters and broadcasters, and the controversy surrounding some cities helped deflect criticism that may otherwise have been directed at other states. According to one interviewee: 'For tabloids and even TV, controversy sells. But no one was talking about Azerbaijan's human rights because fans and politicians in other countries were more interested or more against the rainbow and Black Lives Matter. Maybe Azerbaijan got lucky that countries like Hungary and Russia took the heat.'

Whilst this research gives voice to supporters who attended games in Baku, the perspectives of such a limited number of fans could not be considered necessarily representative of or generalisable to broader populations. Such inherent problems with qualitative methodologies can be mitigated to some degree by combining approaches with processes that facilitate a broader examination, namely search engine analysis. There is only space for brief consideration here. However, at the time of writing, Google searches for 'Euro 2020', 'Azerbaijan Euro 2020' and 'Baku Euro 2020' returned 1.8 billion, 60.4 million and 11.5 million hits respectively, reflecting significant tournament and national exposure; whereas such searches for 'Euro 2020 Azerbaijan corruption' and 'Azerbaijan Euro 2020 whitewashing' returned a respective 4.7 million and 312,000 hits. 'Euro 2020 take the knee' produced 119 million hits, whilst 'Euro 2020 Rainbow' and 'Hungary Euro 2020 Rainbow' returned 54.6 million and 7.8 million hits respectively, reflecting the contextual and political focus on the BLM and LGBTQIA + protests and controversies. This may only represent a brief and broad snapshot, but it does indicate the scale and relativity of popular emphasis.

Sport, statecraft and repression in Azerbaijan

For SME host nations, key objectives typically include staging safe, profitable, memorable and innovative events with sustainable outcomes and legacies which promote sport participation and performance, facilitating modernisation, trade, tourism and revenue growth (Rookwood 2021). However, as with the example of Turkmenistan examined by Horák (2020), Azerbaijan is a resource-rich, authoritarian state that focuses on nation-building, identity formation and other concerns of statecraft in this context. It could be argued that Azerbaijan prioritises domestic control and international influence over return on investment or sport development (Rodríguez-Díaz, Rookwood, and Rojo-Labaien 2020). Azerbaijan finished second in the medal table behind Russia at the 2015 European Games and has invested in its sports infrastructure, but is yet to construct a sustained, internationally renowned sporting culture. The global consumption of mass media coverage as well as social media engagements relating to SMEs can also shape international public opinion and acquisitions of soft power through nation branding and public diplomacy initiatives. In practice, rather than serving as neatly distinct constructs such notions can overlap and prove difficult to articulate, differentiate and measure, whilst attempts to use SMEs in such contexts can have different connotations domestically compared with attempts to exert international influence (Rookwood and Adeosun 2021).

The formation of modern political identities in the post-Soviet sphere is often connected to pursuits of global recognition, including hosting international events (Ismayilov 2012a). Internally, sport-related nationalism can elicit patriotism, and the involvement of 16,000 citizens as volunteers at the 2015 European Games can be seen to reflect a degree of social support for such projects (Rojo-Labaien 2020). Hosting mega-events is particularly significant in Azerbaijan in order to shape national identity, foster patriotism and consolidate power (Makarychev and Yatsyk 2016). This reflects the government's commitment to accentuate national culture and political legitimacy internally and internationally (Ismayilov 2012b). Imposed nation-building policies and practices, implemented through the construction of patriotic landmarks and modern architectural developments are intended to convey the power of the state and its authoritarian president. When it was erected in 2010, the 162-metre-tall flagpole bearing the Azerbaijan flag at Baku's National Flag Square was the highest in the world.

Aspects of post-Soviet Azerbaijan's political culture have remained anchored in Soviet-era features of subordination, reinforced by oppressive, authoritarian leadership, a high dependency on the federal centre and a weakened civil society, producing a pervasive climate of fear among citizens (Rojo-Labaien 2020). Ilham Aliyev's cult of personality and 'clientelistic' presidential system have existed for the majority of Azerbaijan's contemporary statehood, with a strictly unidirectional rule imposed to consolidate the power of the regime and stabilise the country (Hale 2012, 75). This has secured the status of a monolithic elite as the dominant actor over the country's considerable energy resources, over which the government exerts complete control (Gel'man 2008). This in turn has helped shape complex and ambitious nation-building projects, pertinently conveyed through Azerbaijan's event hosting profile.

The limitations imposed by pandemic protocols confined the engagement and impact of Euro 2020 in Baku, whilst one-off contests such as the 2019 UEL final limit the timeframe of international exposure for host cities. Despite the profile of these SMEs therefore, their impact on international public perception was restricted in these cases. However, so too therefore were the prospects for negative publicity. The efforts to acquire soft power, engage in public diplomacy and promote nation branding may have been curtailed, but the unintended and unwelcome outcomes of soft disempowerment, weakened diplomatic ties and critically dissenting voices were also less pervasive (see Brannagan and Rookwood 2016). The 2015 European Games provides a useful frame of reference. It lacked the prestige of the UEFA events, but it did afford Azerbaijan full control, concentrating the focus accordingly. The European Games revealed greater insight into the apparatus of oppression in Azerbaijan: Prior to its inception, the widespread repression of dissent saw numerous regime opponents arrested, whilst many of the remaining NGOs located in Baku were forcibly closed; some western journalists were prevented from entering the country to report on the event; various independent media outlets were closed down; and those who remained operational were subject to close surveillance by national security personnel and feared publishing negative reports, as the event was perceived as a project of Azerbaijan's First Lady Mehriban Aliyeva (Rojo-Labaien 2020).

The Aliyev regime exerts rigid control over mass media outlets which remain the principle means of transmitting information to the Azerbaijani population. This also served to restrict the expression of opposition to the state (Pearce 2014). The 1995 constitution formally declares Azerbaijan a democratic country, yet civil liberties have since eroded severely, shaped by the overriding dogma of stability (Bedford 2014). Azerbaijan's model of governance is presented relative to the perceived position of neighbouring states: 'Call it stability or call it stagnation, but in recent years Azerbaijan has been an island of unchanging continuity as its neighbors, Armenia, Georgia, Iran, and Turkey, have seen tumultuous change' (De Wall 2019, no page).

Conclusion

Azerbaijan is situated at a geopolitical and ethno-cultural intersection. Its Eurasian location shapes a complex range of diverse international influences within and beyond the Caucasus. It borders powerful states such as Russia and Iran, whilst lacking diplomatic relations and open borders with neighbouring Armenia. Azerbaijan's membership to various international political and sporting institutions brings it into contact with numerous entities, whilst its network of partners connected to its lucrative oil industry have helped establish its position on the world stage. The wealth accrued from energy resources has been utilised to consolidate the power and legitimacy of the president and his established monolithic and clientelistic political regime, whilst marking complex and ambitious nation-building projects. The inherited Soviet features of subordination reinforced by oppressive rule have also seen the eradication of pluralism and democratic structures throughout Azerbaijan, whilst the authoritarian modernisation has limited expenditure to Baku.

The concentration of resources and decision-making power has further marginalised those inhabiting the country's interior, where living standards belie the image presented to international audiences through the portfolio of sport sponsorship and event hosting. Some emphasise Azerbaijan's endemic corruption, economic misappropriation and low accountability and transparency standards, framing sport event hosting as attempts to whitewash Azerbaijan's public image under the guise of modernisation by creating connections with international leaders in political and sporting spheres (Ibadoghlu 2019a). The extensive investment in infrastructure and architecture reflect the quest for international recognition, intended to build and transmit Azerbaijan's modernity to the world, and ultimately leverage political influence within and beyond the Caucasus. Two successive but unsuccessful bids to host the Olympic Games testify to the regime's ambition but also the lack of necessary infrastructure and influence. After staging the inaugural European Games, more prestigious sport sponsorships and events were prioritised, notably Formula One and UEFA's 2019 UEL final and Euro 2020 football events. The state was largely spared consequences of soft disempowerment by the racial and sexual inequality controversies that dominated narratives of the latter tournament, primarily centred on other host cities. It remains to be seen whether the return warrants Azerbaijan's considerable investment of state funds and whether subsequent sport event hosting opportunities will be pursued in Baku.

Azerbaijan's wealth has been transformed within the timeframe of this research (2004–2021) which also spans the presidency of Ilham Aliyev. However, relatively little in the way of state resources have been transferred to the general population. The problem is encapsulated by a recent paper by Ibadoghlu (2019b) entitled 'State oil fund of Azerbaijan: huge spending and overwhelming poverty', which states that Azerbaijan spent $100 billion between 2001–2018, and yet the average monthly salary in the country in 2019 was $318. Even in major cities much of the population experience poverty, unemployment and inadequate access to clean water, healthcare, education and transportation systems, and in remote regions the situation is even worse (Ibadoghlu 2019b). Azerbaijan's often neglected and marginalised interior can be difficult to access. This article gives voice to an admittedly limited number of perspectives of those living in its fifth most populous city expressed in 2004, six months after the appointment of President Ilham Aliyev. This offers a geographical, cultural, conceptual and historical frame of reference. Given the diverse focus of this paper there was limited space available to emphasise details of participant perspectives, but it does give voice to a small number of those impacted by the experience and collective memory of war. It also demonstrates that Azerbaijan was, as recently as 2004, 'descending into the Third World after a decade of independence' (Rasizade 2004, 191); a state that welcomed interventive humanitarian aid and development initiatives in response to what is an ongoing conflict that continues to cause death and displacement.

75 per cent of Azerbaijanis live outside of the capital, and much of the population remains impoverished, alienated by or at least marginalised from the statecraft concerns and grand investment projects in Baku. These co-exist alongside a darker reality, the Azerbaijan of poor and displaced people living in underfunded and even splintered communities. Aside from hosting future sports events, the empowerment of civil society – including the protection of basic human rights and the provision of the minimum standards of wellbeing – may well remain elusive until issues of the dogmatic stabilisation of the state, the oppressive authoritarian political infrastructure, the centralised expenditure of national wealth and the settlement of the Nagorno-Karabakh conflict are resolved, all which are firmly entrenched in the contemporary national narrative.

Disclosure statement

No potential conflict of interest was reported by the author.

ORCID

Joel Rookwood http://orcid.org/0000-0002-6510-4519

References

Al Adem, Samar, Paul Childerhouse, Temitope Egbelakin, and Bill Wang. 2018. "International and Local NGO Supply Chain Collaboration: An Investigation of the Syrian Refugee Crises in Jordan." *Journal of Humanitarian Logistics and Supply Chain Management* 8 (3): 295–322. doi:10.1108/JHLSCM-05-2017-0020.
Amnesty International. 2020. "Armenia/Azerbaijan: Civilians must be protected from use of banned cluster bombs." October 5. https://www.amnesty.org/en/latest/press-release/2020/10/armenia-azerbaijan-civilians-must-be-protected-from-use-of-banned-cluster-bombs/.
Askerov, Ali. 2020. "The Nagorno-Karabakh Conflict: The Beginning of the Soviet End." In *Post-Soviet Conflicts: The Thirty Years' Crisis*, edited by Ali Askerov, Stephan Brooks and Lasha Tchantouridzé, 55–82. New York: Lexington Books.
Bedford, Sofie. 2014. "Political Mobilization in Azerbaijan – the January 2013 Protests and Beyond." *Demokratizatsiya* 22 (1): 2–14.
Beilinson, Orel. 2019. "Turkish-Azerbaijani Relations. One Nation – Two States?" *Südosteuropa* 67 (1): 137–139. doi:10.1515/soeu-2019-0009.
Brannagan, Paul, and Joel Rookwood. 2016. "Sports Mega-Events, Soft Power and Soft Disempowerment: International Supporters' Perspectives on Qatar's Acquisition of the 2022 FIFA World Cup Finals." *International Journal of Sport Policy and Politics* 8 (2): 173–188. doi:10.1080/19406940.2016.1150868.

Broers, Lawrence. 2021. *Armenia and Azerbaijan: Anatomy of a Rivalry*. Edinburgh: Edinburgh University Press.
Chatzigianni, Efthalia. 2018. "Global Sport Governance: Globalizing the Globalized." *Sport in Society* 21 (9): 1454–1482. doi:10.1080/17430437.2017.1390566.
Ciarreta, Aitor, and Shahriyar Nasirov. 2012. "Development Trends in the Azerbaijan Oil and Gas Sector: Achievements and Challenges." *Energy Policy* 40: 282–292. doi:10.1016/j.enpol.2011.10.002.
Cornell, Svante. 2017. "Turkey's Role: Balancing the Armenia-Azerbaijan Conflict and Turkish-Armenian Relations." In *The International Politics of the Armenian-Azerbaijani Conflict*, edited by Svante Cornell, 89–105. New York: Palgrave Macmillan.
Croke, Ruaidhrí. 2020. "Dublin to Baku: What's the cost of Euro 2020 for the planet?" *Irish Times*, January 14. https://www.irishtimes.com/sport/soccer/international/dublin-to-baku-what-s-the-cost-of-euro-2020-for-the-planet-1.4138492.
De Wall, Thomas. 2019. "Is Change Afoot in Azerbaijan?" *Carnegie Europe*, November 5. https://carnegieeurope.eu/strategiceurope/80271.
Doyle, Paul. 2019. "Why did UEFA hand Azerbaijan Hosting Rights for the Europa League final?" *The Guardian*, May 16. https://www.theguardian.com/football/2019/may/16/uefa-handed-azerbaijan-europa-league-final-baku-chelsea-arsenal.
ESPN. 2021. "Euro 2020: UEFA bans rainbow advertising at two quarterfinals." *ESPN*, July 3. https://www.espn.com/soccer/uefa-european-championship/story/4425446/euro-2020-uefa-bans-rainbow-advertising-at-two-quarterfinals.
Euronews. 2021. "Europe divided on taking the knee during EURO 2020." *Euronews*, June 11. https://www.euronews.com/2021/06/11/europe-divided-on-taking-the-knee-during-euro-2020-football-tournament.
Evans, Simon. 2021. "UEFA Prohibits 'Rainbow' Protest at Germany vs Hungary Game." *Reuters*, June 23. https://www.reuters.com/lifestyle/sports/uefa-turn-down-request-rainbow-lights-munich-2021-06-22/.
Freizer, Sabine. 2014. "Twenty Years after the Nagorny Karabakh Ceasefire: An Opportunity to Move towards More Inclusive Conflict Resolution." *Caucasus Survey* 1 (2): 109–122. doi:10.1080/23761199.2014.11417295.
Garagozov, Rauf. 2012. "Azerbaijani History and Nationalism in the Soviet and Post-Soviet Periods: Challenges and Dilemmas." *Dynamics of Asymmetric Conflict* 5 (2): 136–142. doi:10.1080/17467586.2012.743030.
Gel'man, Vladimir. 2008. "Out of the Frying Pan, into the Fire? Post-Soviet Regime Changes in Comparative Perspectives." *International Political Science Review* 29 (2): 157–180. doi:10.1177/0192512107085610.
German, Tracey, and Agha Bayramov. 2019. "The (Re)-Politicisation of International Relations in the Post-Soviet Space." *East European Politics* 35 (2): 117–121. doi:10.1080/21599165.2019.1614920.
Guliyev, Farid. 2009. "Oil Wealth, Patrimonialism, and the Failure of Democracy in Azerbaijan." *Caucasus Analytical Digest* 2: 2–5. https://ssrn.com/abstract=1329483.
Gzoyan, Edita, and Regina Galustyan. 2021. "Forced Marriages as a Tool of Genocide: The Armenian Case." *The International Journal of Human Rights* 25 (10): 1724–1743. doi:10.1080/13642987.2021.1874361.
Hale, Henry. 2012. "Two Decades of Post-Soviet Regime Dynamics." *Demokratizatsiya* 20 (2): 71–77.
Heradstveit, Daniel. 2001. "Democratic Development in Azerbaijan and the Role of the Western Oil Industry." *Central Asian Survey* 20 (3): 261–288. doi:10.1080/02634930120095312.
Horák, Slavomír. 2020. "Sports Politics in Authoritarian Regimes: The Synergies of Sport, Ideology and Personality Cult in Turkmenistan." In *Sport, Statehood and Transition in Europe: Comparative Perspectives from Post-Soviet and Post-Socialist Societies*, edited by Ekain Rojo-Labaien, Álvaro Rodríguez-Díaz, and Joel Rookwood, 250–267. London: Routledge.
Hughes, Fergus P. 2009. *Children, Play and Development*. London: Sage.

Human Rights Watch. 2017. "Azerbaijan – anti-gay crackdown: Gay men, transgender women tortured to extort money, intelligence." *Human Rights Watch*, October 3. https://www.hrw.org/news/2017/10/03/azerbaijan-anti-gay-crackdown.

Ibadoghlu, Gubad. 2019a. "Corrupt and Flashy Events Disguised as Modernization in Azerbaijan." *Crude Accountability*, September 13. doi:10.2139/ssrn.3489634.

Ibadoghlu, Gubad. 2019b. "State Oil Fund of Azerbaijan: Huge Spending and Overwhelming Poverty." *Social Science Research Network*. doi:10.2139/ssrn.3489617.

Ismayilov, Murad. 2012a. "The Impact of Energy Resources on Nation-and State-Building: The Contrasting Cases of Azerbaijan and Georgia." In *Beyond the Resource Curse*, edited by Brenda Shaffer and Taleh Ziyadov, 203–224. Philadelphia: University of Pennsylvania Press.

Ismayilov, Murad. 2012b. "State, Identity, and the Politics of Music: Eurovision and Nation-Building in Azerbaijan." *Nationalities Papers* 40 (6): 833–851. doi:10.1080/00905992.2012.742990.

Janmyr, Maja. 2017. "No Country of Asylum: 'Legitimizing' Lebanon's Rejection of the 1951 Refugee Convention." *International Journal of Refugee Law* 29 (3): 438–465. doi:10.1093/ijrl/eex026.

Kalyoncu, Husyhin, Faruk Gürsoy, and Hasan Göcen. 2013. "Causality Relationship between GDP and Energy Consumption in Georgia, Azerbaijan and Armenia." *International Journal of Energy Economics and Policy* 3 (1): 111–117.

Kazaryan, Airazat M., Bjørn Edwin, Ara Darzi, Gevorg N. Tamamyan, Mushegh A. Sahakyan, Davit L. Aghayan, Åsmund A. Fretland, Sheraz Yaqub, and Brice Gayet. 2021. "War in the Time of COVID-19: Humanitarian Catastrophe in Nagorno-Karabakh and Armenia." *The Lancet. Global Health* 9 (3): E243–244. doi:10.1016/S2214-109X(20)30510-6.

Kévorkian, R. 2011. *The Armenian Genocide: A Complete History*. London: I.B. Taurus.

Khalilzada, Javadbay. 2019. "Modernization and Social Change in Azerbaijan: Assessing the Transformation of Azerbaijan through the Theories of Modernity." *New Middle Eastern Studies* 9 (2): 167–188. doi:10.29311/nmes.v9i2.3274.

Kondakov, Alexander, and Evgeny Shtorn. 2021. "Sex, Alcohol and Soul: Violent Reactions to Coming out after the 'Gay Propaganda' Law in Russia." *The Russian Review* 80 (1): 37–55. doi:10.1111/russ.12297.

Krzyzaniak, John S. 2018. "The Soft Power Strategy of Soccer Sponsorships." *Soccer & Society* 19 (4): 498–515. doi:10.1080/14660970.2016.1199426.

Kunti, Samindra. 2021. "Azerbaijan's sportswashing culminates with Euro 2020 quarterfinal." *Forbes*, July 3. https://www.forbes.com/sites/samindrakunti/2021/07/03/azerbaijans-sportswashing-culminates-with-euro-2020-quarterfinal/?sh=69433fdcc1b1.

Lawrence, Amy, and Sean Ingle. 2019. "Arsenal's Henrikh Mkhitaryan to miss the Europa League final over safety fears." *The Guardian*, May 21. https://www.theguardian.com/football/2019/may/21/arsenal-henrikh-khitaryan-miss-europa-league-final-safety-chelsea-baku.

Lillard, Angeline, Ashley M. Pinkham, and Eric Smith. 2011. "Pretend Play and Cognitive Development." In *The Wiley-Blackwell Handbook of Childhood Cognitive Development*, edited by Usha Goswami, 285–311. Hoboken: Wiley-Blackwell.

MacClancy, Jeremy. 1996. *Sport, Identity and Ethnicity*. Oxford: Berg.

Makarychev, Andrey, and Alexander Yatsyk. 2016. *Mega Events in Post-Soviet Eurasia: Shifting Borderlines of Inclusion and Exclusion*. New York: Palgrave Macmillan.

Mammadov, Rashad. 2021. "Political Activist, Citizen's Helper, and Entertainer: A Study of Professional Role Perception of Journalists in Azerbaijan." *Journalism Practice* 15 (7): 911–936. doi:10.1080/17512786.2020.1758189.

März, Julian W. 2021. "Hungary's New Anti-LGBTQ Law: The Medical Profession Must Speak out about the Harm it does to LGBTQ Adolescents' Health." *The Lancet Regional Health. Europe* 8: 100199. doi:10.1016/j.lanepe.2021.100199.

Melton, E. Nicole, and Jeffrey D. MacCharles. 2021. "Examining Sport Marketing through a Rainbow Lens." *Sport Management Review* 24 (3): 421–438. doi:10.1080/14413523.2021.1880742.

O'Conner, Robert. 2021. "Azerbaijan accused of using football as an instrument of war – so should UEFA be taking the Euros there this summer?" *inews*, March 26. https://inews.co.uk/sport/football/euro-2020-fixtures-azerbaijan-uefa-political-concerns-931949.

Öge, Kerem. 2014. "The Limits of Transparency Promotion in Azerbaijan: External Remedies to 'Reverse the Curse.'" *Europe-Asia Studies* 66 (9): 1482–1500. doi:10.1080/09668136.2014.956448.

Open Society Foundations Armenia. 2021. "Request to revoke Azerbaijan's hosting rights of UEFA Euro 2020 games in Baku." *Open Society Foundations Armenia*, June 10. https://www.osf.am/2021/06/request-to-revoke-azerbaijans-hosting-rights-of-uefa-euro-2020-games-in-baku/.

Pearce, Katy. 2014. "Two Can Play at That Game: Social Media Opportunities in Azerbaijan for Government and Opposition." *Demokratizatsiya* 22: 39–66.

Rasizade, Alec. 2004. "Azerbaijan Descending into the Third World after a Decade of Independence." *Journal of Third World Studies* 21: 191–219.

Reinsberg, Bernhard, Alexander Kentikelenis, and Thomas Stubbs. 2021. "Creating Crony Capitalism: Neoliberal Globalization and the Fuelling of Corruption." *Socio-Economic Review* 19 (2): 607–634. doi:10.1093/ser/mwz039.

Roche, Maurice. 2003. "Mega Events, Time and Modernity: On Time Structures in Global Society." *Time & Society* 12 (1): 99–126. doi:10.1177/0961463X03012001370.

Rodríguez-Díaz, Álvaro, Joel Rookwood, and Ekain Rojo-Labaien. 2020. "Interpreting Sport and Transition in Post-Soviet and Post-Socialist Europe: States, Nations and Markets." In *Sport, Statehood and Transition in Europe: Comparative Perspectives from Post-Soviet and Post-Socialist Societies*, edited by Ekain Rojo-Labaien, Álvaro Rodríguez-Díaz, and Joel Rookwood, 1–8. London: Routledge.

Rodríguez-Díaz, Álvaro. 2020. "Sport in the Political and Economic Transition in Belarus: State Nationalism and Mega Events." In *Sport, Statehood and Transition in Europe: Comparative Perspectives from Post-Soviet and Post-Socialist Societies*, edited by Ekain Rojo-Labaien, Álvaro Rodríguez-Díaz, and Joel Rookwood, 179–197. London: Routledge.

Rojo-Labaien, Ekain. 2018. "The Baku 2015 European Games as a National Milestone of post-Soviet Azerbaijan." *Nationalities Papers* 46 (6): 1101–1117. doi:10.1080/00905992.2018.1488826.

Rojo-Labaien, Ekain. 2020. "Oil-Funded Sports Events as the Embodiment of the Evolution of post-Soviet Azerbaijan." In *Sport, Statehood and Transition in Europe: Comparative Perspectives from Post-Soviet and Post-Socialist Societies*, edited by Ekain Rojo-Labaien, Álvaro Rodríguez-Díaz, and Joel Rookwood, 233–249. London: Routledge.

Rookwood, Joel. 2012. "Constructing Peace and Fostering Social Integration through Sport and Play in Azerbaijan." In *Sports, Governance, Development and Corporate Responsibility*, edited by Barbara Segaert, Merc Theeboom, Christiane Timmerman and Bart Vanreusel, 30–43. New York: Routledge.

Rookwood, Joel. 2019. "Access, Security and Diplomacy: Perceptions of Soft Power, Nation Branding and the Organisational Challenges Facing Qatar's 2022 FIFA World Cup." *Sport, Business and Management: An International Journal* 9 (1): 26–44. doi:10.1108/SBM-02-2018-0016.

Rookwood, Joel. 2021. "Diversifying the Fan Experience and Securitising Crowd Management: A Longitudinal Analysis of Fan Park Facilities at 15 Football Mega Events between 2002 and 2019." *Managing Sport and Leisure* 27: 1–19. doi:10.1080/23750472.2021.1985596.

Rookwood, Joel, and Kola Adeosun. 2021. "Nation Branding and Public Diplomacy: Japan's 2019 Rugby World Cup and 2020(21) Olympics, a Global Economic Downturn and COVID-19 Pandemic." *Journal of Global Sport Management* 7: 1–21. doi:10.1080/24704067.2021.1871860.

Rookwood, Joel, and Clive Palmer. 2011. "Invasion Games in War-Torn Nations: Can Football Help to Build Peace?" *Soccer & Society* 12 (2): 184–200. doi:10.1080/14660970.2011.548356.

Scicchitano, Dominic. 2021. "The "Real" Chechen Man: Conceptions of Religion, Nature, and Gender and the Persecution of Sexual Minorities in Postwar Chechnya".*Journal of Homosexuality* 68 (9): 1545–1562. doi:10.1080/00918369.2019.1701336.

Shaw, Malcolm N. 1997. "The Heritage of States: The Principle of 'Uti Possidetis Juris' Today." *British Yearbook of International Law* 67: 75–154. doi:10.1093/bybil/67.1.75.

Sjoberg, Fredrik M. 2014. "Autocratic Adaptation: The Strategic Use of Transparency and the Persistence of Election Fraud." *Electoral Studies* 33: 233–245. doi:10.1016/j.electstud.2013.08.004.

Sommers, Marc. 2003. *Urbanization, War and Africa's Youth at Risk: Towards Understanding and Addressing Future Challenges*. Washington, D.C: United States Agency for International Development.

Spaaij, Ramon, and Nico Schulenkorf. 2014. "Cultivating Safe Space: Lessons for Sport-for-Development Projects and Events." *Journal of Sport Management* 28 (6): 633–645. doi:10.1123/jsm.2013-0304.

Sterchele, Daniel, and Chantal Saint-Blancat. 2015. "Keeping It Liminal. The Mondiali Antirazzisti (anti-Racist World Cup) as a Multifocal Interaction Ritual." *Leisure Studies* 34 (2): 182–196. doi:10.1080/02614367.2013.855937.

Stidder, Gary, and Adrian Haasner. 2007. "Developing Outdoor and Adventurous Activities for Co-Existence and Reconciliation in Israel: An Anglo-German Approach." *Journal of Adventure Education & Outdoor Learning* 7 (2): 131–140. doi:10.1080/14729670701731052.

Ter-Abrahamian, Hrant. 2005. "On the Formation of the National Identity of the Talishis in Azerbaijan Republic." *Iran and the Caucasus* 9 (1): 121–144. doi:10.1163/1573384054068132.

UEFA. 2018. *UEFA Statutes, February 2018 Edition. Rules of Procedure of the UEFA Congress*. UEFA.

Vasilyeva, Olga, and Alexander Libman. 2020. "Varieties of Authoritarianism Matter: Elite Fragmentation, Natural Resources and Economic Growth." *European Journal of Political Economy* 63: 101869–101812. doi:10.1016/j.ejpoleco.2020.101869.

Predicting climate impacts to the Olympic Games and FIFA Men's World Cups from 2022 to 2032

Walker J. Ross ⓘ and ⓘ Madeleine Orr

ABSTRACT
In response to concern for climate change impacting sport competitions and legacies, and the need to consider climate adaptability in event planning, this paper uses a combination of historical weather and air quality data as well as the Intergovernmental Panel on Climate Change Fifth Assessment Report to predict climactic conditions for the mega-events of the 2022 through 2032. In doing so, this paper provides a preliminary overview of environmental conditions (e.g. temperatures, air quality, precipitation) that can be used by event planners to inform contingency plans for the events and their legacies. The most immediate concerns for the mega events between 2022 and 2032 include heat conditions unsuitable for competition and poor air quality, but there may be more harmful environmental concerns for the long-term legacies of these events. It is imperative that event organizers consider creating climate-resilient events, infrastructure, and legacies that can withstand environmental threats in the future.

Introduction

The outbreak of the COVID-19 pandemic forced sport organizations and events to postpone, cancel, and otherwise reconfigure their hosting plans to combat the spread of a sudden and unpredicted contagion (Mastromartino et al. 2020). Highlighted by this muddle of solutions from sport organizations to the pandemic is the need for modern sport organizations to have contingency plans in place to protect stakeholders, minimize financial impacts, and ensure competitive integrity from a variety of potentially disruptive circumstances like pandemics, violence, and natural disasters. Indeed, one area where many sport organizations lack proper contingency planning is in the impact of climate change – more broadly than natural disasters alone – on their operations (Orr and Inoue 2019; Orr 2020).

Sport events are being impacted by climate change already. In 2019, the Rugby World Cup was interrupted by Super Typhoon Hagibis, a Category 5 storm (NASA 2019) that made landfall during the tournament. At the Tokyo 2020 Olympics Games (held in 2021), several events were postponed due to heavy rains from Tropical Storm Nepartak and extreme heat conditions (Dave and O'Connor 2021; Hernandez and Kantchev 2021), both of which were forecast by meteorologists and sport scientists in the years prior to the event (e.g. Kakamu et al. 2017; Matzarakis et al. 2019). And yet, despite ample warnings, little was done to curb the effects of heat and rain on the event. Cyclones (typhoons/hurricanes) and heat waves, like other hazards, have potentially catastrophic impacts on the affected locations. It is clear from just these two examples that the disruptive potential for sudden/fast-onset weather on sports events in the long-term can be arguably crucial and examining these hazards is an important task for effective risk management at events.

The general lack of contingency planning for the natural environment and climate change may be explained by the speed at which these types of disasters occur. While pandemics, violence, and natural disasters (e.g. severe weather, landslides, and wildfires) are sudden, attention-grabbing, and require well-planned responses in order to ensure stakeholder safety, climate change is a slow-moving disaster. Sport organizations may feel that they can delay planning and mitigating the impacts of climate change or even ignore it for the time being since it is a disruption years in the making. Simply put, it may not be viewed as a priority for sport organizations at the moment (e.g. Ross and Mercado 2020). However, it is a disaster with urgent and immediate consequences, and requires a well-planned response the same as the other disasters. This is especially important in light of the reports from the Intergovernmental Panel on Climate Change's (IPCC) Sixth Assessment Report (IPCC 2021) and Special Report on Global Warming at 1.5°C (IPCC 2018) which warn of devastating impacts to human health, lifestyles, biodiversity, food production, and the economy. As such, it will be imperative for sport organizations to begin identifying environmental boundary conditions that provide for safe sporting experiences (e.g. in terms of temperature, precipitation, air quality), and tracking changes to these conditions in their geographic region. This information will allow sport organizations to create contingency plans for their operations to avoid and reduce the negative impacts emanating from climate change, much as they are likely creating contingency plans for pandemic response.

Mega-events are visible symbols of sport for many, command international media attention and significant public investments, and are typically aligned with long-term city planning efforts (Gratton, Dobson, and Shibli 2000). What makes these mega-events particularly vulnerable to the impacts of climate change is that they move to a new location for each iteration of the event, and each new host city has different environmental conditions, introducing new challenges for event organizers to account for. This is particularly salient in the legacy period of the event as legacies are planned for ahead of time as part of the bidding for the events and receive significant levels of funding from hosts (Leopkey and Parent 2012). Contingency planning is therefore necessary for mega-event hosts if the natural environment or climate change creates conditions that are not conducive for play during the event (i.e. fall outside the environmental boundary conditions), or impact its legacy. Due to the funding and interest in these mega-events and legacies, it will be important to protect those legacies in the long run from climate change. The task of planning for climate-related impacts is made even more difficult for the event organizers as they may not be experts in environmental management or climate science, and may be unaware of the available resources to learn about climate change and its impacts, such as the IPCC reports.

It is under these circumstances regarding the lack of clear environmental boundary condition and climate adaptation plans that this paper becomes necessary. The purpose of this research is to provide an interpretation of expected climatological conditions during each of the mega-events scheduled between 2022 and 2032, and in their respective legacy years. Using a combination of historical weather and air quality data to assess climactic conditions in the recent past, and forecasting of climate change in the medium (2050) and distant future (end of 21st century), the objective of this paper is to predict climatological obstacles that mega-events of the 2020s and 2032 ought to consider in preparing their events and subsequent legacy projects to minimize the detrimental impacts of climate change on event operations and outcomes. The rest of the manuscript is organized as follows: first, we introduce and consider the historical and background information relevant to the sport-environment relationship in the context of mega-events. Next, the concepts of climate vulnerability and adaptation are introduced. Third, the methods for historical weather and air quality analysis and forecasting climate impacts are presented, along with the specific approaches used in this study. Finally, predictions for climatological impacts at each mega-event in the 2020s and 2032 are presented and implications for researchers and event managers are discussed, with special attention to possible adaptation options.

Literature review

Environment and mega-events

Sport is considered to have a bi-directional relationship with the natural environment: a concept dubbed 'sport ecology' (McCullough, Madeline Orr, and Kellison 2020). This implies that sport activity impacts the natural environment in which it operates, and that the natural environment impacts the ability of sport to operate. The aforementioned IPCC reports suggest that climate change, a massive shift in global weather patterns driven by human emissions, will impact all sectors (IPCC 2014; IPCC 2018). The logical extension of this warning is that sport organizations will need to adapt to environmental hazards (e.g. warming weather, rising sea levels, extreme weather, and loss of biodiversity), proactively and quickly.

It is understood that most sport organizations are vulnerable to climate-related disruptions (Dingle and Stewart 2018; Orr and Inoue 2019) and that many previous hosts of the Olympic Winter Games may not be climatically viable host candidates for the same event in the future, if climate change trends persist (Scott et al. 2015). Further research has demonstrated the outdoor sports are particularly vulnerable to environmental hazards, such as cross country skiing and baseball (Orr 2020; Kellison and Orr 2020). However, there is perhaps no better setting in which to examine climate change in the context of sport than at mega multi-sport events like the Olympic Games and *Fédération Internationale de Football Association* (FIFA) World Cups.

Sporting mega events

It is prudent to first clarify what qualifies as a mega-event. Gratton, Dobson, and Shibli (2000, 26) offer a typology of major sport events which proposes events that mega-events are 'irregular, one-off, major international spectator events generating significant economic activity and media interest' are Type A events. Additionally, Roche (2000, 1) offers the following definition of a mega event: 'large-scale cultural (including commercial and sporting) events, which have a dramatic character, mass popular appeal and international significance'. Those Type A events and mega-events include the Olympic Games and FIFA

Men's World Cups due to their international scale, popularity, and irregular, one-off nature for host communities (Gratton, Dobson, and Shibli 2000; Roche 2000; Roche 2006). These are the two mega-events that this research will consider. In explaining the relationship between environment and these two mega-events, the Olympic Games environmental history will be examined briefly and then comparisons will be drawn between it and FIFA World Cups.

The relationship between the Olympic Games and the natural environment is fundamental, but it was not until the 1992 Albertville, France Winter Olympic Games mismanaged their environmental impact that there became a full show of support from the International Olympic Committee (IOC) to protect the natural environment (Ross and Leopkey 2017). Before this, and especially during the earliest iterations of the modern Olympic Games, the events were considered by the organizers to be too small in scale to have an impact on the natural environment, though some conservation groups protested this reductionist view (Del Fiacco and Orr 2019). Over time, as the events have grown, there has been more of an encroachment by the Games upon the natural environments in which they take place. After the Albertville Winter Games, the calls for better environmental management planning created changes that lead to the 1994 Lillehammer Winter Olympic Games being considered the first green Olympic Games (Ross and Leopkey 2017). Over time, pressure from many different stakeholders in the Olympic Games (e.g. Organizing Committees, host governments, environmental organizations, and sponsors) has forced the IOC to increasingly include requirements for environmental considerations in the bidding as well as planning stages of the Games (Del Fiacco and Orr 2019; Ross, Leopkey, and Mercado 2019). Through these formal requirements, programs like the Olympic Games Global Impact, initiatives like an Olympic version of Agenda 21 and Agenda 2020, and informal pressures placed on bid cities by the IOC to stand out during the bidding process as sustainable and environmentally conscious hosts, the Olympic Games have slowly produced Games with better environmental initiatives. Games have gone from considering the environment as a problem to manage (Del Fiacco and Orr 2019) to producing robust campaigns such as Oxygen-Plus for the PyeongChang 2018 Winter Olympic Games (Ross and Leopkey 2017). Given this improving trend of environmental management by the Games, it should therefore be expected that Olympic Games of the future will strive for increasingly lofty goals on managing their environmental impact.

To date, the literature examining the environmental impact of FIFA Men's World Cups is underdeveloped compared to that available for the Olympic Games. However, FIFA's Men's World Cups environmental management history mirrors that of the Olympics. The scale of the events and their environmental impact has steadily increased with time as has the scope of environmental initiatives found at these events. For example, the 2006 Men's World Cup held in Germany had the Green Goal programme which addressed water, waste, energy, transportation, and carbon offsetting in an attempt to create the greenest yet Men's World Cup (Collins, Jones, and Munday 2009). Following the 2006 edition, the 2010 South African Men's World Cup was considered at the time to be the most carbon-intensive World Cup ever (Death 2011). Like their Olympic counterparts, the environmental efforts of FIFA World Cups have been widely criticized for their greenwashing and negligibility (Death 2011). Despite the limited action, FIFA does require host cities to consider the environmental impact in the bidding and planning phases of the events (FIFA 2017). These environmental impacts for FIFA Men's World Cups might include, but are not limited to, the impact on climate, transportation, energy use, waste disposal, materials consumption, water use and discharge, land use, noise, as well as food consumption and disposal (Ahmed and Pretorius 2010).

Yet, despite the marked increase in environmental planning and awareness from the Olympic Movement and World Cups, the natural environment is still largely approached by these governing bodies and the event organizers as an issue related to the environmental impact of the event, rather than as a potential threat to the event itself (Ross and Leopkey 2017). This means that event organizers are only seeing one direction of the bidirectional sport-environment relationship: the impact of sport on the environment. They are not seeing the impact of the environment on sport. When viewing the environment as a threat to these mega-events, it has already been shown that while 19 previous Winter Olympic Games host cities (prior to the 2014 Winter Games) had climates suitable for the event from 1981 to 2010, only 10 or 11 of those same cities will remain climatically viable hosts of the Winter Games in the 2050s (Scott et al. 2015). Further, due to rising temperatures from climate change, it has been projected that by 2085 the pool of viable candidate cities to host the Summer Olympic Games will shrink dramatically since athletes will be unable to compete in extreme heat conditions (Smith et al. 2016). These mega-events will be threatened by their natural environments in the future. In consideration of the bi-directional relationship between sport and the natural environment (McCullough, Madeline Orr, and Kellison 2020), there must be environmental planning for how climate and the environment will impact these mega-events in order to avoid a narrowing list of viable host candidates and the potential for selected host cities to become climatically inviable after being awarded the rights to host these events. Therefore, consideration for climate and environmental planning is critical to mega-events of the 2020s and beyond.

Climate vulnerability and adaptation

The United Nations Disaster Risk Reduction office conceptualizes climate vulnerability as a function of (a) potential impact of climate change on a given unit (e.g. a person, an organization, a community, etc.) and (b) adaptive capacity (Adger 2006; Weis et al. 2016).

Potential impact describes the scope and severity of impact that climate change hazards will have on a given unit of observation. Potential impact can be assessed by two factors: exposure (i.e. how likely is the event to be impacted by a hazard?), and sensitivity (i.e. how bad would it be if the hazard were to occur?)(Orr and Inoue 2019). Since hazards are uncontrollable by sport managers, because sports people cannot prevent, change, or contain natural disasters or the weather on a given day, little research has examined environmental hazards or the impacts of climate change on sport events and elite sport performance (Orr 2021). Nonetheless, knowing the exposure of a sport event to environmental hazards (e.g. extreme heat, storm activity, etc.) and the sensitivity to hazards (e.g. the business, health, and performance consequences of heat, storms, etc.), is an important task.

Environmental boundary conditions

While very little research has examined the impacts of climate change on sport (Orr 2021), there is a considerable body of research – along with some sport policies – which aim to establish environmental boundary conditions for sport, including for maximum temperatures for safe summer sport participation, maximum temperatures for winter sports, safe air quality, and acceptable levels of precipitation. These are discussed in the paragraphs below.

A growing line of research has demonstrated that humans perform exercise best in cool, dry environments, with peak performances typically earmarked around 51.8° Fahrenheit (Oikawa et al. 2021). As environmental temperature and humidity increase, both cognitive and physical performance deteriorate, to the point where health can be compromised. The specific risks associated with high temperatures and humidity levels include heat-related illnesses (ranging from heat cramps to heat exhaustion, to heat stroke in extreme cases; Kakamu et al. 2017) and performance decline (e.g. slower pace of play; Miller-Rushing et al. 2012; Tobías et al. 2019). Dehydration can exacerbate these physiological responses (Gifford et al. 2019).

Several thresholds have been proposed for safe temperatures of play, usually measured in wet bulb globe temperature (WBGT) index, which combines dry (Tdb) and wet bulb (Twb) air temperature with radiant (Tg e.g. sunlight) temperature (O'Connor and Casa 2019). This allows researchers to take humidity into consideration, which is important as this can impact heat stress on the human body (Gifford et al. 2019). However, weather forecasts, like historical data, do not typically offer data points for humidity, instead offering only daily average, daily high, and daily low temperatures. So, for the purposes of this research, only air temperature is considered in setting environmental boundary conditions. The air temperature boundary conditions adopted for this study are 78 degrees Fahrenheit (78° F) as a moderate risk threshold, and 82 degrees Fahrenheit (82° F) as the high risk threshold (Roberts 2010; Smith et al. 2016). These thresholds were established by sport medicine specialists and kinesiologists as the points where heat-related illnesses among athletes (especially endurance runners, such as marathoners and road cyclists) become likely and more severe (Roberts 2010; Smith et al. 2016). It should be noted that due to the differences between sports in terms of clothing, equipment, length of exposure to heat, duration of play, and the nature of the sport, there are wide variations in the effects of heat on athletes. However, these thresholds have been identified as useful guidelines for multi-sport event organizers as they provide healthy thresholds for the most at-risk sports (e.g. marathon, road cycling, tennis).

For winter sports, the environmental boundary conditions related to air temperature are linked to the temperatures at which snow naturally falls, and at which snow guns can produce high quality snow. Natural snow falls below the freezing point (32° Fahrenheit), but can typically be maintained on the mountain for a couple of degrees above 32° F, particularly if temperatures drop overnight (Rivera and Clement 2019). Snow guns, which are the most ubiquitous technological innovation used to combat low-snow, can reliably produce snow at temperatures of approximately 28.4° F (with low humidity levels), however, 'ski area operators and snowmaking equipment manufacturers generally identify [23° F] as a threshold for efficient snowmaking' (Scott et al. 2006, p. 386). Thus, for this study we adopt a good snow threshold (preferred environmental condition) of 23° F as this temperature would accommodate both natural and artificial snow, and an acceptable snow threshold (acceptable environmental condition) of 32 °F.

For safe environmental boundary conditions on air quality, limited research exists. It is known that poor air quality can have stronger impacts on people who are exercising compared to sedentary individuals, because when a person is exerting themselves physically, they will typically breathe through their mouths, bypassing their nose's natural filtration system (Tsegaw and Alemayehu 2019). Further, athletes inhale more air while exercising, compared to resting (McKenzie and Boulet 2008). Consequently, athletes who are engaged in outdoor sports are at higher risk of inhaling polluted air than the fans in the stands, or passersby. As reliable guidelines for air quality are not available in the sport research, we turn to the Air Quality Index (AQI) measure for air quality, which is the U.S. national standard method for reporting air pollution levels (Tsegaw and Alemayehu 2019). Because there are several different air pollutants with differing attributes and varying levels of harm, the AQI provides a simple unit of analysis for determining the quality of air. The Pollution standard index (PSI) was developed by the US Environmental Protection Agency to map AQI readings according to human health implications of various levels of air pollution. The six levels of the PSI are organized as follows: Good (AQI < 50), Moderate (AQI of 51–100), Unhealthy for Sensitive Groups (i.e. asthmatics or those with underlying breathing conditions; AQI 101–150), Unhealthy (AQI 151–200), Very Unhealthy (AQI 201–300), and Hazardous (AQI > 300) (Environmental Protection Agency (EPA) 1999). The World Health Organization has repeatedly upheld these classifications as the standard for measuring air quality for health purposes (World Health Organization (WHO) 2006), including for sports.

Regarding precipitation, most outdoor sports leagues and federations have rain and lightning policies to govern responses to rain and storm activity (Spengler, Connaughton, and Earnshaw 2002). Lightning is widely known to present a risk of electrocution, particularly on open fields (Cherington 2001; Roeder and Vavrek 2005) and thus, sports are typically delayed when there is lightning. Rain policies differ on a sport-by-sport basis. For instance, tennis, paddling sports, and baseball stop for rain, while football, rugby, and athletics events typically continue unless rain is very heavy. Consequently, it is challenging to identify clear boundary conditions for precipitation that would hold across sports, however, very heavy rain and storm activity such as cyclones (hurricanes, typhoons) are ill-advised (Brocherie, Girard, and Millet 2015; Murfree and Moorman 2021). The IPCC qualifies heavy rain as > 7.6 mm of rain in an hour.

Adaptive capacity

Adaptive capacity describes 'the ability of a system to adjust to climate change (including climate variability and extremes), to moderate potential damages, to take advantage of opportunities, or to cope with the consequences' (IPCC 2001, 982; see also Brooks, Adger, and Kelly 2005). Research into adaptive capacity seeks to identify and understand relationships between social and biophysical systems, such that response mechanisms to climate change can be created (Adger 2006; Lockwood et al. 2015). Thus, the common purpose of adaptive capacity research is to determine where systems can best direct their efforts to reduce overall climate vulnerability (Parry 2002; Brooks, Adger, and Kelly 2005; Hinkel 2011).

To make climate vulnerability and adaptation concepts more accessible to sport managers, Orr and Inoue (2019) adapted the construct of adaptive capacity to the unique context of sport organizations. The revised construct is organizational climate capacity (OCC), which refers to 'a sport organization's capacity to accommodate changes in climate with minimal disruptions or additional costs' (Orr and Inoue 2019, 455). The new construct of OCC has the same theoretical relationship to overall vulnerability as adaptive capacity. That is, OCC is negatively correlated to overall vulnerability (Orr and Inoue 2019). Further, OCC is conceptualized as existing on a spectrum of low to high, indicating that all organizations have at least some capacity to respond to environmental hazards, even if minimal, but the degree to which they can respond will vary. High OCC imparts resilience to the organization, such that the organization is likely to maintain its key functions despite adverse climate impacts (Folke 2006).

Research on climate adaptation efforts in sport is in its infancy (Orr and Inoue 2019), but growing quickly. Early research has emphasized the importance of matching adaptive measures to the specific environmental and climate hazards an organization is facing (Orr 2021). For instance, it is appropriate to develop a heat policy to address extreme heat waves, or to revise an insurance policy to cover the specific natural disasters most prevalent in a given region (Orr and Inoue 2019).

Early research on climate adaptation in sport has established that heat policies, shading, water breaks, and cooling technologies as possible adaptations to extreme heat conditions (Honjo et al. 2018; Grundstein et al. 2013; Kakamu et al. 2017; Matzarakis et al. 2019; Nybo et al. 2020). For winter sports, the chief climate concern is having cold enough temperatures and sufficient snowfall to produce safe and competitive conditions for snow sports, such as cross-country skiing, alpine skiing, and snowboarding (Goggins et al. 2018; Orr 2020; Orr and Schneider 2018; Scott et al. 2015). As Rutty et al. (2015) indicated, adaptation options for accommodating poor winter conditions include, among others, the production of fake snow, selecting competition venues at higher altitudes, and ensuring the competition program is flexible, to accommodate changes on the day.

In some cases, adaptation involves investments into new infrastructure or equipment. A recent study by Kellison and Orr (2020) illustrated how Major League Baseball franchises are using climate adaptation as a justification for new infrastructures. Specifically, the Texas Rangers constructed a new indoor facility to escape extreme heat, the Miami Marlins build a new ballpark in 2012 that could withstand high winds and hurricanes, and the Oakland A's are in the process of building a facility that can accommodate significant sea level rise in the coming decades (Kellison and Orr 2020). In nearly all cases of climate adaptation research, the focus is on either disaster recovery (Wicker, Filo, and Cuskelly 2013) or the potential climate impacts in the distant future (e.g. 2050 or 2100; Kellison and Orr 2020; Orr 2020). Very little research has examined the possible climate impacts and potential for proactive adaptation efforts in immediate or near-future timeframes (within the next 10–15 years). Overall, research on climate vulnerability and adaptation in sport remains underdeveloped and represents an area ripe for further research.

This research addressed the above research gaps by addressing two research questions:

(1) In the calendar month(s) of the mega-event (i.e. July and August for summer Olympics, February for winter Olympics, November and December for the 2022 Men's FIFA World Cup, and June and July for the 2026 Men's FIFA World Cup), do the average weather conditions in the city meet the environmental boundary conditions of safe and competitive sport performance?
(2) What does the IPCC predict as likely or very likely environmental hazards associated with climate change in the host city's region? Do the environmental hazards identified by the IPCC impact upon the environmental boundary conditions of safe and competitive sport performance?

Methods

Historical weather and air quality analysis

Historical daily weather reports from 1990 to 2020 were collected from publicly accessible National Oceanic and Atmospheric Administration in each Olympic or FIFA World Cup host city, for the given month of the event (e.g. June-August for Summer Olympics, February for Winter Olympics, and either June-July or July-August for FIFA World Cups). In cases where the city had multiple weather stations, the airport weather station was used as the reference. These weather reports include data on daily precipitation (measured in millimetres) and air temperature (daily high, daily low, daily average). The daily weather data for summer events serves as a baseline for determining the expected environmental hazards in an average year (i.e. the likelihood of temperatures, air quality, or precipitation exceeding the environmental boundary conditions for safe sport). Specifically, weather data was analyzed to count the number of days in the event month(s) with temperatures above 78° F and 82° F.[1] Daily precipitation trends were analyzed to identify incidents of heavy rainfall events, which can negatively impact sporting events (Brocherie, Girard, and Millet 2015; Murfree and Moorman 2021). For winter events, daily temperatures were analyzed to count the number of days in the event month(s) with temperatures above freezing (33° F) as warm winter conditions reduce the likelihood of natural snow and create challenges for the production of fake snow, compromising winter sport competitions (Scott et al. 2015; Rutty et al. 2015). Precipitation and snowfall was analyzed for winter events to determine the amount of snowfall and snowpack on the ground. In addition, historical daily air quality data was collected and analyzed using the World AQI platform (waqi.org) and the days with unhealthy or hazardous air quality were counted for the event months.

For all other host cities of 2020s and 2032 Olympic and FIFA events, historical air quality reports from 2015 to 2020 were collected from the World Air Quality Index website (waqi.org), which collates and publishes second-hand data from national weather services. Data for Doha, Qatar is not publicly available and thus was not included in the analysis. Analysis involved counting the days at each level of PSI, to identify the frequency of days with unhealthy conditions, very unhealthy conditions, or hazardous conditions (Environmental Protection Agency (EPA) 1999) in the given event month. Combined with the historical weather data, the historical air quality data helps paint a picture of what types of weather and air quality conditions the host cities might expect in the event year (near future), which might inform proactive adaptation efforts.

Table 1. Boundary conditions for temperature, air quality, and storm activity for olympic sports.

Environmental factor	Boundary condition	Reference
Air temperature for summer outdoor sports	Moderate risk threshold: 78° F High risk threshold: 82° F	Roberts 2010; Smith et al. 2016
Air temperature for winter outdoor sports	Maximum temperature for natural snow: 32° F Maximum temperature for snow guns: 28° F	Scott et al. 2006
Air quality for outdoor sports	Unhealthy threshold: AQI 151-200 Very unhealthy threshold: AQI 201-300 Hazardous threshold: AQI > 300)	Environmental Protection Agency (EPA) 1999; World Health Organization (WHO) 2006
Precipitation	Heavy rain (> 7.6 mm of rain in an hour) and/or lightning.	IPCC, 2014

Forecasting: the IPCC 5th assessment report

In addition to secondary data collected to predict weather and air quality conditions in the month of the events, regional predictions for 2050 and 2080 under low and high emissions scenarios were collected from the IPCC's 5th Assessment Report (summarized for the Olympics and World Cups in Tables 2 and 3, respectfully).

Specifically, the summary results of the IPCC's 5th Assessment Report were collected for the Giorgi-Francisco Region of each Olympic or FIFA host city (Figure 1). Giorgi-Francisco Region regions are climatological regions used to organize the findings of the IPCC's 5th assessment report and represent segments of each continent that have similar climate conditions and challenges (IPCC 2014). Our analysis on future climate conditions and hazards for host cities is limited to simply conveying the most relevant (according to the unique needs of each sport) and likely environmental hazards for each host-city.

Climate impacts to mega-events from 2022 to 2032

Each sport mega-event scheduled between 2022 and 2032 along with their expected climate impacts will be considered in the section that follows. As noted previously, in accordance with the typology of major sport events form Gratton, Dobson, and Shibli (2000), the only mega-events considered for inclusion are the Olympic Games and FIFA Men's World Cups due to their scale, popularity, and cultural significance. This time period of mega-events were chosen as they are the only future sport mega-events to have been awarded thus far, which follows normal bidding timelines.

Olympic games

Beijing 2022 winter Olympic games

There are two potential climate impacts for these Winter Olympic Games: poor air quality and insufficient cold temperatures. In past Olympic Games – particularly in the 2008 Olympic Games previously held in Beijing – air quality has been of concern to athletes and competition (e.g. McKenzie and Boulet 2008). This may yet arise as an issue for athletes who will be competing within the city of Beijing. In the past six years, Beijing has had a total of 74 days with an air quality index (AQI) that reached levels of unhealthy air to hazardous air. Additionally, there should be general concern for temperatures in the region. There is potential for insufficiently low enough temperatures, as nearly every day in February for the past thirty years have been above freezing in Beijing, which may impact snow fall and ice formation. Both are necessary for many of the outdoor sports that are typical of the Winter Olympic program: alpine sports and sledding sports. To combat this, Beijing has already planned to produce artificial snow to ensure the success of the event (Huang 2018), however, warm temperatures may compromise that adaptation plan. In the legacy years of the event, the chief climactic concerns will continue to be insufficient cold weather which may impede winter sport participation. Additionally, the IPCC projects water scarcity concerns in the region (IPCC 2014), which will put pressure on snow production technologies, limiting this adaptation option.

Table 2. Expected environmental hazards at olympic games in the 2020s and legacy years.

Event	Environmental hazards in an average year (based on historical weather data from 1990 to 2020[a,b], and environmental boundary conditions in Table 1)	Expected environmental hazards in legacy years (based on IPCC 5th Assessment Report, table 21-7.)
Beijing 2022 Winter Olympic Games February 4-20, 2022	Poor air quality (about **half the days** in February in the 2010s had poor or hazardous air quality per WHO standards) Insufficient cold temperatures for natural snow (**more than half the days** in February had temperatures above 32° F).	Likely increase in hot days (decrease in cool days). Likely more frequent and/or longer heat waves and warm spells. Increase in heavy precipitation across the region. Future climate change is likely to affect water resource scarcity.
Paris 2024 Summer Olympic Games July 26-August 11, 2024	Extreme heat (**a few days** in July and August each year were hotter than the moderate risk threshold of 78° F)	Very likely increase in hot days (decrease in cool days). Likely more frequent, longer and/or more intense heat waves/warm spells. Likely increase in 20-year return value of annual maximum daily precipitation. Increase in dryness in central Europe and increase in short-term droughts. Studies find that climate change is likely to increase summer tropospheric ozone levels (range 1 to 10 ppb) by 2050s in polluted areas. Impact on other pollutants (e.g. nitrous oxides, volatile organic compounds) is far more uncertain (p.1293).
Milan/Cortina 2026 Winter Olympic Games February 6-22, 2026	Poor air quality (**a few days** in February were in the Unhealthy range, per AQI). Insufficient cold for snow (**more than half days** in February have temperatures above freezing).	Very likely increase in hot days (decrease in cool days). Likely more frequent, longer and/or more intense heat waves and warm spells. Increase in dryness (less precipitation overall). Mass movements (avalanche and landslide) are projected to become more frequent with climate change (p.1281). Natural snow reliability and thus ski season length will be adversely affected, especially where artificial snowmaking is limited (p.1283).
Los Angeles 2028 Summer Olympic Games July 21-August 6, 2028	Extreme heat (**nearly every day** in July and August reached a daily high temperature hotter than the high risk threshold of 82° F, more than half the days had daily average temperatures that exceeded the moderate risk threshold of 78° F)	Very likely large increases in hot days: almost all areas of North America exhibit very likely increases of at least 5 °C in the warmest daily maximum temperature by the late-21st-century (p.1456) Increase in warm spell duration. General increase in heavy precipitation. Drought index projections and climate change regional models show increases in wildfire risk during the summer and fall (p.1461).
Brisbane 2032 Summer Olympic Games July 23-August 9, 2032	No major concerns for temperature, precipitation, or air quality.	Flooding due to sea level rise may become an issue the city. Extreme heat and wildfires during the summer seasons may impeded the safe use of the outdoor facilities year-round.

[a]Historical weather data collected from 1990 to 2020 was collected from the NOAA Climate Data Online database, using each city's international airport meteorology station.
[b]Historical AQI data was collected from 2014 to 2021 from World AQI (waqi.info).

Table 3. Expected environmental hazards at FIFA Men's world cups in the 2020s and legacy years.

EVENT	CITY	Environmental hazards in an average year (based on historical weather data from 1990 to 2020[a,b], and environmental boundary conditions in Table 1)	Expected environmental hazards in legacy years (based on IPCC 5th Assessment Report, table 21-7.)
FIFA Men's World Cup Qatar 2022 November 21-December 18, 2022	Doha, Qatar	Extreme heat (**nearly all the days** in November and December reached daily highs above the threshold of 78° F)	Likely increase in hot days (decrease in cool days) (Table 21.7). Likely more frequent and/or longer heat waves and warm spells (Table 21.7). Studies find that climate change is likely to increase summer tropospheric ozone levels (range 1 to 10 ppb) by 2050s in polluted areas. Impact on other pollutants (e.g. nitrous oxides, volatile organic compounds) is far more uncertain (p.1293).
FIFA Men's World Cup United 2026 June 8-July 3, 2026	North East Cluster: Boston, MA; New York, NY; Cincinnati, OH; Toronto, ON; Montreal, QC	Extreme heat (**more than half the days** in June and July reached daily highs above the threshold of 78° F)	Very likely increase in hot days (decrease in cool days) (Table 21.7): almost all areas of North America exhibit very likely increases of at least 5 °C in the warmest daily maximum temperature by the late-21st-century (p.1456). Likely more frequent, longer and/or more intense heat waves and warm spells (Table 21.7). Projected increases in flooding in metro Boston, NYC (p.1457).
	South East Cluster: Nashville, TN; Atlanta, GA; Orlando, FL; Miami, FL	Extreme heat (**more than half the days** in June and July were hotter than the threshold of 78° F)	Very likely increase in hot days (decrease in cool days) (Table 21.7): almost all areas of North America exhibit very likely increases of at least 5 °C in the warmest daily maximum temperature by the late-21st-century (p.1456). Likely more frequent, longer and/or more intense heat waves and warm spells (Table 21.7).
	Central Cluster: Kansas City, MS; Denver, CO; Dallas, TX; Houston, TX	Extreme heat (**nearly all the days** in June and July reached daily highs above the moderate risk threshold of 78° F)	Spatially varying trends: small increases in hot days in the north, decreases in the south (Table 21.7). Likely more frequent, longer, and/or more intense heat waves (Table 21.7). Increase in consecutive dry days and soil moisture in southern part of central North America (Table 21.7).
	Western Cluster: Edmonton, AB; Seattle, WA; San Francisco, CA; Los Angeles, CA	none	Very likely large increases in hot days (Table 21-7): almost all areas of North America exhibit very likely increases of at least 5 °C in the warmest daily maximum temperature by the late-21st-century (p.1456) Increase in warm spell duration (Table 21-7). General increase in heavy precipitation (Table 21-7). Drought index projections and climate change regional models show increases in wildfire risk during the summer and fall (p.1461).
	Mexico Cluster: Monterrey, Guadalajara, Mexico City	Extreme heat (**nearly all the days** in June and July reached daily highs above the moderate risk threshold of 78° F; half the days in June and July each year were hotter than the high risk threshold of 82 ° F)	Likely increase in hot days (decrease in cool days) (Table 21.7). Likely more frequent, longer and/or more intense heat waves/ warm spells in most of the region (Table 21.7). Increase in dryness (Table 21.7). Much of Mexico exhibits likely decreases in mean annual precipitation beginning in the mid-21st-century (p.1454).

[a]Historical weather data collected from 1990 to 2020 was collected from the NOAA Climate Data Online database, using each city's international airport meteorology station.
[b]Historical AQI data was collected from 2014 to 2021 from World AQI (waqi.info), except for Qatari cities as the data is protected by the government.

Paris 2024 Olympic games

Our analysis of the weather and air conditions in Paris during the months of July and August reveal a moderate risk of extreme heat during the event period. Specifically, the daily high temperature surpassed the 78° F threshold on more than half the days in the event months between 1990 and 2020. As such, organizers should be prepared for the possibility of heat waves and extreme heat days, similar to those experienced in the region during the 2019 Women's FIFA World Cup (Earls 2020). The legacy period for the games is likely to face the same heat-related challenges. Thus, adaptation efforts such as adding shaded areas to outdoor sport venues, or providing cooling options to athletes, that can be implemented for the Games and retained in the legacy period will be especially relevant.

Milan and Cortina 2026 Winter Olympic Games

Only one major climatic hazard may be predicted for Milan hosting the Winter Olympic Games. In the past six years, Milan has had 24 total days with an AQI unhealthy air quality level of concern. Additionally, while Milan's climate is not conducive to hosting outdoor Winter Games' events, the climate of Cortina regularly meets the necessary temperatures and should prove adequate for the purposes of the Winter Games program. In the legacy years of the event, the IPCC specifically notes avalanches and shortened snow seasons as projected challenges for the Mediterranean region of Europe (IPCC 2014), which may impede snow sports participation in the long-term.

Los Angeles 2028 Olympic games

Between 1990 and 2020, nearly every day in July and August in Los Angeles reached a temperature above 78° F. This finding suggests that temperatures are very warm overall and may present a risk of heat-related illness at the event in 2028, should these weather trends continue or worsen (i.e. continue to warm). In the legacy years of the event, the primary concern will continue to be heat, alongside potential air quality issues as wildfire risks increase due to prolonged droughts in California (IPCC 2014).

Brisbane 2032

As the 2032 Summer Olympics will occur during the Southern Hemisphere's winter season, the temperatures not a concern, with daily highs averaging 70° F in July and 73° F in August. A survey of the last ten years' air quality in the city also shows no cause for concern. In the legacy years of the event, however, flooding due to sea level rise may become an issue the city, and extreme heat and wildfires during the summer seasons may impeded the safe use of the outdoor facilities (IPCC 2014).

FIFA men's world cups

Qatar FIFA men's world cup 2022

Heat is the major climactic concern for this particular event. The 2022 Men's World Cup has already been rescheduled form the traditional Northern summer months to November and December to take advantage of cooler temperatures and protect players from heat-related illness as a result of competing (Borden 2015). Another measure that Qatar has taken as hosts is to air condition the stadiums themselves despite being outdoor venues (Knecht 2019). Thus, it does seem that heat is a major concern for this event, but it may also serve as a preview to future mega-events that may face heat-related concerns. Notably, the Persian Gulf region is likely to experience an increased number of hot days and prolonged heat waves in the legacy years of this event (IPCC 2014); thus, the use of the stadiums will be compromised in the long-term unless air conditioning and adaptation efforts are continued for the full lifespan of the facilities. The additional hot days may also worsen ozone pollution in the region, which may worsen air quality (IPCC 2014).

Canada, United States, and Mexico 'UNITED' FIFA men's world cup 2026

Across all regions of the UNITED 2026 World Cup event and in nearly all host cities, extreme heat will be the top climactic concern. With few exceptions (Olympic Stadium in Montreal, Mercedes Bens Stadium in Atlanta, and AT&T Stadium in Dallas), the matches are scheduled to be played in outdoor facilities. Eight of the host cities (Boston, Denver, Kansas City, Mexico City, New York City, Philadelphia, and Toronto), spread across all three host countries, had temperatures above 78° F on more than half the days in the months of June and July between 2015 and 2020. The conditions are even worse (i.e. warmer) in Houston, Baltimore, Nashville, Atlanta, Orlando, Miami, and Guadalajara, where temperatures rose above the 82° F threshold nearly every day in June and July between 1990 and 2020. As discussed above, extreme heat creates a risk of heat-related illness among athletes and spectators (Brocherie, Girard, and Millet 2015; Kakamu et al. 2017). Tobías et al. (2019) have also shown that hot temperatures can negatively impact player performance in football. In each of these cities, it will be important for organizers to develop adaptation strategies that will alleviate heat stress for athletes and spectators, by offering cooling technologies, creating shaded areas, offering additional heat breaks, and so on. The legacy years will similarly face issues of heat across all regions of North America (IPCC 2014). Aside from more days of heat, precipitation trends are expected to change, though the direction of change depends on the region, with the West expected to see more precipitation and Central North America is likely to see more periods of dryness and drought (see Table 2; IPCC 2014).

Discussion

Theoretical contributions

The most important finding of this study is that each mega-event planned for the 2020s will likely facesome environmental hazards either during the event, in the legacy phases (i.e. the years following the event), or both. Most commonly, mega-events will face temperatures that are too warm. At summer sport mega-events, hot temperatures create a risk of heat-related illness among athletes and spectators (i.e. temperatures above 78° F for low-to-moderate risk, and above 82° F for high risk). For winter events, temperatures above freezing and can compromise the tenability and competitiveness of winter sports events (i.e. too warm for natural snowfall, or for fake snow to be produced). Some events may also face air quality concerns, specifically Beijing 2022 and Qatar 2022 where air quality in recent years has been unhealthy or hazardous in the event month. These findings help to illustrate the urgency of addressing climate vulnerability issues in sport and of developing and implementing adaptive strategies to respond proactively to climate-related hazards and their associated challenges.

This further integrates the novel use of historical weather and air quality data techniques from the environmental sciences into sport management and event management literature and creates boundary conditions necessary to safely and successfully hold each event. Previous works have examined environmental and climate hazards in the distant future (e.g. Orr 2020; Rutty et al. 2015; Smith et al. 2016) to provide general assessments for all of sport that are not specific to locations or events. Whereas this assessment of climate conditions and possible hazards has been completed for the near-future term (i.e. 2020s). By including recent historical weather data in the analysis, we were able to identify location-specific weather patterns and air quality challenges that may create challenges for event organizers, athletes, spectators, the media, and more, in the immediate mega-events of the upcoming decade. Given the boundary conditions, this research suggests that upcoming host communities for the mega-events of the next decade may not be able to provide adequate environmental conditions for sport.

Another theoretical contribution of this research builds on work from Orr (2020) and Kellison and Orr (2020) via the use of IPCC reports to predict environmental and climate hazards. Previous research has shown that some sport managers do not prioritize environment in their operations due to a lack of knowledge on the subject or access to information (Ross and Mercado 2020). These IPCC reports provide useful information to both scholars for the study of climate adaptation in sport as well as managers who are charged with creating climate adaptation plans for their businesses, and the present research meaningfully interprets those IPCC reports in the context of these mega-events. Moreover, the IPCC reports (IPCC 2018; IPCC 2021) demonstrate the urgency of climate adaptation efforts for the upcoming decade in addition to those efforts in the distant future. Sport will need to address climate change as part of its future.

Orr (2020) examined climate hazards and adaptation for two sports (baseball and cross-country skiing) across geographic regions, but the hazards experienced for the same sport may differ across locations, as can be observed with the findings for the FIFA Men's World Cup. FIFA Men's World Cups are spread across entire countries or groups of countries, which increases the number of potential hazards that will be faced. Despite football being the only sport played, the climate hazards may differ from one city to the next. Further, as this event is being co-hosted by three different countries, the adaptation strategies (or lack thereof) may also differ between Canada, Mexico, and the United States, due to political and cultural differences. On the flip side, the results of this study show that a multi-sport event held in one location can also face varying hazards: at the Olympic Games, different hazards may impact each sport differently. For instance, precipitation is more of an issue for tennis than rugby sevens, but both will be stopped for lightning or heavy rains (< 7.6 mm per hour). In this case, the scale of hazards, mitigation efforts, and legacy management are confined to the one city and one political and cultural landscape, but must be managed differently due to the diverse needs of each sport.

Based on this research, it is clear each event will have to develop unique adaptation strategies that fit the needs of the event, in the specific political and geographical context of each host city. It is also clear that many of the same climate hazards will be recurring across events: extreme heat, poor air quality, and precipitation during the events in the 2020s and 2032. Very little research has examined approaches to climate adaptation in the sport sector (Orr 2020; Kellison and Orr 2020). However, this is some promising early research on heat policies (Grundstein et al. 2020; Tipton et al. 2019) and cooling technologies (e.g. cooling towels, cooling rooms; Kakamu et al. 2017) as approaches to managing extreme heat. In the case of poor snow conditions for winter sport, organizers are already heavily reliant on snowmaking technologies (Scott et al. 2015, 2019) and events are being scheduled at high-altitude resorts where the likelihood of bad snow is reduced. While these are promising solutions, there is a need for further innovation in climate adaptation strategies in sport.

In the legacy years of each mega-event, heat (warmer weather in winter), variable increased dryness or increased precipitation (depending on the location), and sea level rise top the list of hazards in the legacy years. The managerial implications for the legacy phase are harder to pinpoint as the choices made during the event for how to accommodate safe play will likely influence post-event sporting opportunities and practices in the same venues (e.g. if a cooling room is built at an Olympic tennis venue, we would hope the cooling room would stay in place for those using the venue in the legacy years). Primarily, it is evident that weather policies are needed across sports to identify the safe thresholds for sport participation, with clear actions delineated to guide adaptation when conditions are unsafe (Grundstein et al. 2013; Kakamu et al. 2017), for instance, moving the activity indoors or postponing the activity until conditions become safe.

Practical contributions and recommendations

Building on previous research from Ross, Leopkey, and Mercado (2019) on the Olympic Games, we echo the call that climate-related issues for these mega-events need to be assessed and addressed at the local level. Climates vary from one locality to the next as do the environmental challenges and opportunities presented. What may work to combat climate change or preserve the natural environment in one mega-event host may not work for another situated in a different climate. These communities already have the base of knowledge locally as to what dangers they face and what climate adaptations (e.g. infrastructure and resources) work best for their circumstances. These mega-events ought to utilize that knowledge. Best practices should be developed that may be transferrable from one event to the next (e.g. stakeholder relationships or policies but not necessarily specific environmental actions), but these best practices must be adaptable to the uniqueness of the climates from each host.

For both the IOC and FIFA, despite the efforts that have been made on their part to require candidate host communities to address issues of the environment (Del Fiacco and Orr 2019; Ross, Leopkey, and Mercado 2019), there still remain challenges to the actual implementation of environmental initiatives and responsibility for their success post-event. Both of these organizations ought to consider requiring candidate host communities to address climate-related hazards as well as the capacity of the candidate host communities to utilize the resources they already have available to address those hazards – including addressing those hazards post hoc. Rather than burden these communities with more environmental challenges that result from hosting these mega-events with no means or support from these organizations, require them to have the capacity to address these challenges.

As a final practical implication, these mega-events should consider climate adaption and resiliency with their infrastructure development. Orr and Kellison (2020) discuss the opportunity that sport facilities have in being spaces for emergency response and protection from extreme weather events. Building on the previous point that the infrastructure should not become a burden as the climate changes and environmental disasters occur, this infrastructure should be part of the response to these issues. Host communities should take advantage of the development opportunity these mega-events present to create climate resilient infrastructure that protects their citizens and communities in times of need.

Limitations

The largest and obvious limitation of this work is the evident unreliability of using historical weather data to predict or anticipate current or future weather conditions (Herrera et al. 2017). In other words, this research is based on the assumption that future weather patterns will be similar to those of the recent past. However, as climatological trends have shown, barring a major climactic event (i.e. a hurricane, major wildfire, etc.), recent historical weather data offers a glimpse of what types of conditions might be expected and as such, allow us to paint a picture of general climactic conditions. This paper does not seek to predict specifically the climactic conditions at future sport events, rather, the goal is to identify trends from years past and intuit possible challenges that lie ahead should these trends remain unchanged. Consequently, these findings should be interpreted as 'ballpark' or rough estimates, rather than specific predictions. Thus, caution about knowledge claims for the climate vulnerability of sport will be needed until a larger and more robust research literature is available.

Further, very little is known about the efficacy and risk-reducing potential of climate adaptation options. As of August 2021, very few adaptive measures have been announced at these events to accommodate climactic conditions with the exception of some unique cooling technologies being implemented in some Qatar 2022 football venues (Sofotasiou, Hughes, and Calautit 2015). The degree to which these tactics will be successful in curbing incidents of heat-related illness or the negative impacts of heat on athletic performance is unclear. It is therefore important to highlight that many of the worst climactic impacts may still be avoided through adaptive measures. More research is needed in this area.

Conclusions

This research has provided predictions of the climatological obstacles that the mega-events between 2022 and 2032 may face. Many of those obstacles come in the form of heat conditions unsuitable to competition as well as poor air quality. It should be noted that while these are two impacts, their presence may lead to more severe environmental impacts that manifest over time in other ways like rising sea-levels or loss of biodiversity. The IOC, FIFA, host communities, and the events themselves ought to consider these impacts as part of the planning and legacy management process. Rather than simply addressing the harmful environmental impact of the event, organizers ought to plan their infrastructure and legacies for the long term in anticipation of hazards resulting from climate change.

A difficulty to this research is the ability to predict climatological impacts on host nations for World Cups. In particular, Canada, Mexico, and the United States for the 2026 FIFA Men's World Cup since this is a large, biodiverse region covering much of the North American continent and the final host cities have yet to be selected. With such sizable geographical considerations, it is difficult to make predictions for these mega-events as a whole (c.f., Collins, Jones, and Munday 2009). The impacts will vary from one city or region to the next. Future directions for this research may include a more in-depth look at climatological predictions for these events by looking at them in a city-by-city approach. Additional future directions for this research include a follow up at the end of the 2032 to determine the accuracy of the predictions as well as similar predictions for the 2033 and beyond that respond to changes to our climate as they develop.

Note

1. Thresholds established in previous research using Fahrenheit. Conversion between Fahrenheit and Celsius: (X °F − 32) * 5/9 = °C

ORCID

Walker J. Ross https://orcid.org/0000-0002-4194-8629
Madeleine Orr https://orcid.org/0000-0002-3478-3686

References

Adger, W. Neil. 2006. "Vulnerability." *Global Environmental Change* 16 (3): 268–281. doi:10.1016/j.gloenvcha.2006.02.006.

Ahmed, Fathima, and Leon Pretorius. 2010. "Mega-Events and Environmental Impacts: The 2010 FIFA World Cup in South Africa." *Alternation* 17 (2): 274–296.

Borden, Sam. 2015. "FIFA Confirms Winter World Cup for 2022." *New York Times*, March 19. https://www.nytimes.com/2015/03/20/sports/soccer/fifa-confirms-winter-world-cup-for-2022.html

Brocherie, Franck, Olivier Girard, and Grégoire P. Millet. 2015. "Emerging Environmental and Weather Challenges in Outdoor Sports." *Climate* 3 (3): 492–521. doi:10.3390/cli3030492.

Brooks, Nick, W. Neil Adger, and P. Mick Kelly. 2005. "The Determinants of Vulnerability and Adaptive Capacity at the National Level and the Implications for Adaptation." *Global Environmental Change* 15 (2): 151–163.

Cherington, Michael. 2001. "Lightning Injuries in sports: situations to avoid." *Sports Medicine (Auckland, N.Z.)* 31 (4): 301–308. doi:10.2165/00007256-200131040-00004.

Collins, Andrea, Calvin Jones, and Max Munday. 2009. "Assessing the Environmental Impacts of Mega Sporting Events: Two Options?" *Tourism Management* 30 (6): 828–837. doi:10.1016/j.tourman.2008.12.006.

Dave, Paresh, and Philip O'Connor. 2021. Tropical storm forces Tokyo Olympics organizers to reschedule events. *Global News*, July 26. https://globalnews.ca/news/8059709/olympics-tropical-storm-japan/

Death, Carl. 2011. "'Greening' the 2010 FIFA World Cup: Environmental Sustainability and the Mega-Event in South Africa." *Journal of Environmental Policy & Planning* 13 (2): 99–117. doi:10.1080/1523908X.2011.572656.

Del Fiacco, Anthony Gino, and Madeleine Orr. 2019. "A Review and Synthesis of the Environmentalism within the Olympic Movement." *International Journal of Event and Festival Management* 10 (1): 67–80. doi:10.1108/IJEFM-05-2018-0038.

Dingle, Greg William, and Bob Stewart. 2018. "Playing the Climate Game: Climate Change Impacts, Resilience, and Adaptation in the Climate-Dependent Sport Sector." *Managing Sport and Leisure* 23 (4-6): 293–314. doi:10.1080/23750472.2018.1527715.

Earls, Maya. 2020. As the World Heats Up, Soccer Must Adapt. Scientific American, July 2. https://www.scientificamerican.com/article/as-the-world-heats-up-soccer-must-adapt/

Environmental Protection Agency (EPA). 1999. "Part III: Environmental Protection Agency: 40 CFR Part 58: Air Quality Index Reporting; Final Rule." *EPA*, August 4. https://www.airnow.gov/sites/default/files/2018-06/air-quality-index-reporting-final-rule.pdf

FIFA. 2017. *FIFA Regulations for the Selection of the Venue for the Final Competition of the 2026 FIFA World Cup*. Zurich: FIFA.

Folke, Carl. 2006. "Resilience: The Emergence of a Perspective for Social–Ecological Systems Analyses." *Global Environmental Change* 16 (3): 253–267.

Gifford, Robert T. Todisco, M. Stacey, T. Fujisawa, M. Allerhand, D. R. Woods, and R. M. Reynolds. 2019. "Risk of Heat Illness in Men and Women: A Systematic Review and Meta-Analysis." *Environmental Research* 171: 24–35.

Goggins, Dom, Clara Goldsmith, Caroline Grogan, Jessica Marsh, and Bronwen Smith-Thomas. 2018. "Game Changer: How Climate Change is Impacting Sports in the UK." The Climate Coalition and The Priestley International Centre for Climate.

Gratton, Chris, Nigel Dobson, and Simon Shibli. 2000. "The Economic Importance of Major Sport Events: A Case-Study of Six Events." *Managing Leisure* 5 (1): 17–28. doi:10.1080/136067100375713.

Grundstein, Andrew, Nellie Elguindi, Earl Cooper, and Michael S. Ferrara. 2013. "Exceedance of Wet Bulb Globe Temperature Safety Thresholds in Sports under a Warming Climate." *Climate Research* 58 (2): 183–191. doi:10.3354/cr01199.

Grundstein, A. J., Samatha E. Scarneo-Miller, William M. Adams, and Douglas J. Casa. 2020. "From Theory to Practice: operationalizing a Climate Vulnerability for Sport Organizations Framework for Heat Hazards among US High Schools." *Journal of Science and Medicine in Sport* 24 (8): 718–722. doi:10.1016/j.jsams.2020.11.009.

Hernandez, Daniela, and Georgi Kantchev. 2021. "Sweltering Conditions are a Tough Opponent at the Tokyo Olympics." *The Washington Post*, July 25. https://www.wsj.com/articles/tokyo-olympics-heat-11627186166

Herrera, Manuel, Sukumar Natarajan, David A. Coley, Tristan Kershaw, Alfonso P. Ramallo-González, Matthew Eames, Daniel Fosas, and Michael Wood. 2017. "A Review of Current and Future Weather Data for Building Simulation." *Building Services Engineering Research and Technology* 38 (5): 602–627. doi:10.1177/0143624417705937.

Hinkel, Jochen. 2011. ""Indicators of Vulnerability and Adaptive Capacity": towards a Clarification of the Science–Policy Interface." *Global Environmental Change* 21 (1): 198–208.

Honjo, Tsuyoshi, Yuhwan Seo, Yudai Yamasaki, Nobumitsu Tsunematsu, Hitoshi Yokoyama, Hiroaki Yamato, and Takehiko Mikami. 2018. "Thermal Comfort along the Marathon Course of the 2020 Tokyo Olympics." *International Journal of Biometeorology* 62 (8): 1407–1419. doi:10.1007/s00484-018-1539-x.

Huang, Zheping. 2018. "The Winter Olympics is Pretty Much Over Natural Snow, Which is Great for Their Next Host." *Quartz*, February 23. https://qz.com/1213121/beijing-2022-winter-olympics-will-rely-entirely-on-artificial-snow/

International Olympic Committee (IOC). 2019. "International Olympic Committee Announces Plans to Move Olympic Marathon and Race Walking to Sapporo." https://www.olympic.org/news/international-olympic-committee-announces-plans-to-move-olympic-marathon-and-race-walking-to-sapporo

IPCC. 2001. Climate change 2001: Impacts, adaptation, and vulnerability [McCarthy, J. J., O. F. Canziani, N. A. Leary, D. J. Dokken, & K. S. White (eds.)]. Cambridge University Press.

IPCC. 2021. Summary for Policymakers. In: Climate Change 2021: The Physical Science Basis. Contribution of Working Group I to the Sixth Assessment Report of the Intergovernmental Panel on Climate Change [MassonDelmotte, V., P. Zhai, A. Pirani, S. L. Connors, C. Péan, S. Berger, N. Caud, Y. Chen, L. Goldfarb, M. I. Gomis, M. Huang, K. Leitzell, E. Lonnoy, J. B. R. Matthews, T. K. Maycock, T. Waterfield, O. Yelekçi, R. Yu and B. Zhou (eds.)]. Cambridge University Press.

IPCC. 2014. "Climate Change 2014: Synthesis Report. Contribution of Working Groups I, II and III to the Fifth Assessment Report of the Intergovernmental Panel on Climate Change." [Core Writing Team, R. K. Pachauri and L. A. Meyer (eds.)]. IPCC, Geneva, Switzerland, 151. pp.

IPCC. 2018. "Global Warming of 1.5 °C. An IPCC Special Report on the Impacts of Global Warming of 1.5 °C above Pre-Industrial Levels and Related Global Greenhouse Gas Emission Pathways, in the Context of Strengthening the Global Response to the Threat of Climate Change, Sustainable Development, and Efforts to Eradicate Poverty." [V. Masson-Delmotte, P. Zhai, H. O. Pörtner, D. Roberts, J. Skea, P.R. Shukla, A. Pirani, W. Moufouma-Okia, C. Péan, R. Pidcock, S. Connors, J. B. R. Matthews, Y. Chen, X. Zhou, M. I. Gomis, E. Lonnoy, T. Maycock, M. Tignor, T. Waterfield (eds.)].

Kakamu, Takeyasu, Koji Wada, Derek R. Smith, Shota Endo, and Tetsuhito Fukushima. 2017. "Preventing Heat Illness in the Anticipated Hot Climate of the Tokyo 2020 Summer Olympic Games." *Environmental Health and Preventive Medicine* 22 (1): 1–6. doi:10.1186/s12199-017-0675-y.

Kellison, Timothy, and Madeleine Orr. 2020. "Climate Vulnerability as a Catalyst for Early Stadium Replacement." *International Journal of Sports Marketing and Sponsorship*. 22 (1): 126–141. doi:10.1108/IJSMS-04-2020-0076.

Knecht, Eric. 2019. "World Cup Host Qatar Sees Climate-Controlled Stadiums as the Future." *Reuters*, September 26. https://www.reuters.com/article/us-soccer-worldcup-climate/world-cup-host-qatar-sees-climate-controlled-stadiums-as-the-future-idUSKBN1WB2X1

Leopkey, Becca, and Milena M. Parent. 2012. "Olympic Games Legacy: From General Benefits to Sustainable Long-Term Legacy." *The International Journal of the History of Sport* 29 (6): 924–943. doi:10.1080/09523367.2011.623006.

Lockwood, Michael, Christopher M. Raymond, Eddie Oczkowski, and Mark Morrison. 2015. "Measuring the Dimensions of Adaptive Capacity: A Psychometric Approach." *Ecology and Society* 20 (1): 37. doi:10.5751/ES-07203-200137.

Mastromartino, Brandon, Walker J. Ross, Henry Wear, and Mike L. Naraine. 2020. "Thinking outside the "Box": A Discussion of Sports Fans, Teams, and the Environment in the Context of COVID-19." *Sport in Society* 23 (11): 1707–1723. doi:10.1080/17430437.2020.1804108.

Matzarakis, Andreas, Dominik Fröhlich, Stéphane Bermon, and Paolo Emilio Adami. 2019. "Visualization of Climate Factors for Sports Events and Activities–the Tokyo 2020 Olympic Games." *Atmosphere* 10 (10): 572. doi:10.3390/atmos10100572.

Miller-Rushing, A. J., Primack, R. B., Phillips, N., and Kaufmann, R. K. 2012. "Effects of warming temperatures on winning times in the Boston marathon." *PLoS ONE* 7 (9): e43579.

McCullough, Brian P., M. Madeline Orr, and Timothy B. Kellison. 2020. "Sport Ecology: Conceptualizing an Emerging Subdiscipline within Sport Management." *Journal of Sport Management* 34 (6): 509–520. doi:10.1123/jsm.2019-0294.

McKenzie, Donald C., and Louis-Philippe Boulet. 2008. "Asthma, Outdoor Air Quality, and the Olympic Games." *CMAJ: Canadian Medical Association Journal = Journal de L'association Medicale Canadienne* 179 (6): 543–548. doi:10.1503/cmaj.080982.

Murfree, Jessica R., and Anita M. Moorman. 2021. "An Examination and Analysis of Division I Football Game Contracts: Legal Implications of Game Cancellations Due to Hurricanes." *Journal of Legal Aspects of Sport* 31 (1): 123–146. doi:10.18060/24922.

Nybo, Lars, Andreas D. Flouris, Sebastien Racinais, and Magni Mohr. 2020. "Football Facing a Future with Global Warming: Perspectives for Players Health and Performance." *British Journal of Sports Medicine* 55 (6): 297–298. doi:10.1136/bjsports-2020-102193.

Oikawa, Yoshinori, Victoria Downie, Mike Tipton, David Marlin, Julien Périard, Paloma Castro, and Joanna Dyson. 2021. "Rings of Fire: How Heat Could Impact the 2021 Tokyo Olympics." British Association for Sustainability in Sport. https://basis.org.uk/rings-of-fire

Orr, Madeleine. 2020. "On the Potential Impacts of Climate Change on Baseball and Cross-Country Skiing." *Managing Sport and Leisure* 25 (4): 307–320. doi:10.1080/23750472.2020.1723436.

Orr, Madeleine. 2021. "Finding Consensus on Indicators for Organizational Climate Capacity in Sport." *Managing Sport and Leisure*: 1–19. Advance online publication. doi:10.1080/23750472.2021.1914710.

Orr, Madeleine, and Yuhei Inoue. 2019. "Sport versus Climate: Introducing the Climate Vulnerability of Sport Organizations Framework." *Sport Management Review* 22 (4): 452–463. doi:10.1016/j.smr.2018.09.007.

Orr, Madeleine, and Timothy Kellison. 2020. "Sport Facilities as Sites of Environmental and Social Resilience." *Managing Sport and Leisure*: 1–6. Advance online publication. doi:10.1080/23750472.2020.1855081.

Orr, Madeleine, and Ingrid Schneider. 2018. "Substitution Interests among Active-Sport Tourists: The Case of a Cross-Country Ski Event." *Journal of Sport & Tourism* 22 (4): 315–332. doi:10.1080/14775085.2018.1545600.

Parry, Martin. 2002. "Scenarios for Climate Impact and Adaptation Assessment." *Global Environmental Change* 12 (3): 149–153.

Rivera, Jorge, and Viviane Clement. 2019. "Business Adaptation to Climate Change: American Ski Resorts and Warmer Temperatures." *Business Strategy and the Environment* 28 (7): 1285–1301. doi:10.1002/bse.2316.

Roberts, William O. 2010. "Determining a "Do Not Start" Temperature for a Marathon on the Basis of Adverse Outcomes." *Medicine & Science in Sports & Exercise* 42 (2): 226–232. doi:10.1249/MSS.0b013e3181b1cdcf.

Roche, Maurice. 2000. *Mega-Events and Modernity*. London: Routledge.

Roche, Maurice. 2006. "Mega-Events and Modernity Revisited: Globalization and the Case of the Olympics." *The Sociological Review* 54 (2_suppl): 27–40. doi:10.1111/j.1467-954X.2006.00651.x.

Roeder, William, P., and R. James Vavrek. 2005. "Lightning safety for schools–An update." submitted to 14th Symposium on Education in Meteorology.

Ross, Walker J., and Becca Leopkey. 2017. "The Adoption and Evolution of Environmental Practices in the Olympic Games." *Managing Sport and Leisure* 22 (1): 1–18. doi:10.1080/23750472.2017.1326291.

Ross, Walker J., Becca Leopkey, and Haylee Uecker Mercado. 2019. "Governance of Olympic Environmental Stakeholders." *Journal of Global Sport Management* 4 (4): 331–350. doi:10.1080/24704067.2018.1477524.

Ross, Walker J., and Haylee Uecker Mercado. 2020. "Barriers to Managing Environmental Sustainability in Public Assembly Venues." *Sustainability* 12 (24): 10477. doi:10.3390/su122410477.

Rutty, M., Scott, D., Steiger, R., & Johnson, P. 2015. "Weather risk management at the Olympic Winter Games." *Current Issues in Tourism* 18 (10): 931–946.

Scott, D., McBoyle, G., Minogue, A., and Mills, B. 2006. "Climate change and the sustainability of ski-based tourism in eastern North America: A reassessment." *Journal of Sustainable Tourism* 14 (4): 376–398.

Scott, Daniel, Robert Steiger, M. Michelle Rutty, and Yan Fang. 2019. "The Changing Geography of the Winter Olympic and Paralympic Games in a Warmer World." *Current Issues in Tourism* 22 (11): 1301–1311. doi:10.1080/13683500.2018.1436161.

Scott, Daniel, Robert Steiger, Michelle Rutty, and Peter Johnson. 2015. "The Future of the Olympic Winter Games in an Era of Climate Change." *Current Issues in Tourism* 18 (10): 913–930. doi:10.1080/13683500.2014.887664.

Smith, Kirk R., Alistair Woodward, Bruno Lemke, Matthias Otto, Cindy Chang, Anna Mance, John Balmes, and Tord Kjellstrom. 2016. "The Last Summer Olympics? Climate Change, Health, and Work Outdoors." *The Lancet* 388 (10045): 642–644. doi:10.1016/S0140-6736(16)31335-6.

Sofotasiou, Polytimi, Benjamin R. Hughes, and John K. Calautit. 2015. "Qatar 2022: Facing the FIFA World Cup Climatic and Legacy Challenges." *Sustainable Cities and Society* 14: 16–30. doi:10.1016/j.scs.2014.07.007.

Spengler, John O., Daniel P. Connaughton, and Jeff Earnshaw. 2002. "Perspectives on Lightning Safety Risk Management in Sport and Recreational Activities." *World Leisure Journal* 44 (4): 22–29. doi:10.1080/04419057.2002.9674288.

Tipton, Mike, Russell Seymour, Piers Forster, Jo Corbett, Rob Chave, Kate Sambrook, Dom Goggins, Richard Thelwell, and Hugh Montgomery. 2019. "Hit for Six: The Impact of Climate Change on Cricket." The British Association for Sustainable Sport. https://basis.org.uk/hit-for-six

Tobías, Aurelio, Marti Casals, Javier Peña, and Cristian Tebé. 2019. "FIFA World Cup and Climate Change: Correlation is Not Causation." *RICYDE. Revista Internacional de Ciencias Del Deporte* 15 (57): 280–283.

Tsegaw, Gashaw Tesema, and Yitayal Addis Alemayehu. 2019. "Principal Air Pollutants and Their Effects on Athletes Health and Performance: A Critical Review." *Scientific Research and Essays* 14 (7): 44–52.

Weis, S. W. M., V. N. Agostini, L. M. Roth, B. Gilmer, S. R. Schill, J. E. Knowles, and R. Blyther. 2016. "Assessing Vulnerability: An Integrated Approach for Mapping Adaptive Capacity, Sensitivity, and Exposure." *Climatic Change* 136 (3): 615–629.

Wicker, P., K. Filo, and G. Cuskelly. 2013. "Organizational Resilience of Community Sport Clubs Impacted by Natural Disasters." *Journal of Sport Management* 27 (6): 510–525.

World Health Organization (WHO). 2006. *Air Quality Guidelines for Particulate Matter, Ozone, Nitrogen Dioxide and Sulfur Dioxide: Global Update. Summary of Risk Assessment*. Geneva, World Health Organization, http://www.who.int/phe/air/aqg2006execsum.pdf (accessed 25 November 2006).

Index

Page numbers in **bold** refer to tables and those in *italic* refer to figures.

ABC specialist practitioners 118
active involvement, women and girls 80–3
Active Lives Survey 31
Active People Survey (APS) 31
adaptive capacity 169–70
Air Quality Index (AQI) 169
Aizawa, Kurumi 17, 18
Albertville Winter Games 166
Aleem, Azeem 120
Aliyev, Heydar 145–6
The Aliyev regime 156–7
Alm, J. 2
Annear, M. 29
ANOVA test 54
anti-bribery and corruption (ABC): competition (on-field) and management (governance) 117; competition corruption 126; concepts clarification 119–20; corruption and themes **120**; defined 116; elements of 117; enforcement 125–6; governance assessment 121–4; Greek football clubs 117; ISGB-specific approach 116; legacy 126; media and public scrutiny 118; method 118–19, **119**; monitoring and control 124–5; on-field competition 127–8; procurement 127; risk factors assessment 120–1; stakeholders 119
Antonopoulos, Georgios A. 116, 120, 123, 126
Ap, J. 51
article quality assessment 13
Asian Games 9
#Asone and #Getonside twitter mentions *80*
#AsOne hashtag 78, 77, 79
'As One,' Trans-Tasman bid: audiences and audiences 66; Australia-New Zealand bid 64; bidding narratives 65–6; methodology 73–5; social media presence 76–88; theoretical framework 70–3; Twitter 65
@Asone2023 twitter account *80*, *85*, *87*
AusBid2023.com 77
Australia and New Zealand 83–8, *85*, *87*
Australian Rugby Union (ARU) 86
authoritarian modernisation 149–50

Baku-Tbilisi-Ceyhan (BTC) pipeline 146
Balduck, A. L. 47, 53
Bale, J. 134
Beissel, A. S. 69, 139
Bell, B. 108
Berger, Nicolas 18
'Bid Book' 75, 76
Black, David 70
Black, defined 31
Black, Jack 71
Bloyce, D. 29
Bobina, N. 56
Boolean search string 11
Bourdieu, Pierre 2
Boykoff, J. 2
Brannagan, P. M. 135
Braun, Virginia 118
Brooks, Graham 120
Brown, G. 30
Buelens, M. 47, 53
Butler, O. 137
Button, Mark 120
Byon, K. 57
Byun, Jinsu 67, 68, 71

Chadwick, S. 125
Chalip, Lawrence 67
Chappelet, Jean-Loup 116
Chatziefstahiou, D. 70
Chen, F. 54
Chersulich Tomino, A. 45
Chien, P. M. 51
City of Manchester Stadium 3
Clarke, Victoria 118
climate vulnerability and adaptation: adaptive capacity 169–70; environmental boundary conditions 167–9; potential impact 167
Cochrane Database of systematic reviews 11
Colbeck, Richard 76
Comeau, Gina S. 71, 72
Commonwealth Games 9
Commonwealth of Independent States 145

Conn, D. 122
contingency planning 164
controversies, sport mega-events 3–4
Corbett, Ben 73
Cornelissen, Scarlett 68
corporate governance business processes 123
Crompton, J. 50
Cronje, J. 3
Cush, Adam 18

Dale, A. 31
Deery, M. 52, 54
Desjardins, Bridgette M. 71, 72, 77, 81–3
Devonish, D. 53
digital academic databases 48
Dobson, N. 46, 165, 172
Downs and Black checklist for Quality Assessment 10–11
Downs and Black quality index 12
Drummond, R. 3

Edwards, Allan 73
Ellis, Dawn 67, 68, 71
english media coverage 101–4, **102**
English women's football 99
Environmental Protection Agency (EPA) 169, 171
environment and mega-events 165
Eurasian Economic Community 145
'Extra participants in average quarter' column 33

Faulkner, B. 56
FA Women's Super League (FA WSL) 99
Fédération Internationale de Volleyball (FIVB) Men's World Championships 67
Fielding-Lloyd, Beth 71
FIFA Bid Evaluation Report 79
FIFA Football World Cup 9
FIFA Men's World Cup (FMWC) 3, 67; Canada, United States, and Mexico 'UNITED' FIFA men's world cup 2026 176; Qatar FIFA men's world cup 2022 175–6
FIFA Women's World Cup 2023™ (FWWC 2023™) 64
FIFA Women's World Cup (FIFA WWC) 97–8
Filo, Kevin 73
five-/seven-point Likert scale 52
Fleming, Scott 123
FMWC 2002™ 68–9
Football Association (FA) 99
Football Federation Australia (FFA) 76
Frawley, Stephen 18
Frederick, Evan L. 71, 72
Fredline, E. 52
Fredline, L. 54
Fukuhara, T. 47

Gardiner, Simon 116, 122, 127, 128
Gibson, H. J. 53
Giulianotti, R. 135
glocal consciousness concept 135

Google Scholar 11
Gorse, S. 125
governance 1–2
Gratton, C. 33, 46, 165, 172
Greenidge, D. 53
Gross Domestic Product (GDP) 32
Gursoy, D. 52, 53, 56
Gustavo, N. 52

Hall, C. M. 47, 52
Harada, M. 47
Hayday, E. J. 18, 30
Henry, I. 29, 70
Higgins, V. 31
Higham, J. 52
historical weather and air quality analysis 171, **171**
Horák, Slavomír 144, 155
Horne, J. 2, 5, 136
Huang, H. 56, 57

image leveraging 67–8
Innsbruck Youth Olympic Games 2012 28
Inoue, Y. 52, 169
Intergovernmental Panel on Climate Change's (IPCC) Sixth Assessment Report 164
internally displaced persons (IDPs) 144
International Handball Federation (IHF) 67
International Olympic Committee (IOC) 9, 66, 166
International Rugby Board (IRB) 86
international sport governing bodies (ISGBs) 115
International Tennis Federation investment 115
Ioannides, D. 45
IPCC 5th assessment report 172

Jago, L. 52, 54
Jennings, Andrew 122
joint bidding alliances 68
Jones, I. 52

Kaplanidou, K. 48, 51
Karg, Adam 73
Kassens-Noor, E. 106, 108
Kellison, Timothy 170, 177, 179
Kennelly, M. 45
Kerr, Samantha 76
Kihl, Lisa 116, 122
Kim, H. J. 52, 53
Kim, S. S. 56
Klitgaard, Robert 127
Koenigstorfer, J. 45, 124, 126, 127
Kohe, Geoffrey Z. 69, 139
Kokolakakis, T. 29, 30, 33
Könecke, T. 29, 45
Kulczycki, Wojciech 124, 126, 127
Kunti, Samindra 150

Lajh, Damjan 125
Lee, S. B. 52, 53
legacy claims 3
Leopkey, Becca 67, 68, 71, 178

Lera-López, F. 29, 30, 33
Levi, Michael 116, 120, 123, 126
lightning process 169
Lipicer, Simona 125
Lock, Daniel 73
Lorde, T. 53
Lovett, E. 29

Mackellar, J. 52
Maennig, Wolfgang 117, 118
Maes, M. 47, 53
Mair, J. 45
Manchester City Football Club 3
Manoli, Argyro Elisavet 116, 120, 123, 126
MANOVA test 54
manuscript quality assessment 12
Manzenreiter, W. 2, 5, 77
Mao, L. L. 56
Marxism-Leninism 145
Mason, Daniel S. 116, 122, 123, 126
Masters, Adam 117, 119, 126
McNamee, M. J. 123
mean absolute percentage error statistic (MAPE) 33
Mega event legacy 9
mega-event syndrome 134
mega sporting events (MSEs) 44, 50
Men's Cricket World Cups (MCWC) 85–6
Men's European Football Championships ('Euros') 67
Men's Rugby World Cups (MRWC) 67
Mercado, Haylee Uecker 178
Mingachevir sports complex 148
Misener, Laura 116, 122, 123, 126
Morrow, S. 99
Müller, M. 2, 4, 135
Murthy, Dhiraj 74

Nagorno-Karabakh conflict and sport-for-development 146–9
Narrative synthesis 12
Næss, Hans Erik 128
NCapture, web-browser extension 74
New Zealand Football (NZF) 76
New Zealand Rugby Football Union (NZRFU) 86
Nichols, P. M. 118
Nikou, Chris 76
non-governmental organisations (NGOs) 148
non-mega sporting events (NMSEs) 46
North American Free Trade Agreement (NAFTA) 138
Norwegian Supporters Alliance (2021) 2
Numerato, Dino 117

Ohmann, S. 52
Olympic games: Beijing 2022 winter Olympic games 172, **173**, **174**; Brisbane 2032 175; Los Angeles 2028 Olympic games 175; Milan and Cortina 2026 Winter Olympic Games 175; Paris 2024 Olympic games 175

Olympic Movement and World Cups 167
Olympic World Library 11
organizational climate capacity (OCC) 169–70
Orr, Madeleine 169, 170, 177, 179
Oshimi, D. 47
Oxygen-Plus, robust campaigns 166

Pan-American Games 9
Pappous, A. S. 18, 30
Parry, Jim 116
Patton, M. Q. 75
Paulsson, A. 2
Payne, Geoff 100
Payne, Judy 100
Peacock, Byron 70
Pegoraro, Ann 71, 72
percentage point sport effect 34
Peric, M. 45
Petrick, J. F. 56
petro-state formation 149–50
Pettersson, R. 45
Petty, K. 96, 109
Pfister, G. 97, 98
Philippou, Christina 117, 119, 127
physical activity (PA) legacies: article quality assessment 13; data synthesis and evaluation 12, **13**, **14**, **15–16**; events 9; event type and location 13–14; fixed-duration and costly international competitions 9; limitations at outcome level 19–20; manuscript quality assessment 12; public health researchers 9; regular PA 8; review and assessment protocols 10–11; screening and eligibility assessment 11–12; search strategy and data extraction 11; surveillance efforts 20; systematic review 10
Pielke, Roger Jr. 117, 121
play-for-development (PfD) 148
pollution standard index (PSI) 169
Pope, S. 96, 109
post-sporting event 52
Preferred Reporting Items for Systematic Reviews and Meta-Analyses (PRISMA) 10–11
pre-sporting event 52
Preuß, H. 29
Preuss, H. 28, 45
prospect theory (PT) 51
PubMed/Medline 11

quality of life (QoL) 47

Ramchandani, G. 29, 30, 33
Redeker, Robert 68
The Republic of Azerbaijan: Baghlan Group 144; GDP growth 144; multiple territorial disputes 144; Nagorno-Karabakh 145; political context of 145–6; sport, statecraft and repression 155–7; Turkic states 143
Ritchie, B. J. R. 52

Ritchie, B. W. 51
Robertson, Grant 76
Robinson, Simon 116
Roche, M. 1, 67, 165, 135
Rojo-Labaien, Ekain 144, 150–1
Ross, Walker J. 178
Rowe, D. 139
Rugby World Cup 9
Rutty, M. 170

Salt Lake City (2002) 13
scandals engulfing large national (SGBs) 115
Scelles, N. 99
Scheu, A. 29, 45
Scopus 11
second order SMEs 67
Seidl, M. 28
Shibli, S. 46, 165, 172
single-sport continental/regional events 9
Smith, A. 29, 51
social exchange theory (SET) 51
social impacts 47
social media hashtags 65
social representation theory (SRT) 51
Sport Discuss 11
Sport England's Active Lives Survey 27
sport-for-development (SfD) 145
sport governance officials 118
Sport Industry Research Centre (SIRC) 31
sporting events: analysis 54; countries and cities 44; event legacies and impacts 46–7; journal and fields 48, **49**; literature reviews 48; measurement instruments 52–3; participants and data collection 53–4; referenda/public pressure 44–5; reviewed studies 54, **55**; smaller-scale events 45; social impacts 47; sport tourism events 45; stakeholders 45; study location, data collection methods and sample size 48, **49**; theoretical frameworks and concepts **50**, 50–1; typology 46
sport legacy: data analysis 32–3; decades of 29; ethnic groups 31, **32**, **34**; ethnicity-females **35**; ethnicity-males **35**; facets of 28; health and social inclusion 27; inspirational and motivational effects 28; of London 2012 29–30; measures 32; minority ethnicities and sport participation 30–1; overall female *vs.* female Asian Muslims participation patterns *36*; theoretical perspectives, effects of 28
sport mega-events (SMEs) 65, 115, 165–7; in Baku 150–5; solutions for corruption **129**; stakeholders **117**
sport organizations 164
Sports Marketing Intelligence (2017) 9, 17
staging sport mega events (SMEs) 26
State Oil Company of the Azerbaijan Republic (SOCAR) 151
Student Games 9
Stura, Claudia 68
stylish web-based videos 65
Sugden, John 117, 120, 121
Summer Olympic and Paralympic Games 9

Taks, M. 46
textual and network content analysis 74
Thibault, Lucie 116, 122, 123, 126
Thomson, A. 45, 48
Thorpe, David 128
Tian, L. 54
Tideswell, C. 56
Toffoletti, Kim 72
Tokyo Olympics 5
Tomlinson, Alan 70, 117, 120, 121
Toohey, K. 18, 45
Transatlantic Trade and Investment Partnership 83
Trans-Pacific Partnership 83
triple bottom line (TBL) approach 50–1
Twitter, public opinion: clubs and sports organisations 105; quantity and proportion of tweets sentiment type 105, *105*; word cloud, negative and mixed sentiments *107*; word cloud, positive and mixed sentiments *106*

UEFA Europa League (UEL) 145, 152–3
UEFA Women's Euro 2022: decision-makers 96; description 95; engagement, organisational and inequality issues 96; english media coverage 101–4, **102**; English newspapers 100; inclusion criterias 100; media coverage and public opinion 100; public opinion, Twitter 104–9; Python code, programming language 101; sentiment analysis 101; stadium and television audiences 96; *see also* women's football development
The Union of European Football Associationss (UEFA) 67; *see also* UEFA Women's Euro 2022
'United' 2026: co-hosting 135; description 133–4; mega-events 135–6; NAFTA 138; North American 2026 World Cup 137; Oslo (Norway) 137; Qatar's 2022 World Cup 135; relocations and national allegiances 134; soft power 135; Switzerland and Austria 136; 'Twitter-diplomacy' 134
'United Bid,' North American effort 69
United States–Mexico–Canada Agreement (USMCA) 139
Uvinha, R. R. 52

Valenti, M. 99
Veal, A. J. 18
Vertalka, J. 106, 108
Vetitnev, A. M. 56
Vico, R. P. 52

Wagner, P. 134
Wallstam, M. 45
Wang, Y. 108
Watt, P. 4

Weed, M. 28, 37
wet bulb globe temperature (WBGT) index 168
Wilkes, K. 52
Wilson, M. 106, 108
Winter Olympic and Paralympic Games 9
Wise, N. 45
women's football development 97–9
Women's Football Strategy 65
Women's Rugby World Cups (WRWC) 67
World Air Quality Index website 171

World Games 9
World Health Organization's guidelines 2
World Rugby (WR) 67

Xu, K. 57

Yang, Elaine Chiao Ling 81

Zhang, J. C. 57
Zirin, D. 4

Taylor & Francis eBooks

www.taylorfrancis.com

A single destination for eBooks from Taylor & Francis with increased functionality and an improved user experience to meet the needs of our customers.

90,000+ eBooks of award-winning academic content in Humanities, Social Science, Science, Technology, Engineering, and Medical written by a global network of editors and authors.

TAYLOR & FRANCIS EBOOKS OFFERS:

- A streamlined experience for our library customers
- A single point of discovery for all of our eBook content
- Improved search and discovery of content at both book and chapter level

REQUEST A FREE TRIAL
support@taylorfrancis.com